A COMPLETE GUIDE TO BRASS

INSTRUMENTS AND TECHNIQUE

A COMPLETE GUIDE TO BRASS

INSTRUMENTS AND TECHNIQUE

THIRD EDITION

SCOTT WHITENER
Rutgers University

Illustrations by Cathy L. Whitener

SCHIRMER
CENGAGE Learning

Australia • Brazil • Japan • Korea • Mexico • Singapore • Spain • United Kingdom • United States

A Complete Guide to Brass:
Instruments and Technique, Third Edition
Scott Whitener

Publisher: Clark Baxter

Associate Development Editor: Julie Yardley

Editorial Assistant: Emily Perkins

Executive Technology Project Manager: Matt Dorsey

Executive Marketing Manager: Diane Wenckebach

Marketing Assistant: Marla Nasser

Marketing Communications Manager: Patrick Rooney

Project Manager, Editorial Production: Trudy Brown

Creative Director: Rob Hugel

Executive Art Director: Maria Epes

Print Buyer: Doreen Suruki

Permissions Editor: Kiely Sisk

Production Service: G & S Book Services

Text Designer: Michael Warrell

Photo Researcher: Sue Howard

Copy Editor: Elliot Simon

Cover Designer: Roger Knox

Cover Image: Peter Christopher/Masterfile

Compositor: Newgen

For product information and technology assistance, contact us at
Cengage Learning Customer & Sales Support, 1-800-354-9706.

For permission to use material from this text or product,
submit all requests online at **www.cengage.com/permissions**.
Further permissions questions can be emailed to
permissionrequest@cengage.com.

Library of Congress Control Number: 2005933211

ISBN-13: 978-0-534-50988-0

ISBN-10: 0-534-50988-6

Schirmer
10 Davis Drive
Belmont, CA 94002-3098
USA

Cengage Learning is a leading provider of customized learning solutions with office locations around the globe, including Singapore, the United Kingdom, Australia, Mexico, Brazil, and Japan. Locate your local office at: **www.cengage.com/global.**

Cengage Learning products are represented in Canada by Nelson Education, Ltd.

To learn more about Schirmer, visit **www.cengage.com/Schirmer.**

Purchase any of our products at your local college store or at our preferred online store **www.ichapters.com.**

Printed in Canada
4 5 6 7 10

Dedicated to the memory of my grandmother,
Bertha Schley, who first inspired me to become
a musician

BRIEF CONTENTS

CONTENTS

I**N BRINGING FORTH** the third edition of this book, I wish to express my deep appreciation for the interest shown in this work and the wide acceptance it has received in the field since the original edition was published in 1990. For the third edition the book has been completely revised and rewritten as necessary to reflect the current state of my research and to offer a full presentation of my method of playing and teaching brass instruments. As in the previous editions, the book has three purposes: (1) to serve as a text for college brass techniques and methods courses; (2) to function as a reference book for brass players, composers, conductors, and anyone interested in the world of brass; and (3) most importantly, to set forth my method of brass playing.

The book is divided into two parts. Chapters 1–9 contain discussions of the instruments and an outline of their historical development. Chapters 10–13 are concerned with the techniques of playing and teaching brass instruments as well as care of the instruments. Chapter 14 is directed to conductors. The extensive appendices present a visual impression of the world of brass, lists of recommended recordings, fingering and position charts, and a directory of instrument and mouthpiece makers and sources for brass music.

Many people have contributed to this book, and without their assistance it could not have been written. In particular, I am indebted to Michael Powell, John Rojak, Scott Mendoker, Dr. Travis Heath, Peter DelVecchio, Matthew Paterno, and Philipp Alexander, for their comments and suggestions for this third edition; and to Paul Hlebowitsh, Dr. Richard Plano, Dr. John Bewley, Lawrence Benz, Scott Mendoker, Ann Techan-Mendoker, Dr. B. P. Leonard, Vernon Post, Matthew Paterno, Col. Gilbert Mitchell, Kenneth Kemmerer, Dr. Robert Grechesky, Dr. Jonathan Korzun, Ralph Acquaro, and Dr. William Trusheim for their help with the first two editions.

An important aspect of this book is the photographs of leading brass players to illustrate some of the points emphasized in the text. I would therefore like to express my appreciation to the late Arnold Jacobs, Dale Clevenger, Jay Friedman, the late Philip Jones, Professor Roland Berger of the Vienna Philharmonic, George Coble, Peter Bond, Frøydis Ree Wekre, Barry Tuckwell, Ray Mase, Kevin Cobb, Peter Sullivan, Steven Kellner, Dr. Brian Bowman, Gebr. Alexander, and Yamaha Corporation. Thanks are also due to Steven DeSee, who collected many of the photographs that appeared in the original edition and are continued here, and Brooke McEldowney (Brooke of *9 Chickweed Lane* of the comic strips) for the gift of one of his musical cartoons.

In addition, I am grateful to Charles Schlueter, Vincent Cichowicz, Joseph Hetman, Mrs. Margaret Fletcher, Ursula Jones, my colleague and friend Professor William Fielder, Julie Yardley, Trudy Brown, Katherine Bishop, and Clark Baxter. I am especially grateful to my wife Cathy, who painstakingly prepared all of the line drawings and helped in many other ways, to my daughter Alexandra J. Whitener for expert assistance with computer graphics, and to my daughter Diana M. Whitener for willingness to provide additional drawings for this book.

Scott Whitener

INSTRUMENTS

How Brass
Instruments Work

BRASS INSTRUMENTS are among the oldest of all instruments. In antiquity, simple instruments such as the Scandinavian *lur* and the Roman *buccina* admirably fulfilled their ceremonial and musical functions. As each epoch unfolded, instruments were modified to serve the musical requirements of the new era. The line of development from ancient to modern is a process of refinement of a basic idea: the sounding of a flared tube through the vibration of the lips. Though the outward appearance of the instruments has changed, their internal operation is unaltered from a millennium ago.

In years past, brass instrument makers working with leading players evolved some excellent instruments by trial and error without really understanding the acoustical processes that were taking place. Speculative theories, sometimes inaccurate, surrounded discussions of how the instruments actually functioned. Now, due to the research of acousticians such as Arthur H. Benade,[1] the basic principles at work within the tubing of a brass instrument have been established objectively.

The sound of a brass instrument is created by the vibration of the lips initiating and maintaining a longitudinal standing wave in the air enclosed within the instrument's tubing. The tapered bell flare, which is of great importance, is designed to contain acoustical energy within the instrument in order to set up standing waves at specific frequencies. The player's embouchure may be seen as a flow-control valve acting on the steady airflow coming from the lungs. The closed lips are blown apart, setting them into vibration. Puffs of air are thereby emitted into the mouthpiece, setting in motion a sound wave that eventually reaches the instrument's expanding bell. As the bell flare widens, the wave encounters a drop in impedance (resistance) that, perhaps surprisingly, causes it to reflect back toward the mouthpiece (Figure 1.1). It is then reflected at the mouthpiece, where it is modified by the motion of the lips, encouraging a specific frequency dependent on the effective length of the vibrating air column. The oscillation of the lips (vibration) is itself modified by the reflecting wave so that its pattern of vibration corresponds to the instrument's timbre and the desired pitch. As the wave bounces back and forth while interacting with the instrument and the vibrating lips, the standing wave characteristic of brass instrument sound is formed. In reality, the process takes only a few hundredths of a second.

Although some acoustical energy leaks through the "barrier" in the expanding bell flare, most is reflected in the middle and low frequencies. As frequencies rise, the

---

[1]See Arthur H. Benade, *Fundamentals of Musical Acoustics* (New York: Oxford University Press, 1976), pp. 391–429, and Benade's article, "The Physics of Brasses," *Scientific American* (July 1973), pp. 24–35. Another source is John Backus, *The Acoustical Foundations of Music*, 2nd ed. (New York: W. W. Norton, 1977), pp. 259–280. I am grateful to Dr. Richard J. Plano, professor of physics at Rutgers University, for enlightening discussions on this subject.

FIGURE 1.1
Approximate point
of wave reflection
in a horn bell

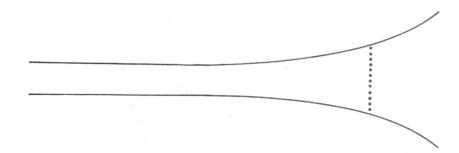

reflective threshold moves ever closer to the mouth of the bell and less energy is reflected. At this point the bell flare begins to operate more like an old-fashioned megaphone. This is why high notes are more difficult to play than pitches in the middle register.

In the production of a sustained tone, the fluctuations in pressure within the mouthpiece brought about by the standing wave help the embouchure to open and close in its vibrational pattern.[2] The player adjusts the embouchure and the force of the air stream so that vibration at a specific frequency is favored. The changes in pressure within the mouthpiece act on the adjusted embouchure to produce a steady tone. The embouchure's vibrations per second correspond to the cycles per second of a specific pitch. The pressure variations have been measured inside the mouthpiece and the peaks that occur at specific frequencies (indicating greater input impedance) recorded on a graph.[3] The resonance peaks—points at which the standing wave's amplitude is greatest—closely approximate the harmonic series in a well-designed brass instrument. (These are the notes that can be played without using the valves.) The length and shape of the instrument govern the pitches produced at the resonance peaks, but in each brass instrument the peaks always appear in the same pattern.

■ THE HARMONIC SERIES

Notes of the harmonic series are familiar to all brass players because a considerable amount of practice time is usually devoted to exercises based on them. Prior to the invention of valves, these were the only notes available to the natural trumpet and horn, although a technique of handstopping (used after c. 1750) allowed hornists to fill in the gaps between harmonics. What is not often recognized is the importance of the bell flare in deriving a usable harmonic series. If one attempts to play a harmonic series by inserting a mouthpiece into an appropriate length of cylindrical pipe, such as a garden hose, the following musically unusable series (approximating the odd-numbered harmonics) will result:[4]

[2]An important step forward was taken about 15 years ago by Ellis Wean, tubist of the Vancouver Symphony Orchestra, who obtained clear pictures of the opening and closing motion of the lips in vibration on a videotape using his TRU-VU transparent mouthpieces for each brass instrument. A strobe light was used to isolate the motion of the lips inside the mouthpiece while the instrument was being played. The subjects were leading players from the Montreal Symphony Orchestra.
[3]See Benade, *Fundamentals.*
[4]See Richard Merewether, *The horn, the horn . . .* (London: Paxman Musical Instruments Ltd., 1978), p. 36. The application of a mouthpiece to a cylindrical tube also influences the resultant harmonic series; see Backus, *The Acoustical Foundations of Music,* pp. 260–268.

If a well-designed flared bell is attached, the harmonics will be raised to form the standard harmonic series:[5]

Although different fundamental pitches can be used, depending on the length of the instrument, the structure of the harmonic series is always the same. For example, the series for the horn in F (written in concert pitch) is:

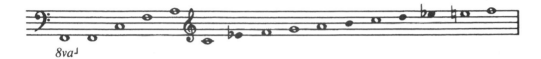

8va⌐

During the 17th and 18th centuries, trumpets were made of sufficient length to enable the player to utilize the area of the harmonic series that more or less resembles a diatonic scale. In modern trumpets, which are of shorter overall length, the fundamental is placed proportionally an octave higher, because the spaces between harmonics can be filled by notes played with the valves. The fundamental is positioned similarly in the other brass instruments, with the exception of the horn, which retains the octave-lower fundamental of the natural horn.

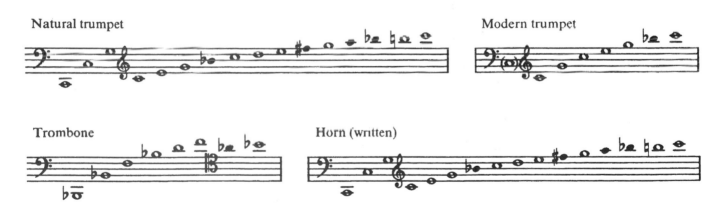

Another important aspect of the harmonic series is that partials of the series also sound in greater or lesser degree when a note is played. This is what defines the characteristic tone quality of an instrument. Also, notes with less sharply defined resonance peaks (making these notes more difficult to produce) are made more stable by the participation of other harmonically related peaks when the instrument is played at medium and loud dynamic levels.

■ VALVES

The valve is an ingenious device that opens an additional section of tubing for the vibrating air column to pass through, thus lengthening the wind path within the instrument and making available notes of the harmonic series of a different fundamental (this is

---

[5]Pitches are approximate for the two series shown. Certain harmonics do not agree with the equal-tempered scale (the most obvious of these are shown as quarter notes).

accomplished on the trombone by extending the slide). The segments of tubing that can be added by the valves lower the fundamental by a tone (first valve), a semitone (second valve), and a tone and a half (third valve).[6] The valves can also be used in combination by depressing valves simultaneously. The air column is then directed in turn through the tubing of each valve that has been opened, making accessible up to three additional harmonic series (2–3, 1–3, 1–2–3).

By utilizing the various overtones of the seven harmonic series, the instrument is made fully chromatic.

Since the 7th, 11th, 13th, 14th, and 15th harmonics of the series are not in tune within the equal temperament system in use today, they are substituted by valve notes. In the interest of finger dexterity, the 1–2 combination, which also lowers the fundamental a tone and a half, is normally used in place of the third valve alone. A basic problem of the valve system is inadequate tube length when the valves are used in combination, causing sharpness. Various approaches are used to correct this deficiency.[7]

Three principal types of valve are in use today. All function similarly, but they differ in their method of opening and closing the ports between the main tube and the tubing that can be added by the valve. In each, the vibrating air column runs down the valve section from one end or the other (depending on the construction of the instrument) and, with the valves closed, continues directly into the bell flare. If a valve is depressed, the air column is sent through the valve tubing before it proceeds toward the bell. The operation of the principal valve types can be seen in Figures 1.2, 1.3, and 1.4.

Piston valves offer a light, quick action but have less direct and accurate windways than the other two types. A shorter finger stroke may be used on rotary valves, but their action is not quite as immediate as that of piston valves. An advantage of the rotary type is that the diameter of the windway is maintained with somewhat greater consistency (although there is still some constriction), providing less resistance. Vienna valves (now found only on Vienna horns) cause the least disturbance to the air column,

---

[6] This is true of a descending valve system. In France and parts of Belgium, a system was in use on the horn in which the third valve raises the pitch by one tone. In this system, the third valve is set to direct the air column through its tubing; when depressed, the third valve tubing is bypassed, raising the overall pitch of the horn one tone (F to G; B♭ to C). Ascending horns began to fall out of fashion during the 1970s and were largely replaced by instruments constructed with the usual descending system. Players are still sometimes seen using ascending horns, and the idea (which offers some genuine advantages) may be revived in future. The *cor ascendant* is discussed in Chapter 4. A fourth ascending valve was at one time used on the Merri Franquin system trumpets. When depressed, the pitch of the trumpet is raised from C to D.

[7] This problem is discussed in depth under "Intonation" in Chapter 6; related discussions appear under the same heading in Chapters 3 and 7.

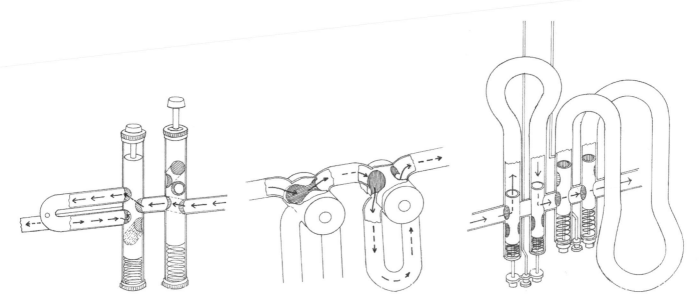

FIGURE 1.2 Piston valve   **FIGURE 1.3** Rotary valve   **FIGURE 1.4** Vienna valve

enabling the Vienna horn to play and sound more like the natural instrument. With the valves closed, the air column goes straight through the valve section, avoiding the angles and inconsistent windways inherent in rotary and piston designs. (When the valve is opened, however, the vibrating air column must make a sharp turn into the valve tubing.) Although their action is not as fast as that of other valve types, Vienna valves contribute great fluency and smoothness to slurred passages.[8]

In recent years, attention has been directed toward improving the response and the timbre of the trombone's F attachment (and attachments in other keys). Previously, it had been somewhat difficult to match the timbre of notes played on the attachment and those played in B♭. This led to the development of new types of change valves, with better windways. The first of these was the Thayer axial-flow valve, which received wide acceptance among trombonists. In this valve design, the diameter of the windway remains constant as it rotates from port to port. This offers improved response and tone quality. The success of the Thayer valve led many firms to develop improved valves for the trombone, and today most trombones are equipped with a valve that offers more accurate and free-blowing windways. Improved windways have been developed for rotary valves on horns in recent years, as well.

In using any type of valve, it is important to recognize that there are only two positions: open and closed. Therefore, valves should always be depressed as quickly as possible to avoid an audible discontinuity between notes. In slow passages, students often have a tendency to move their valves sluggishly. This produces an unattractive sound, particularly on slurs. Sometimes placing the fingertips slightly above the valve caps or levers encourages a quicker motion.

■ DESIGN CONSIDERATIONS

Every brass instrument consists of four basic parts: the mouthpiece (with its tapered backbore), a conical leadpipe, a section of cylindrical tubing containing the valves or slide, and the gradually expanding bell flare. The diameter of the bore, the shape and size of the tapered sections, the thickness and type of material, and overall mass are variables that cause instruments of the same type to play and sound differently.

[8]The Vienna valve is discussed further in Chapter 4.

Bore size is determined by the diameter of the tubing of the instrument's cylindrical section, although the bell throat and leadpipe taper usually conform to the main bore and contribute to an instrument's being designated as of large, medium, or small bore. Instruments of smaller bore generally respond with less effort and have a lighter tone. Although their timbre is exceptionally pure and clear, they can be overblown at high dynamic levels, causing an overlay of edge on the sound. Large-bore instruments typically have a darker, weightier tone that remains more consistent from soft to loud, but they require more effort to play.

Along with the leadpipe taper, how the bell is shaped is of primary importance in determining both the quality of an instrument and the character of its timbre. The size of the bell, how sharply it is flared, and especially the diameter and taper of the bell throat strongly influence tone, intonation, and response. The rate of expansion of the bell section from the valves onward also has a significant effect on timbre. (Bell tapers are discussed in relation to the horn in Chapter 4.) How the bell is made is also a factor governing the overall quality of the instrument. The finest bells are formed from sheet brass, which is beaten on a mandrel and then spun and brought to final shape on a lathe by hand. This work requires the skill of a master craftsperson and this must be reflected in the instrument's price. Bells of this type have a strong, resonant tone that carries well.

Brass instruments are primarily made from yellow brass, gold (red) brass, and nickel-silver alloys.[9] Each of these materials contributes certain qualities to the timbre, and players usually have clear preferences. The Physikalisch-technische Bundesanstalt of Braunschweig, Germany, has investigated the influence of different alloys on horn timbre. While the findings tend to confirm the views expressed in Chapter 4, more research is needed to arrive at firm conclusions.[10] Other alloys, such as beryllium and sterling silver, are sometimes used as trumpet bell materials, and ambronze has been used in the construction of horns.

The finish that is applied to the metal is another issue of personal preference. Some feel that any type of finish degrades an instrument's tone and response, while others find no important difference or welcome the effect that either lacquer or silver plating contributes. Plating and lacquer do serve as protective coatings and resist deterioration of the metal. Gold plating is more rarely used because of its cost.

An instrument's mass also affects its playing and tonal qualities. A heavier instrument will have a darker and more solid timbre but will require somewhat more exertion to play than one of lesser weight. Lighter instruments often feel more responsive and flexible to the player but exhibit tonal differences from those of greater mass. Whether the difference is positive or negative is a subjective question that must be answered by the player in consideration of the music being performed. In general, instrument designers seek a careful balance between lightness and sufficient weight to produce a full, resonant tone. The thickness of the walls of the tubing and bell flare also has a significant effect on both timbre and playability.

Another area where the question of mass has come under consideration is in the design of mouthpieces. Heavy-mass or heavy-wall mouthpieces are now available. Some players find definite advantages to this type of mouthpiece, while others retain their preferences for mouthpieces of traditional shape and weight.[11]

Attention has also been given to the effects of stress reduction both in the construction of instruments and in the metal itself. Stress pressures are often built into an instrument through the soldering process when it is assembled. These can be relieved to a certain extent by taking the instrument apart and meticulously reassembling it with minimal stress. Another approach (which is also directed to the alloy) is either heavy annealing or bringing the instrument to a subfreezing temperature. Opinion is quite

---

[9] The relative contents of the alloys are yellow brass, 70 percent copper and 30 percent zinc; gold (red) brass, 85 percent copper and 15 percent zinc; nickel-silver, 63 percent copper, 27 percent zinc, and 10–12 percent nickel.

[10] The effect of different materials on timbre is considered in Chapters 4 and 5.

[11] The variables of mouthpiece design are discussed in Chapter 2.

divided on the merit of these procedures. Though some players find improvements through these methods, many reaffirm the importance of traditional "work hardening" in the making of brass instruments. "Work hardening" is traditionally believed to contribute resonance and carrying power to the timbre.

The bends in the tubing and how it is arranged within the overall pattern of the instrument is another design factor now being given consideration. Open-wrap designs emphasize broad, gentle bends in the tubing. This is believed to create lessened resistance and to contribute greater flexibility in changing notes. In trombone F and other attachments, the open-wrap configuration is considered to improve the sound. While it is generally agreed that sharp, tight bends are best avoided, some designers feel that more squared-off bows give the timbre firmness and a more ringing tone that projects well in a concert hall (earlier Vincent Bach trumpets, for example).

ANATOMY OF THE MOUTHPIECE

AS WAS DISCUSSED in Chapter 1, the mouthpiece forms a chamber in which air coming from the lungs is converted into acoustical energy to create sound within the flared and cylindrical tubing of the instrument. (See Figure 2.1.) This is why the mouthpiece plays so crucial a role in influencing tone quality, response, and intonation. It is also the interface between player and instrument. Therefore, the selection of a mouthpiece is not only an important consideration, but a highly individual and personal one. Not only must a particular mouthpiece enable a player to produce a good tone quality (and one that is appropriate to the music being performed), but it must offer a quick response in all ranges without undue effort, as well as clear tonguing, reliable intonation, and good endurance. Individuals vary considerably in their embouchure formation, due to differences in facial musculature, lips, and teeth. Consequently, a mouthpiece that works well for one player will not necessarily produce comparable results with another. The important thing is that along with being of effective design, the mouthpiece must *suit* the player. Choosing the right mouthpiece can make an important difference in a player's advancement, while a wrong choice can hold progress back. The best way to select a mouthpiece is first to consider the variables of mouthpiece design and their effects.

The five basic components of a mouthpiece are shown in Figure 2.2. The main points to consider are:

- Rim: inner diameter, width, contour, and edge (bite)
- Cup: depth and shape; air volume
- Throat and bore: shape of opening, diameter, length of bore
- Backbore: rate and shape of taper
- Shank: length in relation to the instrument and accuracy of fit into receiver

Each of these factors significantly influences how a mouthpiece will perform and the timbre it will produce.

Carefully study Figures 2.3 through 2.6; these are side views of actual mouthpieces (not drawings) that have been cut in half to reveal their inner contours.

■ INNER RIM DIAMETER (CUP DIAMETER)

Although it is often identified as the diameter of the mouthpiece cup, this measure is the distance between the inner edges of the rim and will be considered with other aspects of rim design. This distance defines the area in which the lips vibrate and, in conjunction with the depth of the cup and its shape, determines the air volume of the cup. Consequently, inner rim diameter is a key factor influencing the size of the sound (breadth and

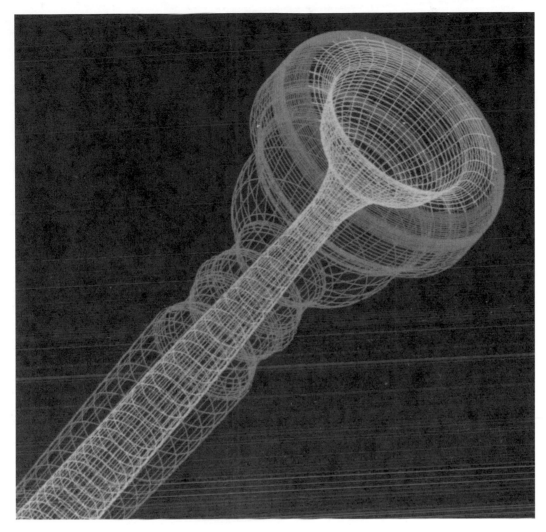

FIGURE 2.1 Wireframe mouthpiece

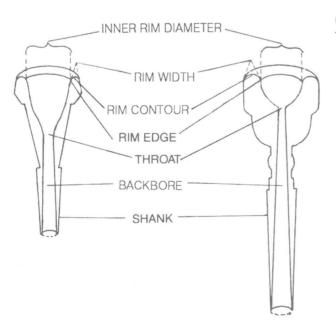

INNER RIM DIAMETER

RIM WIDTH

RIM CONTOUR

RIM EDGE

THROAT

BACKBORE

SHANK

FIGURE 2.2
The parts of a mouthpiece

FIGURE 2.3
Trumpet

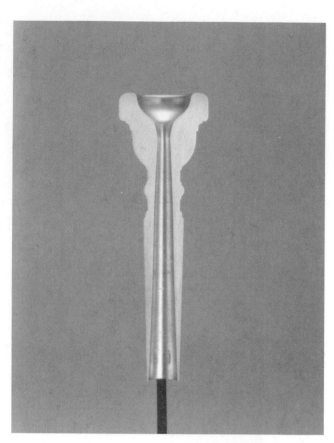

FIGURE 2.4
Horn

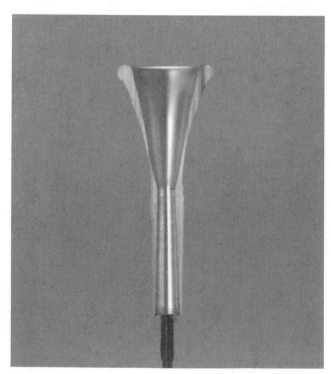

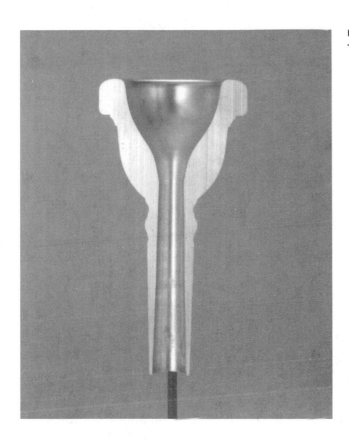

FIGURE 2.5
Trombone

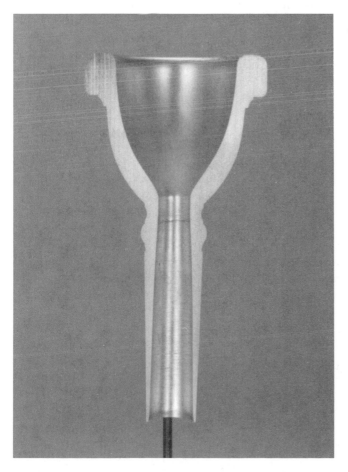

FIGURE 2.6
Tuba

fullness), although the throat and backbore are also important factors. The opening and closing motion of the embouchure in vibration is affected by the inner rim diameter. A larger diameter encourages the embouchure to open more in its oscillation for a given pitch. This creates a greater range of vibrational motion (at the same *frequency* of vibration) than a smaller diameter, thereby contributing a fuller, more resonant tone.

Brass players, especially trumpet and horn players, are extraordinarily sensitive to small differences in inner rim diameter. The ability to detect differences of two-tenths of a millimeter is not uncommon. The very broad range of inner rim diameters in use on mouthpieces of each brass instrument is, among other things, an indication of the significant individual variability in the dental arch. This can best be understood by visualizing the arch-shaped line of the upper teeth as if viewed downward from the top of the head. In some individuals, this arch is flatter at the center, where the mouthpiece rests. Players with this type of arch can use a wider inner rim diameter without compromising the seal at each side of the rim. Individuals with a more pronounced arch usually require mouthpieces within a slightly narrower range of inner diameters in order to maintain a balanced seal at the sides without increased mouthpiece pressure. (The circumference of the mouthpiece rim is symmetrical; if the area of seal at each side of the rim is significantly rearward of the central seal area due to the shape of the dental arch, more pressure must be applied to create a stable seal. This produces a greater level of mouthpiece pressure at the center of the embouchure.) Any decrease in inner rim diameter can be compensated for in the mouthpiece's tone by increasing the depth (or altering the shape) of the cup, increasing the throat diameter, or enlarging the backbore.

There is variability, too, in the thickness of the lip tissue itself and the size and placement of the teeth. These factors also must be taken into account in the choice of an inner rim diameter. Players with fuller lip tissue and larger teeth usually require a wider inner rim diameter to allow sufficient space for unrestricted vibration. An inner diameter that is too narrow inhibits free vibration and can cause the mouthpiece placement to shift downward[1], creating problems in tone production (mouthpiece placement is discussed in Chapter 10). An inner rim diameter that is too wide for an individual will cause a feeling of loss of control, and the high range will suffer. It should be recognized, however, that in changing to a larger inner rim diameter, there will be a period of adjustment in which these same effects will be present to some degree until the muscles at the sides of the rim (where the rim contacts the lips) and just inside the rim adjust to the new diameter. The key is whether this proves to be a temporary condition or one that lingers. Usually, this can be determined within a couple of weeks. If the condition persists, it might be an indication that the inner rim diameter is too wide.

An experienced player will usually determine by trial and error a particular inner rim diameter that suits his or her embouchure and one that (along with the other mouthpiece variables) offers sound and playing qualities consistent with what the player is trying to achieve. In general, modern brass players try to use as large an inner diameter as possible, as long as the criteria described earlier are met. Aside from the fullness and resonance of tone that a wider diameter offers, greater comfort and flexibility are provided by having more room for the embouchure to make adjustments for higher and lower pitches. Additionally, mouthpiece pressure (only enough to create a stable seal) is distributed across a wider area rather than being concentrated in the center.

Wider diameters do at first require somewhat greater embouchure strength and more air than smaller diameters. Mouthpieces with narrow diameters generally produce a lighter tone and require less effort. At one time, narrow diameters were thought to facilitate high range, but this idea is largely discredited today. In fact, an overly narrow inner rim diameter can restrict the vibration of the embouchure and impede the airflow in the upper register. Most professional players use fairly large inner rim diameters for

---

[1]Trumpet and horn players must be particularly careful that the inner edge of the upper rim does not shift downward onto the red part of the upper lip. This inhibits the free vibrational motion of the embouchure and can sometimes be caused by an inner rim diameter that is too narrow for the player.

all of their playing, including the higher trumpets and descant horn, although cups of shallower depth are usually substituted on these instruments.

As important as the inner rim diameter is in the choice of a mouthpiece, it is surprising that the measurements listed by manufacturers in their catalogs are not more precise. The approximations that appear in such lists make comparisons between mouthpieces of different makers based on their stated measurements very different from comparisons made by actual testing. The reason for the lack of precision on this vital measurement is that there is no standardized depth (from the top of the rim into the cup) at which the measurement is taken. The problem is compounded by differences in rim contour (rim contour is discussed later). In some contours, the inside of the rim slopes inward and the inner diameter constantly changes (narrows), with no clearly defined point at which the rim ends and the cup begins. Consequently, measurements made at a shallower depth will be wider than those made deeper into the cup. Ideally, the inner diameter should be measured at the rim edge (bite); but again, in some designs the edge is smoothly blended into the contour without a clear point of definition. In others, the edge is placed higher or lower along the face of the inner rim. The net effect of these variables is that manufacturers' inner rim measurements should be understood to be approximate, and only by playing a mouthpiece can a meaningful evaluation and comparison with other mouthpieces be made.

Ranges of Modern Inner Rim Diameters	Most Common Range
Trumpet: 15.8–18.29 mm	16.2–17.2 mm
Cornet: 16–17 mm	16–16.4 mm (conical cup type)
Horn: 16.2–18.5 mm	16.8–18 mm[2]
Tenor trombone: 24.3–26.9 mm	25.4–26 mm
Bass trombone: 26.52–29.5 mm	26.4–28.52 mm
Euphonium: 25.1–26 mm	25.4–26 mm
Tuba: 30–33.7 mm	Bass tuba: 30–32 mm
	Contrabass tuba: 31.4–32.76 mm

◼ RIM WIDTH

The thickness of the mouthpiece rim is a prime factor in the interface between player and instrument. Rim width cannot be considered in a vacuum, however, since there is a subtle interplay between the shape of the rim (rim contour) and its thickness. A carefully designed contour can give a wider rim some of the qualities of a narrower rim and make a narrow rim more comfortable to the embouchure. In general, wide rims (except those with sophisticated contours[3]) tend to be somewhat less responsive and flexible. They are comfortable, however, and the added support contributes to security and endurance. Narrow rims offer excellent flexibility and faster response, but the smaller contact area does not provide the support of a wider rim. Usually, a mouthpiece designer will strive for a balance of these features by finding a compromise between wide and narrow, along with an effective contour.

Most rims for trumpet, trombone, euphonium, and tuba are designated as medium or medium-wide rims. These offer a good balance of flexibility, comfort, and endurance.

[2] A current trend in the design of horn mouthpieces is to produce inner rim diameters in increments of 0.5 mm—for example, 16.5, 17, 17.5, and 18 mm. As a result, there are too few sizes in the range of 17–17.5 mm, where many horn players fall. A better approach is taken in the Stork Orval series. The basic mouthpiece is available in diameters of 17, 17.25, 17.5, 17.75, and 18 mm, with both American and European shanks. The Denis Wick range now includes rim diameters of 17, 17.25, 17.5, and 18 mm.
[3] Such as the Paxman Halstead Chidell and Denis Wick wide-rim horn mouthpieces.

Somewhat narrower rims have been used of late on some of the larger bass trombone mouthpieces and on a few tuba mouthpieces. The greatest diversity in rim width is among horn mouthpieces. Horn rims vary from around 3.5 to 5.7 mm! To interpret such a broad range of rim thicknesses, it would be fair to say that 3.9- to 4.0-mm rims could be considered standard medium-narrow rims and 4.2- to 4.3-mm widths as medium-wide rims. Widths that are less than 3.9 mm should be regarded as quite narrow, and anything greater than 4.4 mm is a wide rim. The divergence in rim thicknesses in use on horn mouthpieces is an indication of the vastly different approaches designers have followed to balance the level of flexibility needed in horn playing with comfort and endurance.

The medium and medium-wide rim widths in use on the other brass instruments fall proportionally into smaller ranges:

Trumpet	5.05–5.50 mm
Cornet	5.17–5.30 mm
Tenor Trombone	6.26–6.80 mm
Bass Trombone	6.09 (narrow) to 6.73 mm
Euphonium	6.26–6.72 mm
Tuba	6.89–8.11 mm

Rim widths outside these parameters should be considered as narrow or wide.

■ RIM CONTOUR

How the rim is shaped is known as the rim contour. Contours can be round, fairly flat, oval, or with the high point or peak shifted toward the inside or outside on the rim face. These variations affect individuals differently, so the player should be aware of this variable in trying various mouthpieces. The only generalizations that can be made are that somewhat flat rims, if not too wide, tend to be responsive and offer a clear attack and that very round contours are often less responsive and limit endurance. Balanced-contour rims (semiflat and semiround) are probably the most widely used today.

The shape of the rim on the outside is also a consideration. On some trumpet mouthpieces the outer edge of the rim is rounded off to promote flexibility. Horn players who use an inset mouthpiece placement are particularly sensitive to the shape of the outer rim surface, since some of the lower lip tissue is in contact with this part of the rim when they play in the low register.

While finding a suitable rim contour can only be accomplished by trial and error, it should be recognized that this, along with the rim thickness and edge, is one of the most important factors in determining how a mouthpiece will work for an individual. This is the actual interface between the player's embouchure and the instrument.

■ RIM EDGE (BITE)

The inner edge of the rim is part of the rim contour. This edge can be designed so that its presence is clearly detected by the lips or reduced to imperceptibility. It can also be placed higher or lower on the inner face of the rim contour. Some performers believe that a slightly discernible edge improves response and attack, while others find such a rim uncomfortable and tiring to play. There may be a relationship between rim width and the need for some definition in its edge. Medium rims probably require a subtle edge to feel responsive. Narrower rims, with their more direct response, cause discomfort if the edge is noticeable. Rims, of course, can be altered to suit individual preferences. Often, the rim of one model is substituted on another cup, usually through the use of a screw-rim (component) mouthpiece.

◼ CUP DEPTH AND SHAPE

Of all the elements of mouthpiece design, the shape and depth of the cup have the greatest influence over the quality of tone. Deeper cups lend fullness to the sound and a somewhat darker character. Shallow cups produce a timbre that is both lighter in weight and brighter in color. Instrument designer Vincent Bach attributed these differences to the way in which partials are present in the sound. With deep cups, the fundamental tends to predominate, with fewer of the highest partials present. A tone more endowed with upper partials results when a shallow cup is used. The goal is to find the right balance of these qualities to achieve a full and characteristic timbre, consistent with good intonation and response.

The quickness of response and ease of playing in different registers are additional factors influenced by the depth and shape of the cup (in combination with a well-designed backbore). Mouthpieces vary significantly in their ease and directness of response and how they center the production of sound in the middle, upper, and lower ranges. Some mouthpieces are superior in this respect, and this is an important criterion in the selection of a mouthpiece.

The two hypothetical cup shapes are the bowl and the cone; in actuality, most brass mouthpieces are carefully derived combinations of these two basic configurations. By comparing Figures 2.3 through 2.6, one can clearly see the differences in cup shape among brass instruments. The horn mouthpiece is the most conical. In earlier periods, horn mouthpieces were totally conical; but today, most incorporate a very slight cup while preserving a basic funnel shape. Cornet and euphonium mouthpieces are more conical than the corresponding trumpet and trombone mouthpieces in order to give these instruments their sweet, mellow tone. Although the trumpet cup is the most bowl-like, the bottom of the cup has a conical shape to contribute a characteristically clear, ringing sound. For much of their previous history, conical mouthpieces, more like those used on the horn, were favored by trombonists. These produced a pure, centered tone quality that was particularly effective on smaller-bore trombones.

As shown in Figures 2.3, 2.5, and 2.6, the trombone mouthpiece is proportionally more conical for its depth than the trumpet, the tuba even more so. (The area at the bottom of the cup that opens into the throat and backbore is discussed later.) What this reveals is that the way in which the theoretical bowl and cone shapes have been combined for each instrument is different and has evolved independently.

The depth of the cup also affects to some extent the high and low ranges. Very deep cups are normally used, for example, by fourth horn players and bass trombonists to facilitate the low register. Conversely, trumpeters often substitute shallow cups when performing on the piccolo trumpet. Jazz and studio players usually prefer shallower cup depths to cope with the high range demands of these fields and to produce an appropriately brilliant timbre. (At times, the latter has had a negative effect on students who use shallow mouthpieces, hoping to gain range quickly. Shallow cups are not conducive to good development in the formative stages, and they wreak havoc in school bands and orchestras. A shallow mouthpiece should be viewed as a specialized tool for a specific performance situation.) With the exceptions noted, most brass players look for a cup depth that produces the fullest and most resonant tone, so long as the full range of the instrument can be played reliably, with good intonation, and without excessive effort.

The shape of the cup for a given depth is a less obvious, but vitally important variable. Some cup shapes produce more resonant and darker tones. Others produce lighter sounds. The ease of response, too, is affected by how the cup is shaped. Unfortunately, little useful information can be gained by visually examining the shape of the cup. How this shape influences the tone and playing characteristics of a mouthpiece can only be determined by playing several mouthpieces and comparing their qualities.

■ THROAT AND BORE

The main considerations are how the opening to the bore is shaped, the diameter of the bore, and its length. Mouthpiece makers are not consistent in how these two components are identified. For a long time the mouthpiece's narrowest diameter was designated the throat or throat bore. The conical opening between the bottom of the cup and the short cylindrical bore were not considered separate entities. Many manufacturers continue to designate both components as the throat. However, there is a recent trend toward considering the shaped opening to the bore as the throat and the cylindrical passage as the bore.

How the throat is shaped and how it opens from the bottom of the cup into the bore influences sound and response. In the 18th century, trumpet mouthpieces were bowl-shaped, with sharp-edged throats drilled directly into the bottom of the cup. In modern trumpet mouthpieces, a conical interface from the bottom of the cup flows smoothly into the cylindrical bore without any presence of an edge. In some designs, more of a shoulder is left at the throat opening; but in others, the opening itself takes on a smooth, conical shape. The latter lessens resistance and adds depth to the sound. At least one maker refers to this conical opening as a second cup, whereas others consider this the throat of the mouthpiece. At one time, double-cup mouthpieces were popular among trumpet players in the jazz field. Rarely seen today, such mouthpieces had an actual smaller cup cut into the bottom of the primary cup. It was felt that this facilitated the high range.

The bore is the narrowest diameter in the mouthpiece and can be made in a variety of diameters. It is cylindrical in shape. Its length can be negligible or of a specific calculated length. The latter affects the placement of the pitches, especially in the high register. The length of the bore must be carefully worked out in relation to the backbore and cup depth to ensure good intonation.

Large bores darken the tone and give it body. Smaller diameters have the opposite effect. The bore's diameter can be measured by inserting numbered (or metric) drill bits into the bore until the correct size is found. Drill bits are numbered such that the higher the number, the smaller the diameter. For example, the standard bore of Bach trumpet mouthpieces is 27 (3.67 mm; 0.144"). Symphony players typically use larger bores, in the range 25 to 23. There is less consistency among horn mouthpieces, with bores usually varying from 1 to 17 (5.79–4.39 mm; 0.227–0.172"). The bores of trombone and euphonium mouthpieces usually run from 6.4 mm (0.252") to 7.4 mm (0.291"), and tuba bores run from 7.4 mm to 8.85 mm (0.348"). Most professional brass players determine their preference in bore diameter through experimentation and either order their mouthpiece with the appropriate bore or have an existing mouthpiece drilled to that size.

■ BACKBORE

Because it is impossible to gain any really useful information from visual inspection, the backbore is the least understood aspect of the mouthpiece and all judgments must be made by trial and error. No system of measurements is in use to guide the player and allow for comparisons, so one must rely on catalog descriptions such as "large," "medium," "symphony," "Schmidt," " barrel," and others or on letter or number identifications (b, c, d; 10, 24, 87) that apply only to a particular manufacturer. However, response, intonation, flexibility, tone, and endurance are all greatly influenced by the backbore. To stress the importance and the variability inherent in this aspect of mouthpiece design, it should be noted that Vincent Bach developed 107 different backbores for trumpet, and the firm normally offers one standard and seven other backbores to special order.

It might be assumed that backbores are drilled to a constant rate of taper, but this is rarely the case. Larger backbores expand at a steeper rate during the first third, or less, of their length and thereafter very gradually until the final diameter is reached. The final diameter should match the leadpipe taper. Smaller backbores employ a much more gradual taper over approximately the first two-thirds of their length. So-called standard backbores represent a compromise between these extremes. The larger bores, such as "symphony" and "Schmidt" models, offer a fuller tone but require more air and greater embouchure strength than the standard models. Endurance is the critical factor. A player's embouchure can become quickly exhausted due to lack of resistance if the backbore is too large. Backbore experimentation should only be undertaken by experienced players who are well accustomed to a particular mouthpiece.

▪ SHANK

The purpose of the mouthpiece shank and instrument receiver is to bring the backbore into contact with the leadpipe without interruption so that a continuous taper is formed. If it were not so inconvenient, mouthpieces and leadpipes would probably be made in one piece to ensure the accuracy of this taper. Any inexactness at this point can influence the instrument's performance, so it is essential that the shank fit the receiver accurately. The player should check the fit carefully; there should be no wobbles, and the mouthpiece should go into the receiver the correct distance.

American shanks are normally made with Morse 0 or number 1 tapers. This does not automatically ensure that the correct interface will be formed with the leadpipe. Sometimes a gap will occur between the end of the mouthpiece and the leadpipe. There is a difference of opinion among designers of trumpet mouthpieces as to the negative or positive effect of such a gap. Although no acoustical explanation has been forthcoming, it does appear that certain mouthpiece–instrument combinations produce far better results with a gap than without one. Horn mouthpieces sometimes go into the leadpipe too far or not far enough, affecting the instrument's pitch center on certain notes.

No single standard similar to the Morse taper is used among European makers. On German and British horns, for example, American-made mouthpieces (which have a smaller shank) usually go too far into the mouthpipe. Similar fit problems sometimes arise with rotary valve trumpets and tubas. A mouthpiece maker can correct any problems of this sort by copying the mouthpiece with a larger or smaller shank or by altering the cup, rim, and throat of a European mouthpiece to the player's requirements while leaving the original shank unchanged. Some progressive firms offer mouthpieces with either American or European shanks.

▪ COMPONENT MOUTHPIECES

Screw-rim mouthpieces have been available for many years.[4] These allow different combinations of cup and rim to be used by the player, usually when switching between instruments (for example, C trumpet to piccolo trumpet or double horn to descant horn). This is accomplished by creating a threaded joint between the rim and cup so that the rim can be removed from one cup and attached to another. Normally, the player will use one rim with different cups (including the throat and backbore). In recent years, the possibilities inherent in this principle have been extended by creating three-piece component mouthpieces. These have threaded joints that subdivide the mouthpiece into rim, cup, and throat-backbore, permitting three-way combinations to be assembled.

▪ HEAVY-WALL MOUTHPIECES

Mouthpieces purposely constructed with greater mass and weight have recently gained popularity. Players who favor these designs feel that they offer increased power and do not distort at high volume levels. Another possible benefit is better centers ("slots") for

---

[4]It is believed that the first screw-rim mouthpieces were made by the late German trumpet and mouthpiece maker Josef Monke, of Cologne.

the notes of the upper and lower registers. Many other players continue to prefer traditional designs, and it is likely that both types of mouthpiece will continue to coexist in the future.

■ GENERAL MOUTHPIECE SUGGESTIONS

- Choose a high-quality mouthpiece of a recognized manufacturer.
- Remember that no single manufacturer produces the best mouthpieces for all brass instruments.
- Choose a mouthpiece that responds easily, plays well and without undue effort in all ranges, promotes clear tonguing, and has a good tone quality.
- Do not choose a mouthpiece solely for its tone quality. It must also play well for the individual player.
- Keep in mind that, while the upper range may suffer temporarily after a change to a larger mouthpiece, it should soon return.
- Avoid shallow mouthpieces.
- Do not choose a mouthpiece simply because it works well for another player, even a famous one. Mouthpieces work differently for individual players. The mouthpiece must suit the individual.
- Test every mouthpiece individually. Different examples of the same mouthpiece may not be identical, due to the way mouthpieces are made.
- Because mouthpiece makers do not use a consistent system of numbering, the only way to determine the characteristics of a particular model is to study the catalog description and dimensions, if given. Only by play-testing can useful comparisons be made between mouthpieces.
- Although searching for the ideal mouthpiece is unwise, it is important to try different mouthpieces at regular intervals in your development to see if they offer any improvements.

■ MOUTHPIECE RECOMMENDATIONS

Trumpet and Cornet

It is important to understand how models are identified by various manufacturers. Bach, Denis Wick, and Stork indicate progressively larger cup diameters as the numbers become smaller. Schilke and Yamaha use an opposite system. The system used by other firms should be determined by studying their catalogs. Cup depths on Bach mouthpieces are frequently misunderstood:

A = Very deep

Number without letter = medium-deep

B = medium

C = medium-shallow

D = shallow

E = extremely shallow

The medium-deep cups identified by number only were intended by Vincent Bach as a standard model for the B♭ and C trumpets. In recent years, they have tended to be overlooked in favor of the C cup. While both cups yield excellent results, unlettered models offer a fuller, more resonant tone.

Cornet mouthpieces must be made with the smaller cornet shank; this should be specified when ordering if the mouthpiece is offered for both trumpet and cornet. In reality, a cornet mouthpiece must be constructed quite differently from a trumpet mouthpiece if a true cornet tone is to be achieved. The darker, more mellow tone of the cornet should contrast to the brilliant, ringing tone of the trumpet. This is achieved by the depth and conical shape of the cornet mouthpiece's cup, along with a larger bore and slightly narrower rim. The most authentic cornet mouthpieces currently available (with sufficient cup depth and traditional shape) are the Denis Wick models.

Trumpet

Beginner	Intermediate	Advanced
Bach 7 or 7C	Bach 6, 5, 5C, or 3C	Bach 2, 2C, 1, X1, 1¼C, or 1C
Stork Vacchiano 7C	Stork Vacchiano 3C	Stork Vacchiano 1, 2C, 2B, 3B
Denis Wick 4	Denis Wick 3	Denis Wick 2W, 1CW, or 1W
Josef Klier 77C	Josef Klier 66B	Josef Klier 44C, 44B
Tilz 200-S5	Tilz 200-S5	Tilz 200-S8 or -S9
Yamaha 11C4–7C	Yamaha 15B4	Yamaha 16C4, 17C4
Schilke 9 or 11	Schilke 14 or 17	Schilke 18, 20, or 20D2d

Cornet

Beginner	Intermediate	Advanced
Denis Wick 5B	Denis Wick 5B, 4B	Denis Wick 5 or 4 or RW 4 or 3
Yamaha 11E4		Lewington–McCann Model[5]

Flugelhorn

Intermediate	Advanced
Denis Wick 5BFL, 4FL, 4F	Denis Wick 2F, 4FL, RW3FL

Horn

Beginner	Intermediate	Advanced
Josef Klier W3DK, W3CK	Josef Klier W3DK, W3CK, W2DK	Josef Klier W2DK, W2CK, W2CM
Tilz B3	Tilz B4, McWilliam 1	Tilz B4, McWilliam 1 or 1W
Tilz E. Schmid 55	Tilz E. Schmid 8 or 85	Tilz Schmid 8 or 85
Denis Wick 7, 7N	Denis Wick 7, 7N, 6N	Denis Wick 6N, 5N
Laskey 70G	Laskey 725G or 75G	Laskey 75G
Paxman 3B, 3C	Paxman 3B, 3C, 4B, 4C	Paxman 4B, 4C[6]
		Paxman Halstead-Chidell 22A-AS or 23A-AS
Yamaha 30C4	Yamaha 30C4	Yamaha 31D4
Schilke 30	Schilke 30	Schilke 31

E♭ Alto (Tenor) Horn

Intermediate	Advanced
Denis Wick 5	Denis Wick 5, 3, 2

[5] Lewington–McCann cornet mouthpieces are available from Bill Lewington Ltd., London.
[6] Paxman mouthpieces are also available as screw-rim models with standard and narrow rims. E. Schmid models are available from both mouthpiece maker Bruno Tilz and horn maker Engelbert Schmid.

Trombone

Before purchasing a trombone mouthpiece, it is necessary to know whether the instrument's receiver has been designed to accept a large or a small shank. Large-bore tenor trombones, such as the Conn 88H and Bach 42B, require large shanks, while medium- and small-bore tenors normally accept the smaller size. Bass trombones invariably take the large shank. Most mouthpieces for tenor trombone (with the exception of the largest models) are available with either shank, so the correct size must be specified when ordering.

Tenor Trombone

Beginner	Intermediate	Advanced
Denis Wick 12CS, 9BS	Denis Wick 6BS or 6BL	Denis Wick 5BS or 5BL, 4BL, 4AL
–	Greg Black Alessi Models 6M, 5.5	Greg Black Alessi Models 6M, 3.5, 2
Bach 12C, 12, 11	Bach 7C, 7, 6½ AL	Bach 5G, 4G
Schilke 46	Schilke 47, 50	Schilke 51B, 51
Josef Klier P89C	Josef Klier P77B	Josef Klier P66B, P55A

Bass Trombone

Beginner	Intermediate	Advanced
–	Denis Wick 5AL, 4AL, or 3AL	Denis Wick 2AL, 1AL, or 0AL
–	Schilke 57	Schilke 58, 59, 60
–	Bach 5G, 3G	Bach 2G, 1G, 1½ G
–	–	Josef Klier P33AK, P22AK

Euphonium and Baritone

Again, the question of shank sizes arises. Formerly, many American instrument manufacturers and Yamaha used a standard size equivalent to the small trombone shank. In the Denis Wick catalog, these are identified by the letter Y (the last letter of the mouthpiece's number indicates shank size). Boosey and Hawkes/Besson euphoniums made since 1974 accept the normal large trombone shank (L), but earlier models required a special shank size that the Wick catalog designates by the letter M. The popular Denis Wick Steven Mead models fit all modern euphoniums. When ordering Bach and Schilke mouthpieces, it is necessary to indicate whether a large or small shank is to be used.

Most trombone and euphonium mouthpieces are not interchangeable, since an authentic euphonium tone can only be achieved with a deeper, more conical cup.

Euphonium[7]

Beginner	Intermediate	Advanced
Denis Wick 6BY, 6BM, 6BL	Denis Wick SM5	Denis Wick SM4, SM3
Schilke 46D	Schilke 46D	Schilke 51D
Bach 12C, 11	Bach 6½ A, 6½ AL	Bach 5G, 4G
Yamaha 48	Yamaha 48D, 51	Yamaha 51, 51D

[7]See David R. Werden, "Euphonium Mouthpieces–A Teacher's Guide," *The Instrumentalist* (May 1981), pp. 23–26.

Baritone

Beginner	Intermediate	Advanced
Denis Wick SM9	Denis Wick SM6	Denis Wick SM4

Tuba

Beginner	Intermediate	Advanced
Bach 30E, 32E	Bach 22	Schilke S-H (Helleberg II)
Denis Wick 4L, 5L	Denis Wick 3L	Dillon M1C
Yamaha 65	Schilke 66	Denis Wick 2L, 1L
–	Yamaha 66	Monette 95, 97, 98, 99
–	Conn 7B Helleberg	Perantucci 44, 48, 50
–	–	Josef Klier T55A, T44B
–	–	Bach 18, 12, 7
–	–	Laskey 30G, 30H
–	–	Yamaha 67C4
–	–	Conn Helleberg

CHAPTER 3

TRUMPET AND CORNET

TRUMPETERS TODAY have a wide assortment of specialized instruments available to help them meet the exacting performance standards now routinely expected. (See Figure 3.1.) This is in sharp contrast to earlier periods. When the author's teacher, William Vacchiano, joined the New York Philharmonic in the 1930s, only one player in the trumpet section owned a C trumpet, and every trumpeter was expected to play all of the standard repertoire on the B♭ instrument. Today, there are trumpets pitched in the keys of every scale note of a full octave above the B♭ instrument. These fall into two basic categories: B♭ and C trumpets for general use and higher trumpets pitched in D, E♭, E, F, G, piccolo B♭/A, and C for orchestral and solo literature demanding a high tessitura.

It is fair to ask why so many trumpets are necessary. The answer can best be illustrated by an example. While a strong player might possibly be able to sustain the high range called for in Bach's *B Minor Mass* on a B♭ trumpet, the notes would be produced fairly high on the harmonic series, with considerable effort. By changing to a piccolo trumpet in A, the same notes would be played lower in the most stable part of the harmonic series, where response is easiest and the harmonics are more widely separated. This facilitates making entrances and playing in the high register, and it improves accuracy. Also, the undue effort required to maintain the high tessitura of this work on the larger instrument would prove severely fatiguing. A smaller, higher-pitched trumpet brings such parts much more under the player's control.

Aside from these considerations, the larger and weightier tone of the B♭, while well suited to the works of composers of the Romantic and later periods, would be out of place within the lighter textures and balances required by Bach's compositional style and orchestration. The evolution of trumpets pitched in higher keys has come about in response to the need for specialized instruments designed to enable trumpeters to adapt to the demands of the diverse repertoire performed by today's orchestras. Along with the need for these instruments in orchestras, the now greatly expanded solo literature has provided a further stimulus for their development. For example, the Haydn *Trumpet Concerto* is now usually played on the E♭ trumpet; the Hummel *Trumpet Concerto* is played either on the E♭ or on the E trumpet when it is performed in its original key. The Baroque solo literature written for the natural trumpet in D is invariably performed on the piccolo A trumpet, except in performances using historical instruments.[1]

Although these instruments have come into wide use in recent years, the idea of trumpets in higher keys is not new. Teste, solo trumpeter of the Paris Opera, performed Bach's *Magnificat* on a G trumpet as early as 1885. The great Belgian trumpeter Théo Charlier gave the first modern performance of Bach's *Brandenburg Concerto No. 2* in 1898 using a Mahillon G trumpet. French, Belgian, and German makers led the way in the

---

[1] The natural trumpet is discussed in Chapter 8.

FIGURE 3.1   The trumpets in use today (left to right): Piccolo B♭/A, G, F bell and slides, E bell, E♭, D bell and slides (Schilke), E♭, C, and B♭ (Bach)

development of the higher trumpets well into the 20th century. During the last 35 years, however, high trumpets have undergone extensive research and development everywhere in the quest for improved instruments to cope with the mounting demands placed on modern orchestral trumpeters.

Several factors have combined to create these pressures. The trend toward longer orchestral seasons, an oversupply of well-trained players, and the expectation by conductors and audiences of the note-perfect accuracy in live performances that they are accustomed to on recordings have all had their effect. Most important, however, is that principal trumpeters are now regularly expected to perform the demanding Baroque literature with the flawless skill that was previously reserved for exceptional players and Baroque specialists.

Another important influence is the emergence of the trumpet as a major solo instrument. Just as Jean-Pierre Rampal popularized the solo flute and Dennis Brain the horn, Maurice André brought the trumpet into a new era of solo recordings and international concert appearances. The torch has been carried forward by today's generation of brilliant soloists, who require responsive, reliable, and in-tune high trumpets.

■ THE B♭ AND C TRUMPETS

By the end of the 19th century, the modern B♭ trumpet had replaced the longer F trumpet[2] as the standard orchestral instrument. While the passing of the old F trumpet timbre was lamented by many,[3] trumpeters were confronted with parts of increasing difficulty by composers such as Strauss and Mahler, and the new instrument proved more effective in meeting these demands. The popularity of the B♭ cornet also contributed to the change, since many orchestral players also played the cornet and were accustomed to the technical advantages of an instrument in B♭. Trumpets in C also made their appearance about this time and became established as the standard orchestral instrument in France, Belgium (piston valve), and Austria (rotary valve).

[2] The instrument was built in the key of G but was mostly played through the use of crooks in the keys of F, E, E♭, and D.
[3] See, for example, the discussion of the horn and trumpet by Ralph Vaughan Williams in *The Making of Music* (Ithaca, N.Y.: Cornell University Press, 1955), p. 29.

The present widespread use of the C trumpet in American orchestras can be traced to the appointment in 1920 of Georges Mager as first trumpet of the Boston Symphony Orchestra. A graduate of the Paris Conservatory in the class of Jean-Joseph Mellet (a student of Arban) and one of the greatest players of his time, Mager used the C trumpet, rather than a B♭, as his primary instrument during his entire 30-year tenure in Boston. He led a section composed of his French colleagues Gustav Perret, Marcel LaFosse, René and (later) Roger Voisin playing C trumpets. This was unique in orchestras of the time and established the pattern that has become standard in American orchestras today.

Among the first major figures beyond Boston to adopt the C trumpet was William Vacchiano, who joined the New York Philharmonic in 1935 and served as principal trumpet from 1942 to 1973. The use of the C trumpet has increased internationally (except in France, Belgium, and Austria, where the instrument has long been established) as a result of the influence of American brass playing, in particular that of Adolph Herseth, former principal trumpet of the Chicago Symphony.[4]

The trend is not universal, however. British trumpeters, following in the great tradition of Ernest Hall, have maintained their allegiance to the B♭, preferring its rounder tone and blending qualities. British orchestral brass sections are renowned for the fullness, resonance, and balance of timbre between B♭ trumpets and trombones. When particularly high tessituri are required, British trumpeters often make use of the E♭ trumpet. The B♭ has to some extent retained its position in German and Eastern European orchestras as well. In bands, the B♭ remains the primary instrument, due to its fuller timbre and greater ability to blend within an ensemble of wind instruments. The literature for band is primarily written for the B♭ instrument and would have to be transposed if C trumpets were used.

Another area where the C trumpet has failed to gain a foothold is in the jazz and studio fields. The C trumpet's timbre and playing characteristics do not seem to be particularly adaptable to the musical requirements of jazz performers.

Given the trend toward C trumpets in orchestral playing in the United States, it is important to emphasize that most trumpeters are in agreement that students should begin and play through their formative years on the B♭ instrument and continue to play it alongside the C trumpet as adults. In this way a good tonal concept and tone production will be established and maintained.

It would be well to consider what specific advantages the C trumpet has to offer an orchestral player. The primary factor underlying the trend to C trumpets is related to the nature of orchestral playing, with its long periods of rest. The response of the C instrument seems to be better suited to making "cold" entrances than the B♭, and it provides a greater feeling of security and control. This feeling is augmented for many players by the instrument's being in the same key as the string section, particularly in the sharp keys in which orchestras often play. The C trumpet also seems to be somewhat more compatible with the range in which the first trumpet plays and the extreme dynamic contrasts required. The timbre carries well, and this allows the player to project the sound with slightly less effort than would be required by the B♭.

C trumpets are now available with a number of leadpipe and bell combinations, and these have contributed to an improved instrument. American orchestral players generally prefer a large-bore C, and a medium-large B♭. There is still an important role for the B♭, and the parallel use of B♭ and C trumpets is likely to continue indefinitely. By having two primary instruments available, the player is afforded maximum flexibility in adapting to the requirements of the part to be performed. There has been and continues to be (especially in Britain) superb orchestral playing on the B♭ trumpet as well as the C. How the player utilizes these instruments to best advantage ultimately will remain a matter of individual preference.

---

[4] Adolph Herseth is a former student of Georges Mager.

■ THE D TRUMPET

The high trumpet in D was developed in the late 19th century in response to the enthusiasm of the time for performing the choral works of Bach and Handel. It was often referred to as a "Bach trumpet," but this name is now discouraged, to avoid confusion with the natural trumpet, which has enjoyed a revival in recent years. (The fundamental of the natural trumpet in D is an octave below the valve trumpet.) The D trumpet offered an excellent solution to the problem of performing the difficult parts in Bach's *B Minor Mass,* Handel's *Messiah,* and other Baroque works. Modern composers, such as Ravel (*Boléro*) and Stravinsky (*The Rite of Spring* and *Petrushka*), also utilized the instrument for colorful high-range effects.

At present, three types of D trumpet are available: a medium-bore and bell model suitable as a Baroque instrument, a large-bore that can be used in place of the B♭ or C in regular orchestral passages, and a D–E♭ combination (actually an E♭ trumpet provided with a main tuning slide or bell, to change the pitch to D, and a set of longer valve slides).

Students are sometimes under the impression that the higher trumpets provide "instant high range." Actually, trumpeters usually only add a note or two above what can be played on their regular instrument. What is gained, however, is better control and consistency in performing high-register passages.

In recent years, the D trumpet has largely been replaced in the Baroque literature by the piccolo trumpet in A. The smaller instrument has brought the difficult Baroque trumpet parts within the capability of a greater number of performers. While it offers greater security and ease of playing, the inherent smaller bore and bell of the piccolo results in a timbre that tends to be of lesser body and fullness than that of the D trumpet; it is also far removed from the tone of the natural trumpet of Bach's time. The D trumpet is a more effective substitute for the natural trumpet, combining the advantages of a valve instrument with a fuller tone quality that is closer to the Baroque instrument. However, the use of the piccolo in A in place of the D trumpet is likely to continue, since most players find that it offers greater ease and security in performance.

■ THE E♭ TRUMPET

E♭ trumpets are used today primarily in the performance of the Haydn and Hummel[5] concertos, in brass ensembles, and for orchestral passages requiring a high tessitura. There is an additional aspect of the use of high trumpets that is unrelated to tessitura: Some passages lie better (in regard to fingering and tone production) on one instrument than on another. For example, the aforementioned Haydn and Hummel concertos can be played fluently on the B♭; however, they are much more oriented to the E♭, which places the player in the key of C. Many trumpeters feel that this facilitates fingering (especially on trills) and accuracy.

The principle of substituting one trumpet for another applies to the entire range of trumpets and affords the performer a choice in matching the instrument to the part:

Haydn, *Trumpet Concerto*

[5] The Hummel concerto was composed for a keyed trumpet pitched in E. It is most often performed in editions transposed to E♭ so that it may be played comfortably on the B♭ or E♭ trumpet.

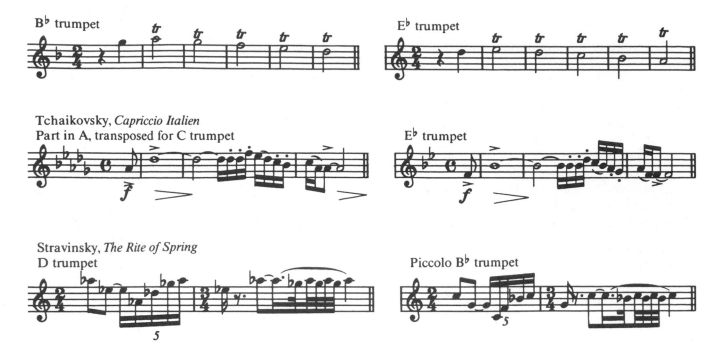

B♭ trumpet

E♭ trumpet

Tchaikovsky, *Capriccio Italien*
Part in A, transposed for C trumpet

E♭ trumpet

Stravinsky, *The Rite of Spring*
D trumpet

Piccolo B♭ trumpet

Professional orchestral trumpeters often make use of both the D and E♭ trumpets for passages ordinarily played on the C or B♭ when the tessitura tends to be high or when the part clearly lies better on the higher trumpet. The same practice is followed in brass quintets and large brass ensembles. The choice between D and E♭ trumpet depends on which instrument places the player in a more fluent key. In addition to the C and B♭, the D and E♭ trumpets are essential tools for the professional player.

The E♭ trumpet is becoming a standard feature of the 10-piece brass ensemble, developed by Philip Jones. Many new compositions and arrangements for this type of ensemble call for an E♭ on the first trumpet part to cope with a higher tessitura and to provide a brilliant tonal color to the overall sound. In many of these pieces the E♭ trumpet is treated with great virtuosity.

■ TRUMPETS IN E, F, AND G

The E trumpet was developed specially for players who wish to perform the Hummel trumpet concerto in its original key of E major. At present, models are available from Blackburn, Schilke (part of a bell-tuned G–F–E combination consisting of a G trumpet with interchangeable bells and valve slides for G, F, and E), and Yamaha (a bell-tuned E–E♭ combination with corresponding bells and valve slides).[6]

F trumpets were originally constructed for the difficult trumpet part in Bach's *Second Brandenburg Concerto*. They have now been superseded by the piccolo B♭ in that work. Their chief use today is for occasional orchestral passages.

The G trumpet is preferred as a Baroque instrument by players who want the tone and feel of an instrument larger than the piccolo. The G combines a timbre more like that of the D trumpet with some of the playing advantages of the piccolo.

■ THE PICCOLO TRUMPET

Of all the high trumpets, the piccolo B♭/A is the most widely used today. This is due to the extensive development of these instruments over the three decades. Trumpeters first used the piccolo B♭ more or less exclusively for the *Second Brandenburg Concerto* and for

---

[6]Bell tuning allows bells in different keys or sizes to be used on the same basic instrument. Tuning is accomplished by moving the bell section rather than a movable slide. Many players consider that this option offers improved playing qualities and intonation.

other Baroque parts that did not require the written low C of the D trumpet. Since this note is beyond the compass of the three-valve piccolo and figures in a number of scores, the piccolo's use was fairly limited. (D or G trumpets were normally used for these parts.) It was soon found that by lengthening the piccolo B♭ to A (through interchangeable leadpipes), parts written for the D trumpet could be played in the key signature of F, a more fluent and responsive key than the B♭ piccolo's E major:

Bach, *B Minor Mass*
Trumpet in D

Piccolo B♭ trumpet

Piccolo A trumpet

With the addition of a fourth valve, which extended the range of the piccolo downward a perfect fourth, standard Baroque works such as Bach's *Christmas Oratorio* and Handel's *Messiah* (which require the written low C of the D trumpet) began to be performed on the piccolo. The fourth valve adds five notes to the player's range below the limit of the three-valve piccolo. The fourth valve makes available some alternate fingerings to improve intonation. The sharp 1–2–3 and 1–3 combinations can be improved by fingering 2–4 and 4, respectively, a procedure normally used on four-valve euphoniums and tubas. There are two configurations of four-valve piccolo. The most common consists of four in-line valves. This adds some mass to the instrument in comparison to a three-valve design, and some players feel that this contributes a bit more weight and fullness to the tone. Others feel that the in-line fourth valve creates added and unnecessary resistance and therefore prefer a three-valve pattern in which a fourth (rotary) valve is placed within the third valve loop.[7] The third valve tubing is extended to lower the fundamental pitch a perfect fourth whenever the fourth valve is opened. The latter arrangement offers the same compass and alternate fingerings but eliminates the added resistance of the fourth valve in the main windway. The instrument plays like a three-valve design, with additional mass created by the weight of the fourth rotary valve.

[7]See Vincent Cichowicz, *The Piccolo B♭—A Trumpet* (The Selmer Co.); David Hickman, *The Piccolo Trumpet* (Denver, Colo.: Tromba, 1973); Roger Sherman, *The Trumpeter's Handbook* (Athens, Ohio: Accura Music, 1979); Gerald Webster, *Piccolo Trumpet Method* (Nashville, Tenn.: Brass Press, 1980).

Orchestral players soon began to use the piccolo for high passages in later works, for example, Ravel's *Boléro* and Stravinsky's *Petrushka* and *The Rite of Spring*, in place of the D trumpet. At the same time, the piccolo was brought into prominence by solo artists like Adolph Scherbaum and Maurice André. Most recently, the piccolo has been enjoying widespread popularity in the film and recording fields.

As stated earlier, the piccolo trumpet does not automatically bestow high range. What it does is to bring these notes down into the trumpet's most secure register by raising the fundamental. While comparable skill is required in performing in the upper register from one instrument to another, the piccolo trumpet offers the player the acoustical advantage of producing these notes in the instrument's middle range, providing greater control and security.

The choice of a mouthpiece for the piccolo trumpet is highly individual. A piccolo trumpet mouthpiece must have a shallow cup combined with a smaller throat and backbore. It is best to use a mouthpiece that has been specifically designed for the piccolo trumpet.[8] Component mouthpieces are sometimes used; these allow the player to retain the same rim while altering cup, throat, and backbore. Some players use their standard rim for all the high trumpets, while others change to a rim of narrower inner width.

Choosing a piccolo trumpet (or any high trumpet) for the first time poses difficulties, since it requires experience to evaluate the playing and sound qualities of different instruments. The best way of selecting a piccolo is by trying a number of instruments. Certain instruments will work better for individual players than others, and this should be the focus of the selection process (it is unwise to choose a particular model because another player uses it). *The first consideration is that the instrument play easily and be in tune.* Only if this requirement is met should the instrument's tone quality be weighted as a consideration. Players are often misled by an attractive tone quality and overlook the instrument's playing deficiencies. The player will obviously want an instrument with a first-rate tone quality; however the best-sounding instrument is useless if it does not produce the notes reliably and is not well in tune.

There is also a piccolo trumpet built in C. Normally this is built as a combination trumpet with leadpipes and valve slides for C, B♭, and A, thereby offering an additional choice of key to the player.

■ ROTARY VALVE TRUMPETS

German-type rotary valve trumpets are now standard equipment for a significant portion of the repertoire of most major American orchestras. This has come about in response to the desire by conductors and players to produce a more authentic sound in 19th century literature by German and Austrian composers. While the rotary valve trumpet is perhaps somewhat less flexible in technical passages, it possesses a much broader and slightly darker timbre that is ideally suited to the works of Beethoven, Brahms, Bruckner, Strauss, and others. Also, these instruments have a greater capacity to blend with woodwinds and strings. When called for, they produce a larger volume of tone than piston instruments and tend to hold more of the core of the sound in forte passages.

The rotary valve trumpet followed a separate line of development and has been used as the primary instrument in central European orchestras for over a century and a half. Piston valve instruments, on the other hand, were originally centered in France and England and from there came to the United States. Today, rotary valve trumpets can be heard with great distinction in the Vienna Philharmonic and Berlin Philharmonic as well as in leading orchestras in the United States.

Although the cylindrical bore of the rotary valve trumpet is slightly smaller than its piston valve counterpart, the leadpipe and bell are decidedly larger. The instrument is

---

[8]Suggested piccolo mouthpieces are the Stork 2P, 3P, or 7P and Josef Klier 4 EP or 5 EP.

FIGURE 3.2 Rotary valve trumpets (left to right): Heckel models: B♭ (Ganter) and C (Yamaha), and Monke C and D

designed with a wider pattern to avoid sharp curves in the tubing. These factors, combined with the less resistant rotary valves, create the impression of a much larger instrument, requiring greater air support.

There are two traditional designs of rotary valve trumpet, and, although they appear similar, they have much different proportions in their tapered sections and produce quite dissimilar tonal characteristics. One type is made by the Cologne firm of Josef Monke. Others often follow the style of instrument perfected by F. A. Heckel (and, later, Windisch) of Dresden. Schagerl and Lechner (Austria) fall into this category. Instruments are built in all of the standard keys. Heckel-type rotary valve trumpets often have a vent key for high C and sometimes one for high D. Players who favor these additions feel these notes are made more secure by opening the vent keys.

■ THE CORNET

There has been a remarkable resurgence of interest in America in recent years in traditional cornets (see Figure 3.3) and cornet playing. Most of the major manufacturers have developed new models of short "shepherd's crook" cornets, and they form a vital part of the developing brass band movement. The latter constitutes a growing market for high-quality cornets. In wind bands they are also being revived to lend authenticity to repertoire originally written for them. Wind band conductors are now interested in achieving a more authentic timbre in such works as Gustav Holst's suites for military band and Ralph Vaughan Williams's *Toccata Marziale*, for example. Orchestral players are using cornets more frequently when specified by the composer. In the past, these parts were usually played on trumpets, thus negating the effect of contrasting tone colors between cornets and trumpets that was intended by Berlioz, Franck, Debussy, and others.

There should be a great difference in tone and style between trumpet and cornet. Genuine cornet tone is darker and much softer in timbre than the clear, ringing trumpet

FIGURE 3.3
Cornets in B♭ and E♭
(Besson)

sound and should be colored with an expressive, vocal-style vibrato. Such a timbre can only be achieved through the use of a mouthpiece with a distinctly deeper and more conical cup. Trumpet players often try to use the same mouthpiece (with a smaller cornet shank) when performing on the cornet, thereby losing the essential beauty and mellowness of the true cornet tone. In fact, many cornet mouthpieces available today are in reality trumpet mouthpieces with a cornet shank. The most authentic cornet mouthpieces available are the Denis Wick models, particularly the numbers 4 and 5, which were designed in collaboration with Thomas Wilson, former principal cornet of H. M. Scots Guards Band, about 40 years ago. The Denis Wick mouthpieces are also available with a shallower cup (designated by number and the letter B) that is midway between a true cornet cup and that of the trumpet. The hybrid B cups are popular in the United States, but they tend not to be used in Britain, due to the inevitable sacrifice in tone quality brought on by the shallower cup. It is hoped that as the brass band movement develops, the deeper cups will become standard in America, as they are in Britain. The best advice for brass band cornetists is to choose a Denis Wick 4 or 5 or a Denis Wick Roger Webster model RW5, RW4, or RW3.

Most manufacturers still produce "long-model" cornets; these are constructed in more of a trumpet pattern and omit the traditional "shepherd's crook" of the bell section. The changes unfortunately affect the timbre, which is closer to that of the trumpet than to the cornet's.

The cornet is at its best in melodic passages, where its sweet, voicelike tone can bring a depth of expression and beauty that is difficult to equal on the trumpet. Another asset is its extraordinary agility, which surpasses that of the trumpet. The best way to form a concept of genuine cornet tone and style is to seek out recordings of the many superb British brass bands. These bands have an unbroken performance tradition reaching back to the 19th century and have maintained their style independent of the influence of the trumpet and modern orchestral brass playing. (Appendix B lists representative recordings.) Salvation Army brass bands, where a premium is placed on melodic expression, also offer good examples of traditional cornet playing. Of particular interest are two recordings produced by the International Trumpet Guild. One features performances of the legendary Herbert L. Clarke dating from 1904 to 1921 (Crystal 450 TCCH01). The other is a collection of recordings by great cornetists from the turn of the century, such as Walter Rogers, Allesandro Liberati, and Bohumir Kryl, among others (International Trumpet Guild-ITG 004). Both recordings should be carefully studied by all cornet and trumpet players.

Cornets are also made in Eb; these are used exclusively in brass bands. The Eb soprano cornet is the highest voice of the brass band and plays an important solo part. Cornets are occasionally made in C, but they are rare today, used mostly by orchestral trumpeters accustomed to playing the C trumpet.

WHICH TRUMPETS DOES THE PLAYER NEED?

With the wide range of trumpets available, it might be helpful to know which instruments are needed by players in various situations. Students should have little need for any instrument other than a Bb trumpet or cornet unless they aspire to major in trumpet on the college or conservatory level. In such cases, four trumpets will be needed: Bb, C, Eb/D, and piccolo Bb/A. Professional symphonic players usually have more than one instrument in these keys, each offering different playing qualities. In addition, the professional might own several rotary valve trumpets, a G trumpet, a Bb cornet, and a flugelhorn. Jazz and studio players generally prefer a Bb trumpet with lighter playing qualities and sound than do orchestral performers, and they also have available a flugelhorn.

It is worthwhile for conductors of high school and college bands to make available a set of cornets for loan, to aid performances of works in which cornets play an important role. Similarly, conductors of school and youth orchestras should have a few C trumpets available and possibly some higher trumpets, as well.

INTONATION

Before going into the specific problems of trumpet intonation, it would be useful to consider more generally the problem of playing brass instruments in tune. By far, the most common difficulty is that students tend to allow the instrument to determine intonation rather than controlling it themselves. Many notes require very subtle adjustments of embouchure, vowel formation, and air pressure to bring them into tune. Certain notes must also be corrected by some mechanical means, such as extending a valve slide or using an alternate fingering. (The acoustical problem of sharpness when valves are used in combination is discussed in Chapter 6.)

The aural–mental process that enables the brass player to start the sound on a specific pitch and to play in tune involves an ability to prehear the note that is to be played. A pitch signal is sent from the "mental ear" to bring the embouchure and other elements of tone production into a specific adjustment for a note. Tone and style are guided in the same way. Missed notes or poor intonation occur when the elements of tone production are not in the right adjustment for a specific pitch; this is often the result of an unclear or inaccurate pitch signal.

The procedure used by brass players is the same as is used in singing. The time-honored method of training is the study of solfège, or sightsinging. This study serves to fix pitches definitely in the mind so that a clear signal will be sent to the voice. Any lack of clarity will be revealed by the intonation of the melody or interval being sung. By learning to reproduce exact vocal pitches, the ability to predetermine pitch will rapidly develop, and this will carry over to the instrument. It is a good practice for brass players to sing as well as play the etudes and exercises being studied.

It is unfortunate that the study of solfège is rather neglected in the United States, and this accounts for a great deal of the intonation difficulties in school and college ensembles. More emphasis could be given to working on chorales and chords in school groups, since the practical experience of matching pitches with those of other players is the primary means of developing the skills necessary for good ensemble playing. In addition, one of the best ways for brass players to develop a good sense of pitch is to join a choir. By learning to sing in a choral ensemble, the player will rapidly develop the ability to control intonation on the instrument.

In examining intonation charts for the trumpet, one can become dismayed by the number of notes apparently needing correction. In practice, most of these are controlled by the adjustment of the embouchure, vowel formation, and wind speed. This is an unconscious process that is controlled by the mental ear as it focuses on the exact pitch to be played. Technical demands limit the number of notes that can be altered by lengthening the first and third valve slides. There are, however, certain notes that require this type of correction to bring them into tune:

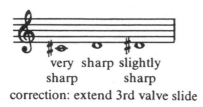

very sharp slightly
sharp   sharp

correction: extend 3rd valve slide

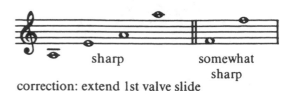

sharp   somewhat
                               sharp

correction: extend 1st valve slide

Obviously, valve slides cannot be moved in very rapid passages. In these situations the player selects notes that have sufficient duration to make correction practicable. Another approach is to preset the slide for a prominent note within a moving passage. This focuses the passage on a corrected pitch center and makes the entire passage sound more in tune. While some players must make greater use of the slides than others, the general tendency is not to use them enough.[9]

Specific notes needing correction can be identified through the use of an electronic tuner. This is an essential piece of equipment that should be purchased by all serious students and made available in school music rooms. In working with the tuner, the degree of correction necessary for all out-of-tune notes should be determined by observing the meter. Next, scales, intervals, and arpeggios should be slowly played while making the necessary corrections against various reference pitches sounded by the tuner. This will do a lot to improve a player's general intonation.

The low F♯, G, and G♯ tend to vary in pitch from player to player. Some must use the third valve slide, while others can play these notes in tune with minimal or no adjustment.

A more complex problem involves the D, E♭, and E, particularly on the C trumpet:[10]

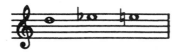

These notes are the fifth harmonics of their respective series, which tend to be low in pitch. In a well-designed trumpet, the lengths of the first and second valve slides have been calculated as a compromise intended to raise the D and E♭ slightly (shortened) but not so much as to render the other notes played with the first and second valves uncontrollably sharp. This is a primary reason why the first valve slide must be extended on the pitches shown in the preceding chart. In spite of this, the D and E♭ as well as the E are only minimally up to pitch and require an adjustment of embouchure and air stream to bring

[9]To facilitate moving the first valve slide, the player might consider replacing the ring with a spring trigger. The trigger offers an advantage, in that only one motion is necessary, rather than the double movement required by the ring.
[10]The author is indebted to Professor Clifford Lillya for clarifying this problem.

them into tune. On the C and higher trumpets, alternate fingerings are often used to raise the pitch of these notes, but the fingerings are awkward when executing fast passages. The problem is aggravated by too high a pitch placement on the third-space C, which has a wide "band width" or "slot," and by not using the trigger on the F above. These factors cause some players to have fairly severe intonation problems in the range of C to G.

The solution is to cultivate a lower pitch placement on the C and to make certain that the first valve slide is extended on the sharp notes. A lower placement on the C can be accomplished by centering the C between the G below and E above. As a temporary measure, the C might be fingered 2–3 until the feel of a lower C is established. (The 2–3 combination should be considered only an exercise, since its pitch is too low for actual use.) When tuning, it is advisable to check the D, E♭, and E against the tuning note. If they seem flat, the main tuning slide should be brought inward until these notes form accurate intervals with the reference pitch. It is essential to use the first valve trigger on the top-line F and A above, to bring them into a better pitch relationship with the D, E♭, and E. In the end, many players will still prefer to use the fingering 1–2 on E and 2–3 on E♭. It is important when doing this that the first valve slide be extended slightly on the E and the third on E♭ to avoid sharpness on these notes. The problem of low fifth harmonics is present on the B♭ trumpet as well as the C trumpet but in lesser degree. It is also quite acute on the D and E♭ trumpets, but for some reason the problem is less severe on rotary valve trumpets. This probably has to do with differences in the tapers and windways of rotary valve instruments.

Playing in tune is, above all, a practical skill that requires careful listening and experience in matching other players in ensembles. Too much analysis often creates further problems. It is best to adopt a relaxed, natural approach to intonation, as one would in singing, and to seek a consensus among the players. Playing in small ensembles provides invaluable experience and improvement, as do sectional rehearsals. A useful rehearsal procedure is to have two or three parts play alone. In this way, problems in intonation and balance can be clearly heard and corrected.

■ TRANSPOSITION

A question often asked is why trumpet players must study transposition. Would it not be simpler to provide parts already transposed for B♭ or C trumpet?

The origin of the problem goes back to the era of the natural (valveless) trumpet, when it was customary (with certain exceptions) for notes of the harmonic series to be written and read in C. A length of tubing known as a *crook* would be inserted to obtain the desired sounding pitch. For example, Mozart notated the trumpet parts to the *Prague Symphony* (No. 38 in D, K. 504) in the key of C with the instruction that the D crook be used. By always keeping the notation of the harmonic series the same, irrespective of the key of the composition, the parts were made easier for the players to read and perform using the harmonic series of the natural trumpet. The tradition of writing the fundamental and its harmonics in C continued into the valve era and continues today with B♭ trumpet notation. Trumpeters must be prepared to transpose from parts originally written for trumpets in A, D, E♭, E, and F, to name some of the common keys.

Transposed parts for B♭ or C trumpet are not ordinarily provided, for several reasons. There is a reluctance within the classical music world to tamper with a composer's notation. Additionally, orchestral trumpeters often substitute trumpets in different keys on various parts, and it would be difficult for publishers to keep up with individual preferences. Also, switching instruments is made easier for the player by having learned the part in its original notation. Above all, there is a certain tradition and pride of craftsmanship in being able to play from the part as the composer wrote it; therefore, professional trumpeters tend to look down on the use of transposed parts. New compositions, however, should be notated at concert pitch, leaving the choice of which trumpet to use to the player. Piccolo trumpet parts can either be written at concert pitch or transposed specifically for the B♭ or A piccolo. Band parts are best written for the B♭ trumpet.

Two methods are used in transposition: interval and clef. In the interval system, the notes are mentally moved upward or downward the correct distance between the key of the trumpet specified in the part and the trumpet that will be used. The key signature must be altered in the same way. For example, in Strauss's *Ein Heldenleben,* the part for E♭ trumpet must be read up a perfect fourth when played on a B♭ trumpet, since the B♭ sounds a fourth below the E♭ instrument. If the part is to be played on a C trumpet, the notes must be moved upward a minor third:

When the distance is only a half step, as in transposing A parts on the B♭ trumpet, one of two procedures can be used, depending on the key signature. If the part is written without key signature or in a sharp key, the passage may be read in the parallel flat key by altering the key signature:

If the passage is written with a flat key signature, the notes are visually moved downward to the next line or space and the key is lowered a half step:

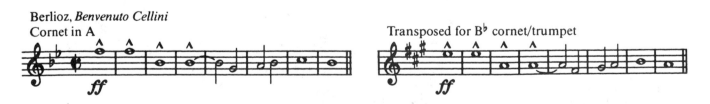

In the clef method, the notes need not be moved on the staff. Only the appropriate clef and key signature are mentally inserted at the beginning of the line:

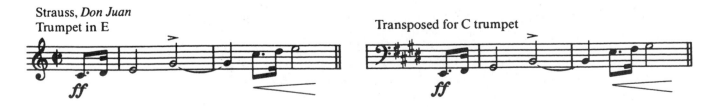

The common transpositions are shown in the following tables:

Transposition Table: Interval Method

Key of Part	Played on B♭ Trumpet	Played on C Trumpet
A	Half step lower	Minor 3rd lower
B♭	–	Major 2nd lower
C	Major 2nd higher	–
D	Major 3rd higher	Major 2nd higher
E♭	Perfect 4th higher	Minor 3rd higher
E	Augmented 4th higher	Major 3rd higher
F	Perfect 5th higher	Perfect 4th higher

Note: Key signature must also be changed.

Transposition Table: Clef Method

Key of Part	Played on B♭ Trumpet	Played on C Trumpet
A	Tenor clef	–
B♭	–	Tenor clef
C	Alto clef	–
D	Bass clef	Alto clef
E♭	Mezzo-soprano clef	Bass clef
E	Mezzo-soprano clef	Bass clef
F	–	Mezzo-soprano clef

Note: Key signature must also be changed.

In performing Baroque works written for trumpet in D on the piccolo trumpet in A, the part should be read a perfect fifth lower in the key of F. C parts may be read on the A piccolo by using the bass clef.

Ultimately, it is the time that can be given to the study of transposition that is important, rather than the method used. Not all of the study time must be with the instrument. Although some daily instrumental work is necessary to orient the ear to different pitch levels, eye and finger coordination may be developed by reading silently and pretending to press the valves. In this way, nonpractice hours can be used to further transposition skills. Simple materials, such as familiar etudes and melodies, should be used at first, gradually progressing to studies specifically designed for transposition.[11]

■ MUTES

In scores where no specific instruction is given other than that a passage is to be muted, it is assumed that the straight mute is intended. To achieve a blend in muted sound, it is best if mutes of different materials or makers are not mixed within the same section, since they tend to vary in intonation and timbre. The conventional straight mute is usually made from aluminum (although sometimes plastic and other metals are now used) and produces a resonantly pungent timbre. Straight mutes are also constructed from fiber; these have a softer, less cutting sound. It is customary for a composer to specify when a fiber mute is to be used in place of the customary metal type.

[11] See Lucien Thévet, *Cinquante exercices à changement de ton (Fifty Exercises with Changes of Key)* (Alphonse Leduc); Ernst Sachse, *100 Studies* (International Music Co.); Bordogni-Porret, *24 Vocalises* (Alphonse Leduc); Mel Broiles, *Have Trumpet . . . Will Transpose* (Charles Colin), Ernest Williams, *Method of Transposition* (Charles Colin).

FIGURE 3.4
Assorted mutes for
brass instruments
(Denis Wick)

Because the bell throats of various trumpets differ, it may be necessary to sand a mute's corks to obtain good intonation. A properly adjusted mute will usually still play slightly sharp; the best method of correcting this is to place a pencil mark on the trumpet's main tuning slide at the beginning of rehearsal. The slide can then be extended for muted passages and returned to the mark for open playing. The amount of correction necessary can be determined by playing open and muted pitches into an electronic tuner. A special mute must be used on the piccolo trumpet due to its small bell.

There is an entire range of specialized mutes, each producing its own specific timbre. Of these, the cup mute and harmon, or wa-wa, mute are the most common. The latter incorporates an extendable tube that may be covered and uncovered to create the wa-wa effect. The tube can be adjusted to different lengths for distance effects or omitted entirely for yet another color. The notation used for the wa-wa effect, and also with hats and plungers, is + (closed), and o (open).

Occasionally, a cloth bag is placed over the bell to dull and soften the sound. A very useful mute is the Charlie Spivak Whispa-Mute, which allows the performer to play comfortably, yet produce an extremely soft sound. It is sometimes used as a substitute for the straight mute in very quiet passages. Mutes designed for practicing have appeared recently and these are helpful on tours and in other difficult practice situations.

Trumpet Mutes

Straight mutes:	Fiber derby
Metal	Felt hat
Fiber	Cloth bag
Plastic	Clear or solo tone mute
Piccolo trumpet mute	Rubber plunger
Cup mute	Fiber plunger
Felt-lined cup mute	Plunger straight mute
Harmon, or wa-wa, mute (also version for piccolo trumpet)	Bucket mute
Whispa-mute	Buzz-wow mute

RECOMMENDED LITERATURE[12]

Complete Methods

Arban: *Complete Conservatory Method*, ed. Goldman and Smith (C. Fischer)

*Arban: *Méthode complète*, ed. Maire, 3 vols. (A. Leduc)

Clodomir: *Méthode complète*, ed. Job (A. Leduc)

Forestier: *Grande Méthode*, 3 vols. (Salabert)

*Franquin: *Méthode complète* (Enoch et cie)

*Petit: *Grande méthode de cornet à pistons* (Salabert)

*Saint-Jacome: *Grand Method* (C. Fischer)

Schneider: *Schule für Trompete* (Schott)

Plog: *Method for Trumpet* (Balquidder)

Elementary Methods

Clarke: *Elementary Studies* (C. Fischer)

Fricke: *104 Progressive Exercises* (Balquidder)

Gordon: *Physical Approach to Elementary Brass Playing* (C. Fischer)

*Lillya: *Method for Trumpet or Cornet*, 2 vols. (Balquidder)

Longinotti: *l'Etude de la trompette* (Editions Henn)

McDunn and Rusch: *Méthode de Trompette*, 2 vols. (A. Leduc)

Plog: *Method for Trumpet* (Balquidder)

Ridgeon: *Brass for Beginners* (Boosey & Hawkes)

Robinson: *Rubank Elementary Method* (Rubank)

Rosenfeld: *A Method for Trumpet* (Schaffner)

Wiggins: *First Tunes & Studies* (Oxford)

Williams: *Modern Method* (Colin)

*Vannetelbosch: *Trumpet for Beginners*, vol. 1 (A. Leduc)

Vizzuti: *Trumpet Method*, 3 vols. (Alfred)

Studies

Medium to Medium-Difficult

Bennett: *14 Melodic Studies* (R. King) (A. Leduc)

Bennett: *18 Preliminary Studies* (R. King) (A. Leduc)

*Bordogni: *24 Vocalises*, trans. Porret (transposition) (A. Leduc)

*Bousquet: *36 Celebrated Studies*, ed. Goldman (C. Fischer)

*Brandt: *34 Studies and 24 Last Studies*, ed. Vacchiano (Belwin-Mills)

Broiles: *Have Trumpet . . . Will Transpose* (transposition) (C. Colin)

*Busser: *12 Melodic Studies* (A. Leduc)

*Caens: *Basic Systems*, vols. 1–5 (A. Leduc)

*Chavanne: *25 Characteristic Studies* (A. Leduc)

*Clarke: *Setting Up Drills* (C. Fischer)

*Clarke: *Technical Studies* (C. Fischer)

*Clodomir: *Études caractéristiques* (A. Leduc)

*Clodomir: *Petits exercices* (A. Leduc)

*Clodomir: *Vingt études chantantes* (A. Leduc)

*Clodomir: *Vingt études de mécanisme* (A. Leduc)

*Clodomir: *Vingt études mignonnes* (A. Leduc)

*Colin: *Advanced Lip Flexibilities* (C. Colin)

Concone/Korak: *The Complete Solfeggi* (Balquidder)

*Dokchidzer: *Methode de trompette* (A. Leduc)

*Endresen: *Supplementary Studies* (Rubank)

*Gallay: *22 exercices*, ed. Maire (A. Leduc)

Gekker: *Articulation Studies* (C. Colin)

*Goldman: *Practical Studies* (C. Fischer)

Gower and Voxman (eds.): *Rubank Advanced Method* (Rubank)

*Gresham: *Plainchant for Trumpet* (Balquidder)

*Groth: *Etudes on New Tonguing and Breathing Techniques* (Zimmermann)

Hering: *32 Etudes* (C. Fischer)

Hovaldt: *Lip Flexibility* (R. King)

Johnson: *Progressive Studies for the High Register* (H. Gore)

*Kopprasch: *60 Studies*, ed. Gumbert and Herbst, 2 vols. (C. Fischer)

*Laurent: *Études pratiques*, 3 vols. (A. Leduc)

*Laurent: *Soixante études et exercices* (multiple tonguing) (A. Leduc)

*Laurent: *Vingt études faciles et de moyenne force* (preparatory to *Études pratiques*) (A. Leduc)

Lillya: *Trumpet Technique* (Balquidder)

Lin: *Lip Flexibilities* (Balquidder)

*McGregor: *Daily Scale Builder* (Balquidder)

*Pares: *Scales* (Rubank)

Salvation Army: *101 Technical Exercises* (Salvation Army)

*Schlossberg: *Daily Drills and Technical Studies* (M. Baron)

Skornicka: *Rubank Intermediate Method* (Rubank)

Smith: *Lip Flexibility* (C. Fischer)

Snedecor: *Low Etudes* (PAS Music)

Snedecor: *Lyrical Etudes* (PAS Music)

Staigers: *Flexibility Studies*, 2 vols. (C. Fischer)

Stamp: *Warm-ups Plus Studies* (BIM)

Stamp/Wiener: *How to Play J. Stamp's Warm-ups* (BIM)

*Thévet: *Cinquante exercices à changement de ton* (*Fifty Exercises with Changes of Key*) (A. Leduc) (transposition)

*Vannetelbosch: *Trumpet for Beginners*, vol. 2 (A. Leduc)

*Vannetelbosch: *20 Melodic and Technical Studies* (Leduc)

*Williams: *The Best of Ernest Williams* (Colin)

*Williams: *Method of Transposition* (Colin)

---

[12] Essential material is indicated by an asterisk. Repertoire lists appear in the texts by Dale and Sherman.

Vacchiano: *The Art of Double Tonguing* (Peters)

Vacchiano: *The Art of Solo Playing* (Tromba Publications)

Vacchiano: *The Study of Intervals* (Manduca)

*Vacchiano: *Trumpet Routines* (C. Colin)

Zauder: *Embouchure & Technique Studies* (C. Colin)

Difficult

André: *12 Études caprices dans le style baroque* (piccolo trumpet) (Editions Billaudot)

*André/Lopez: *Exercices journaliers* (Billaudot)

Bach/Glover: *24 Studies* (BIM)

Bach/Sawyer: *12 Etudes* (BIM)

Balasanyan: *20 Studies*, ed. Foveau (International)

Balay: *15 Etudes* (A. Leduc)

*N. Bizet: *12 Grandes études de perfectionnement* (A. Leduc)

Bodet: *16 Études de virtuosité d'après J. S. Bach* (A. Leduc)

Bodet: *25 Reading Exercises* (A. Leduc)

*Bozza: *16 Etudes* (A. Leduc)

Broiles: *Trumpet Baroque*, 2 vols. (piccolo trumpet) (Queen City)

*Charlier: *Études transcendantes* (A. Leduc)

*Clarke: *Characteristic Studies* (C. Fischer)

Duhem: *24 Etudes* (C. Fischer)

*Gallay: *12 Grand caprices*, ed. Maire (A. Leduc)

*Gallay: *39 Preludes*, ed. Maire (A. Leduc)

Gekker: *Endurance Drills for Performance Skills* (C. Colin)

*Glantz: *48 Studies* (C. Colin)

*Harris: *Advanced Studies* (C. Colin)

Hickman: *The Piccolo Trumpet* (Tromba Publications)

*Longinotti: *Studies in Classical and Modern Style* (International)

Maxime-Alphonse: *Études nouvelles*, 3 vols. (Leduc)

McGregor: *Audition & Performance*, 4 vols. (Balquidder)

*Petit: *15 Études techniques et mélodiques* (A. Leduc)

*Petit: *Grandes études* (A. Leduc)

Roditi: *The Book of Articulations* (Roditi)

*Sabarich: *10 Etudes* (Selmer)

*Sachse: *100 Studies* (transposition) (International)

*Smith: *Top Tones* (C. Fischer)

*Tarr: *The Art of Baroque Trumpet Playing*, vols. 1 & 2 (Schott)

*Thibaut: *Chromatic Exercises* (Balquidder)

*Thibaut: *Method for the Advanced Trumpeter*, 3 vols. (Balquidder)

Trognée: *15 Grandes etudes* (BIM)

*Vacchiano: *Orchestral Rhythms* (Balquidder)

Vizzuti: *Advanced Etudes* (BIM)

Webster: *Method for Piccolo Trumpet* (BIM)

Williams: *Method of Transposition* (Colin)

*Zorn: *Exploring the Trumpet's Upper Register* (Kendor)

Unaccompanied Trumpet (Cornet)

Difficult

Adler: *Canto I* (Oxford)

Anon.: *Last Post and Reveille* (Boosey & Hawkes)

*Arnold: *Fantasy* (Faber)

Bach: *Six Short Solo Suites for Trumpet* (R. King)

Bartles: *Sonatina* (BIM)

*Bourgeois: *Fantasy Pieces for Trumpet* (Brass Wind Publications)

Bozza: *Graphismes* (A. Leduc)

Burrell: *5 Concert Studies* (Oxford)

*Cheetham: *Concoctions* (Presser)

Chkolnik: *Monologue* (BIM)

Della Peruti: *Elegy Set* (Wimbledon)

*Dokshitser: *Images romantiques* (M. Reift)

Friedman: *Poem for a fallen Hero* (BIM)

Friedman: *Solus* (BIM)

Gallagher: *Sonata* (BIM)

Graap: *Missa* (Haas)

Henze: *Sonatina* (Dunster Music)

Hvoslef: *Tromba Solo* (BIM)

Janetzki: *Sonate* (Haas)

Mabboux: *Triptyque* (BIM)

*Michel: *Oriental Express* (M. Reift)

*Persichetti: *Parable* (Presser)

*Plog: *Postcards* (BIM)

Powell: *Alone* (BIM)

Presser: *Second Suite* (Presser)

Rabe: *Shazam* (Reimer)

Reiche: *Abblasen* (Philharmusica)

Renwick: *Encore Piece* (Tromba Publications)

Schmidt: *White Sun Lady* (Western International)

*Sampson: *Litany of Breath* (BIM)

Sampson: *Notes from Faraway Places* (BIM)

Schuman: *25 Opera Snatches* (Presser)

Searby: *Lament and Dance for Solo Trumpet* (Brass Wind Publications)

*Vizzuti: *Cascades* (BIM)

Trumpet and Cornet with Piano

Easy

Bach: *Aria: Bist du bei mir*, arr. Fitzgerald (Belwin-Mills)

Bakaleinikoff: *Serenade* (Belwin-Mills)

Barsham (ed.): *Shore's Trumpet* (Boosey & Hawkes)

Barsham and Jones: *Trumpet Solos*, 2 vols. (Chester)

Beechey (ed.): *Trumpet Tunes of the English Baroque* (Schott)

Borst and Bogar (eds.): *Trumpet Music for Beginners* (Editio Musica)

Dearnley (ed.): *8 Easy Pieces* (Chester)

Dexter and de Smet: *First-Year Trumpeter*, 2 vols. (E. Ashdown)

Gregson: *Ten Miniatures for Trumpet and Piano* (Brass Wind Publications)

Haydn: *A Haydn Solo Album*, arr. Lawrence (Oxford)

Haydn: *Andante*, arr. Voxman (Rubank)

Handel: *A Handel Solo Album*, arr. Lethbridge (Oxford)

Hering (ed.): *Easy Pieces for the Young Trumpeter* (C. Fischer)

Keynotes Album for Trumpet (Brass Wind Publications)

Lawrance: *Easy Winners for Treble Brass* (with CD accompaniment) (Brass Wind Publications)

Lawrance: *Winners Galore for Treble Brass* (Brass Wind Publications)

Lawton (ed.): *Old English Trumpet Tunes*, 2 vols. (Oxford)

Lawton (ed.): *The Young Trumpet Player*, 3 vols. (Oxford)

Lowden: *Easy Play-Along Solos* (recording included) (Kendor)

Mills and Romm: *Beginning Trumpet Solos*, 2 vols. (with cassette accompaniment) (H. Leonard)

Mozart: *Concert Aria*, arr. Voxman (Rubank)

Mozart: *A Mozart Solo Album*, arr. Lethbridge (Oxford)

Philips (ed.): *Classical & Romantic Album*, vol. 1 (Oxford)

Tenaglia: *Aria*, arr. Fitzgerald (Presser)

Up-Front Album for Trumpet, vols. 1 & 2 (Brass Wind Publications)

VanderCook: *Marigold* (C. Fischer)

VanderCook: *Morning Glory* (C. Fischer)

Wallace and Miller: *First Book of Solos* (Faber)

Wallace and Miller: *Second Book of Solos* (Faber)

Willner (ed.): *Classical Album* (Boosey & Hawkes)

Medium to Medium-Difficult [13]

Adams: *The Holy City* (Boosey & Hawkes)

Ancelin: *Six chants populaires de basse-Bretagne* (Leduc)

Anderson: *Trumpeter's Lullaby* (Belwin-Mills)

Archibald: *Fiesta Española* (Brass Wind Publications)

Archibald: *Russian Roulette* (Brass Wind Publications)

Arutunian: *Elegy* (BIM)

Bakaleinikov: *Polonaise* (Belwin-Mills)

Balakireff: *Georgian Song*, trans. Smedvig (International)

Balay: *Petite pièce concertante* (Belwin-Mills)

*Barat: *Andante et Scherzo* (A. Leduc)

Barat: *Orientale* (A. Leduc)

*Bozza: *Badinage* (A. Leduc)

*Bozza: *Lied* (A. Leduc)

Burgon: *Brideshead Revisited* (Chester)

Burgon: *Lullaby & Aubade* (Galaxy)

Burgon: *Toccata* (Galaxy)

Busser: *Variations* (A. Leduc)

Butterworth: *Knightly Pieces* (Brass Wind Publications)

Chance: *Credo* (Boosey & Hawkes)

*+J. Clarke: *Trumpet Voluntary*, arr. Voisin (International)

*Clerisse: *Noce villageoise* (A. Leduc)

Cools: *Solo de Concours* (A. Leduc)

Corelli: *Prelude & Minuet*, arr. Powell (Southern)

*Delmas: *Choral et variations* (Billaudot)

*Delmas: *Variation tendre* (Billaudot)

*Dello Joio: *Sonata* (Associated)

Ellerby: *Mercurial Dances* (Brass Wind Publications)

Forbes (ed.): *Classical & Romantic Album*, vols. 2 and 3 (Oxford)

*Georges: *Légende d'armor* (Enoch)

Getchell (ed.): *Master Solos* (H. Leonard)

Gregson: *Cameos* (Brass Wind Publications)

Fiocco: *Arioso* (Presser)

*Fitzgerald: *English Suite* (Presser)

*Fitzgerald: *Gaelic Suite* (Presser)

Floore: *9 Simple Pieces* (Tierolff)

*Gaubert: *Cantabile et scherzetto* (C. Fischer)

Gedalge: *Contest Piece* (International)

Gibbons: *Suite* (Galaxy)

Gorb: *A Tango to Bali* (Brass Wind Publications)

*Handel: *Aria con variazioni*, arr. Fitzgerald (Belwin-Mills)

Handel: *Sonata #3*, arr. Powell (Southern)

Herrmann: *Andante e polacca* (BIM)

*Hovhaness: *Prayer of Saint Gregory* (Southern)

*James: *Windmills* (B. Ramsey)

*Jacob: *4 Little Pieces* (Emerson)

Lancen: *Quatre soli* (A. Leduc)

Lawton: *Old English Trumpet Tunes* (Oxford)

Ledger (ed.): *Warlike Music 1760* (Oxford)

LeGron: *Cloches de Bretagne* (Billaudot)

*Miller: *Trumpet Basics* (Faber)

Mills and Romm: *Intermediate Trumpet Solos* (with cassette accompaniment) (H. Leonard)

Mortimer (ed.): *Souvenir Album* (Boosey & Hawkes)

*Persichetti: *The Hollow Men* (Presser)

---

[13] Works requiring the use of high trumpets are noted with a plus sign (+).

*Purcell: *Sonata,* ed. Voisin (transposed) (International)

Ramskill: *Absolutely Trumpet* (Brass Wind Publications)

Ramskill: *Some Might Say Prokofiev* (Brass Wind Publications)

Richardson (ed.): *6 More Trumpet Tunes* (Boosey & Hawkes)

Richardson (ed.): *6 Trumpet Tunes* (Boosey & Hawkes)

*Ropartz: *Andante et allegro* (Southern)

Simon: *Willow Echoes* (C. Fischer)

+Stanley: *Suites No. 1, 2, 3 of Trumpet Voluntaries* (BIM)

Telemann: *Heroic Music,* arr. Lawton (Oxford)

Top Line Album for Trumpet (Brass Wind Publications)

Voxman (ed.): *Concert and Contest Collection* (Rubank)

Wastall (ed.): *First Repertoire Pieces for Trumpet* (Boosey & Hawkes)

Wiggins: *Trumpeter's Tune* (Chester)

Woolfenden: *Landmarks* (Brass Wind Publications)

Difficult

Adams: *Concerto* (BIM)

Adams: *Sonata* (BIM)

*+Albinoni: *Concerto in D Major,* arr. Thilde (Billaudot)

*+Albinoni: *Sonata in C* (Music Rara)

*+Albinoni: *Sonata No. 11 (St. Mark)* (BIM)

+Albrechtsberger: *Concertino in E♭* (BIM)

*André-Bloch: *Meou-Tan Yin* (A. Leduc)

Antheil: *Sonata* (Weintraub)

*Arban: *Carnival of Venice* (C. Fischer)

*Arban: *Piano Accompaniments to 12 Celebrated Fantasies* (C. Fischer)

*Arnold: *Concerto* (Faber)

Arutiunian: *Aria et scherzo* (A. Leduc)

*Arutiunian: *Concerto* (International)

Arutiunian: *Concert scherzo* (BIM)

Arutiunian: *Elegy* (BIM)

Arutiunian: *Rhapsody for Trumpet* (Peters)

Bach, trans. Tambyeff: *Concerto en ut majeur* (with organ) (A. Leduc)

Bach: *Wir glauben all' an einen Gott* (with organ) (BIM)

V. Bach: *Hungarian Melodies* (PP Music)

Balay: *Pièce de Concours* (A. Leduc)

Baratto: *Helvetia* (BIM)

+Baratto: *Stella maris* (BIM)

Beauchamp: *Rhapsodine* (Combre)

Bellstedt: *La Mandolinata* (Southern)

Bellstedt: *Napoli* (Southern)

*Bitsch: *Quatre Variations sur un thème de Domenico Scarlatti* (A. Leduc)

Blazhevich: *Concerto No. 5* (International)

Blazhevich: *Scherzo* (Reift)

*Bloch: *Proclamation* (Broude Bros.)

Boehme: *Konzert in F Moll* (Benjamin)

*Borgo, Cima, and Perllegrini: *13 Canzoni Strumentali Milanesi* (with organ) (BIM)

R. Boughton: *Trumpet Concerto* (Brass Wind Publications)

*Bourgeois: *Sonata for Trumpet and Piano* (Brass Wind Publications)

*Boutry: *Concertino* (A. Leduc)

*Boutry: *Préludes* (Salabert)

*Boutry: *Trompetunia* (A. Leduc)

*Boutry: *Trumpeldor* (A. Leduc)

*Bozza: *Caprice* (A. Leduc)

*Bozza: *Caprice No. 2* (A. Leduc)

*Bozza: *Concertino* (A. Leduc)

*Bozza: *Cornettina* (A. Leduc)

*Bozza: *Frigariana* (A. Leduc)

*Bozza: *Rhapsodie* (A. Leduc)

*Bozza: *Rustiques* (A. Leduc)

Brandt: *Konzertstück No. 1* (Reift)

Brandt: *Konzertstück No. 2* (Reift)

*+Buxtehude: *Komm, Heiliger Geist, Herr Gott* (with organ) (BIM)

Cellier: *Chevauchee fantastique* (Billaudot)

Charlier: *Solo de concours* (Schott Frères)

+Charpentier: *Marche et triomphe et second air de trompette* (A. Leduc)

*+Charpentier: *Prelude to Te Deum* (with organ) (BIM) (Emerson)

Chitchyan: *Armenian Sketch* (BIM)

Chitchyan: *Humoresque* (BIM)

Chkolnik: *Concerto* (BIM)

*H. Clarke: *Music of Herbert L. Clarke,* 2 vols. (Warner Bros.)

+J. Clarke: *Suite in D Major* (Musica Rara)

+J. Clarke: *Trumpet Voluntary in D* (International)

Clerisse: *Andante et Allegro* (Billaudot)

Clerisse: *Theme Varie* (A. Leduc)

Cords: *Concert Fantasie* (C. Fischer)

+Corelli: *Sonata in D* (Musica Rara)

Cosma: *Concerto* (Billaudot)

Davies: *Sonata* (Schott)

D. Davis: *Quotation* (BIM)

Delerue: *Concertino* (A. Leduc)

Donato: *Prélude et allegro* (A. Leduc)

Emmanuel: *Sonate* (A. Leduc)

*Enesco: *Legend* (International)

*Ewazen: *Sonata* (Southern)

*+Fasch: *Concerto No. 2* (BIM)

*+Fasch: *Konzert in D* (Sikorski)

Filas: *A Very Short Love Story* (BIM)

Filas: *Concerto* (BIM)

Filas: *Sonata* (BIM)

+Frackenpohl: *Sonatina* (BIM)

Friedman: *Sonata* (BIM)

*+D. Gabrieli: *Sonata No. 2 in D*, ed. Tarr (Musica Rara)

*+D. Gabrieli: *Sonata No. 4 in D*, ed. Tarr (Musica Rara)

Gimeno: *Concerto No. 3* (BIM)

Gimeno: *Sonata* (BIM)

Gliere: *Concerto*, ed. Dokshitser (Reift)

*Goedicke: *Concert Etude* (Belwin-Mills) (BIM)

Goedicke: *Concerto* (International)

Gregson: *Concerto* (Novello)

+Grossi: *Sonata* (Musica Rara)

Hailstock: *Sonata* (Presser)

*+Handel (and others): *A Suite of Trumpet Voluntaries* (with organ) (BIM)

Haug: *Concertino* (BIM)

*Haydn: *Concerto in E♭*, ed. Robbins-Landon and Tarr (Universal Edition); also version with cassette accompaniment (H. Leonard)

+M. Haydn: *Concerto in D* (A. Benjamin)

+M. Haydn: *Concerto No. 2*, ed. Tarr (Musica Rara)

Hedge: *Sonata* (Westfield)

Herrmann: *Andante e polacca* (BIM)

+Hertel: *Concerto No. 1*, ed. Tarr (BIM)

+Hertel: *Concerto No. 2*, ed. Tarr (Musica Rara)

*Hindemith: *Sonate* (Schott)

Hoddinott: *Little Suite* (Brass Wind Publications)

*Honegger: *Intrada* (Salabert)

*Horovitz: *Concerto* (Novello)

Howarth: *The Amazing Mr. Arban* (Chester)

*Howarth: *Concerto* (Chester)

*Hubeau: *Sonate* (Durand)

*Hummel: *Concerto*, ed. Tarr (Universal); also version with cassette accompaniment (H. Leonard)

Husa: *Concerto* (Associated)

*Ibert: *Impromptu* (A. Leduc)

*+Jacchini: *Deux Concertos-Sonates* (A. Leduc)

*+Jacchini: *Sonata in D* (Musica Rara)

+Jevtic: *Quasi una passacaglia* (with organ) (BIM)

+Jevtic: *Que le Jour est Beau!* (BIM)

Jolivet: *Air de Bravoure* (International)

Jolivet: *Concertino* (Durand)

*Jolivet: *Concerto No. 2* (A. Leduc)

Kassatti: *Espagnolade* (BIM)

Kassatti: *In petto* (BIM)

Kassatti: *Kino concertino* (BIM)

*Kennan: *Sonata* (Warner Bros.)

Koetsier: *Concertino* (BIM)

Koetsier: *Sonatina* (Donemus)

Kovacs: *Capriccio Brasiliano* (BIM)

Kreutzer: *Variationen in G* (BIM)

Krol: *Concerto classico* (Haas)

Kryzwicki: *Concerto* (A. Leduc)

Laburda: *Concerto per tromba* (Haas)

Laburda: *Sonatine* (Haas)

Larsson: *Concertino* (Gehrmans)

Laue: *Trumpet Concerto in D Major* (Brass Wind Publications)

Liebermann: *Concerto* (Presser)

*Longinotti: *Scherzo Iberico* (BIM)

Luening: *Introduction und Allegro* (Peters)

Lukas: *Concerto* (BIM)

*Mager (ed.): *9 Grand Solos de Concert* (Southern)

McDowall: *The Night Trumpeter* (Brass Wind Publications)

Meier: *Konzertstück* (BIM)

Mendez: *Jota* (C. Fischer)

Mendez: *La virgen de la Macarena* (Koff Music)

Mendez: *Mexican Hat Dance* (C. Fischer)

Meyer-Selb: *5 Bagatelles virtuos* (BIM)

Michel: *Chant du Berger* (Woodbrass)

+Molter: *Concerto No. 1 in D* (Musica Rara) (BIM)

+Molter: *Concerto No. 2* (BIM)

Mouquet: *Légende Héroïque* (A. Leduc)

*+L. Mozart: *Concerto in D*, ed. Thilde (Billaudot) (Haas)

+Mudge: *Concerto in D* (Musica Rara)

*+Neruda: *Concerto in E♭*, (BIM) (Brass Wind Publications)

*+Otto: *Trumpet Concerto in E♭* (Brass Wind Publications)

*Patterson: *Trumpet Concerto* (Josef Weinberger)

Pachmutova: *Konzert* (Reift)

Peaslee: *Nightsongs* (Margun)

Pilss: *Concerto* (King)

Pilss: *Sonate* (Universal)

Plog: *Concerto No. 1* (with large brass ensemble and perc.) (BIM)

Plog: *Concerto No. 2* (BIM)

Plog: *Nocturne* (BIM)

Plog: *3 Miniatures* (BIM)

Ponchielli: *Concerto per tromba* (BIM)

Porrino: *Concertino* (Ricordi)

Presser: *Sonatina* (Presser)

*Proctor: *The Huffle* (Brass Wind Publications)

Proctor: *Trumpet Concerto* (Brass Wind Publications)

*+Purcell: *Sonata* (original key) (Schott)

Rauber: *Concerto "Humeurs"* (BIM)

Riisager: *Concertino* (W. Hansen)

Sachse: *Concertino in E♭* (BIM)

Saint-Saëns-Busser: *Fantaisie en Mi Bémol* (A. Leduc)

Sampson: *The Mysteries Remain* (with organ) (BIM)

Sampson: *Serenade* (flugelhorn) (with string orch.) (BIM)

Saryan: *Serenade* (BIM)

Schlaepfer: *Ascensus* (BIM)

Schuller: *Concerto* (Associated)

Schuller: *Pavane* (Margun)

Shakhov: *Scherzo* (BIM)

Staigers: *Carnival of Venice* (C. Fischer)

+Stanley: *Suite No. 1 of Trumpet Voluntaries* (with organ) (BIM)

*+Stanley: *Trumpet Tune*, arr. Coleman (Oxford)

*Stevens: *Sonata* (Peters)

+Stoelzel: *Concerto in D* (Billaudot)

+Stradella: *Sinfonia*, 2 vols. (Musica Rara)

+Stradella: *Sonata* (Haas)

Szentpali: *Pearls* (BIM)

*+Tartini: *Concerto in D* (Selmer) (Brass Wind Publications) (Billaudot)

Telemann: *Air de trompette* (with organ) (BIM)

*+Telemann: *Concerto in D* (Musica Rara)

Telemann: *Heroic Music*, arr. Lawton (Oxford)

Tisnè: *Heraldiques* (Billaudot)

*Tomasi: *Concerto* (A. Leduc)

Tosi: *Mundial-Concerto* (BIM)

*Torelli: *Concertino in C* (International)

*+Torelli: *Concerto in D*, ed. Tarr (Musica Rara)

*+Torelli: *Sinfonia (G1)* (Sikorski)

*+Torelli: *Sinfonia (G2)*, ed. Tarr (Musica Rara)

*+Torelli: *Sinfonia (G3)*, ed. Tarr (Musica Rara)

*+Torelli: *Sinfonia (G4)*, ed. Tarr (Musica Rara)

*+Torelli: *Sonata*, ed. Neilson (International)

*+Torelli: *Sonata (G5)*, ed. Tarr (Musica Rara)

*+Torelli: *Sonata (G6)*, ed. Tarr (Musica Rara)

*+Torelli: *Sonata (G7)*, ed. Tarr (Musica Rara)

*+Torelli: *2 Concertos (G8, G9)* (Sikorski)

Trognée: *Valse lente* (BIM)

Turrin: *Caprice* (BIM)

Turrin: *Elegy* (BIM)

Turrin: *Four Miniatures* (trumpet or flugelhorn) (BIM)

Turrin: *Intrada* (BIM)

Turrin: *2 Portraits* (Flugelhorn) (BIM)

Tuthill: *Sonata* (Warner Bros.)

Valero: *Concierto No. 1* (BIM)

+Vejvanovsky: *Sonata* (Edition Ka We)

Voegelin: *Encuentro y Danza* (BIM)

Wilder: *Sonata* (Margun)

Wilder: *Suite* (Margun)

Williams: *Adirondacks Polka* (C. Colin)

Williams: *Concerto No.2* (C. Colin)

Williams: *Prelude & Scherzo* (C. Colin)

Williams: *Sonata* (Colin)

Zbinden: *Concertino* (Schott)

Zingg: *Album* (BIM)

Zwilich: *American Concerto* (Presser)

Recommended Books on the Trumpet and Cornet[14]

Altenburg, Detlef. *Untersuchungen zur Geschichte der Trompete in Zeitalter der Clarinblaskunst (1500–1800).* Regensburg: G. Bosse, 1973.

*Altenburg, Johann Ernst. *Trumpeters' and Kettledrummers' Art.* Trans. by Edward H. Tarr. Nashville: Brass Press, 1974.

* Anstutz, Allan Keith. "A Videofluorographic Study of the Teeth Aperture, Instrument Pivot, and Tongue Arch and Their Influence on Trumpet Performance." D.M.E. Thesis, University of Oklahoma, 1970.

*Bach, Vincent. *The Art of Trumpet Playing.* Elkhart, Ind.: Vincent Bach Corporation, 1969.

Barclay, R. L. *The Art of the Trumpet-Maker: The Materials, Tools, and Techniques of the Seventeenth and Eighteenth Centuries in Nuremberg.* Oxford, UK: Clarendon Press, 1992.

*Bate, Philip. *The Trumpet and Trombone: An Outline of Their History, Development, and Construction,* 2nd ed. New York: W. W. Norton, 1978.

Bellamah, Joseph L. *A Trumpeter's Treasury of Information.* San Antonio, Tex.: Southern Music Co., 1969.

*Bendinelli, Cesare. *Tutta l'arte dell trombetta (1614).* Facsimile, ed. E. H. Tarr. Kassel: Bärenreiter, 1975.

---

[14]Many interesting articles appear in the *International Trumpet Guild Journal* and other periodicals listed in Appendix C.

Booth, Matthew. *Sound the Trumpet: The John Wilbraham Method.* London: Stainer & Bell, 2000.

*Brownlow, Arthur. *The Last Trumpet: A History of the English Slide Trumpet.* Stuyvesant, N.Y.: Pendragon Press, 1996.

Bush, Irving. *Artistic Trumpet Technique and Study.* Hollywood, Calif.: Highland Music, 1962.

Bush, Irving. *Trumpet Players Blow with Good Vibrations.* Montrose, Calif.: Balquidder Music, 2003.

Campos, Frank Gabriel. *Trumpet Technique.* New York: Oxford University Press, 2005.

Cardoso, Wilfredo. *Ascending Trumpets: The Use of Trumpets with Ascending Valves in Symphonic Music, Opera, and Ballet.* Buenos Aires: Cardoso, 1978.

Cardoso, Wilfredo. *High Trumpets: Practical Applications of High Trumpets in Trumpet Solos in the Works of J. S. Bach, Baroque Music, Symphony Orchestra and Opera Repertoire.* Buenos Aires: Cardoso, 1977

Carnovale, Norbert, and Paul F. Doerksen. *Twentieth Century Music for Trumpet and Orchestra*, 2nd rev. ed. Nashville, Tenn.: The Brass Press, 1994.

Cassone, Gabriel. *La Tromba.* Varese, Italy: Zecchini, 2002.

*Clarke, Herbert L. *How I Became a Cornetist.* Kenosha, Wis.: Leblanc Educational Publications, n.d.

Dale, Delbert A. *Trumpet Technique.* London: Oxford University Press, 1967.

*D'Ath, Norman W. *Cornet Playing.* London: Boosey & Hawkes, 1960.

*Davidson, Louis. *Trumpet Profiles.* Bloomington, Ind.: Davidson, 1975.

Davidson, Louis. *Trumpet Techniques.* Rochester: Wind Music, 1970.

Davidson, Todd. "The Introduction of the High Trumpet into the Late-Nineteenth and Early-Twentieth-Century Orchestra." D. Mus. thesis, Indiana University, 2002.

Davies, Rick. *Chappottín, Chocolate, and the Afro-Cuban Trumpet Style.* Lanham, Md.: Scarecrow Press, 2003.

Dokshizer, Timofei. *The Memoires of Timofei Dokshizer: An Autobiography.* Westfield, Mass.: International Trumpet Guild, 1997.

*Eldredge, Niles. *A Brief History of Piston-Valved Cornets.* New York: Historic Brass Society, 2002. [Reprinted from 2002 *Historic Brass Society Journal* 14:337–390.]

*Fantini, Girolamo. *Modo per imparare a sonare di tromba tanto di guerra quanto musicalmente in organo, con tromba sordina, con cimbalo e con orgn'altro strumento* (1638). New York: Performers' Facsimiles, 2002. Nashville, Tenn.: The Brass Press, 1972.

*Farley, Robert, and John Hutchins. *Natural Trumpet Studies.* Oakham, Rutland, England: Brass Wind Publications.

Foster, Robert E. *Practical Hints on Playing the Trumpet/Cornet.* Melville, N.Y.: Belwin Mills, 1983.

Hajdinjak, Reinhard. *Solo-Trompete und Blasorchester: Verzeichnis von über 500 Solowerken für* Trompete(n) *und Blasorchester.* Vienna, Austria: J. Kliment, 1991.

Handel's Trumpeter: The Diary of John Grano (c.1692–1748). Stuyvesant, N.Y.: Pendragon Press, 1998.

Hanson, Fay. *Brass Playing.* New York: Carl Fischer, 1975.

*Harper, Thomas. *Instructions for the Trumpet* (1837). Homer, N.Y.: Spring Tree Enterprises, 1988.

Hiller, Albert. *Trompetenmusiken aus drei Jahrhunderten (ca.1600 nach 1900): Kompositionen für 1 bis 24 (Natur-) Trompeten mit und ohne Pauken.* Cologne, Germany: W. G. Haas, 1991.

Hyatt, Jack H. "The Soprano and Piccolo Trumpets: Their History, Literature, and a Tutor." D.M.A. thesis, Boston University, 1974. UM 74–20, 473.

Johnson, Keith. *The Art of Trumpet Playing.* Ames, Iowa: Iowa State University Press, 1981.

Kay, Jackie. *Trumpet.* New York: Pantheon Books, 1998.

*Laird, Michael. *BrassWorkBook for Natural Trumpet.* Gt. Dunmow, England: BrassWorks.

Lindner, Andreas. *Die Kaiserlichen Hoftrompeter und HofPauker in 18. und 19. Jahrhundert.* Tutzing, Germany: H. Schneider, 1999.

Lowrey, Alvin. *Lowrey's International Trumpet Discography.* Columbia, S.C.: Camden House, 1990.

*Mathez, Jean-Pierre. *Joseph Jean-Baptiste Laurent Arban, 1825–1889: Portrait d'un musicien Française du XIXe siècle.* Moudon, Switzerland: Editions BIM, 1977.

Mathie, Gordon. *The Trumpet Teacher's Guide.* Cincinatti, Ohio: Queen City Brass Publications, 1984.

*Meidt, Joseph Alexis. *A Cinefluorographic Investigation of Oral Adjustments for Various Aspects of Brass Instrument Performance.* M.A. thesis, University of Iowa, 1967.

Musique pour trompette: Catalogue thematique. Paris: Alphonse Leduc, 1994.

Poper, Roy. *Roy Poper's Guide to the Brasswind Methods of James Stamp.* Montrose, Calif.: Balquidder Music, 2001.

Ryan, Marc. *Trumpet Records: An Illustrated History, with Discography.* Milford, N.H.: Big Nickel Publications, 1992.

Seraphinoff, Richard, and Robert Barclay. *Making a Natural Trumpet: An Illustrated Workshop Guide.* Edinburgh University Collection of Historic Musical Instruments, 2003.

*Sherman, Roger. *The Trumpeter's Handbook.* Athens, Ohio: Accura Music, 1979.

*Smithers, Don. *The Music and History of the Baroque Trumpet Before 1721.* London: J. M. Dent, 1973.

*Snell, Howard. *The Trumpet: Its Practice and Performance: A Guide for Students.* Hollington, England: Rakeway Music, 1997.

*Steele-Perkins, Crispian. *The Trumpet.* London: Kahn & Averill, 2001.

*Tarr, Edward. *The Art of Baroque Trumpet Playing: Exercises from the Schola Cantorum Basiliensis (Die Kunst des Barocktrompeten-spiels: Übungen aus der Schola Cantorum).* New York: Schott, 1999. [3 volumes]

*Tarr, Edward. *East Meets West: The Russian Trumpet Tradition from the Time of Peter the Great to the October Revolution, with a Lexicon of Trumpeters Active in Russia from the Seventeenth to the Twentieth Centuries.* Hillsdale, N.Y.: Pendragon Press, 2000.

*Tarr, Edward. *The Trumpet.* Portland, Ore.: Amadeus Press, 1988.

Weast, Robert. *Famous Trumpet Players (from 1584 to the present)*. Johnston, Iowa: Brass World.

Webster, Gerald. *Method for Piccolo Trumpet*. Nashville, Tenn.: Brass Press, 1980.

Yanow, Scott. *The Trumpet Kings: The Players Who Shaped the Sound of Jazz Trumpet*. San Francisco: Backbeat Books, 2001.

Other Books of Interest to Brass Players [15]

Anderson, Paul G. *Brass Solo and Study Material Music Guide*. Evanston, Ill.: The Instrumentalist Co., 1976.

*Baines, Anthony. *Brass Instruments: Their History and Development*. London: Faber & Faber, 1976.

Barbour, J. Murray. *Trumpets, Horns, and Music*. East Lansing, Mich.: Michigan State University Press, 1964.

Bellamah, Joseph L. *Brass Facts*. San Antonio, Tex.: Southern Music, 1961.

Bernstas, Bob. *Top Brass: Interviews and Masterclasses with Jazz's Leading Brass Players*. New York: Boptism Music Publishers, 2002.

Brass Anthology: A Collection of Articles Published in the Instrumentalist Magazine from 1946 to 1999. Northfield, Ill.: The Instrumentalist Co., 1999.

Brown, Merrill E. *Teaching the Successful High School Brass Section*. West Nyack, N.Y.: Parker, 1981.

Carse, Adam. *Musical Wind Instruments*. New York: Da Capo Press, 1965 (Originally published in London by Macmillan, 1940.

Devol, John. *Brass Music for the Church*. Plainview, N.Y.: Harold Branch, 1974.

Dundas, Richard J. *Twentieth Century Brass Musical Instruments in the United States*, rev. ed. Rutland, Vt.: R. Dundas, 1998.

Eliason, Robert E. *Early American Brass Makers*. Nashville, Tenn.: Brass Press, 1981.

*Farkas, Philip. *The Art of Brass Playing*. Rochester, N.Y.: Wind Music, 1962.

Farkas, Philip. *The Art of Musicianship*. Bloomington, Ind.: Musical Publications, 1976.

*Frederiksen, Brian. *Arnold Jacobs: Song and Wind*. Gurnee, Ill.: WindSong Press Limited, 1996.

*Herbert, Trevor. *The British Brass Band: A Musical and Social History*. Oxford, England: Oxford University Press, 2000.

*Herbert, Trevor, and John Wallace, eds. *The Cambridge Companion to Brass Instruments*. Cambridge, England: Cambridge University Press, 1997.

Johnson, Keith: *Brass Performance and Pedagogy*. Upper Saddle River, N.J.: Prentice-Hall, 2002.

Lawrence, Ian. *Brass in Your School*. London: Oxford University Press, 1975.

*Macdonald, Donna. *The Odyssey of the Philip Jones Brass Ensemble*. Moudon, Switzerland: Éditions BIM, 1986.

Meckna, Michael. *Twentieth-Century Brass Soloists*. Westport, Conn.: Greenwood Press, 1994.

Mende, Emilie. *Pictorial Family Tree of Brass Instruments in Europe*. Moudon, Switzerland: Éditions BIM, 1978.

Méndez, Rafael: *Prelude to Brass Playing*. Boston: C. Fischer, 1961.

Perspectives in Brass Scholarship: Proceedings of the International Historic Brass Symposium, Amherst, 1995. Stuyvesant, N.Y.: Pendragon Press, 1997.

Rasmussen, Mary. *A Teacher's Guide to the Literature for Brass Instruments*. Durham, N.H.: Brass Quarterly, 1968.

Severson, Paul, and Mark McDunn. *Brass Wind Artistry*. Athens, Ohio: Accura Music, 1983.

*Stewart, Dee. *Arnold Jacobs: The Legacy of a Master*. Northfield, Ill.: The Instrumentalist Publishing Co., 1987.

Swain, John. *The Brass Instruments: A Reference Manual*. Portland, Maine: Manduca Music Publications, 1997.

*Taylor, Arthur R. *Brass Bands*. London: Granada Publishing, Ltd., 1979.

Trusheim, William H.. "Mental Imagery and Musical Performance: An Inquiry into Imagery Use by Eminent Orchestral Brass Players." Ed.D. dissertation, Rutgers University, New Brunswick, N.J., 1987.

Watson, J. Perry. *The Care and Feeding of a Community British Brass Band*. Farmingdale, N.Y.: Boosey & Hawkes, n.d.

Watson, J. Perry. *Starting a British Brass Band*. Grand Rapids, Mich.: Yamaha International Corp., 1984.

Weast, Robert. *Keys to Natural Performance for Brass Players*. Des Moines, Iowa: Brass World, 1979.

---

[15] A very useful guide to articles, books, and dissertations on brass instruments is Allen B. Skei's *Woodwind, Brass, and Percussion Instruments of the Orchestra: A Bibliographic Guide* (New York: Garland, 1985).

CHAPTER 4

THE HORN

OF THE FIVE PRINCIPAL VARIETIES OF HORN available today,[1] some may be categorized as student instruments, others as general-purpose horns, and still others as specialized high-register models, known as *descant horns*. There are differences in the keys in which the instruments are built: single horns in F or B♭; full or compensating double horns in F/B♭; double descant horns in B♭/F-alto, B♭/E♭-alto, and B♭/B♭-soprano; and full or compensating triple horns in F/B♭/F- or E♭-alto (or B♭ soprano). Horns are made with rotary, piston, and Vienna valves, and the third valve can be descending or ascending. There are also variations in bore and bell-throat taper as well as in the material from which the instrument is made (yellow brass, gold brass, and nickel silver). Today's horn players have a wide array of excellent equipment at their disposal. To clarify the choices available and to gain an understanding of how each horn is used, the various types will be considered individually.

FIGURE 4.1 Single and double horns (left to right): single F, single B♭ with stopping valve, compensating F/B♭ double, and full F/B♭ double (Alexander)

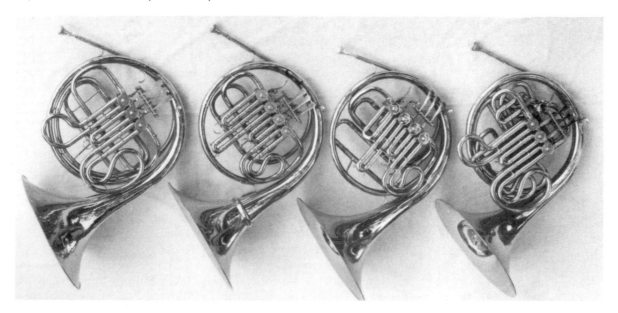

[1] Paxman's catalog at one time listed no fewer than 39 models. The present Alexander catalog offers 22 different horns. The options of added stopping valves, F extensions for single B♭ horns, ascending third valve systems, differing bells, and wrapping patterns account for the availability of so many models. The output of most other firms is considerably smaller.

▪ THE SINGLE F HORN

With the exception of the Vienna Horn (discussed later), single F horns are today intended specifically for beginners. Horn players tend to be more diverse in their playing and tonal concepts than other brass players; it is surprising, therefore, that there is such a unanimity of opinion as to the importance of beginning on the F horn. It is felt that in this way the student will develop a good concept of horn tone and that the fundamental elements of horn playing, particularly accuracy and flexibility,[2] will be developed. Agreement on this point is far from universal, however. Many horn players feel that the B♭ horn offers important advantages to beginning students. Because of the more widely spaced harmonics, finding the right notes is much easier for students in the early stages of playing. In addition, the ease of response of the B♭ is a positive aid to tone production.

▪ THE DOUBLE HORN

The most widely used horn today is the F/B♭ full double. Earlier, single B♭ horns were frequently utilized on first and third (high) parts in orchestras and full doubles on second and fourth (low), but now entire sections of full doubles are found almost everywhere.

The first double horn was developed by a German hornist, Edmund Gumpert,[3] in collaboration with instrument maker Fritz Kruspe, whose firm introduced it at Erfurt, Germany, in 1897. At that time, German horn players were increasingly using the B♭ horn (or a B♭ crook) in order to cope with the endurance and high range demands of parts being written by Strauss, Mahler, and other late 19th century composers. Although the greater responsiveness, ease, and better high register of the B♭ horn made performing such parts less taxing, many horn players missed the intonation and tone of the F horn in the middle and lower register.

Gumpert had the idea of building a B♭ horn with longer rotors and valve casings so that two ranks of valve tubing could be accommodated. A change valve directed the air column to one or both ranks of valve tubes. When the change valve was in the F position, the air column went through both sides of the instrument—the normal B♭ tubing plus additional lengths to convert the horn's pitch to F. With the change valve in the B♭ position, the F section was bypassed and the instrument functioned as an ordinary B♭ horn. This original type of double horn is known as a *compensating double,* to distinguish it from the full double horn that appeared a short time later. The full double horn is a simpler and more direct system that provides a better F section, but it is heavier due to the extra tubing required. In the full double configuration, the change valve routes the air column directly through either the F or the B♭ ranks of tubing before it reenters the bell section. (See Figures 4.2 and 4.3.)

Although the double horn consists of two complete horns in one, it is not approached in that way by the player. A crossover point is established (usually written G♯ above middle C or, more rarely, C♯, a fourth higher) and the instrument is considered (in the player's mind) one horn. The appropriate B♭ and F fingerings are used above and below the crossover point. Every effort is made to minimize differences in timbre between the F and B♭ sides, and it is difficult to detect when a skilled player passes from one side to the other. The double horn combines the tone and intonation of the F horn in the low and middle ranges with the B♭ horn's tone and security in the high register.

Another common way to use the double horn is to play it essentially as a B♭ horn, reserving certain notes for the F horn (usually G in and below the staff, F♯ below middle C, and from low C downward). This is often the practice in Europe, and it is growing in America. Horns made in England and Germany are designed to be played in this way, if desired. The bores of European double horns were enlarged to 12 or 12.1 mm some

---

[2] If a single F horn is unavailable, the F section of a double horn will serve equally well.
[3] Edmund Gumpert is often confused in the literature with his more renowned uncle, Fritz Gumpert, and credit for developing the double horn is misattributed to the elder Gumpert.

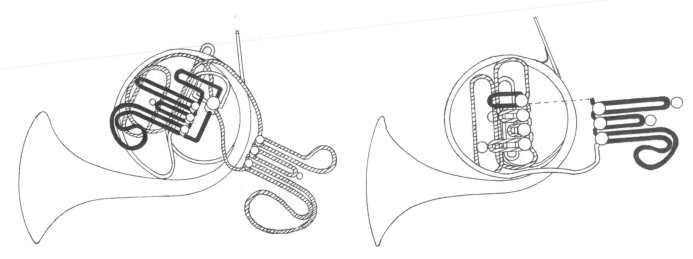

FIGURE 4.2 Windways of a full double horn   **FIGURE 4.3** Windways of a compensating double horn

years ago in order to give the B♭ section a fuller tone and improved intonation in the lower middle range and to contribute greater resonance overall. Both types of double horn are in use today, although compensating doubles are now fairly rare. The latter are sometimes favored by hornists who play primarily on the B♭ horn and prefer a lighter-weight instrument, but want the availability of an F section. The compensating double is a good solo instrument, due to its lighter weight, and is occasionally found in orchestras, particularly in Scandinavia.

■ THE SINGLE B♭ HORN

In the period following the introduction of the double horn there was not a total changeover to the new instrument. Single F horns were replaced, but single B♭ instruments continued in use. Many high horn players (those who played the first and third parts in orchestras) preferred the lighter B♭ horn and felt that it offered better endurance and clarity of tone. Use of the single B♭ continued to be widespread, especially in Germany (and high horn players who adopted double horns continued to play primarily on the B♭ side). It was found that a good blend of sound could be achieved with a mixture of single B♭s and full doubles. The Berlin Philharmonic used this effective format well into the 1950s, and the same arrangement was popular in England after German horns began to be played there. The single B♭ horn was less common in the United States due to a preference for double horns, but one of the greatest players during the first half of the 20th century, Willem Valkenier, solo horn of the Boston Symphony in the Koussevitzky era, played a single B♭ throughout his long career with that orchestra. Another important early player who used the single B♭ was Franz Xaver Reiter (a student of Franz Strauss[4]), who played with the New York Philharmonic.

The single B♭ has always been a favorite solo instrument for its lightness, technical agility, and accuracy. The great soloist Dennis Brain used an Alexander single B♭ exclusively for both orchestral and solo work after switching from a French-type single F piston horn around 1950. A similar single B♭ was used by his colleague and successor Alan Civil. B♭ horns are still found in orchestras: Tim Brown, principal of the BBC Symphony Orchestra, usually plays on a single B♭, and Jeffrey Bryant, former principal of the Royal Philharmonic, uses an Alexander five-valve model. The single B♭ also offers definite advantages in chamber music, where its light response is an asset in balancing with just a few instruments.

[4] Franz Strauss, father of composer Richard Strauss, was in the second half of the 19th century considered one of the greatest German horn players. He was an early exponent of the B♭ horn.

Single B♭ horns must be fitted with a stopping valve (handstopping is discussed later). This valve routes the vibrating air column through an additional length of tubing to lower the pitch three-quarters of a tone to produce an in-tune stopped note (this can be accomplished on the F horn by transposing down one half-step). With the slide of the stopping valve pushed in, the horn can be played in A, which is useful for high-register parts such as Beethoven's Seventh Symphony. An F extension is often added to enable the player to reach notes below the ordinary B♭ range and to provide an improved low C. The extension can be either attached to the stopping valve or built into the instrument through an added fifth valve. Another innovation is the addition of a C valve, which bypasses some of the tubing and raises the overall pitch of the horn by one tone. This offers positive advantages in the high register.

■ THE ASCENDING THIRD VALVE HORN

The final two instruments that might be termed general-purpose horns are not in general use but have flourished in specific geographical areas. The first of these, known in France and Belgium as the *cor ascendant,* is constructed with an ascending third valve. This type of instrument dates from 1848, when Jules Halary invented a horn in which the air column was normally directed through the tubing of the third valve (without the valve's being depressed). With a G crook, the extra length (one tone) of the third valve loop allowed the instrument to be played in F so long as only the first two valves were used. By depressing the third valve, the extra tubing was bypassed and the instrument's pitch was raised one tone to G. This offered a significant improvement in the upper register of the F horn. Around 1930, Louis Vuillermoz developed a compensating double horn based on this principle, and this instrument was widely used in France and Belgium until the middle 1970s.[5]

Aside from the ascending third valve feature,[6] French-type horns have traditionally been made with piston valves and narrower bore and bell, although the Vuillermoz design increased these dimensions slightly. The famous French makers, Selmer, Courtois, and Couesnon, all produced models of this type. The ascending third valve system has also been made available on regular medium- and large-bore rotary valve models by Alexander (Germany), Engelbert Schmid (Germany), and Paxman (England). For the past three decades, the usual descending rotary valve full double horns that are used elsewhere have most often been seen in French orchestras rather than traditional piston valve ascending instruments. Modern rotary valve ascending instruments do offer decided advantages in the upper register and for certain orchestral passages. These are occasionally used by individual players today in France, Belgium, Germany, and the United States as a general-purpose horn that incorporates some of the high-register advantages of the descant or triple horn within a double horn.

■ THE VIENNA HORN

The most distinctive horn in use today is actually a survivor from an earlier epoch. The principal instrument of the Vienna Philharmonic, the Vienna horn is unchanged from the instrument introduced by Leopold Uhlmann around 1830. Of similar bore and bell to the natural horns of that era and incorporating a removable F crook, or *bogen,* the Vienna horn retains an authentic 19th century tone quality and requires all of the playing skill of the great hornists of that period. It would obviously have been easier for the Viennese players to have adopted the B♭ or double horn when these replaced single F horns elsewhere, but, to their credit, they have over the last century remained steadfast

[5]The controversy over the changes in the horn playing and instruments used in France is best represented in two articles: André Cazalet, "The Horn, the Brasses and France," *Brass Bulletin,* 81 (1993), pp. 48–55; and Lucien Thévet, "On the French School of Horn Playing," *Brass Bulletin,* 84 (1993), pp. 54–61. M. Thévet's thoughtful article raises issues that are important to all brass players.
[6]The use of the ascending third valve is fully covered in Lucien Thévet's *Méthode complète de cor* (Paris: Alphonse Leduc, 1960).

in their commitment to maintain the special traditional timbre of the Vienna horn. In fact, the Vienna horn has become the trademark of the Vienna Philharmonic Orchestra.

At low and medium volume levels, the Vienna horn has a pure, classic F horn tone; as the volume increases, the sound is transformed to a bright, heroic quality at a lower dynamic level than on the B♭ or double horn. The lower threshold of the brighter timbre enables the Viennese players to bring a strong, brilliant horn sound to bear that stands out from the orchestral texture much more frequently in works of Bruckner, Wagner, and other 19th century composers than players in other orchestras.

An important stylistic feature of Viennese horn playing is the glissando-like slur, which adds expressive character to romantic compositions. The double-piston Vienna valve[7] is believed to improve slurring by providing a better continuity of the air column through valve changes than the rotary valve. Perhaps due to a combination of bore, bell, and its more direct airways, the high register of the Vienna horn is usually far better than that of other types of single F horn. This is a reason for its survival as a viable professional instrument. For demanding high passages, a small F alto descant horn or a Paxman double F/F-alto is usually substituted for the Vienna horn.

Considering today's exacting standards for accuracy and the difficulty of playing the single F horn, it should be noted that Viennese hornists achieve a technical standard comparable to sections composed of modern horns, while retaining their special sound. Viennese horn playing is held in great esteem by all hornists, especially the performances of its greatest players, such as the late Gottfried von Freiberg and Roland Berger (see Figure 4.4).

FIGURE 4.4
Vienna horn with F crook, played by Professor Roland Berger of the Vienna Philharmonic

---

[7] The Vienna valve is discussed in Chapter 1.

■ DESCANT HORNS

In the years following 1900, horns pitched an octave above the F horn appeared in Germany to aid the performance of Baroque horn parts, which are notorious for their high-register demands. The small bore and bell of these instruments were not ideal; but in the absence of an alternative, these horns served well enough until the late 1950s. At that time, the ingenious horn player-designer Richard Merewether collaborated with Robert Paxman, a London horn maker, in an effort to develop an improved descant horn using a standard-sized bell.

The idea of a double descant horn had been tried earlier in Germany, but the instrument was generally unsatisfactory in intonation due to the differences in length between its two sides in relation to its bell and leadpipe tapers. From their work on a single descant with a normal-sized bell, Merewether and Paxman developed a successful dual-bore double descant in F/F-alto. A B♭/F-alto soon followed, which allowed most of the range to be played on the B♭ side, with the F-alto side reserved for the highest register. This stimulated other firms to reexamine their designs, and Alexander produced compensating and full double descants in which the F-alto could be played for most of the range when desired. This offered surprising technical possibilities along with high-register advantages. The German soloist Hermann Baumann made a worldwide impression with these instruments. Today, descant horns are a normal part of a professional horn player's equipment. They are widely used for the Baroque repertoire, some Mozart and Haydn symphonies, concertos, and other works requiring a high tessitura. Most manufacturers now produce descant horns (see Figure 4.5).

The descant horn is comparable to the higher trumpets, in that it does not provide automatic high range but places these notes lower in the harmonic series, where there is greater distance between notes of the series. This allows the player to produce high notes in the most reliable and responsive part of the horn's harmonic series. For unusually high parts, as are found in a few of Bach's cantatas, or as an alternative to the B♭/F-alto, a B♭/B♭-soprano and an F-alto/B♭-soprano are available. A recent innovation has been the substitution of E♭-alto for F-alto. This makes possible a longer leadpipe, and several of the notes correspond to normal B♭ fingerings.

■ THE TRIPLE HORN

Not really a descant horn in the usual sense but a general-purpose instrument that can be used as an alternative to the double horn, the triple horn was developed by the late Richard Merewether from his work with descant horns. The full triple is constructed by lengthening the rotary valves still further to accommodate three ranks of valve tubing. This results in a horn that incorporates three independent sections in F, B♭, and F alto (or B♭ soprano) (see Figure 4.6). There is also a compensating model consisting of an independent F-alto section combined with the B♭ and F parts of the normal compensating double. The difficulty of designing a workable triple horn was the problem of the weight of the required extra tubing. Merewether was able to bring the instrument's weight down to an acceptable level through the use of hollow valve rotors. The problem of weight has received great attention from today's leading makers, and through various means the best triple horns now weigh only slightly more than a double horn.

■ OTHER DESIGN FACTORS

Aside from the various types of instruments available, there are other important factors affecting the design of a horn that must be considered by the player. Chief among these are the size and rate of an instrument's tapered sections, such as the leadpipe and bell throat, the length of the leadpipe, how the tubing is arranged, and the metal alloy from which it is made.

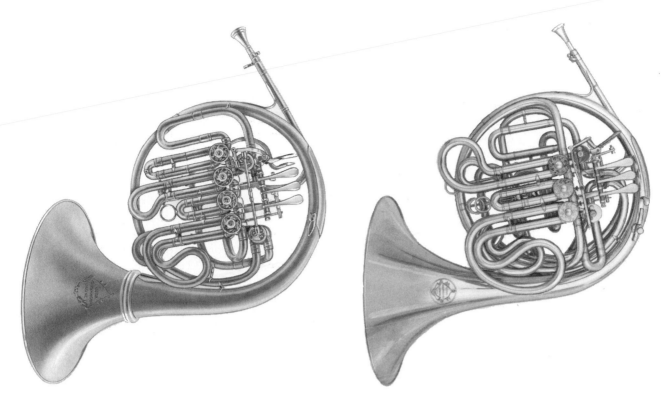

FIGURE 4.5 B♭/F-alto descant horn (Alexander)   **FIGURE 4.6** F/B♭/F-alto triple horn (Alexander)

Small bells, such as those found on old French piston valve horns and natural horns, are no longer made, except for modern reproductions of historical instruments. The bell throats of the horns in use today may be classified as medium, medium-large, large, and extra-large. The variation is in the bell's inner dimensions, not its over-all diameter at the end, which averages between 12⅛ inches (309.2 mm) and 12⅜ inches (314.6 mm). Horn makers are not entirely consistent in how their models are identified. The middle-size bell is designated as large by some and medium-large by others. At least one maker refers to their extra-large bell model as a large. (The classification of bell throats is at the center of the confusion concerning bore sizes, discussed later.)

The shape and dimensions of the bell throat have a profound influence on the horn's tone and playing qualities. Extra-large profiles often give the impression of a fuller sound at close range but fail to project well into the hall in comparison with medium and medium-large bell throats, which produce a more focused tone with greater carrying power. Because the sound radiates away from the audience and undergoes a complex reflective interaction with the acoustics of the hall, horn timbre must be evaluated from a distance. The bell throat also influences the color and character of the horn's timbre. Medium and medium-large bells have a warm, well-defined sound that projects clearly within an orchestral, band, or brass ensemble texture. The large bell compromises some of this definition for a greater degree of fullness combined with a somewhat darker color. Many feel that the extra-large bell goes too far in this respect and the horn sound loses clarity. Large-belled instruments also require greater effort to play. The present international trend seems to favor the medium and medium-large bells.

Of equal importance to bell size is the alloy used in the construction of the horn. The three materials—yellow brass, gold (red) brass, and nickel silver—impart different qualities to the sound. Yellow brass consists of 70% copper/30% zinc; gold brass is 85%

copper/15% zinc; and nickel silver is 63% copper/27% zinc/10–12% nickel.[8] Yellow brass is the most widely used material and, along with gold brass, is preferred by a majority of professional players worldwide. It contributes a warm, characteristic horn tone that can be modified for various musical contexts. Gold brass endows the timbre with a richer, more veiled quality of darker color. Nickel silver was once believed to darken the tone, but this has now been attributed to the extra-large bell throats of the horns usually made with this material. In the author's opinion, nickel silver imbues the timbre with a drab, metallic quality, in comparison with the greater color and character of yellow or gold brass.

Confusion often surrounds the subject of horn bore sizes. This is primarily because manufacturers and players tend to refer to only the horn's tapered portions (leadpipe and bell section) as the bore. This is not incorrect, but the tapered portions must be considered in relation to the horn's main bore. The main bore is determined by the diameter of the cylindrical tubing in the middle of the instrument containing the valves. Most manufacturers offer two or three bell sizes (with appropriate leadpipes), but only one main bore. European horns usually have a main bore of 12 or 12.1 mm. Other horns are often smaller in main bore. Thus it is not uncommon for horns identified as large bore to combine a smaller main bore with a large or extra-large bell throat. The timbres that result from the medium, large, and extra-large bells differ considerably, depending on the diameter of the main bore to which they are attached. Outward appearances can be deceiving, as well. Some horns are wrapped more compactly than others, but this gives no indication of their internal bore dimensions, which might be larger than an instrument wound in a more open pattern.

The configuration of the tubing of the double horn is another factor in the design of high-quality horns. Modern full double horns have evolved from the four widely copied patterns of double horns dating from the early years of the 20th century: Kruspe (model 9),[9] Alexander (model 103), C.F. Schmidt (which used a piston change valve), Knopf (usually known as a Geyer model in the United States). Players and designers often have a preference for one configuration over another. For example, the Knopf–Geyer type has smooth, wide bends in the tubing arrangement, due to the placement of the change valve at the far end of the valve cluster and a longer leadpipe. This results in lessened resistance, a quality that is preferred by many players but rejected by others. Each of the layouts has its merits, and the choice of one over another is purely a matter of preference. Many firms make instruments in more than one configuration. Over the years, various alterations have been made to the basic designs.

Most horns are available with either a fixed or a detachable bell. With the latter, the horn may be carried in a flat case rather than the usual form-fitting type. The threaded rings of the detachable bell add some weight to the horn. Some players find no important difference in the playing qualities of detachable-bell models, while others either prefer the difference or have a negative view of this option.

By far, the most important recent development in horns (and other brass instruments) has been improvement in the basic acoustical design and construction of the instruments. Around 1984, Anton Alexander, head of the well-known horn-making firm Gebr. Alexander, came into contact, through his activities in the Research Union of German Musical Instrument Makers, with Prof. Klaus Wogram of the

---

[8] Richard Merewether, *The Horn, the Horn . . .* (London: Paxman Musical Instruments, Ltd., 1979), p. 14. Walter A. Lawson gives the percentages for nickel silver as 65 percent copper, 17 percent zinc, and 18 percent nickel. Walter A. Lawson, *Development of New Mouthpipes for the French Horn* (Boonsboro, Md.: Lawson, n.d.), p. 14.
[9] There is some confusion about the models made by Kruspe. Listed in Kruspe's 1933 catalog are four models of double horn: No. 9 full double (232038), Model Horner, Philadelphia, with extra-wide bell and leadpipe; No. 10 full double (1027 194), Model Walter Kruspe (this appears to be a medium or medium-large bell model); No. 11 compensating double (295 125), Model Gumpert–Kruspe (this is the original double horn); and No. 12 compensating double (888 990), Model Professor Wendler, Boston (Georg Wendler was Kruspe's son-in-law and was first horn of the Boston Symphony for some years. He later took over direction of the Kruspe firm. The Wendler model is often incorrectly thought to have been the first double horn).

Physikalisch-Technische Budesanstalt, Braunschweig.[10] Wogram had developed a new software system that allowed brass instruments to be tested acoustically and located irregularities in the tapers of the conical tubing and the cylindrical tubing in areas where the tubing had been bent. Anton Alexander worked closely with Prof. Wogram to develop a mathematical model for testing horns. Turbulence could for the first time be detected and precisely located where an inconsistency existed in a tapered section. The system also was able to identify places in the forms for bending tubing in which deviations occurred that prevented a perfect cylindrical shape. Alexander set about incorporating these findings into the design and manufacture of their instruments. The results of this work led to significant improvements in the intonation, response, high range, and tone of their horns and Wagner tubas. The groundbreaking achievements of Klaus Wogram and Anton Alexander represent the wave of the future in the design and construction of brass instruments.

LINKAGES

The way in which motion from the valve levers is delivered to turn the valves is another consideration involving preference on the part of individual players. Before the development of the Unibal and Minibal mechanical linkages, string action afforded a more positive, quicker action. The new linkages are equally quick and have the advantage of durability and trouble-free operation. Players usually have a preference for one type over another, and some manufacturers offer both types.

RIGHT-HAND POSITION

The use of the right hand in horn playing is now being recognized for its acoustical function, actually forming part of the instrument by narrowing the bell throat. As described in Chapter 1, in sounding the instrument, a longitudinal standing wave is set up between the mouthpiece and a reflective threshold created by the expanding bell flare. As the pitch rises, the threshold moves increasingly toward the bell opening; on the horn, at written G above the staff, it has reached the player's hand. From this point upward, the hand essentially lengthens the bell throat by reducing its diameter so that the standing wave can continue to operate without encountering a drop in impedance (caused by the widening of the bell flare) within the horn's compass.[11] This can be confirmed by trying to play the range above G without the hand in the bell. The note centers seem to disappear, making production of the notes difficult.

The need to form an acoustically effective passageway dictates how the hand should be formed in the bell. The position described in Chapter 11 will ensure good results and should be carefully imitated. If the hand position is incorrect, the instrument's intonation and note centers will be affected. The right hand also refines the timbre by absorbing some of the higher partials and deflecting the sound toward the body. The player can control these effects still further by covering the bell to a greater or lesser degree to create a more mellow or brighter timbre. Intonation is controlled in the same way—opening to raise the pitch and closing to lower it.

HANDSTOPPING AND MUTING

The pungent, metallic timbre produced when the hand completely seals the bell is an effect unique to the horn. During the late 18th and early 19th centuries, playing with the hand open and closed to various degrees, including the full stopped position, was the

---

[10] Letter to the author from Philipp Alexander.
[11] See Richard Merewether, *The Horn*, pp. 28–32; Arthur Benade, "The Physics of Brasses," *Scientific American*, July 1973, pp. 24–35; and B. Lee Roberts, "Some Comments on the Physics of the Horn and Right-Hand Technique," *The Horn Call*, VL, no. 2 (May 1976), pp. 41–45.

primary means of playing diatonic and chromatic notes on the horn. It is important to distinguish between handstopping and the use of a mute. Separate and distinct sounds are produced by stopping and muting, and these effects are employed differently by composers. The horn mute functions the same as other mutes and causes no acoustical change within the instrument, as is caused by handstopping. The acoustical aspects of handstopping and the controversy surrounding this subject are discussed later. For readers who wish only to know how to produce the stopped effect, the next section will suffice.

Producing the Handstopped Effect

The stopped sound is made by bringing the palm of the hand around into the bell opening to completely seal the bell. Since the bell throat is fully closed, it is essential to blow harder than normal and to concentrate intensely on the desired pitch. As described later, a shift of harmonic series takes place, so it is necessary to transpose down one half-step. When playing on the B♭ side of the double horn, the stopped note is usually played one half-step lower on the F side. The intonation of the stopped note should be carefully matched to the same pitch played open. While the playing of stopped notes exclusively on the double horn's F side is the orthodox procedure, and the one that makes theoretical sense, one should nonetheless take a flexible approach to fingering, trying all of the fingerings available on both sides of the horn. Whichever fingering yields the best intonation and stopped timbre should be used.

Stopping with the hand is most effective in the written range from E above middle C to the top of the staff. There is a brass stopping mute available that efficiently produces an in-tune stopped sound (notes must still be transposed downward one half-step) (see Figure 4.7). The stopping mute is generally preferred in the lower register, and many favor the mute in all ranges whenever there is sufficient time in the music to insert and remove it. Some horns are equipped with a special stopping valve. This permits stopped notes to be played without transposition. The pitch of stopped notes can be carefully adjusted by means of a tuning slide. It is particularly intended for stopping on the B♭ horn, where three-quarters of a tone are theoretically required for in-tune stopped notes. Stopping valves are normally fitted to single B♭ and B♭/F-alto (B♭ soprano) descants. For double and triple horns, there is a trade-off between the obvious benefits of a stopping valve and the weight it adds to the horn.

FIGURE 4.7
Stopping mute
(Denis Wick)

Handstopping: Acoustical Considerations

There has been a long-term dispute over whether the pitch rises or descends when the bell is stopped. The rising-pitch hypothesis appears logical, since the instrument is shortened by this process. It would seem to be verified by the observation that, if the player transposes downward a half-step and stops the bell, the same pitch results as the open tone.

Actually, the pitch has not risen. It can be demonstrated that as the hand is gradually closed, the pitch descends until, at full seal, it settles exactly one-half step above the next *lower* harmonic. This phenomenon can be seen in the following chart:[12]

Harmonic series—F horn

To take a practical example: To sound a stopped G, the player transposes downward a half-step, using the second valve of the F horn. Although this appears to be an F♯, in reality it is the seventh partial of the harmonic series of the second valve. If the bell were open, this note would sound as an A, but through the process of sealing the bell it has descended to G. This can be confirmed by playing the stopped harmonic series of the second valve; it will be found to conform to the series shown here:

2nd valve harmonic series: open

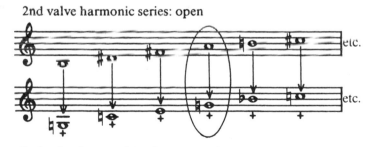

2nd valve harmonic series: stopped

Muting

The standard horn mute (nontransposing) is basically a straight mute, but its timbre is less incisive than those used on the trumpet and trombone. Usually, they are made of fiber, although plastic and metal alloys have been tried recently. Mutes must be selected with care, since good intonation is possible only if the mute is well designed and fits the bell throat exactly. The best mutes are made to fit specific bells. Also, there is some variation of timbre between different brands of mute.[13]

---

[12] Adapted from Richard Merewether, *The horn,* p. 40.

[13] For detailed information on horn mutes, see Nicholas E. Smith, "The Horn Mute: An Acoustical and Historical Study" (D.M.A. thesis, University of Rochester, 1980) UM 80-19, 070.

■ USING THE F AND B♭ SECTIONS OF THE DOUBLE HORN

The main concern in combining the sides of the double horn is to match the timbres of the F and B♭ sections so that one unified tone is produced throughout the range. The usual crossover is at written G♯, although a minority of players prefer C♯, a fourth higher. The B♭ side is sometimes used for several low notes, particularly the low C♯, to improve intonation and response.

When good tonal matching has been achieved, the changeover is almost impercep-tible. An effective way of developing this ability is to play individual notes and passages first on the F side and then on the B♭ side while concentrating on retaining the timbre of the F horn. It is helpful to occasionally practice solely on the F horn or B♭ horn. It is ad-visable to be fluent with B♭ fingerings in all ranges, for there are tricky passages that can be facilitated through the use of the B♭ horn. The following chart indicates the most com-mon procedure for combining the F and B♭ sections:

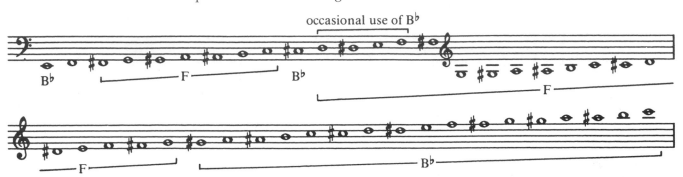

Another approach to the double horn is to play primarily on the B♭ side, reserving the F side for certain individual notes for better intonation and for low notes beyond the B♭'s range. This has long been a standard procedure among German, British, and other European players and it is becoming more widely used in the United States. The greater mass of the double horn played in B♭ contributes a broader tone than does a single B♭, and it has the advantage of an F section available when desired. The change valves of German and British horns are made to be reversible so that the horn can stand in either F or B♭ without having to depress the thumb valve (change valve). The widespread use of the B♭ horn was the primary reason European makers enlarged the main bore to 12 mm or more. The enlarged bore produces good intonation and a fuller tone, particu-larly in the B♭'s lower middle range, where horns of smaller bore tend to sound hollow. Players who use the double horn in this way prefer the sound and response of the B♭ side and feel that playing on one side offers a greater consistency of sound. Usually, only a few notes are played on the F side: G in the staff, G and F♯ below the staff, and low notes from low C downward.

There is an inherent difference in response between the F and B♭ sides of the double horn. This is caused by the significant difference in length between the F and B♭ tubing in relation to the tubing's diameter. The response of the B♭ side is immediate and direct, while the F side tends to be slower and more distant. Greater resistance is created in the longer tubing of the F horn by being of the same diameter as the B♭ side. This problem has been addressed by Paxman with a "dual-bore" system for double and triple horns in which the bore is increased from the B♭ horn's 12 mm to 12.7 mm for the F side in order to equalize the response of the two sides.

■ TRANSPOSITION AND NOTATION

As was discussed in Chapter 3, the practice surviving from the prevalve era of notating parts in the key of C and using crooks to obtain the desired sounding pitch has left trum-pet and horn players with a legacy of parts in a variety of keys. Therefore, transposition skills must be developed as a normal part of the horn player's training. The following table presents the common transpositions.

Transposition Table

Key of Part	Interval Method	Clef Method
B♭	Perfect 5th lower	Mezzo-soprano
C	Perfect 4th lower	–
D	Minor 3rd lower	–
E♭	Major 2nd lower	Tenor clef
E	Half-step lower	Tenor clef
G	Major 2nd higher	Alto clef
A	Major 3rd higher	Bass clef

Note: The key signature must also be changed.

The current practice of notation for the horn consists of writing for the F horn (sounding a fifth below concert pitch, therefore written a fifth above) regardless of whether a double horn, a single B♭, or one of the descant horns will be used. It is helpful to the player if the bass clef is used below G:

As in treble clef notation, notes in the bass clef are written a fifth above where they are to sound. This manner of using the bass clef is known as *new notation*. This is to distinguish the present system from a 19th century tradition of writing bass clef notes an octave lower (*old notation*).

concert pitch   old notation   new notation

■ HORN CHORDS

A curious phenomenon associated with the horn is that a haunting three- or four-note chord can be made to sound by simultaneously singing a fifth or sixth above or below a played note in the lower register. Soloists in the natural horn era apparently sometimes inserted this effect into cadenzas. Eugene Vivier caused a stir in Paris with this phenomenon in 1843. In fact, most horn players can develop the technique, but it requires a great deal of patient practice and concentration. Its chief interest today is that Carl Maria von Weber included horn chords in the cadenza of his *Concertino in E Minor*. It has also been revived here and there by contemporary composers and a few soloists. For those wishing to hear this effect, the late Alan Civil used it in a cadenza in his superb recording of the Mozart horn concertos.

■ INTONATION AND TUNING

As with the trumpet, subtle adjustments of embouchure and air pressure are required to achieve good intonation. Since the pitch of any note may be raised or lowered by opening or closing the hand position in the bell, the horn player has a further means available of controlling intonation; this is used as necessary as a normal aspect of playing procedure. The horn exhibits the same deficiencies as other valve brass instruments; unlike them, however, the outer tubing of the valve slides is shortened to allow a slide to be brought inward as well as pulled outward to find the best position for good intonation when the valve is used alone and in combination. Students sometimes mistakenly assume that the valve slides of the horn are similar to those of the trumpet or euphonium and try to play the horn with the slides fully in; this results in disastrous intonation.

The best settings for the valve slides must be determined through a tuning procedure. To do this, unisons and various intervals should be played against a reference pitch and each slide moved as necessary. An electronic tuner is essential in this process.

To set the valve slides of the F horn or F side of a double horn, adjust the main tuning slide to a reference pitch of written G (concert C). The main tuning slide is usually at the end of the leadpipe. Play the slurred or tongued interval G–C to see if a good fourth results and readjust the slide, if necessary. In general, by playing intervals rather than matching single notes, a more consistent and accurate tone placement will result and the pitch of the second note will be more clearly revealed. The reference pitch should be set to sound the note circled. This note is played first, followed by either slurring to or tonguing the second note. The slide should be moved to whatever position produces the most exact interval.

If discrepancies are found between the positions needed for single valve notes and valve combinations, a compromise setting should be used.

To set the B♭ slides, it is necessary first to bring the B♭ section into agreement with the F section through the use of a common open tone. Play the third-space C on one side of the horn and then change to the other side. The separate F and B♭[14] tuning slides should be adjusted so that the two pitches match.

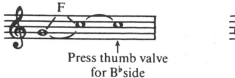
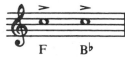

Once the correct settings for the F and B♭ tuning slides have been determined, the player should move only the main tuning slide when tuning with the orchestra or band. The B♭ valve slides can be set using the following procedure:

The D and A should be checked for possible sharpness, and the E and E♭ for flatness:

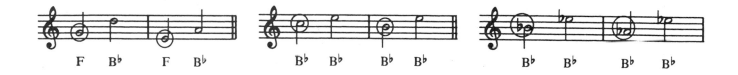

A few books attempt to give measurements for the slide settings, but these usually prove of little use due to the variability of instruments and players. In a professional horn section, some differences in slide settings can be noted, yet the section will achieve a high standard of intonation.

The 1–2 valve combination can often be played better in tune in the low register by using the third valve. The sharp 1–2–3 combination on the low C♯ can be avoided by playing this note 2–3 on the B♭ side.

[14]Separate tuning slides for the B♭ section of the double horn are not absolutely necessary, and some models of double horn do not have them. Horns of this type are tuned by adjusting the F tuning slide so that the written C played on the F side matches the pitch of that note played on the B♭ side.

FIGURE 4.8   Wagner tuba (tenor in B♭; Alexander)

FIGURE 4.9   Wagner tuba (bass in F; Alexander)

To develop good intonation in school and college horn sections, it is essential that the slide settings be checked and brought into agreement with each other. This can be done by tuning to a reliable open tone, such as middle G, and then playing single notes, intervals, and chords together while making the necessary adjustments. It is useful to play a diatonic or chromatic scale slowly in unison from middle C to fourth-space E, stopping when necessary to change the slide settings.[15] After the slide settings have been established, some careful work on trios, quartets, and quintets should be undertaken. A

[15] A useful book for establishing some of these fundamentals is Robert W. Getchall and Nilo Hovey, *Section Studies for French Horns* (Melville, N.Y.: Belwin-Mills, 1967).

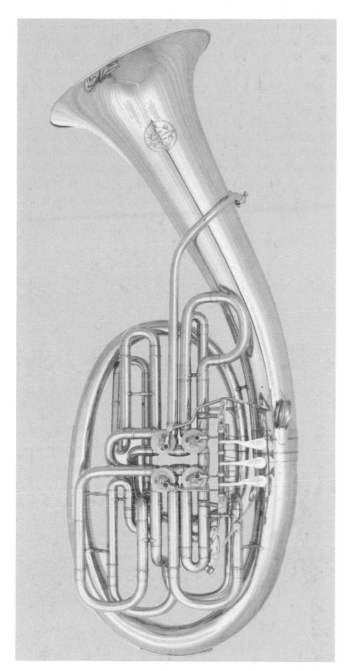

FIGURE 4.10
Wagner tuba (double; Alexander)

progressive program of quartet playing can do a great deal to improve a horn section in a relatively short time. In the final analysis, good intonation is achieved by careful listening and adjusting to other players.

■ THE WAGNER TUBA

The Wagner tuba should be considered with the horn since this instrument, although technically a member of the tuba family, was intended to be played by hornists. (See Figures 4.8, 4.9, and 4.10.) In 1853, during the composition of *Das Rheingold*, the idea occurred to Richard Wagner to expand the brass section in certain places. The composer had become acquainted with the saxhorns during a visit with Adolphe Sax in Paris. The Berlin firm of Moritz is believed to have supplied the original set of Wagner tubas for the first complete performance of *Der Ring des Nibelungen* in 1875. These were made in the traditional oval shape of the German military *Tenorhorn* and *Bariton*, but with the valves on the left so that they could be played by horn players. The mouthpipe is constructed to accommodate a regular horn mouthpiece. Eight horns were called for in the score, four of which doubled on the new instruments. The quartet included two tenors in B♭ (of similar length to the B♭ horn) and two basses in F (which correspond to the F horn).

Wagner was followed by Bruckner and Strauss in using the instrument. The solo in *Don Quixote*, which today is usually played on the euphonium, was originally intended for this instrument. In an effort to improve intonation, the bell tapers of most modern Wagner tubas have been enlarged, thereby losing some of the haunting intensity of timbre envisioned by the composer. An authentic set can be heard in the Vienna Philharmonic. The latest development is an F–B♭ double tuba based on the compensating principle.[16]

RECOMMENDED LITERATURE[17]

Complete Methods

Franz: *Complete Method* (C. Fischer)

*Freund: *French Horn Method for the Young Beginner* (Waldhornschule), 3 vols. (Doblinger)

Graham-Crump: *Complete Horn Method*, 2 vols. (Oxford)

Hoeltzel, Michael: *Horn-Schule*, 2 vols. (text in German) (Schott)

*Huth, Fritz: *School for Horn* (Benjamin-Rahter)

*Neuling, Hermann: *Grosse F und B Hornschule*, 2 vols. (text in German) (Pro Musica)

Pottag and Hovey: *Pottag–Hovey Method*, 2 vols. (Belwin-Mills)

*Stern and Schneider: *Schule für Waldhorn* (Schott)

Elementary Methods

*Hauser: *Foundation to Horn Playing* (C. Fischer)

*Horner: *Primary Studies* (Elkan-Vogel)

Clevenger, McDunn, and Rusch: *Dale Clevenger Method*, 2 vols. (Kjos)

Goldstein: *Book of Exercises* (Cor)

*Howe: *Method* (Marvin C. Howe)

Skornicka: *Rubank Elementary Method* (Rubank)

*Tuckwell: *50 First Exercises* (Oxford)

Williams: *Enjoy Playing the Horn* (Oxford)

Studies

Medium to Medium-Difficult

Brophy: *Technical Studies for Solving Special Problems on the Horn* (C. Fischer)

*Burden: *Horn Playing—A New Approach* (Paterson's Publ.)

DeGrave: *Etudes for Modern Valve Horn* (Wind Music) (med. to diff.)

*Gallay: *22 Studies* (International)

*Gallay: *24 Studies* (International)

Goldstein: *Etudes*, 2 vols. (Cor)

Gounod: *Dix études* (Billaudot)

Gower and Voxman: *Rubank Advanced Method*, 2 vols. (Rubank)

*Huth: *Tonleiter-Studien* (Hofmeister)

*Kopprasch: *60 Selected Studies*, 2 vols. (C. Fischer) (medium to difficult)

*Levet: *La technique journalière du corniste* (Lemoine)

*Maxime-Alphonse: *Deux cents études nouvelles*, vols. 1–3 (A. Leduc)

*Miersch: *Melodious Studies for French Horn* (C. Fischer)

*Moore and Ettore: *Master Warm-Up and Flexibility Studies* (Mel Bay)

*Mueller: *34 Studies*, 2 vols. (International) (medium to difficult)

*Parès: *Parès Scales* (Rubank)

Pottag: *Daily Exercises* (Belwin-Mills)

*Pottag (ed.): *Preparatory Melodies to Solo Work* (Belwin Mills)

Pottag and Andraud (eds.): *Selected Melodious, Progressive, and Technical Studies*, vol. 1 (Southern)

*Schantl: *Grand Theoretical and Practical Method* (Wind Music) (medium to difficult)

*Schantl: *92 Übungen für Ventilanfänger* (Pizka)

Singer: *Embouchure Building* (Belwin-Mills) (medium to difficult)

*Thévet: *Fifty Exercises with Changes of Key* (Transposition) (Leduc)

---

[16] For additional information on the historical background of the Wagner tuba, see James Harvey Keays, "An Investigation into the Origins of the Wagner Tuba" (D.M.A. thesis, University of Illinois, 1977), UM 78-4044.

[17] Essential literature is noted with an asterisk. Repertoire lists appear in the texts by Brüchle, Gregory, and Schuller.

Difficult

Artôt: *19 Progressive Etudes* (Belwin-Mills)

*Belloli: *8 Studies* (International)

Bergonzi: *Capricci*, 2 vols. (Doblinger)

Brahms: *10 Horn Studies* (Belwin-Mills)

*Cugnot: *30 Études* (Wind Music)

*Gallay: *12 Études brillantes* (International)

*Gallay: *12 Grand Caprices* (International)

*Gallay: *12 Studies for Second Horn* (International)

*Gallay: *40 Preludes* (International)

Gugel: *12 Studies* (International)

Hackleman: *21 Characteristic Etudes for High Horn Playing* (BIM)

Hackleman: *34 Characteristic Etudes for Low Horn Playing* (BIM)

Jeurissen: *4 Characteristic Studies* (McCoy)

*Kling: *40 Studies* (International)

*Maxime-Alphonse: *Deux cents études nouvelles*, vols. 4–6 (A. Leduc)

*Neuling: *30 Special Studies for Low Horn*, 2 vols. (Pro Musica)

Pottag and Andraud: *Selected Melodious, Progressive, and Technical Studies*, vol. 2 (Southern)

Proust: *25 Etudes* (Combre)

*Ranieri: *Etuden* (Pizka)

*F. Strauss: *17 Concert Studies* (Eulenburg)

Unaccompanied Solos

Difficult

Adler: *Canto XI* (Ludwig)

Apostel: *Sonatine* (Universal)

*Arnold: *Fantasy* (Faber)

Bach: *Cello Suites*, transcribed by Hoss (Southern)

Baratto: *3 kleine Stücke* (BIM)

Barboteu: *5 pieces poetiques* (Choudens)

Berge: *Horn Call* (Norsk Oslo)

*Bissill: *Lone Call and Charge* (Warwick)

Bozza: *Graphismes* (A. Leduc)

*Buyanovsky: *Pieces* (McCoy)

Chasalow: *Winding Up* (BIM)

*Davies: *Sea Eagle* (Chester)

*Dodgson: *Cor Leonis* (BIM)

Faust: *Prelude* (Faust)

Halstead: *Suite* (Dunster)

Kauder: *3 Melodies for Solo Horn* (Seesaw)

McGuire: *Prelude 17* (Warwick)

Orval: *Libre–Free–Frei* (McCoy)

Persichetti: *Parable* (Presser)

Plog: *Postcards* (BIM)

Schlaepffer: *Instances II* (BIM)

Slavicky: *Tre Pezzi* (BIM)

Horn and Piano

Easy

Anderson: *Prelude and March in Canon* (Boosey & Hawkes)

Bakaleinikoff: *Canzona* (Belwin)

Bakaleinikoff: *Cavatina* (Belwin)

Brightmore: *3 Easy Solos* (Taurus)

Carse: *2 Easy Pieces* (Galaxy)

Franck: *Panis Angelicus* (Warner Bros.)

Gregson and Ridgeon: *Nine Miniatures* (Brass Wind Publications)

Gunning and Pearson: *The Really Easy Horn Book* (Faber)

Handel and Haydn: *8 Solos from "Messiah" and "The Creation,"* arr. Lethbridge (Oxford).

Jones (ed.): *First Solos for the Hornplayer* (Schirmer)

Langrish (ed.): *8 Easy Pieces* (Oxford)

Lawrance: *Easy Winners for Treble Brass* (with CD accompaniment) (Brass Wind Publications)

Lawrance: *Six Modern Pieces* (Brass Wind Publications)

Lawrance: *Winners Galore* (Brass Wind Publications)

Lawton (ed.): *The Young Horn-Player*, 3 vols. (Oxford)

Marshall (ed.): *An Album for the Horn* (Oxford)

Ohanian: *Beginning Horn Solos* (with cassette accompaniment) (H. Leonard)

Ohanian: *Easy Horn Solos* (with cassette accompaniment) (H. Leonard)

Onozo and Kovacs (ed.): *Horn Music for Beginners* (Editio Musica)

Phillips (ed.): *Classical and Romantic Pieces* (Oxford)

Up-Front Album for F Horn, vols. 1 and 2 (Brass Wind Publications)

Medium to Medium-Difficult

Baker: *Cantilena* (Chester)

Baratto: *Andantino romantico* (BIM)

Baratto: *Hirte und sein Horn* (BIM)

Beethoven: *Little Rondo* (Schirmer)

*Bissill: *Absolutely Horn* (Brass Wind Publications)

*Bissill: *Horn Talk* (Brass Wind Publications)

*Bissill: *O Solo Mio* (Brass Wind Publications)

*Butterworth: *Romanza* (Hinrichsen)

Campbell: *Horn Solos*, 2 vols. (Faber)

*Chabrier: *Larghetto* (Salabert)

Dishinger: *Masterworks Solos* (Medici)

*Dunhill: *Cornucopia* (Boosey & Hawkes)

Forbes (ed.): *Classical and Romantic Album*, vols. 2 and 3 (Oxford)

Françaix: *Canon in Octave* (International)

*Glazounov: *Reverie* (Belwin-Mills)

*James: *Windmills* (B. Ramsey)

*James and DeHaan (ed.): *Horn Solos* (Chester)

Johnson (ed.): *Intermediate Horn Book* (Oxford)

Jones (ed.): *Solos for the Hornplayer* (Schirmer)

Lawrance: *In Concert* (Brass Wind Publications)

Ledbury: *Cornucopia* (Brass Wind Publications)

Marshall (ed.): *An Album for the Horn* (Oxford)

Moore: *Second Book of Horn Solos* (Faber)

*Mozart: *Concerto No. 1 in D* (Breitkopf & Härtel)

*Mozart: *Concerto No. 3 in E♭* (Breitkopf & Härtel); also version with cassette accompaniment (Ohanian) (H. Leonard)

*Mozart: *Concert Rondo in E♭* (Breitkopf & Härtel)

Ohanian: *Intermediate Horn Solos* (with cassette accompaniment) (H. Leonard)

Ployhar (ed.): *Horn Solos,* 2 vols. (Belwin-Mills)

Read: *Poem* (C. Fischer)

Richardson (ed.): *6 Horn Tunes* (Boosey & Hawkes)

*Saint-Saëns: *Romance* (Belwin-Mills)

Stout (ed.): *Master Solos* (with cassette accompaniment) (H. Leonard)

Top-Line Album for Horn (Brass Wind Publications)

Woolfenden: *Horn Dances* (Brass Wind Publications)

Voxman (ed.): *Concert and Contest Collection* (Rubank)

Difficult

*Abbott: *Alla Caccia* (Josef Weinberger)

Adler: *Sonata* (R. King)

*Albrechtsberger: *Concerto* (International)

*Arnold: *Concerto* (Lengnick)

Artunian: *Concerto* (International)

Aubin: *Concerto* (A. Leduc)

Balay: *Chanson du Forestier* (A. Leduc)

Baratto: *Andantino romantico* (BIM)

Baratto: *Hirte und sein Horn* (BIM)

*Beethoven: *Sonata,* ed. Tuckwell (Schirmer)

Bellini: *Concerto* (Billaudot)

Bitsch: *Variations* (A. Leduc)

Blanc: *Sonata* (Pizka)

*Bourgeois: *Fantasy Pieces for Horn* (Brass Wind Publications)

*York Bowen: *Two Preludes* (Josef Weinberger)

*Bozza: *Chant lointain* (A. Leduc)

*Bozza: *En Forêt* (A. Leduc)

Bush: *Autumn Poem* (Schott)

Carr: *Soliloquy* (Broadbent and Dunn)

*Cherubini: *2 Sonatas,* ed. Tuckwell (Schirmer)

Cosma: *Concerto* (BIM)

Cosma: *Sonatine* (BIM)

Czerny: *Andante e Polacca* (Doblinger)

Danzi: *Concerto* (Heinrichshofen)

Danzi: *Sonata* (International)

Delmas: *Ballade Feerique* (Billaudot)

Deutschmann: *Marsch und Variationen* (Haas)

Ducommun: *Sonata da Chiesa* (organ) (BIM)

*Dukas: *Villanelle* (International)

Duvernoy: *Concerto No. 3* (Ka We)

Eccles: *Sonata in G Minor,* transcribed by Eger (International)

Farnon: *Conversation and Games* (Warwick)

Foerster: *Concerto* (Schirmer)

Friedman: *Jerusalem Fugue* (BIM)

Gallay: *Concerto* (Ka We)

Ghidoni: *Mississippi Souvenir* (A. Leduc)

*Gliere: *Concerto* (International)

Goedicke: *Concerto* (International)

*Haydn: *Concerto No. 1* (Boosey & Hawkes)

*Haydn: *Concerto No. 2* (Boosey & Hawkes)

*M. Haydn: *Concertino,* ed. Tuckwell (Schirmer)

Hidas: *Concerto* (Editio Musica)

*Hindemith: *Concerto* (Schott)

Hindemith: *Sonata for Alto Horn* (Schott)

*Hindemith: *Sonate* (Schott)

Hoddinott: *Sonata* (Oxford)

*Jacob: *Concerto* (Galaxy)

Janetzki: *Sonate* (Haas)

Jevtic: *Concerto* (BIM)

Jevtic: *Danse d'été* (BIM)

Kling: *Concerto* (H. Pizka)

Koetsier: *Concertino* (BIM)

Koetsier: *Romanza* (Reift)

Koetsier: *Sonatina* (Reift)

Krivitsky: *Konzert* (Reift)

Lees: *Concerto* (Boosey & Hawkes)

Lefebvre: *Vallée* (Salabert)

Lewy: *Concerto* (H. Pizka)

Lukas: *Concerto* (BIM)

Madsen: *Sonata* (Musikk-Huset)

*Marais: *Le Basque* (Paxman)

McCabe: *Floraison* (Novello)

McCabe: *Shapeshifter* (Novello)

Meier: *Concerto* (BIM)

Milde: *Concertino* (Haas)

Molter: *Concerto in D* (BIM)

*L. Mozart: *Concerto in D*, ed. Tuckwell (Schirmer)

*Mozart: *Concerto No. 2 in E♭* (Breitkopf & Härtel)

*Mozart: *Concerto No. 4 in E♭* (Breitkopf & Härtel)

Musgrave: *Music for Horn and Piano* (Chester)

*Neruda: *Concerto in E♭* (BIM)

Nielsen: *Canto Serioso* (Skandinavisk Musikforlag)

*Patterson: *Horn Concerto* (Josef Weinberger)

Perrin: *Sonate* (BIM)

Pilss: *Concerto* (R. King)

Pilss: *Tre pezzi* (Doblinger)

Plog: *Nocturne* (BIM)

Plog: *3 Miniatures* (BIM)

Porter: *Sonata* (R. King)

Proust: *Gamins d'Paris* (Billaudot)

Punto: *Concerto No. 11* (Medici Music)

*Rosetti: *Concerto No. 1* (Ka We)

*Rosetti: *Concerto No. 2* (International)

*Rossini: *Prelude, thème et variations* (Schirmer)

*Saint-Saëns: *Concertpiece* (International)

Sampson: *Sonata Forty* (BIM)

Schuman: *3 Colloquies* (Presser)

Sor: *3 Seguidillas* (A. Leduc)

Sperger: *Concerto in D* (BIM)

Sperger: *Concerto in E♭* (BIM)

*F. Strauss: *Concerto*, ed. Tuckwell (Schirmer)

*R. Strauss: *Concerto No. 1* (Schirmer); also version with cassette
accompaniment (Ohanian) (H. Leonard)

*R. Strauss: *Concerto No. 2* (Boosey & Hawkes)

*Telemann: *Concerto in D*, ed. Tuckwell (Schirmer)

Tisné: *Lied* (A. Leduc)

*Tomasi: *Concerto* (A. Leduc)

Turner: *Concerto for Low Horn in F* (BIM)

Turok: *Sonata* (BIM)

*Vinter: *Hunter's Moon* (Boosey & Hawkes)

*Weber: *Concertino*, ed. Tuckwell (Schirmer)

Wilder: *First Sonata* (CFG)

Wilder: *Suite* (Margun)

Woolfenden: *Horn Dances* (Brass Wind)

Zbinden: *Episodes* (Création) (BIM)

Recommended Books on the Horn [18]

*Bourgue, Daniel. *Conversations About the Horn*. Paris: International Music Diffusion, 1996.

Bushouse, David. *Practical Hints on Playing the Horn*. Melville, N.Y.: Belwin-Mills, 1983.

Brüchle, Bernhard. *Horn Bibliographie* (3 vols.). Wilhelmshaven: Heinrichshofen's Verlag, 1970.

*Coar, Birchard. *A Critical Study of the Nineteenth-Century Horn Virtuosi in France*. DeKalb, Ill.: Coar, 1952.

*Coar, Birchard. *The French Horn*. DeKalb, Ill.: Coar, 1947.

*Cousins, Farquharson. *On Playing the Horn*. London: Samski Press (distributed by Paxman Musical Instruments), 1983.

*Domnich, H. *Méthode de premier et second cor*. Geneva: Minkoff Reprints, 1974.

*Duvernoy, Frédéric. *Méthode pour le cor*. Geneva: Minkoff Reprints, 1972.

Fako, Nancy Jordan. *Philip Farkas and His Horn: A Happy, Worthwhile Life*. Elmhurst, Ill.: Crescent Park Music Publications, 1998.

*Farkas, Philip. *The Art of Horn Playing*. Evanston, Ill.: Summy-Birchard, 1956.

Farkas, Philip. *A Photographic Study of 40 Virtuoso Horn Players' Embouchures*. Rochester, N.Y.: Wind Music, 1970.

*Fitzpatrick, Horace. *The Horn and Horn-Playing and the Austro-Bohemian Tradition 1680–1830*. London: Oxford University Press, 1970.

Gardner, Randy C. *Mastering the Horn's Low Register*. Richmond, Va.: International Opus, 2002.

Gourse, Leslie. *Blowing the Changes: The Art of the Jazz Horn Players*. New York: Franklin Watts, 1997.

*Gregory, Robin. *The Horn*. London: Faber & Faber, 1969.

Heyde, Herbert. *Hörner und Zinken*. Leipzig: VEB Deutscher Verlag für Musik, 1982.

Hill, Douglas. *Collected Thoughts on Teaching and Learning, Creativity, and Horn Performance*. Miami, Fla.: Warner Bros. Publications, 2001.

Hill, Douglas. *Extended Techniques for the Horn*. (Hialeah, Fla.: Columbia Pictures Publications, 1983.

*Humphries, John. *The Early Horn: A Practical Guide*. Cambridge: Cambridge University Press, 2000.

Janetzky, Kurt. *Das Horn: Eine Kleine Chronik seines Werdens und Wirkens*. Stuttgart: Hallweg Verlag, 1977.

Janetzky, Kurt, and Bernhard Brüchle. *The Horn*. Portland, Ore.: Amadeus Press, 1988.

Kaslow, David M. *Living Dangerously with the Horn: Thoughts on Life and Art*. Bloomington, Ind.: Birdalone Books, 1996.

McBeth, Amy. *A Discography of 78 rpm Era Recordings of the Horn: Solo and Chamber Music Literature with Commentary*. Westport, Conn.: Greenwood Press, 1997.

---

[18] Many interesting articles appear in *The Horn Call* (published by the International Horn Society), *The Horn Magazine* (published by the British Horn Society), and other periodicals listed in Appendix C.

Meek, Harold. *Horn and Conductor: Reminiscences of a Practitioner with a Few Words of Advice.* Rochester, N.Y.: University of Rochester Press, 1997.

*Merewether, Richard. *The Horn, the Horn. . . .* London: Paxman Musical Instruments, 1979.

*Morley-Pegge, Reginald. *The French Horn.* London: Ernest Benn, 1973.

*Pettitt, Stephen. *Dennis Brain.* London: Robert Hale, 1976.

*Pizka, Hans. *Das Horn bei Mozart.* Kirchheim bei München: Hans Pizka Edition, 1980.

*Pizka, Hans. *Hornisten—Lexikon/Dictionary for Hornists 1986.* Kirchheim bei München: Hans Pizka Edition, 1986.

*Prichard, Paul, ed. *The Business: The Essential Guide to Starting and Surviving as a Professional Hornplayer.* Surrey, England: Open Press Books, 1992.

Reynolds, Verne. *The Horn Handbook.* Portland, Ore.: Amadeus Press, 1997.

Schuller, Gunther. *Horn Technique,* 2nd ed. London: Oxford University Press, 1992.

Schwarzl, Siegfried. *The Development of Horn Ensemble Music from the Romantic Era to the Present Time in Vienna and in Other Cultural Circles.* Vienna: Wiener Waldhornverein, 1987.

Secrist-Schmedes, Barbera. *Wind Chamber Music, for Two to Sixteen Winds: An Annotated Guide.* Lanham, Md.: Scarecrow Press, 2002.

Stewart, Dee. *Philip Farkas: The Legacy of a Master.* Northfield, Ill.: The Instrumentalist Co., 1990.

Tuckwell, Barry. *Horn.* New York: Schirmer Books, 1983.

*Tuckwell, Barry. *Playing the Horn.* London: Oxford University Press, 1978.

*Wekre, Frøydis Ree. *Thoughts on Playing the Horn Well.* Oslo: Frøydis Ree Wekre, 1994.

Weyse, Volker. *Solo-Horn und Blasorchester: Verzeichnis von über 200 Solowerken für ein oder mehrere Hörner (inklusiv Jagdhorn, Signalhorn, Alphorn, Lure) und Blasorchester.* Vienna, Austria: Kliment, 2000.

Whaley, David R. "The Microtonal Capability of the Horn." D.M.A. thesis, University of Illinois, 1975. UM 76-7010.

Yancich, Milan. *An Orchestra Musician's Odyssey: A View from the Rear.* Rochester, N.Y.: Wind Music, 1995.

Yancich, Milan. *A Practical Guide to French Horn Playing.* Rochester, N.Y.: Wind Music, 1971.

CHAPTER 5

THE TROMBONE

THE TREND IN TROMBONE PLAYING since the 1950s has been toward larger and, in the case of the bass trombone, more complex and specialized instruments. In earlier years, small-bore trombones, following the pattern established by the French instrument maker Antoine Courtois and other French firms in the mid-19th century, enjoyed great popularity in Britain and America. When used with a conical mouthpiece, the instrument offered the pure tone and agile technique demanded by famous soloists of the era, such as Arthur Pryor (1870–1942).

Although trombones of this type were the mainstay of American bands and theater orchestras around the turn of the 20th century, players in symphony orchestras of that era used instruments of considerably larger bore and bell dimensions. This was probably a result of the strong German influence in American orchestras at that time. Large-bore German trombones served as the prototypes from which the modern American symphonic trombone was developed.

Today, there are four general categories of trombone, based on their bore and bell dimensions (see Figure 5.1):

Type	Bore	Bell
Small-bore tenor	Up to 0.500″ (12.7 mm)	7–8″ (177.8–203.2 mm)
Medium-bore tenor	0.510–0.525″ (12.9–13.3 mm)	0″ (203.2 mm)
Large-bore tenor	0.547″ (13.8 mm)	8.5″ (216 mm)
Bass	0.562″ (14.2 mm)	9.5–10.5″ (241–267 mm)

In the trombone sections of symphony orchestras, one would typically find two large-bore tenors and a bass, all having a basic pitch of B♭. An F attachment might, or might not, be found on the principal player's instrument[1], but it is likely that one would be included on that used by the second player. The bass trombonist would be using one of the recent in-line double valve instruments or an earlier double- or single-trigger model. (The instruments with F attachments or double valves would be equipped with Thayer, Hagmann, or Conn CL2000 valves, discussed in Chapter 1.) Similar instruments would be used in concert bands and wind ensembles. In jazz and studio work, small- and medium-bore trombones are usually preferred for their more responsive upper register and brighter tone. Beginners generally start on the small- or medium-bore and later move to an instrument more specifically suited to their performance interests.

---

[1] First trombonists often prefer the response and sound of a large-bore trombone without F attachment for the range in which they play. For certain repertoire, an F attachment would be used. The F attachment does not determine whether a trombone is designated as large-bore or medium-bore or as a bass. This is determined by the diameter of the cylindrical tubing, the size of the taper of the bell throat, and the overall width of the bell. Often, the same model of tenor trombone is made with and without F attachment. Some instruments are made with removable F attachments.

FIGURE 5.1

Bass and tenor trombones (left to right): bass with dual in-line independent valves (F, G♭, and D) (King), large-bore tenor with F attachment (Conn), medium-bore tenor (Conn), and small-bore tenor (King).

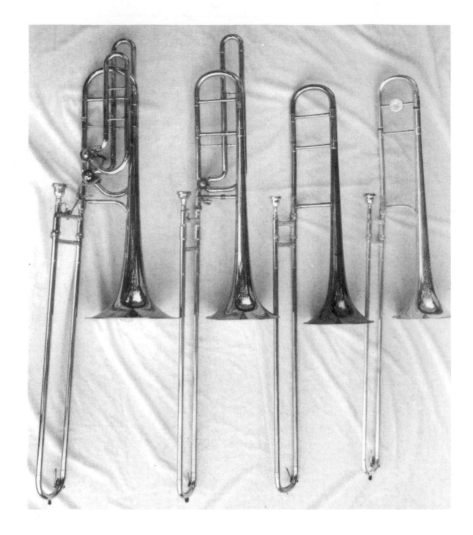

The situation is similar in Europe, where American-type symphonic trombones displaced small-bore instruments in England during the 1950s and in France slightly later. In Germany and Austria, however, traditional German trombones have developed along somewhat independent lines (see Figure 5.2). Constructed with wider, more gently curved bows and large bells, these instruments incorporate a more conical bore that includes a dual-bore slide (the lower slide is of larger diameter than the upper slide and is connected by a tapered bow).[2]

American-style trombones are also used in these countries. The leading orchestras, however, such as the Berlin Philharmonic and Vienna Philharmonic, generally favor traditional German instruments. The use of German trombones is important in achieving a blend of sound and matching the broader projection patterns of the rotary valve trumpets that are characteristic of these orchestras.

German trombones produce a dark, almost somber tone quality at softer dynamic levels and assume a resonant brightness at *fortissimo*. This contrasts with American-style trombones, which tend to hold a more consistent timbre throughout the dynamic range. (A similar change of timbre related to dynamics occurs in rotary valve trumpets and the horns used in the German and Austrian orchestras—particularly the Vienna horn.)[3] The distinctive qualities of the German trombone contribute a great deal to the overall effect the Vienna and Berlin brass sections achieve in Wagner, Bruckner, and Mahler.

[2] Leading examples are made by the German firms of Lätzsch, Thein, Pfretzschner, and Glassl, among others.
[3] The Vienna horn is discussed in Chapter 4.

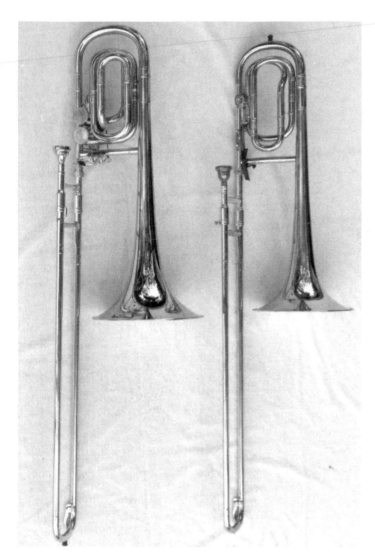

FIGURE 5.2
German trombones (left to right): bass with dual in-line independent valves, large-bore tenor with removable F attachment (Lätzsch).

Along with the trend in modern trombone playing to larger bore and bell diameters, more highly developed and efficient bass trombones have come into regular use. The inadequacy of the F attachment in completely filling the gap between low E and the fundamental (pedal) range has led to the development of the double-valve bass trombone.

■ THE ALTO TROMBONE

At the other end of the scale is the E♭ alto trombone, which, during the late 18th and early 19th centuries, led the orchestral trio of alto, tenor, and bass. It is used today in solo playing and for orchestral parts requiring a high tessitura and lightness of tone (see Figure 5.3). The alto trombone allows the player to achieve delicate balances without strain, and it makes high entrances more secure. Its timbre blends well with woodwinds and strings and is particularly effective with voices.

In Germany, the alto trombone has always been used for parts that were originally written for it, but the instrument has been less frequently employed in the past in the United States and Britain. Since the alto is pitched in E♭, the player must learn a different set of positions. Players have, therefore, in the past often preferred to play such parts on their regular instrument or a small-bore tenor. In recent years, however, the alto has come into general use in the orchestras of America and Britain. This has come about in response to the general desire to perform orchestral music in a way that is more faithful

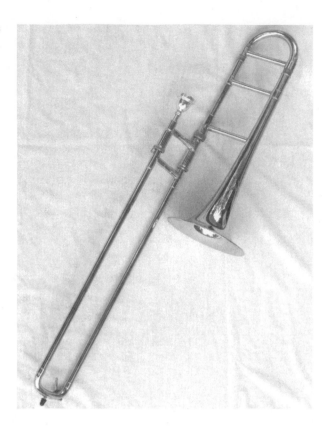

FIGURE 5.3
Alto trombone (Bach).

to the original intentions of the composer and for the important solo literature written for the instrument.[4] When the alto trombone is used in early 19th century works, it is preferable if the second and bass parts are played on somewhat smaller-bore instruments to facilitate a blend of tone. As high-quality alto trombones continue to become more widely available, there will undoubtedly be even greater use of this instrument.

A soprano trombone pitched in B♭ appeared in Germany in the late 17th century. Its principal use was to play chorale melodies in trombone choirs, and it can still be found there fulfilling this function. In America, the instrument is sometimes used in trombone choirs associated with the Moravian Church.

■ THE F ATTACHMENT

The origin of the F attachment can be traced to the bass trombone in F, which was used throughout the 19th and early 20th centuries. The idea of fitting additional F tubing to a B♭ trombone dates from 1839, when the first instruments of this type were produced by C. F. Sattler of Leipzig. The purpose of the F attachment is to extend the compass of the B♭ trombone downward to the pedal range and to provide some alternate positions to improve technical fluency in the low register. It consists of a rotary (or Thayer, Hagmann, Greenhoe, or Conn CL2000) valve that diverts the air column through a secondary section of tubing to lower the instrument's pitch a perfect fourth. Unfortunately, the F attachment is unable to completely bridge the gap between the normal and pedal ranges. The low C is theoretically beyond the standard-length slide, and a much longer slide would be needed to reach the low B immediately above the first pedal tone (B♭).

The reason for this is that the distance between positions increases as the slide is extended. By adding the extra tubing to lower the trombone's pitch a perfect fourth, a slide

[4] A list of literature and a discography for the alto trombone are provided in Stephen C. Anderson, "The Alto Trombone, Then and Now," *The Instrumentalist* (November 1985), pp. 54–62.

of greater length would be necessary to obtain the full seven positions (the F bass trombone had such a slide). As it is, the trombonist must play the more widely spaced F positions on the shorter B♭ slide, where it is scarcely possible to fit six positions. In practice, finding the F positions is not as difficult as it may appear since the player thinks of them as altered B♭ positions: 1, ♭2, ♭3, ♯5, 6, ♭7.

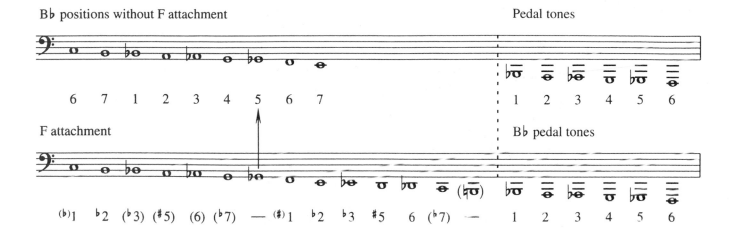

The problem of the absent low B and overextended C is not serious for the tenor player, but it presents a formidable obstacle to the bass trombonist since the literature calls for chromatic tones down and into the pedal range. This has led to the development of the double-valve bass trombone, discussed later. Both the low C and B can (almost) be played on the single-valve F attachment, provided that sufficient time is allowed to pull out the attachment's tuning slide (in effect making it an E attachment). The low B, however, is still theoretically beyond the end of the slide.

Another problem with the F attachment is that there is usually a difference in tone quality between normal B♭ notes and those played with the attachment. For this reason, trombonists generally restrict its use to the lower register and spend a good deal of practice time attempting to equalize the sound. This problem has been improved in recent years by new valves that feature more accurate and direct windways.

One of the chief advantages of the F attachment is that alternate positions are provided so that awkward movements can be avoided:

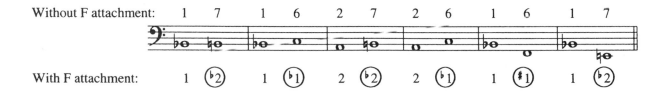

The most effective way to learn to use the F attachment is to work through one of the books of studies designed for this purpose.[5]

A common method of tuning the F attachment is to play the middle F alternately in B♭ and F and then to adjust the attachment's tuning slide as necessary. In using this tuning

[5] A. Ostrander, *The F Attachment and Bass Trombone* (C. Colin); O. Blume (ed.) and R. Fink, *36 Studies for Trombone with F Attachment* (C. Fischer); R. Fote, *Selected Kopprasch Studies for Trombone with F Attachment* (Kendor Music).

procedure, however, the low F on the F attachment tends to be flat and the main slide must be brought inward to bring it into tune (this is possible only on instruments with spring barrels or if the first position is played without being completely closed). Also, the second-space C is usually sharp, so the first position must be lowered accordingly. An alternative method of tuning the F attachment that is favored by many players is to tune the low F against the B♭ a perfect fourth above. This ensures that the low F will be in tune when needed. With this tuning, the low C will be sharp and even more difficult to reach in the flat seventh position. Therefore a decision must be made as to which is more important, an in-tune F or a more attainable low C. Tenor trombonists usually favor the F, and bass trombonists the C. (Bass trombonists often tune the low C in first position and pull in for the F.) On some trombones, the low D♭ is a bit sharp when played in sixth position on the F attachment. In such cases, the D♭ should be considered a flat sixth.

■ BASS TROMBONES

Bass trombonists must be able to play with a full, clear sound into the pedal range. Prior to the development of the double-valve bass trombone, the player had to extend the tuning slide of the F attachment to produce a usable low C, and, even with this measure plus embouchure adjustment, the low B was generally unsatisfactory in pitch and tone quality.[6]

By incorporating a second valve and added tubing within the F attachment, the pitch could be instantaneously lowered a half-step to E.[7] The two problem notes could be played on the E attachment without pulling out the tuning slide, but this still required considerable embouchure adjustment.

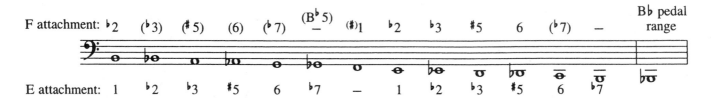

It was soon found that by lengthening the tubing of the second valve to E♭ or D, the low notes could be played with less extension of the main slide, yielding better tone and response as well as improved slide motion.

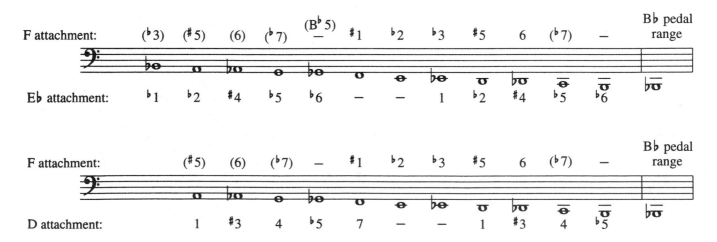

---

[6] The low C and B were easily accessible on the 19th century bass trombone in F, which had a longer slide fitted with a handle. As a result, these notes are found in the literature.

[7] The second valve cannot be used independently since the added tubing is an extension built into the F attachment. Both triggers must be depressed to use the E (E♭ or D) valve.

The latest development is the in-line double-valve bass trombone, in which both valves are located in the main tubing of the bell section. This allows the valves to be used independently. The instrument is usually available in two forms, depending on whether G♮ or G♭ is chosen as the pitch of the second valve. (Some models come with both a G♮ and a longer G♭ tuning slide for the second valve tubing so that either format is available to the player.) Although these are the usual formats, there have been many experiments with other tunings.

When the first valve (operated by the thumb) is activated, the normal F attachment positions may be played. If the lever of the second valve is depressed by the middle finger, an alternative set of G♮ or G♭ positions are made available. Using both valves together lowers the trombone's pitch to either E♭ (G♮ format) or D (G♭ format). It is essentially four trombones in one: B♭, F, G♭ (G♮), D (E♭). The G♭–D tuning is the most common.

G attachment:

G♭ attachment:

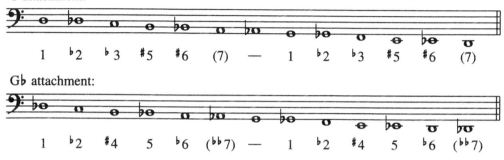

Additional improvements in the design of bass trombones are the use of larger, more direct valves, such as those made by Thayer, Hagmann, Greenhoe, and others, and shaping the tubing from the valves in a more open pattern to provide better response with less resistance.[8] Some recent experiments have lengthened the second valve's tubing so that C is in first position when the valves are used together.

▪ OTHER ATTACHMENTS

Sattler's choice of the key of F for the attachment fitted to the B♭ tenor trombone in 1839 was probably made because F was the standard key of the bass trombone at that time (earlier instruments were often tuned lower, to E♭ or D). While Sattler's purpose for the tenor-bass was the same as it is today (to enable the trombonist to play notes in the lowest register in F with less slide extension and to fill in the missing notes between low E and pedal B♭), he probably did not anticipate that the F attachment would provide the added benefit of a few optional positions for the tenor range, assisting technical facility. Thus, the F attachment has been accepted by succeeding generations of trombonists without giving much thought as to whether F is the optimum key for the attachment. Recently, an engineering professor, Dr. B. P. Leonard, has shown that F is *not* the best choice of key for either of the attachment's purposes. For technical facility, a G attachment offers more alternative positions as well as the added possibility of being constructed with a shorter slide (six positions in B♭ and five in G). The lower inertia of the shorter slide combined with the G positions constitutes a clear improvement over the conventional F attachment. To bridge the gap between low E and pedal B♭, a single-valve E♭ attachment is superior to either the F attachment or the double-trigger-dependent (contained within the F attachment) E or E♭ attachments.[9] In addition to B♭/G and B♭/E♭ models, Dr. Leonard

---

[8] See Douglas Yeo, "The Bass Trombone: Innovations on a Misunderstood Instrument," *The Instrumentalist*, (November 1985), pp. 22–28.

[9] B. P. Leonard, "Rational Design of Trigger Attachments," Center for Computational Mechanics, The University of Akron, Akron, Ohio. Dr. Leonard has patented the B♭–E♭ (perfect fifth) and (in-line) B♭/G♮–E♭–D♯ tunings.

designed an in-line B♭/G♮–E♮–D♮ instrument (actually the first U.S. in-line design), which features a shorter slide. This offers the technical advantages of the B♭/G configuration along with the capability to effectively bridge the gap to the pedal range.[10]

■ SLIDE MOVEMENT

How effectively the trombonist is able to move the slide from position to position will determine both the quality of technique and intonation. The slide must obviously be in excellent condition and free of any tendency to bind. The instrument's weight should be supported and balanced by the left arm and hand so that the right hand is free to control the slide.

To achieve clarity in moving passages, the player must make the slide reach a precise position before each note begins without shortening the duration of the previous note. Due to the distances involved, it takes a great deal of practice to develop the necessary coordination to place the slide in position with accuracy. Through practice, the player develops an automatic feel for the location of each position but must continually strive for the quickest possible movement between positions. A helpful technique for improving slide movement is to occasionally practice scales, arpeggios, and melodies in the dark. Students are often dependent on visual reference points such as the bell in making slide movements. When the visual crutch is removed, the player must rely on the ear and feel of the hand to locate the positions. This will accelerate a student's mastery of slide motion.

In legato, quickness of slide motion is essential. Students sometimes interrupt the air flow to compensate for slow slide motion. Although this eliminates obvious glissandos, the legato is unsatisfactory. Developing good intonation is a continual process of careful listening. In practicing, trombone students should make it a policy not to accept notes that reflect any fault in slide movement or intonation. (Trombone legato is discussed more fully in Chapter 10.)

■ OPTIONAL POSITIONS

Optional positions play a more important role in trombone technique than do alternate fingerings in the playing of valve instruments. Through their use, a number of changes of slide direction and long shifts between positions can be avoided. For example: in a fast-moving passage, if sixth-position C is followed by the F above, it is preferable to play the F also in sixth rather than return the slide to first position. Unlike most alternate fingerings, differences in intonation between the regular and optional position can be corrected by the trombone slide.

By selecting optional positions, the trombonist tries to maintain the direction of slide motion where possible. These patterns become established through the practice of scales and arpeggios. Students often resist using different positions and cling to familiar positions no matter how awkward the slide motion. It is important, therefore, that the use of optional positions be included within their normal technical development to avoid problems when more difficult literature is encountered. Most method books incorporate this skill progressively within their studies.

Since they are played on different harmonic series, there will be some discrepancy in timbre between the regular and optional position. In rapid passages, small variations in timbre may not be noticed; but in notes of longer duration, tone quality must be the primary consideration, even if a somewhat awkward shift of the slide is necessary.

---

[10]The first in-line independent double-trigger trombone was invented by Hans Kunitz (British Patent, 1965). This is a large F bass intended to function as a contrabass incorporating the keys of F/C–D–B♭. In the early 1970s, B. P. Leonard independently invented the in-line configuration with the tuning B♭/G♮–E♮–D♮. The prototype was built by J. Onqué, of the Giardinelli Band Instrument Company in New York. Giardinelli subsequently made several alterations in the tuning of Leonard's design—B♭/F–G♮–E♭ and B♭/F–G♭–D♮. In the latter forms, the double-trigger design has been adopted by instrument manufacturers for bass trombones.

Positions that involve long extensions of the slide tend to be less resonant and more difficult to control physically, due to the imbalance of the instrument. With a few exceptions, a more consistent tone will be achieved by minimizing the intermixing of notes taken in B♭ or F on trombones with F attachments. Ordinarily, the F attachment is rarely used above second-space C. Practice must be directed toward matching the timbre and intonation of regular and optional positions. By playing a note in each position, the trombonist can equalize tone, stability, and intonation to an acceptable level on most notes.

The following are the most commonly used optional positions:

Normal position: 2   1   2   1   2   1   1   ♯2   1   1

Optional position: 7   6   6   5   5   4   ♯4   4   3   3

■ INTONATION

The trombone is unique among wind instruments in being capable of completely variable pitch. This is both an advantage and a challenge to the player. Having a greater capacity to adjust intonation than other brass players, the trombonist must rely more on the ear in locating exact pitch centers. In this sense, trombone playing is similar to string playing, where it takes considerable time and effort to learn to play in tune. Apart from the general suggestions presented in the discussion of the trumpet in Chapter 3, the following notes will most often need correction:

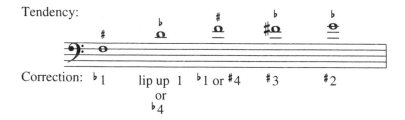

Tendency:

Correction: ♭1   lip up 1   ♭1 or ♯4   ♯3   ♯2
                     or
                     ♭4

The highest octave will vary with individual players and instruments and will require fine adjustment. It is common for students to exhibit a tendency to sharpness in the upper register; this is usually the result of too much embouchure adjustment in proportion to air pressure and volume.

Within a brass section, the first trombone must concentrate carefully on the pitches played by the first trumpet. It is helpful if these players can sit next to each other in order to hear each other as clearly as possible. Likewise, the bass trombone should be seated next to the tuba since the parts often double. Specific guidelines for seating the brass section for optimum balance and intonation are presented in Chapter 14.

In large ensembles, the trombone section must work outside of full rehearsals if good intonation is to be achieved. Only through sectional rehearsals is adequate time available for careful tuning and balancing of chords. It is helpful if the tubist occasionally joins these sessions, since the low brass must work as a team. In bands, euphoniums should also be included.

■ TRILLS ON THE TROMBONE

Trills are occasionally called for in the literature for the trombone; when they are, the player must be able to produce a smooth and reliable lip trill. Fortunately, the upper register of the trombone lends itself to whole-tone lip slurs, and these, with work, can be refined into usable trills.

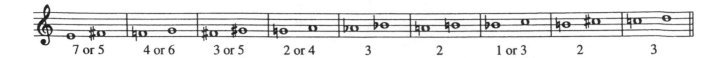

Lip trills are difficult for everyone at first. Above all, a great deal of patience is needed for this work. By working slowly and by gradually increasing the speed, the trill can be developed over time. The great hornist Barry Tuckwell has suggested that if the usual way of practicing lip trills is reversed, the trill can be developed more easily[11]:

Trombonist Michael Powell has suggested that the player visualize standing in the middle of a seesaw, with the two notes of the trill at opposite ends. The goal is to decrease the distance between the two ends and consequently between notes.

■ THE GLISSANDO

The special capability of the trombone's moving slide to produce a glissando has not been lost on composers who like to make use of this effect. There are, however, instances in the repertoire where glissandos have been written without an adequate awareness of what the instrument can do. Continuous glissandos can only take place within the seven positions of the slide:

Occasionally, problematic glissandos are found that cross over the first (ascending) or seventh (descending) positions. Experienced trombonists have found their way around such "broken glissandos,"[12] but it would be better if composers considered the length of slide available above or below the starting note before writing this effect.

Another problem is, for example, the glissando from low B to F in Bartók's *Concerto for Orchestra*, which was written for the longer slide of the obsolete F bass trombone. While this is impossible on the B♭–F bass due to the length of the slide, it can be managed on the in-line double-valve instrument with some adroit handling of the valves in conjunction with the slide (some bass trombonists play this on a contrabass trombone,

---

[11] Barry Tuckwell, *Playing the Horn* (London: Oxford University Press, 1978), pp. 17–18.

[12] Some solutions, as well as a table of glissandos, may be found in Denis Wick, *Trombone Technique* (London: Oxford University Press, 1971), pp. 62–66. See also Edward Kleinhammer, *The Art of Trombone Playing* (Evanston, Ill.: Summy-Birchard, 1963), pp. 58–61.

if one is available). The various configurations of double-valve bass trombone have created new possibilities for glissandos.

■ THE F, C, AND G CLEFS

Although the trombonist is free of the burden of transposition that confronts horn and trumpet players, parts in tenor, alto, and occasionally treble clef will be encountered in addition to the usual bass clef. An advanced player must be prepared to function comfortably in the tenor and alto clefs (parts written in alto, tenor, and bass clef were originally intended for alto, tenor, and bass trombone). In writing for the trombone today, the use of clefs is extremely helpful as a means of avoiding excessive ledger lines:

More use could be made of the nontransposed treble clef, particularly in the jazz and studio fields, as an alternative to the ledger lines required in bass clef by high-register parts. An anomaly is the transposed treble clef, in which the trombone sounds down a ninth from where it is written. Trombone parts in brass bands (other than the bass trombone) are written in this manner. Players familiar with tenor clef can perform such parts by replacing the treble clef with a tenor clef and subtracting two sharps (or adding two flats).

Students of orchestration are often confused when they are told that the trombone is a nontransposing instrument sounding an octave below the B♭ trumpet (a transposing instrument). The trombone (with its movable slide) predates the horn and trumpet as a chromatic instrument and did not go through a "natural" era during which notes were limited to the harmonic series. To make performing on the harmonic series easier, natural trumpet and horn parts were mainly notated in C and crooks were inserted to make the notes sound in the key of the orchestra. The practice of writing the fundamentals of the horn and trumpet as C continues today. Consequently, when the trumpeter plays open (written) C on the B♭ trumpet, concert B♭ sounds. Open position on the trombone (first position) has always been notated and read as concert B♭, the fundamental pitch.

■ MUTES

Trombone mutes follow the same patterns as those for trumpet but are constructed in appropriately larger dimensions (see Figure 5.4). Mutes are now made from various metals, plastic, and fiber. Composers sometimes specify the mute material in their scores to achieve different sounds.

With the variety of bell sizes available, it is important to use a mute that has been designed for a specific type of bell. Even with a well-designed mute, it may be necessary to make further adjustments by sanding the corks. The low register, particularly F attachment notes, should be checked when selecting a mute since some will work better than others in this range. Where possible, the same brand of straight mute should be used between trumpets and trombones to ensure evenness of tone color. Cup mutes, harmon mutes, and so forth may not blend as well between the two sections.

One irritating problem that seems to occur with regularity is where the composer has failed to allow adequate time to insert or withdraw the mute. Composers should check their muting instructions carefully and mentally go through the motions they are asking of the performer. Generally, more time is needed for mute changes by trombonists than by trumpeters.

FIGURE 5.4
Assorted mutes for brass (Jo-Ral).

■ MISCELLANEOUS

Although some trombones are produced with a silver-plated finish, most professional performers prefer lacquered brass. The latter is considered to offer a warmer, fuller tone. Some players favor bells made of gold (red) brass. This material includes a greater percentage of copper and produces a darker, somewhat softer timbre.

Another matter of preference used to be whether rotary valves were operated by string action, which is still found on horns, or by mechanical connection such as the ball and socket. It was felt that string action delivered a quicker valve change. The ball and socket was easy to maintain but tended to be noisy. The new mechanical actions, such as the Unibal and Minibal linkages and similar devices, have solved these problems, and mechanical connections are now felt to be equal to string action.

Leadpipes are the subject of experimentation, and some instruments are made with removable leadpipes to allow performers the option of selecting one that is more suited to their specific requirements. Existing instruments can be modified to accept different leadpipes.

■ THE TROMBONE IN MUSIC COMPOSED SINCE THE 1960S

In recent decades, composers have shown a great deal of interest in the trombone's unlimited capacity to vary pitch and produce novel sounds. Microtonal effects, singing or speaking through the instrument, and passing air through the tubing are a few of the devices that have been employed. A number of solo compositions have appeared and have been received with interest. Works such as Luciano Berio's *Sequenza V*, Adler's *Canto II*, Erickson's *General Speech*, and others have brought the trombone into a new era as a solo instrument admirably suited to today's compositional techniques. There has been a comparable reawakening in the traditional literature. Soloists such as Christian Lindberg and Joseph Alessi and others have popularized the trombone as a solo instrument through recordings and concert appearances. This has been of immense service to young trombonists, who now can look forward to a widening circle of opportunities for the future.

RECOMMENDED LITERATURE FOR THE TROMBONE[13]

Complete Methods

*Arban: *Complete Method*, ed. Alessi and Bowman (Encore Press)

*Arban: *Famous Method*, ed. Randall and Mantia (C. Fischer)

Arban: *First and Second Year*, ed. Prescott (C. Fischer)

Flandrin: *Méthode complète de trombone à coulisse ténor* (Salabert)

Josel: *Posaunenschule*, 3 vols. (L. Krenn)

*LaFosse: *Méthode complète*, 3 vols. (A. Leduc)

Elementary Methods

Beeler: *Method*, 2 vols. (Warner Bros.)

Cimera: *Method* (Belwin-Mills)

E. Clarke: *Method* (C. Fischer)

Coombes: *Simply Brass for Trombone* (Brass Wind Publications)

Long: *Rubank Elementary Method* (Rubank)

McDunn: *Methode de trombone*, 3 vols. (A. Leduc)

Ostrander: *Method* (bass trombone) (C. Fischer)

Ridgeon: *Brass for Beginners* (Boosey & Hawkes)

Slokar: *Method for Trombone* (Reift)

Studies

Medium to Medium-Difficult

Barbez: *Technique du trombone basse* (A. Leduc)

Becquet: *6 Exercises* (warm-ups) (BIM)

Blume: *36 Studies*, vols. 1 and 2 (C. Fischer)

Bordogni: *43 Bel Canto Studies*, transcribed Roberts (bass trombone) (R. King)

*Bordogni: *Melodious Etudes*, transcribed by Rochut, vol. 1 (C. Fischer)

*Bourgeois: *Bone of Contention* (medium-difficult) (Brass Wind Publications)

*Bourgeois: *Splinters of Bone* (very easy to medium) (Brass Wind Publications)

*N. Clarke: *Featuring Rhythm for Trombone* (Brass Wind Publications)

Colin: *Advanced Lip Flexibilities* (C. Colin) (med. to diff.)

Concone/Korak: *The Complete Solfeggi* (Balquidder)

*Crees and Gane: *How Trombonists Do It* (Brass Wind Publications)

*Edney: *Melodic Studies for Trombone*, 2 vols. (Brass Wind Publications)

Endresen: *Supplementary Studies* (Rubank)

*Faulise: *The F and D Double-Valve Bass Trombone Daily Warm-Up and Maintenance Exercises* (PF Music)

*Fink: *Introducing the Tenor Clef* (Accura Music)

Fink: *Studies in Legato* (C. Fischer)

*Gower and Voxman: *Rubank Advanced Method*, 2 vols. (Rubank)

*Gregson: *20 Supplementary Tunes for Beginner Brass* (Brass Wind Publications)

*Gresham: *Plainchant for Trumpet/Trombone* (Balquidder)

Hansen: *Solobuch für Posaune*, 4 vols. (Benjamin)

Mantia: *Trombone Virtuoso* (C. Fischer)

McGregor: *Daily Scale Builder* (Balquidder)

Josel: *Special Legato Exercises* (Krenn)

Josel: *Technical Exercises*, 2 vols. (Krenn)

Josel: *Tonleiter* (Krenn)

*LaFosse: *School of Sightreading and Style*, 5 vols. (A. Leduc) (easy to difficult)

*Little: *Embouchure Builder* (Pro Art Publ.)

*Maenz: *20 Studies for Bass Trombone or Tuba* (Hofmeister)

Mantia: *Trombone Virtuoso* (C. Fischer)

*Mowat: *Unlocking the Tenor Clef* (Brass Wind Publications)

Mueller: *Technical Studies*, vols. 1 and 2 (C. Fischer)

Nightengale: *Warm-up Book* (Warwick)

Ostrander: *Basic Techniques* (bass trombone) (R. King)

*Ostrander: *F Attachment and Bass Trombone* (C. Colin)

Ostrander: *Melodius Etudes* (bass trombone) (C. Fischer)

*Parés: *Scales* (Rubank)

Reift: *Warm-Ups* (Reift)

*Remington: *Warm-up Exercises* (Accura Music) (bass trombone) (easy to difficult)

*Remington: *Warm-up Studies* (Accura Music) (easy to difficult)

*Rochut, *Melodius Etudes* (see Bordogni)

*Schlossberg: *Daily Drills and Technical Studies* (M. Baron) (medium to difficult)

*Schwartz: *The Bordogni Vocalises* (7 vols.) (with CD accompaniment) David A. Schwartz

[13]Essential literature is noted with an asterisk.
Repertoire lists may be found in the texts by Fink, Gregory, Griffiths, Kleinhammer, and Wick.

*Schwartz: *Breakfast: Intonation Practice for Trombonists* (with CD accompaniment) (David A. Schwartz)

Slama: *66 Etudes in All Keys* (C. Fischer)

Slokar: *Warm-Ups and Technical Routines* (Reift)

Slokar and Bachmann: *Schule für Bass Posaune* (Reift)

Skornicka and Boltz: *Rubank Intermediate Method* (Rubank)

*Tyrrell: *40 Progressive Studies* (Boosey & Hawkes)

Voxman (ed.): *Selected Studies for Trombone* (Rubank)

Wiggins: *First Tunes and Studies* (Oxford) (easy to medium)

Difficult

Aharoni: *New Method for the Modern Bass Trombone* (Noga Music)

Anderson: *Complete Method for Alto Trombone* (Modern Editions)

Bach: *Suites*, transcribed by LaFosse (A. Leduc)

*Bitsch: *15 Etudes de rhythme* (A. Leduc)

*Blazhevich: *Clef Studies* (International)

*Blazhevich: *Sequences* (International)

*Blazhevich: *70 Studies* (tuba) (bass trombone) (R. King)

Blume: *36 Studies*, vol. 3 (C. Fischer)

*Bordogni: *Melodious Etudes*, transcribed by Rochut, vols. 2 and 3 (C. Fischer)

*Boutry: *12 Etudes de haut perfectionnement* (A. Leduc)

Dufresne and Voisin: *Sightreading Studies* (C. Colin)

Fink: *Introducing the Alto Clef* (Accura Music)

Fink: *Studies in Legato for Bass Trombone and Tuba* (C. Fischer)

*Green: *ProSlide Studies* (Warwick)

Gillis: *20 Etudes for Brass Trombone* (Southern)

Gillis: *70 Progressive Studies for the Modern Bass Trombone* (Southern)

Kahila: *Advanced Studies* (alto and tenor clef) (R. King)

Kahila: *Semester of Studies* (bass trombone) (R. King)

Kopprasch: *Selected Studies*, ed. Fote (bass trombone) (Kendor)

*Kopprasch: *60 Selected Studies*, 2 vols. (C. Fischer)

*Marsteller: *Advanced Slide Technique* (Southern)

*Marsteller: *Basic Routines* (Southern)

*Maxted: *20 Studies for Tenor Trombone* (E. Williams)

Mueller: *Technical Studies*, vol. 3 (C. Fischer)

*Ostrander: *Double-Valve Bass Trombone Low-Tone Studies* (C. Colin)

*Ostrander: *Shifting Meter Studies* (bass trombone) (R. King)

*Pederson: *Unaccompanied Solos* (bass trombone) (Kendor)

*Raph: *Double-Valve Bass Trombone* (C. Fischer)

*Rochut: *Lectures* (Fetter)

*Rochut: *Melodius Etudes* (see Bordogni)

*Sauer: *20 Orchestral Etudes* (E. Williams)

Sluchin: *Study Material for Alto Trombone* (Warwick)

Toulon: *10 Etudes* (bass trombone) (A. Leduc)

Watrous: *Trombonisms* (C. Fischer)

Unaccompanied Solos

Difficult

Adler: *Canto II* (bass trombone) (Oxford)

Agrell: *Temperamental Suite* (bass trombone) (BIM)

*Arnold: *Fantasy* (Faber)

Bach: *6 Cello Suites*, transcribed by Brown (tenor trombone) (International)

Bach: *6 Cello Suites*, transcribed by Marsteller, 2 vols. (bass trombone) (Southern) (original cello editions are available from Peters and Bärenreiter)

Berio: *Sequenza V* (Universal Ed.)

Bernstein: *Elegy for Mippy II* (Schirmer)

*Bourgeois: *Coat de Bone* (Warwick)

*Bozza: *Graphismes* (A. Leduc)

Brink: *Exegesis* (bass trombone) (BIM)

Buss: *Time Capsule* (Brixton)

Cage: *Solo for Sliding Trombone* (Peters)

Childs: *Sonata* (Presser)

Cope: *3 Pieces* (BIM)

*Crespo: *Improvisation I* (Lydke)

Dubois: *Music for a Sliding Trombone* (bass trombone) (Donemus)

*Erickson: *General Speech* (Seesaw Music)

Fetter: *Bass Lines* (Fetter)

Fetter: *Variations on Palestrina's Dona Nobis Pacem* (Fetter)

Globokar: *Exchanges* (Peters)

Hartley: *Sonata brève* (bass trombone) (Presser)

Heider: *D.E. Memorial* (bass trombone) (Peters)

Hidas: *Fantasia* (Editio Musica)

*Hidas: *Meditation* (bass trombone) (Editio Musica)

*Horowitz: *Concert Study* (Warwick)

Johnston: *Revelstoke Impressions* (bass trombone) (BIM)

Kenny: *Sonata for Bass Trombone* (Warwick)

Másson: *Cadenza* (BIM)

Másson: *Monologue* (BIM)

Michel: *Hommage à Jean Tinguely* (Reift)

Naulais: *L'homme aux 3 visages* (IMD)

Nightengale: *Undertones* (Warwick)

Pacciani: *Ritornelli* (BIM)

Persichetti: *Parable XVIII* (Presser)

*Plog: *Postcards* (BIM)

*Premru: *Prelude and Dance for Solo Bass Trombone* (Emerson)

Presser: *Partita* (Philharmusica)

Presser: *3 Folk Tales* (bass trombone) (Presser)

Rabe: *Busta* (Reimer)

Ross: *Prelude, Fugue, and Big Apple* (with tape) (bass trombone) (Boosey & Hawkes)

Skolnik: *3 Pieces* (Presser)

Stockhausen: *In Freudenschaft* (Stockhausen)

Sturzenegger: *B.A.C.H. Fantaisie* (BIM)

Telemann: *12 Fantasies* (C. Fischer)

Watson: *Zhindt* (Warwick)

Xenakis: *Keren* (Salabert)

Trombone and Piano

Easy

Adams: *The Holy City* (Boosey & Hawkes)

Bach: *Aria, Bist du bei mir*, transcribed by Fitzgerald (Belwin-Mills)

Bakaleinikoff: *Andantino Cantabile* (Belwin-Mills)

Bakaleinikoff: *Meditation* (Belwin-Mills)

Barnes: *The Clifford Barnes Trombone Album* (Boosey & Hawkes)

Dearnley (ed.): *More Easy Pieces* (Chester)

Goodwin and Pearson: *First Book of Trombone Solos* (Faber)

Goodwin and Pearson: *Second Book of Trombone Solos* (Faber)

Keynotes Album for Trombone (Brass Wind Publications)

Lawrance: *Badinage* (Brass Wind Publications)

*Lawrance: *Easy Winners for Trombone* (with CD accompaniment) (Brass Wind Publications)

Lawrance: *Winners Galore for Trombone* (Brass Wind Publications)

Lawton (ed.): *The Young Trombonist*, 3 vols. (Oxford)

Laycock: *The Dove* (Boosey & Hawkes)

Mendelssohn: *On Wings of Song* (Boosey & Hawkes)

*Mowat: *Slide Show for Trombone* (Brass Wind Publications)

Mozart: *A Mozart Solo Album*, arranged by Lethbridge (Oxford)

Perry (ed.): *Classical Album* (Boosey & Hawkes)

Phillips (ed.): *Classical and Romantic Album* (Oxford)

Smith (ed.): *First Solos for the Trombone Player* (Schirmer)

Snell: *Belwin Master Solos*, Easy (Belwin)

Strauss: *Allerseelen* (Rubank)

Up-Front Album for Trombone, Baritone, Euphonium, 2 vols. (Brass Wind Publications)

Verdi: *A Verdi Solo Album*, arranged by Lethbridge (Oxford)

Watts: *Beginning Trombone Solos* (with cassette accompaniment) (H. Leonard)

Watts: *Easy Trombone Solos* (with cassette accompaniment) (H. Leonard)

Medium to Medium-Difficult

Bach: *Sinfonia*, transcribed by Fote (bass trombone) (Kendor)

Baker (ed.): *Master Solos* (H. Leonard)

*Barat: *Andante and Allegro* (C. Fischer)

Barnes: *Trombone Album* (Boosey & Hawkes)

Berlioz: *Recitative and Prayer* (Presser)

Carr: *Cool Cat and Friends* (Brass Wind Publications)

*Clack: *First Repertoire Pieces* (Boosey & Hawkes)

N. Clarke: *Sketches from Don Quixote for Trombone* (Brass Wind Publications)

Fauré: *Elégie* (A. Leduc)

Galliard: *6 Sonatas*, 2 vols. transcribed Brown (International)

*Gaubert: *Cantabile et Scherzello* (C. Fischer)

Graves: *Sarabande* (Emerson)

Handel: *Sonata 3*, arranged by Powell (Southern)

*Horovitz: *Adam-Blues* (Novello)

Iveson: *A Little Light Music for Trombone* (Brass Wind Publications)

*Iveson: *Trombone Solos* (Chester)

*Lusher: *Sweet and Sour* (Warwick)

Lusher and Norton: *Trombone Album* (Boosey & Hawkes)

Marcello: *Sonata in C* (International)

Marcello: *Sonata in E Minor* (International)

*Mowat: *Bach for Trombone* (Brass Wind Publications)

Ostrander (ed.): *Concert Album* (Editions Musicus)

Snell: *Belwin Master Solos, Intermediate* (Belwin)

Proctor: *On Your Metal* (Brass Wind Publications)

*Pryor: *Annie Laurie* (Ludwig)

Rachmaninoff: *Vocalise* (International)

Ramskill: *From Vivaldi to Fats Waller for Trombone* (Brass Wind Publications)

Richardson (ed.): *6 Classical Solos* (Boosey & Hawkes)

*Smith (ed.): *Solos for the Trombone Player* (Schirmer)

Still: *Romance* (International)

Tanner: *Trombone Solos*, 2 vols. (Belwin)

*Tcherepnine: *Andante* (Belaieff)

Telemann: *Sonata in F Minor* (International)

Top-Line Album for Trombone, Baritone, Euphonium (Brass Wind Publications)

Voxman (ed.): *Concert and Contest Collection* (Rubank)

Watts: *Intermediate Trombone Solos* (with cassette accompaniment) (H. Leonard)

Difficult

*Albrechtsberger: *Concerto* (alto trombone) (Rosehill) (Editio Musica)

*Arutiunian: *Concerto* (BIM)

*Bach/Mowat: *A Bach Recital for Trombone* (Brass Wind Publications)

Baratto: *Andante Cantabile* (BIM)

Baska: *Trombone Sonata* (Presser)

Berlioz, arranged by Mowat: *Recitative and Prayer* (Brass Wind Publications)

Blank: *Esquisse* (BIM)

Bloch: *Symphony* (Broude Bros.)

Blazhevich: *Concerto No. 1* (BIM)

Blazhevich: *Concerto No. 2* (International)

*Bourgeois: *Fantasy Pieces for Bass Trombone* (Brass Wind Publications)

*Bourgeois: *Fantasy Pieces for Tenor Trombone* (Brass Wind Publications)

*Bourgeois: *Sonata* (Warwick)

*Bozza: *Allegro et finale* (bass trombone) (A. Leduc)

*Bozza: *Ballade* (A. Leduc)

*Bozza: *Ciaccona* (A. Leduc)

*Bozza: *Hommage à Bach* (A. Leduc)

*Bozza: *New Orleans* (bass trombone) (A. Leduc)

*Bozza: *Prelude et allegro* (bass trombone) (A. Leduc)

*Bozza: *Theme varié* (bass trombone) (A. Leduc)

Brown: *Sonata* (BIM)

*Carr: *Two Folk Songs for Trombone and Piano* (Brass Wind Publications)

*Castérède: *Fantaisie Concertante* (bass trombone) (A. Leduc)

*Castérède: *Sonatine* (A. Leduc)

Chavez: *Concerto* (Schirmer)

Corelli: *Sonata in F,* transcribed by Brown (International)

Cosma: *Concerto* (BIM)

*Creston: *Fantasy* (Schirmer)

Curnow: *Fantasy for Trombone* (Rosehill)

*David: *Concertino* (C. Fischer)

DeFaye: *A la manière de Vivaldi* (A. Leduc)

Defaye: *2 danses* (also for bass trombone) (A. Leduc)

Eccles: *Sonata in G Minor* (International)

Ewazen: *Ballade* (bass trombone) (Southern)

*Ewazen: *Concerto for Bass Trombone* (Southern)

*Ewazen: *Rhapsody for Bass Trombone* (ITA Manuscript Press)

*Ewazen: *Sonata* (Southern)

Filas: *Concerto* (BIM)

Filas: *Romance Concertante* (bass trombone) (BIM)

Filas: *Sonata "At the End of the Century"* (BIM)

*Finger: *Sonata in E♭* (BIM)

Friedman: *Sonata* (BIM)

Gabel: *Fantasie* (Billaudot)

*Gaubert: *Morçeau symphonique* (International)

Gedalge: *Solo de concours* (Salabert)

George: *Concerto* (bass trombone) (Accura)

George: *Sonata* (Southern)

*Gregson: *Concerto* (Novello)

*Grondahl: *Concerto* (Samfundet til Udgivelse Af Dansk Musik)

*Guilmant: *Morçeau symphonique* (Warner Bros.) (Schott) (Brass Wind Publications)

Hartley: *Arioso* (bass trombone) (Fema Music)

Hartley: *Sonata Concertante* (Fema Music)

Hidas: *Concerto* (Editio Musica)

*Hidas: *Rhapsodie* (bass trombone) (Editio Musica)

*Hindemith: *Sonate* (Schott)

Hoddinott: *Ritornelli* (Oxford)

*Holst: *Concertante* (Warwick)

*Horovitz: *Concert Piece for Bass Trombone* (Warwick)

Hovorka: *Concertino* (BIM)

*Howarth: *Concerto* (Chester)

*Ibert: *Histoires* (A. Leduc)

*Jacob: *Cameos* (bass trombone) (Emerson Ed.)

*Jacob: *Concertino* (Emerson Ed.)

*Jacob: *Concerto* (Stainer & Bell)

*Jacob: *Sonata* (Emerson Ed.)

Jevtic: *Actus tragicus* (BIM)

Kassatti: *Sonatine* (BIM)

Kalke: *Concertino in F* (bass trombone) (Uetz)

*Kelly: *Sonatina* (Josef Weinberger)

Kenny: *Sonata for Alto Trombone* (Warwick)

*Koetsier: *Allegro Maestoso* (bass trombone) (Reift)

Koetsier: *Concertino* (BIM)

Koetsier: *Falstaffiade* (Reift)

Koetsier: *Sonatina* (Donemus)

Krenek: *5 Pieces* (bass trombone) (Bärenreiter)

Krol: *Capriccio da Camera* (Simrock/Schauer)

Larsson: *Concertino* (Gehrmans Musikforlag)

*Lebedev: *Concert Allegro* (bass trombone—originally for tuba) (Editions Musicus)

Lipkis: *Harlequin* (bass trombone) (Warwick)

Loudova: *Sonata Angelica* (BIM)

Mahler, arranged by Mowat: *Trombone Solo from Mahler Symphony No. 3* (Brass Wind Publications)

Manen: *15 Moments musicaux,* vols. 1 and 2 (Combre)

*Martin: *Ballade* (Universal)

McDougall: *Concerto for Bass Trombone* (Warwick)

Meier: *Musique pour trombone* (BIM)

*Milhaud: *Concertino d'hiver* (Associated)

*L. Mozart: *Concerto* (alto trombone) (Kunzelmann)

Naulais: *Latitude* (Martin)

Nelhybel: *Concerto* (bass trombone) (Southern)

Nielsen: *2 Fantasy Pieces* (International)

Oestreich: *Concertino* (BIM)

Pichaureau: *Seringa* (bass trombone) (Choudens)

Pichaureau: *Trombontests* (A. Leduc)

*Pilss: *Concerto* (bass trombone) (R. King)

Plog: *Four Themes on Paintings of Goya* (BIM)

Plog: *Nocturne* (BIM)

Plog: *3 Miniatures* (BIM)

*Pryor: *Blue Bells of Scotland* (C. Fischer)

*Pryor: *Thoughts of Love* (C. Fischer)

Raum: *Fantasy for Trombone* (Warwick)

Raum: *Olm Ütz Concerto* (BIM)

Richards: *Rainy Day in Rio* (bass trombone) (Studio)

*Rimsky-Korsakoff: *Concerto* (Boosey & Hawkes) (ed. Mowat, Brass Wind Publications)

*Ropartz: *Piece in E♭ Minor* (International)

*Rota: *Concerto* (Ricordi)

Rueff: *Concertstück* (bass trombone) (A. Leduc)

Ruswick: *The Velvet Slide* (Brass Wind)

Saglietti: *Concerto Classico* (Warwick)

*Saint-Saens: *Cavatine* (Durand) (ed. Mowat, Brass Wind Publications)

*Salzedo: *Pièce Concertante* (A. Leduc)

Sampson: *In Time* (bass trombone) (with percussion) (BIM)

Sanders: *Sonata in E♭* (Warwick)

Sandstrim: *Bombibone Brassbit* (Warwick)

Siekmann: *Concerto* (bass trombone) (Brelmat)

Sikorski: *Concerto* (Polski wydawnictwo Muzyczne)

Smita: *Concertino in E♭* (BIM)

Snell: *Belwin Master Solos,* advanced (Belwin)

Spillman: *Concerto* (bass trombone) (Editions Musicus)

Spillman: *Two Songs for Bass Trombone* (Editions Musicus)

Stevens: *Sonata* (Southern)

Stevens: *Sonatina* (Southern)

Stojowski: *Fantasie* (A. Leduc)

Sulek: *Sonata "Vox Gabrieli"* (BIM)

Thilloy: *Rojo y Negro* (Warwick)

*Tomasi: *Concerto* (A. Leduc)

*Tomasi: *Danse Sacrée* (bass trombone) (A. Leduc)

Tomasi: *Être ou ne pas être* (bass trombone) (A. Leduc)

Tuthill: *Concerto* (R. King)

Voegelin: *Méditation sur B.A.C.H.* (with organ) (BIM)

*Wagenseil: *Concerto* (Boosey & Hawkes)

White: *Sonata* (Southern)

White: *Tetra Ergon* (bass trombone) (BIM)

Wilder: *Sonata* (bass trombone) (Margun Music)

Uber: *Skylines* (bass trombone) (Hidalgo)

Uber: *Sonata* (Southern)

Zbinden: *Triptyque* (BIM)

Zwilich: *Concerto* (Presser)

Books on the Trombone [14]

Arling, Harry J. *Trombone Chamber Music,* 2nd ed. Nashville, Tenn.: Brass Press, 1983.

Bahr, Edward. R. *Trombone/Euphonium Discography.* Stevens Point, Wis.: Index Horse, 1988.

Baker, David. *Contemporary Techniques for the Trombone.* 2 vols. New York: Charles Colin, 1974.

*Bate, Philip. *The Trumpet and Trombone: An Outline of Their History, Development, and Construction,* 2nd ed. London: Ernest Benn, Ltd., 1978; New York: Norton, 1978.

*Dempster, Stuart. *The Modern Trombone: A Definition of Its Idioms.* Athens, Ohio: Accura Music, 1994.

Everett, Thomas G. *Annotated Guide to Bass Trombone Literature,* 3rd ed. Nashville, Tenn.: Brass Press, 1985.

Fadle, Heinz. *Looking for the Natural Way: Thoughts on the Trombone and Brass Playing.* Detmold, Germany: Edition Piccolo, 1996.

*Fink, Reginald H. *The Trombonist's Handbook.* Athens, Ohio: Accura Music, 1977.

Fischer, Henry George. *The Renaissance Sackbut and Its Use Today.* New York: Metropolitan Museum of Art, 1984.

*Gregory, Robin. *The Trombone.* New York: Faber & Faber, 1973.

Griffiths, John R. *The Low Brass Guide.* Hackensack, N.J.: Jerona Music, 1980.

Guion, David M. *The Trombone: Its History and Music 1697–1811* New York: Gordon & Breach, 1988.

*Harvey, Roger. *BrassWorkBook for Alto Trombone.* Gt. Dunmow, England: BrassWorks.

*Harvey, Roger. *BrassWorkBook for Trombone Section.* Gt. Dunmow, England: BrassWorks.

Heyde, Herbert. *Trompeten, Posaunen, Tuben.* Leipzig: VEB Deutscher Verlag für Musik, 1980.

Kagarice, Vern L., et al. *Solos for the Student Trombonist: An Annotated Bibliography.* Nashville, Tenn.: Brass Press, 1979.

Kehle, Robert. *Alto Trombone Literature: An Annotated Guide.* Warwick, England: Warwick Music, 2000.

---

[14]Many interesting articles appear in the *International Trombone Association Journal* and other periodicals listed in Appendix C.

*Kleinhammer, Edward. *The Art of Trombone Playing.* Summy-Birchard, 1996.

*Kleinhammer, Edward. *Mastering the Trombone.* Hannover, Germany: Edition Piccolo, 1997.

Knaub, Donald: *Trombone Teaching Techniques,* 2nd ed. Athens, Ohio: Accura Music, 1977.

Lane, G. B. *The Trombone: An Annotated Bibliography.* Lanham, Md.: Scarecrow Press, 1999.

Lane, G. B. *The Trombone in the Middle Ages and the Renaissance.* Bloomington, Ind.: Indiana University Press, 1982.

Lupica, Benedict. *The Magnificent Bone: A Comprehensive Study of the Slide Trombone.* New York: Vantage Press, 1974.

*Maxted, George. *Talking About the Trombone.* London: J. Baker, 1970.

Naylor, Tom L. *The Trumpet and Trombone in Graphic Arts, 1500–1800.* Nashville, Tenn.: Brass Press, 1979.

Schöck, Ralf F. *Solo-Posaune und Blasorchester Verzeichnis von über 750 Solowerken für Eine oder Mehrere Posaunen und Blasorchester.* Vienna: Musik Verlag J. Kliment, 1999.

Senff, Thomas E. "An Annotated Bibliography of the Unaccompanied Solo Repertoire for Trombone." D.M.A. thesis, University of Illinois, 1976. UM 76-16, 919

Thompson, J. Mark. *French Music for Low Brass Instruments.* Bloomington, Ind.: Indiana University Press, 1994.

*Wick, Denis. *Trombone Technique,* 2nd ed. London: Oxford University Press, 1984.

*Wigness, C. Robert. *The Soloistic Use of the Trombone in Eighteenth Century Vienna.* Nashville, Tenn.: Brass Press, 1978.

THE BARITONE
AND THE EUPHONIUM

THE ORIGIN OF THE EUPHONIUM and baritone (see Figures 6.1 and 6.2) is more obscure than that of the tuba, which has a definite starting point and clear lines of development.[1] It is known that tenor-range brass instruments built in B♭ with three valves were part of German military bands during the late 1820s. The next clue is an instrument called the *Euphonion*, which was developed in 1843 or 1844 by Sommer of Weimar.[2] This may be the same Sommer (his first name is unknown) who caused a stir with a similar instrument at the 1851 Crystal Palace Exhibition in London.

About the same time, Adolph Sax patented his complete family of saxhorns, which included two low B♭ instruments: the *Saxhorn Baryton*, which was of similar dimensions to the modern baritone, and the *Saxhorn Basse*, a larger instrument originally of greater bore size than the euphonium. The originality of Sax's instruments was disputed at the time, and it is clear that the German instruments both preceded them and developed independently. Sax's instruments were, however, distinct in their tone and playing qualities as well as in their use of piston valves. Sax should also be credited with developing a complete group of instruments of this type, and he is largely responsible for their acceptance in countries west of the Rhine.

Today, the baritone and euphonium (both are in the key of B♭) are constructed similarly but differ significantly in their bore and bell dimensions. Consequently, there are important differences in timbre and playing characteristics between the two instruments. Baritones from British and European manufacturers, and others based on these designs, are made with distinctly narrower bores than euphoniums. For example, top-level Besson baritones are built with a 13.89-mm (0.547″) main bore, as opposed to 14.72 mm (0.580″) for their euphoniums.

It should be noted, however, that the "bore" of a brass instrument is more than just the diameter of the main bore. The latter is the width of the cylindrical tubing in the middle of the instrument, after the leadpipe and before the bell flare where the valve section is located. Cylindrical tubing is of one consistent diameter throughout its length. Conical tubing expands continuously. The conical lead pipe gradually increases in diameter until it reaches the valve section. Tuning slides and valve tubing are of necessity constructed of cylindrical tubing. On instruments in which the tuning slide is after the valves, cylindrical tubing leads to the beginning of the conical bell flare. The rate of expansion of the bell flare can be more gradual (narrow) or open broadly into a large bell. By comparison, the bell flare of the baritone is much more slender than that of the euphonium. The difference in main bore can readily be seen by comparing the cylindrical tubing of the valve sections

---

[1] The development of the baritone and euphonium is sketched as clearly as it probably can be in Clifford Bevan's *The Tuba Family* (New York: Scribner's, 1978), pp. 90–94.

[2] It is likely that the name *euphonium* for instruments of this type in English derives from Sommer's instrument and his presence in London in 1851.

FIGURE 6.1
Baritone (Besson).

FIGURE 6.2
Euphonium (Besson).

of the two instruments. If slide tubing from the baritone is inserted into the euphonium, it will not fit and will rattle within the larger tubing. These factors give the baritone its lighter, less expansive tone in comparison with the darker, weightier timbre and more tuba-like appearance of the euphonium. The brass band is the only ensemble where a clear distinction between the instruments is made. Brass band scores include separate baritone and euphonium parts, and players specialize on one instrument or the other. The baritone plays more of an ensemble role, with most of the important solos going to the euphonium.

In the United States, differences between the two instruments are less defined than between British-type baritones and euphoniums. This is due to a lack of clarity in identifying the instruments as well as a tendency for American firms to produce larger-bore

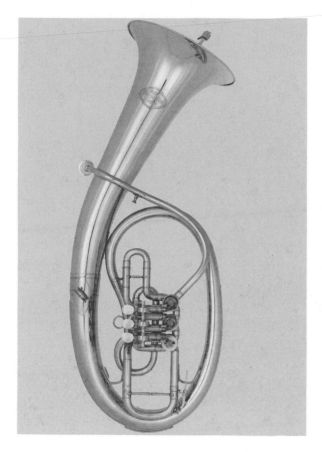

FIGURE 6.3
German Tenorhorn (Alexander).

baritones and smaller euphoniums than those used in Great Britain. This is changing, however, due to the preference for British-type euphoniums in American wind and brass bands. Greater precision would prevail if the name *euphonium* was reserved for instruments with a bore greater than 14 mm (0.551″). Further confusion is generated by the habit among conductors and players of referring to both instruments as baritones or baritone horns.

Still more confusion is created by the names applied to these instruments in other countries. In Germany, the baritone is known as the *Tenorhorn* (see Figure 6.3) and the euphonium as the *Baryton* (see Figure 6.4). In England, the tenor horn is the E♭ alto horn. Sax's original designation of *Baryton* (baritone) and *Basse* (euphonium) is still used in France.

■ INTONATION

The degree to which a player can correct intonation by lipping a faulty note into tune decreases as the vibrating air columns become longer, the diameter of the bore increases, and greater quantities of air are used. Hence, intonation on the trumpet can be more readily influenced by subtle adjustments of the player's embouchure than on the lower brass. Hornists have the further ability to affect pitch by altering the right-hand position, and trombonists can correct pitches by varying the position of the slide. Intonation problems on the baritone, euphonium, and tuba, however, require some form of mechanical correction, and how this is approached is an important consideration in the design of the instrument.

Aside from problems with the harmonic series itself (which should be minimal in a well-designed instrument), errors occur when the valves are used in combination. For example, the total length of a euphonium in B♭ is 115.325″ (2929.25 mm). When the first valve

FIGURE 6.4
German Baryton
(Meinl Weston).

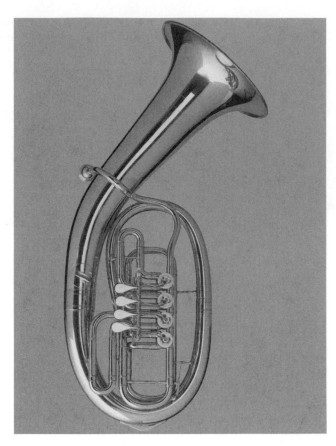

is depressed, 14.175″ (360.4 mm) of tubing are added to lower the pitch one tone to A♭. When the third valve is depressed, the instrument's pitch is lowered one and one-half tones to G, adding 21.825″ (554.35 mm). The difficulty arises when the first and third valves are used together to lower the instrument to F. Just as progressively more tubing is required between each trombone position to arrive at the correct measurement for a given pitch, so the valve tubing would need some means of extending itself for the lower pitch. The length of the vibrating air column necessary for the low F is 153.960″ (3910.58 mm). If 14.175″ (360.4 mm) of the first valve and the third valve's 21.825″ (554.35 mm) are added to the euphonium's fundamental length of 115.325″ (2929.25 mm), the total tubing available for the F is 151.325″ (3843.65 mm)—that is, 2.635″ (66.93 mm) too short, producing a sharp pitch. When all three valves are used to play a low E, the discrepancy is even greater.[3]

The usual way around this problem is for the manufacturer to increase the length of the third valve tubing to more than the one-and-one-half-tone extension it was originally intended to provide; this introduces a compromise that is workable on high brass instruments due to their greater responsiveness to embouchure control. The third valve is, however, diverted from its original purpose and is almost never used alone. In its place, the first and second valves are used in combination for the one-and-one-half-tone extension, but their combined length is a little short, producing some sharpness in pitch. This is why trumpeters must use the first valve trigger on notes played with this combination. (The first valve is usually constructed slightly long to reduce the amount of correction necessary.)

There have been various approaches to finding a practical solution to the problem of insufficient tube length when valves are used together. For the trumpet, the compromises

---

[3]F. C. Draper, *Notes on the Besson System of Automatic Compensation of Valved Brass Wind Instruments* (Edgware, England: Besson, 1953).

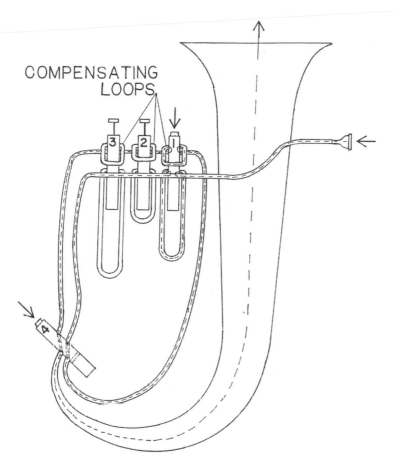

COMPENSATING
LOOPS

FIGURE 6.5
Blaikley's four-valve
compensating system.

work well enough, provided that the instrument is fitted with both a first- and third-valve trigger or ring and that the player makes use of them. A similar approach has been taken at times by some euphonium manufacturers by adding rings to the third and/or first valve slides or the main tuning slide. While these offer some measure of correction, they are awkward to use in an instrument of this size and do not offer a very viable solution. Most commonly, a fourth valve is incorporated into the design; this affords some improvement by providing alternate fingerings for the 1–3 and 1–2–3 combinations (4 and 2–4, respectively) by lowering the pitch of the instrument by a perfect fourth, thereby incorporating greater tube length in the alternate fingerings. Since the requisite tube lengths are only approximated by the increase provided by the fourth valve, the overall improvement is limited. This has led tubists to consider the further addition of a fifth valve to be essential.

The most effective solution of all for the euphonium is the system of automatic compensation designed by David J. Blaikley for the Boosey company in 1874. In this system, each valve contains a second loop of tubing of sufficient length to correct intonation when the valve is used in combination with the compensating (master) valve. There are both three- and four-valve compensating systems. In the preferable four-valve system (see Figure 6.5), the fourth valve acts as the compensating valve and has its compensating tubing routed through the other valves. The valves perform normally when used independent of the fourth valve. In combination with the fourth valve, however, the vibrating air column is directed a second time through the regular valves' compensating loops, thereby adding the exact length of corrective tubing for accurate intonation.

The advantage of the compensating system may be seen in the following chart, which compares the intonation of compensated and uncompensated four-valve systems:

uncompensated

degree sharp
or flat *   0   #1.08   #.68   #.326   b.036   #.008   b.234

fingering   0   1 2 3 4   1 3 4   2 3 4   3 4   1 4   2 4

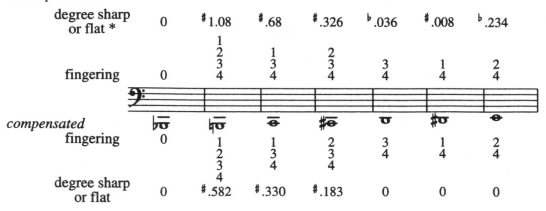

compensated
fingering   0   1 2 3 4   1 3 4   2 3 4   3 4   1 4   2 4

degree sharp
or flat   0   #.582   #.330   #.183   0   0   0

* Of a semitone.

uncompensated †

b.052   b.211   #.112   0   0   0   b.243   b.052   b.211   #.112   0   0   0

1 3   2 3   1 2   1   2   0   2 4   1 3   2 3   1 2   1   2   0

4   2 3   3   1   2   0   2 4   4   2 3   3   1   2   0

0   #.147   0   0   0   0   0   0   #.147   0   0   0   0

compensated

† The fourth valve would normally be used in place of the 1 – 3 combination
on uncompensated instruments, providing improved intonation.

uncompensated

b.211   #.112   0   0   0   #.112   0   0   0   0   0   0   b.211

2 3   1 2   1   2   0   1 2   1   2   0   1   2   0   2 3

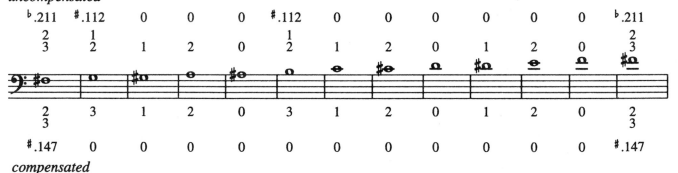

2 3   3   1   2   0   3   1   2   0   1   2   0   2 3

#.147   0   0   0   0   0   0   0   0   0   0   0   #.147

compensated
uncompensated

#.112   0   0   0

1 2   1   2   0

3   1   2   0

0   0   0   0

compensated

Comparison of intonation of compensated and uncompensated four-valve systems.
Adapted from Draper, *Notes on the Besson System*.

An additional advantage of the compensating system is that on instruments of this type, the third valve is constructed in the exact length for the one-and-one-half-tone extension (not longer, as in uncompensated instruments) as originally intended, and may be used in place of the sharp 1–2 combination, whenever the fingering pattern or the duration of the note permits. (The 1–2 combination is still often preferred, since it follows the first finger more naturally in rapid fingering sequences.) The accurate tuning of the third valve gives the player of a compensated instrument an advantage in intonation (it is a pity that many players are unaware of this feature and still cling to the 1–2 combination).

While it does not solve all problems, the four-valve compensating system does greatly improve intonation. On one of the top compensating models available today,[4] a thumb trigger is added so that the main tuning slide can be extended as necessary. This is a useful addition and gives the player even more mechanical control over intonation. As with all brass instruments, good intonation ultimately depends on the player's developing a keen ear to hear pitches, knowledge of the instrument's intonation tendencies, and the skill to adjust inaccurate pitches.

■ TONE AND PLAYING STYLE

Euphonium playing bears a relationship to cornet playing, in that the main emphasis should be melodic and expressive. While both instruments are especially suited to technical display—and this is exploited in the literature—their most important quality is a subtle capacity to emulate the human voice. This can best be heard by listening to some of the finest British brass bands, where all 25 players (regardless of instrument) play with an essentially vocal concept. The use of a natural, singing vibrato is fundamental to this style and lends expressiveness and sensitivity to the tone.

The euphonium was originally created to blend with the other conical-bore instruments of the brass band, so it should have a deep, mellow tone quality, without any trace of edge or hardness. If the trombone tone needs a certain "ring" in the timbre, the euphonium and baritone timbre should have softness and richness. The difference in tone quality between euphonium and baritone is one of degree: The sound is similar, but the baritone timbre is somewhat lighter in both color and weight.

To achieve a characteristic tone quality, it is essential to use a mouthpiece of adequate depth and throat-bore. It is quite common to find students using trombone mouthpieces that are too small to yield a satisfactory tone. (In orchestras, a trombonist usually volunteers to perform the euphonium parts, and this often results in a hollow, rather hard timbre.) By examining the expanding tubing along the bell section, one can grasp the need for a large-capacity mouthpiece. In order to fill flared tubing of this size, a great quantity of air is necessary. A small mouthpiece places a restriction on the air column and results in a thin, fairly colorless tone. A large backbore (as on the Denis Wick SM 3, 4, or 5) is helpful in achieving the characteristic rich, dark timbre.

In orchestral circles, the euphonium is known as the tenor tuba and is generally played without vibrato. The Bydlo solo in *Pictures at an Exhibition* (Mussorgsky–Ravel), originally written for the French C tuba (and is in the tuba part),[5] however, gains character from the addition of some vibrato and a full, rich euphonium tone. In other passages, such as those found in Janáček's *Sinfonietta* and Holst's "Mars" (*The Planets*), a pure, haunting, straight tone is more effective. In Strauss's *Don Quixote*, the vibrato question is less clear, and some experimentation is called for. Sometimes a German rotary valve euphonium (known as *Baryton* in Germany) is employed. This instrument has an unusually sturdy tone but lacks an effective system of

---

[4] Besson Prestige, BE 2051 and 2052.
[5] The French C tuba is discussed in Chapter 7.

compensation.[6] For this reason, it is important that a four-valve model be used and that the fit of the mouthpiece into the receiver be carefully checked. (This problem is discussed in Chapter 2.)

The euphonium is in its natural element in bands, where it is treated as a leading solo voice. Composers have taken advantage of the instrument's technical agility, and the player is provided with many interesting and challenging parts. This is even more true of euphonium writing in the brass band. The instrument is employed in truly virtuosic fashion in the leading British bands, such as Black Dyke Mills, Seller's Engineering, and Grimethorpe Colliery, to name only a few.

The euphonium is a superb solo instrument with a long tradition, although it has mostly been associated with brass and wind bands. In the days when bands like Sousa's and Gilmore's toured the United States, euphonium players were featured as soloists alongside the cornetists and gained considerable fame. In subsequent years, the solo euphonium was rather forgotten in America, as it fulfilled its ensemble role in concert bands. In Britain, the euphonium remained fairly prominent due to the popularity of brass bands and the leading role given the instrument in this type of group. Euphonium solos have always been a standard feature of brass band concerts, and there were always excellent soloists around. Today's generation of soloists both in Britain and America, such as the Childs brothers, Steven Mead, and Dr. Brian Bowman, have brought about a rebirth of interest in the solo euphonium on a wide scale. New solo works with orchestra as well as band have been introduced, and there is a rising tide of enthusiasm for this medium. What is needed now is more exposure and perhaps a more broad-minded attitude on the part of conductors and concert managements. Concert programs of both orchestras and bands can be enriched by occasional offerings of something new and unusual, and the euphonium never fails to make a hit with audiences.

■ MISCELLANEOUS

The first use of a mute for the euphonium can be found in Strauss's *Don Quixote.* Mutes are infrequently called for in the literature, and it is probably necessary for the band or orchestra to make one available when required. An example of muted writing can also be found in Karel Husa's *Music for Prague 1968* (for band).

The baritone and euphonium are obviously bass clef instruments, and this should be the normal practice of notation. Beginners should be taught in bass clef. There is, however, a longstanding tradition of writing for euphonium and baritone as transposing B♭ instruments in the treble clef (like the cornet), sounding a ninth lower. This is the case in brass bands, and it is common for wind band parts for euphonium to be furnished in both treble and bass clefs. This practice probably came about in order to make it easier for cornet players to switch to other instruments within the brass band. It is important, therefore, for euphonium players to be equally comfortable in bass or treble clef. An important reason for learning the treble clef in addition to bass clef is that a great quantity of vital study and solo literature for cornet, trumpet, and horn will be made accessible. The tenor clef is useful, as well, for trombone and bassoon literature and is beginning to appear in band writing for euphonium. Orchestral players will occasionally have to deal with transposed bass clef parts and other oddities.

Passing mention might be made of the double-bell euphonium, although this instrument is now considered a valuable collector's item. It was popular as a solo instrument during the Sousa–Pryor era, and the normal tone of the instrument could be modified by being directed through a second, smallish bell to produce echo and trombone-like effects. Superior instruments in their time, double-bell euphoniums are sought after today as much for their playing qualities as for the novelty of their design.

---

[6] At least one German maker is now producing a five-valve *Baryton,* which should offer improved intonation. The instrument is intended for orchestral use.

RECOMMENDED LITERATURE FOR BARITONE AND EUPHONIUM[7]

Complete Methods

*Arban: *Complete Method*, ed. Alessi and Bowman (Encore Press)

*Arban: *Method*, ed. Mantia and Randall (trombone) (C. Fischer)

Saint-Jacome: *Grand Method* (cornet) (C. Fischer)

Elementary Methods

*Beeler: *Method* (Warner Bros.)

Long: *Elementary Method* (Rubank)

Ridgeon: *Brass for Beginners* (Boosey & Hawkes)

Uber: *70 Beginning and Early Studies* (PP Music)

Wiggins: *First Tunes and Studies* (Oxford)

Williams: *Little Classics* (Colin)

Studies

Medium to Medium-Difficult

Blume: *36 Studies*, vol. 1 (trombone) (C. Fischer)

*Bordogni: *Melodious Etudes*, ed. Rochut, vols 1 and 2 (trombone) (C. Fischer)

*H. L. Clarke: *Technical Studies*, ed. Gordon (C. Fischer)

N. Clarke: *Featuring Rhythm* (Brass Wind Publications)

*Davis: *Polished Brass* (treble clef) (Brass Wind Publications)

*Edney: *Melodic Studies for Trombone* (Brass Wind Publications)

*Fink: *From Treble to Bass Clef* (Accura)

*Gregson: *20 Supplementary Tunes for Beginner Brass* (Brass Wind Publications)

Komischke: *Daily Drills* (Reift)

*Kopprasch: *60 Selected Studies* (trombone) (C. Fischer) (medium to difficult)

*Lawrance: *Featuring Melody* (Brass Wind Publications)

Miller: *60 Studies* (R. King)

Mueller: *Technical Studies*, vols. 1 and 2 (trombone) (C. Fischer)

Mueller: *30 Leichte Etuden* (F. Hofmeister)

*Parés: *Scales* (Rubank)

Reift: *Warm-Ups* (Reift)

Ronka: *Modern Daily Warm-Ups and Drills* (C. Fischer)

*Sparke: *Scales and Arpeggios* (Studio Music)

*Tyrrell: *40 Progressive Studies* (trombone) (Boosey & Hawkes)

Voxman (ed.): *Selected Studies* (Rubank)

Wastall: *Scales and Arpeggios* (Boosey & Hawkes)

Difficult

Blume: *36 Studies*, vol. 2 (trombone) (C. Fischer)

*Bordogni: *Melodious Etudes*, ed. Rochut, vol. 3 (trombone) (C. Fischer)

Charlier: *32 Études de perfectionnement* (H. Lemoine)

*Gordon: *30 Velocity Studies* (trombone) (C. Fischer)

*Green: *Euphonium Eurhythmics* (Warwick)

*Harris: *Advanced Daily Studies* (C. Colin)

Komischke: *Virtuosity Drills* (Reift)

Mueller: *Technical Studies*, vol. 3 (trombone) (C. Fischer)

Uber: *Symphonic Studies* (REBU)

Unaccompanied Solos

Difficult

Bach: *Dance Movements from the Cello Suite*, transcribed by Torchinsky (Schirmer)

Baxley: *Ronald McDifficult* (Clark-Baxley)

Constantinides: *Fantasy* (Whaling)

Croley: *Sonata* (Philharmusica Corp.)

Frackenpohl: *Bonebits* (Anglo-American)

Globokar: *Echanges* (Peters)

Grainger: *Walking Tune* (Philharmusica)

Paganini: *Caprice 24* (Cimarron Music)

Paganini: *Four Caprices* (Cimarron Music)

*Sparke: *Pantomime* (Studio Music)

Stevens: *Soliloquies for Euphonium Solo* (Tuba Press)

Baritone/Euphonium and Piano[8]

Easy

Adams: *The Holy City* (trombone) (Boosey & Hawkes)

Dearnley (ed.) *More Easy Pieces* (trombone) (Chester)

Gluck: *2 Classic Airs* (trombone) (Editions Musicus)

Haydn: *Aria and Allegro* (Rubank)

Johnson (ed.): *Sacred Solos* (trombone) (Rubank)

Keynotes Album for Trombone (Brass Wind Publications)

Laycock: *The Dove* (trombone) (Boosey & Hawkes)

Mendelssohn: *On Wings of Song* (trombone) (Boosey & Hawkes)

Mozart: *Arietta and Allegro* (Southern)

Perry (ed.): *Classical Album* (trombone) (Boosey & Hawkes)

---

[7]Essential material is noted with an asterisk. For additional literature, see the *Brass Music Guide* (Robert King) and texts by Bevan, Griffiths, Louder, and Winter.

[8]See Earle L. Louder, "Original Solo Literature and Study Books for Euphonium," *The Instrumentalist* (May 1981), pp. 29–30; also "Begged, Borrowed, and Stolen Solo Euphonium Literature," by Paul Droste in the same issue (pp. 30–32).

Strauss: *Allerseelen* (Rubank)

Up-Front Album for Trombone, Baritone, Euphonium, 2 vols. (Brass Wind Publications)

Wagner: *Song to the Evening Star* (Kendor)

Medium to Medium-Difficult
Amos: *Cavatina for Euphonium* (Oxford)

*Barat: *Andante and Allegro* (trombone) (C. Fischer)

*Bridge: *Meditation* (Obrasso)

Campbell: *Master Solos* (H. Leonard)

*Capuzzi: *Andante and Rondo* (Hinrichsen)

Carr: *Cool Cat and Friends* (Brass Wind Publications)

Corelli: *Prelude and Minuet* (Southern)

*Cowell: *Tom Binkley's Tune* (Presser)

*Denwood: *4 Folksongs from Provence* (Emerson)

Dishinger: *Masterworks Solos* (Medici)

Elgar/Werden: *Salut d'amour* (Cimarron Music)

Elgar/Wilson: *Romance* (Rose)

*Ewald: *Romance* (Editions Musicus)

Galliard: *6 Sonatas,* transcribed by Brown, 2 vols. (trombone) (International)

Gliere: *Russian Sailors' Dance* (C. Fischer)

Handel: *Andante and Allegro* (Southern)

Handel: *Sonata 3* (Southern)

*Handel/Wilkinson: *Harmonious Blacksmith* (Studio Music)

Kreisler/Werden: *Liebesfreud* (Cimarron Music)

Lawrance: *Badinage* (Brass Wind Publications)

Lawrance: *Easy Winners for Trombone* (Brass Wind Publications)

Lawrance: *Winnders Galore for Euphonium, Baritone* (Brass Wind Publications)

Marcello: *Adagio* (Whaling)

Martin/Werden: *Come to the Fair* (Cimarron Music)

Mendelssohn/Werden: *For the Mountains Shall Depart* (Cimarron Music)

Mendelssohn/Werden: *On Wings of Song* (Cimarron Music)

*Mowat: *Bach for Trombone* (Brass Wind Publications)

Proctor: *On Your Metal* (Brass Wind Publications)

*Pryor: *Annie Laurie* (trombone) (Ludwig)

*Pryor: *Blue Bells of Scotland* (trombone) (C. Fischer)

*Pryor: *Starlight* (trombone) (C. Fischer)

Ramskill: *From Vivaldi to Fats Waller for Trombone* (Brass Wind Publications)

Roper: *Sonata for Euphonium* (Studio Music)

Rossini: *Largo al Factotum* (Boosey & Hawkes)

*Senaille: *Allegro Spiritoso* (Southern)

*Simon: *Willow Echoes* (C. Fischer)

*Sparke: *Aubade* (Studio Music)

*Sparke: *Song for Ina* (Studio Music)

Top-Line Album for Trombone, Baritone, Euphonium (Brass Wind Publications)

Voxman (ed.): *Concert and Contest Collection* (Rubank)

Difficult
*Alary: *Morçeau de concours* (C. Fischer)

*Bach: *Prelude No. 22,* arranged by Hilgers (Reift)

Bach: *Sonatas 1, 2, 3,* arranged by Marsteller (Southern)

Barat: *Andante and Allegro* (CBCI)

Barat: *Introduction et serenade* (A. Leduc)

*Barat: *Morçeau de concours* (A. Leduc)

*Baratto: *Euphonissimo* (BIM)

*Baratto: *Romanze in F* (BIM)

*Bellstedt: *Napoli* (Southern)

Benson: *Aubade* (H. Leonard)

Blazhevich: *Concerto No. 2* (C. Fischer)

Boda: *Sonatina* (tape) (Whaling)

*Bourgeois: *Concerto for Euphonium* (R. Smith) (Brass Wind Publications)

*Boutry: *Mosaïques* (Tabor Press)

*Bowen: *Euphonium Music* (Rosehill)

Bozza: *Allegro et finale* (A. Leduc)

*Brasch: *Fantasy on Weber's Last Waltz* (H. Brasch)

*A. Butterworth: *Partita* (Comus)

Carr: *Two Folk Songs for Trombone and Piano* (Brass Wind Publications)

*Childs and DeVita: *Softly As I Leave and Other Favorites* (Rosehill)

N. Clark: *Concerto* (Maecenas)

*R. and N. Childs: *Childs' Choice* (Rosehill)

*Clarke: *Music of Herbert L. Clarke* (cornet) (Warner Bros.)

*Clarke: *Sounds from the Hudson* (cornet) (C. Fischer)

Cords: *Concert Fantasie* (original for cornet) (Cundy Bettoney)

*Cosma: *Concerto* (L.A.M. Larghetto)

*Curnow: *Rhapsody for Euphonium* (Rose)

*Curnow: *Symphonic Variants* (Billaudot)

*Ellerby: *Concerto* (Studio Music)

*Filas: *Concerto* (BIM)

*Frackenpohl: *Sonata* (Dorn)

*George: *Sonata* (Alphaeus)

*Guilmant: *Morçeau symphonique* (trombone) (Warner Bros.) (Ed. Mowat, Brass Wind Publications)

*Hartley: *Sonata Euphonica* (Presser)

Hartley: *2 Pieces* (Presser)

*Horovitz: *Concerto* (Novello)

*Hoshina: *Fantasy for Euphonium and Piano* (TUBA)

*Jacob: *Fantasia* (Boosey & Hawkes)

Johnsen: *Preludium* (Norsk)

*Kassatti: *By Gaslight* (BIM)

*Kassatti: *Kino Concertino* (BIM)

Klengel-Falcone: *Concertino No. 1 in B♭* (Belwin)

Koetsier: *Allegro Maestoso* (original for bass trombone) (Donemus)

*Kroll: *Banjo and Fiddle* (Obrasso)

*Madsen: *Sonata* (MusikHF)

Mancone: *Bel automne au Canada* (Billaudot)

*Mantia/Werden: *Believe Me If All Those Endearing Young Charms* (Cimarron Music)

*Marcello (Mead): *Sonata in F Major* (Studio Music)

Marcello/Mortimer: *Sonatas 1 and 2* (Reift)

*Michel: *Scherzo* (Reift)

*Nelhybel: *Concerto* (TUBA)

*Newsome: *Sound of Switzerland* (Obrasso)

de la Nux: *Concert Piece* (SMC)

Poot: *Impromptu* (Andel Uit.)

Presser: *Sonatina* (Presser)

*Pryor: *Thoughts of Love* (trombone) (C. Fischer)

*Reeman: *Sonata for Euphonium* (Studio Music)

*Ross: *Concertino* (with percussion) (Whaling)

Saint-Saens: *Morçeau de concert* (Shawnee)

Saint-Saens/Mowat: *Cavatine, Op. 144* (Brass Wind Publications)

Schubert/Werden: *Arpeggione Sonata* (Cimarron Music)

Schumann/Werden: *Romance No. 2* (Cimarron Music)

*Sparke: *Concerto* (Studio Music)

*Sparke: *Fantasy* (R. Smith)

*Sparke: *Rhapsody from Baritone* (Studio Music)

Szentpali: *Pearls* (BIM)

Takacs: *Sonate* (Sidemton)

Townsend: *Chamber Concerto No. 2* (Mercury)

Uber: *Sonata* (Editions Musicus)

*Vaughan Williams: *6 Studies in English Folksong* (Galaxy)

*Vaughan Williams: *A Winter's Willow* (Medici)

*White: *Lyric Suite* (Schirmer)

*Wilby: *Concerto* (Rosehill)

*Wilder: *Concerto* (Margun)

*Wilder: *Sonata* (Margun)

*Wilhelm: *Concertino* (Manu)

Woodfield: *Double Brass* (Obrasso)

Young: *Euphonium Sonata* (R. Smith)

Young: *Euphonium Suite* (R. Smith)

Baritone and Euphonium Books[9]

Bahr, Edward R. *Trombone/Euphonium Discography*. Stevens Point, Wis.: Index House, 1988.

*Bevan, Clifford. *The Tuba Family*. New York: Scribner's, 1978.

*Bowman, Brian L. *Practical Hints on Playing the Baritone (Euphonium)*. Melville, N.Y.: Belwin-Mills, 1983.

*Childs, Robert and Nicholas. *A Method for Brass Players*. Kirklees Music/Obrasso Verlag AG.

Griffiths, John R. *The Low Brass Guide*. Hackensack, N.J.: Jerona Music, 1980.

*Lehman, Arthur. *The Art of Euphonium Playing*. Poughkeepsie, N.Y.: Robert Hoe.

*Louder, Earle L. *Euphonium Music Guide*. Evanston, Ill.: The Instrumentalist Co., 1978.

Miles, David Royal. *An Annotated Bibliography of Selected Contemporary Euphonium Solo Literature by American Composers*. Tuba Press, 1992.

*Phillips, Harvey, and W. Winkle. *The Art of Tuba and Euphonium Playing*. Secaucus, N.J.: Summy-Birchard (Warner Bros. Publications), 1992.

Preinsperger, Ewald. *Solo-Tenorhorn und Blasorchester: Verzeichnis von über 500 Solowerken für ein oder mehrere Tenorhörner/Euphonien und Blasorchester*. Vienna, Austria: J. Kliment, 1995.

Rose, W. H. *Studio Class Manual for Tuba and Euphonium*. Houston, Tex.: Iola Publications, 1980.

Werden, D. *Euphonium Music Guide*. New London, Conn.: Whaling Music

Werden, D. *Scoring for Euphonium*. New London, Conn.: Whaling Music

*Winter, Denis. *Euphonium Music Guide*. New London, Conn.: Whaling Music, 1983.

[9]Articles of interest to the euphonium players appear in *The Instrumentalist,* the ITEA *Journal,* and other periodicals listed in Appendix C.

CHAPTER 7

THE TUBA

TO THE NONTUBIST, today's tuba world is a confusing jumble of instruments of differing keys, types and numbers of valves, sizes, and so forth. As with the rest of the brass family, the great variety of tubas now available reflects the need for more specialized and improved instruments to fit different performance situations.

There are two broad categories of tuba: bass tubas in F and E♭ and contrabass tubas in C and B♭. (The latter are usually identified as CC and BB♭ tubas; large-bore E♭ instruments are sometimes designated EE♭.) In the United States, orchestral tubists generally prefer a five-valve CC as a standard instrument (see Figures 7.1 and 7.2) but also use a five-valve F or four-valve E♭ for high passages and some solo work. The BB♭ serves primarily as a band instrument, but it is widely used in orchestras in Germany and Eastern Europe. The E♭ tuba, once familiar in American bands, is the principal tuba in British symphony orchestras, brass ensembles, and brass and military bands. In the United States, the E♭ increasingly serves as an alternative to the F tuba and as a solo instrument.

■ VALVE TYPES

Among the most obvious differences in tubas is that some are built with rotary valves and others with piston valves. Piston valves offer a cleaner articulation and are generally better in technical passages. Rotary valves, on the other hand, encourage a smooth legato. The difference between rotary and piston tubas is more than just the valve types, however. The tapered portions of the instruments, including leadpipes and bell contours, as well as the layouts of the tubing are quite different between the two instruments. These variables, along with the effects of the valve systems, impart different timbres and distinctive playing qualities to the two types of tuba, irrespective of key.

For a number of years, rotary valve tubas were used in most American symphony orchestras. This was due primarily to the unavailability of large-bore piston valve CC tubas suitable for orchestral use. To fill this void, orchestral tubists turned to large-bore German tubas, which are traditionally made with rotary valves. As these became standardized in American orchestras, they were also adopted by bands and wind ensembles. The picture today is quite different. Due to the persistent efforts of several eminent American orchestral players and as a result of new design improvements, excellent CC and F piston and rotary valve instruments are widely available. The choice of valve type now centers more on personal preference than on practicality. Makers such as Alexander, Hirsbrunner, B&S, Kurath, Yamaha, Meinl-Weston, and others offer both types of instrument in a variety of sizes. The American firms Conn and King now produce high-quality piston tubas in BB♭ and CC. The large-bore piston valve CC tubas are based in their design to some extent on an old, well-known American York tuba that was played by the great tubist Arnold Jacobs during his long career in the Chicago Symphony Orchestra.

FIGURE 7.1
Five-rotary-valve CC tuba
(Alexander).

The placement of the valves is an important consideration for the player. On rotary valve tubas, the valve levers are arranged vertically at the center of the instrument. This allows the right arm and hand to be in a relaxed position, assisting finger dexterity. An additional benefit of this layout is that the valve slides are directed upward so that they can be moved by the left hand in making adjustments in intonation. The opposite of this is the top-action piston valve tuba, in which the valves are placed in line beneath the top bow. Some tubists feel that this places the right hand in an uncomfortable position, creating tension. Front-action (side-action) piston valve tubas have the valves located so that the valve caps face outward, permitting a similar hand position as on rotary valve tubas, and also have upward-directed valve slides, permitting intonation adjustment. This arrangement is generally considered preferable.

■ DIMENSIONS AND BORE

There is substantial variation in the size of tubas, not only in bore and bell diameter, but in overall dimensions and weight. For example, BB♭ tubas are made with main bore diameters of 0.610″ (15.5 mm) to 0.920″ (23.4 mm). Bell diameters may vary from 14³⁄₈″ (365.55 mm) to 24″ (609.6 mm). Weights range from 6.132 to 14.512 kg.[1]

[1]Clifford Bevan, *The Tuba Family* (New York: Scribner's, 1978), p. 126.

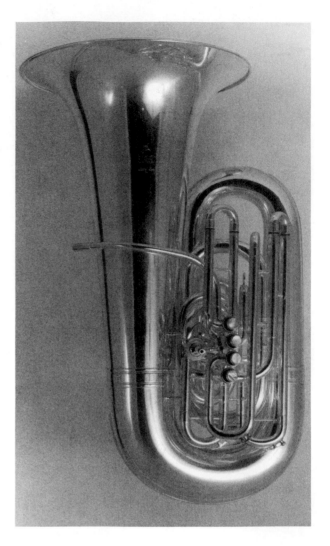

FIGURE 7.2
Five-piston-valve CC tuba
(Hirsbrunner).

Among rotary valve tubas, three general sizes can be distinguished: a smaller bore of approximately 0.740″ (17.8 mm), a standard bore of 0.778″ (19.7 mm), and an extra-large bore of 0.835″ (21.2 mm). These are sometimes identified as 3/4, 4/4, and 5/4 models. There is, however, considerable diversity among manufacturers as to the actual bore used under each label. The largest bore sizes are descendants of Václav Červeny's *Kaiserbass*, introduced in the 1880s. (Červeny produced the first contrabass tubas in CC and BB♭ in 1845.)

CC tubas are built in the same large bore sizes as BB♭s. This gives the CC an equal volume of tone while preserving its advantages in fingering and projection. The bores of orchestral (five-rotary-valve CC) tubas are usually in the range of 0.778 to .835,″ but even larger bores are sometimes used. The largest piston valve CC tubas are in the range of 0.748 to 0.787″ (19–20 mm). Typical F tuba bore sizes are 0.681″ (17.3 mm) to 0.770″ (19.5 mm). E♭ tuba bores usually average around 0.730″ (18.5 mm). In comparison, three-valve student models in BB♭ generally run from 0.610″ (15.5 mm) to 0.670″ (17 mm).

Tubas may be wrapped in a compact or more open pattern, with heights varying from 33″ (838.2 mm) to 48″ (1219.2 mm). Some players feel that the more compact instruments are rather stuffy in response, due to sharp bends in the tubing. The height of the largest instruments sometimes presents problems to individual players, who must alter their playing position to reach the mouthpiece.

The variables of key, size, and bore allow tubists to adapt more fully to the needs of differing repertoire. For example, an orchestral tubist might use a large-bore CC in performances of Bruckner and Wagner and other large-scale works but change to a smaller instrument for compositions having a light, transparent texture. Similarly, an F or E♭ tuba would probably be chosen for high-register solos, such as are found in Stravinsky's *Petrushka*. For brass ensemble playing, a large bore EE♭ might be used.

▣ VALVE SYSTEMS

If the valve systems fitted to modern tubas appear complex, it should be noted that the first tuba (of 1835) by Wieprecht and Moritz was a five-valve model in F. Today, tubists generally agree that three valves are inadequate and six valves excessive. On standard four- and five-valve models, the purpose of the added valves is to extend the low range and improve intonation.

Unlike the trumpet, the fundamental of the tuba's harmonic series is a fully usable note. A fourth valve is added to extend the range downward[2] from the lowest valve combination (1–2–3; fingered 2–4 when a fourth valve is added) to the fundamental, since notes of the chromatic octave from the fundamental to the second harmonic are called for by composers. The sharpness caused when valves are used in combination is severe in this octave, although intonation can be corrected to some extent by pulling valve slides on individual notes. The best solution is a fifth valve, which affords a greater selection of fingerings and yields the most accurate intonation in this range. Six-valve tubas were developed for players who wish to use the F tuba as their principal instrument. The sixth valve enables this instrument to cover the same range as the CC. Most professional tubists (outside France) find the six-valve arrangement overly complex and prefer a five-valve system.

▣ USING THE FOURTH AND FIFTH VALVES

Greater mechanical correction is necessary on the tuba than on other brass instruments, due to the length of the vibrating air columns. The most effective method of controlling intonation is by moving valve slides while playing. In order to do this, the valve slides must go upward, as on rotary valve and front-action tubas. On instruments of this type, all but the second valve slide are accessible to the left hand, with the first slide being used most often. The fourth and fifth valves come into play in the lowest octave and are used in combination with the adjustment of valve slides to center pitches in this range.

The fourth valve not only extends the range down to the fundamental but offers an alternative to the sharp 1–3 and 1–2–3 fingerings:

To correct intonation, the valve slide should be pulled out for all fingerings circled (◯). When an arrow is added to the circle (⬆), the valve slide should be pushed inward.

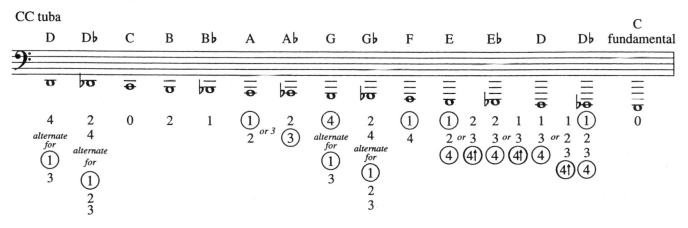

[2] This is done by lowering the basic pitch of the instrument downward a perfect fourth.

BB♭ tuba

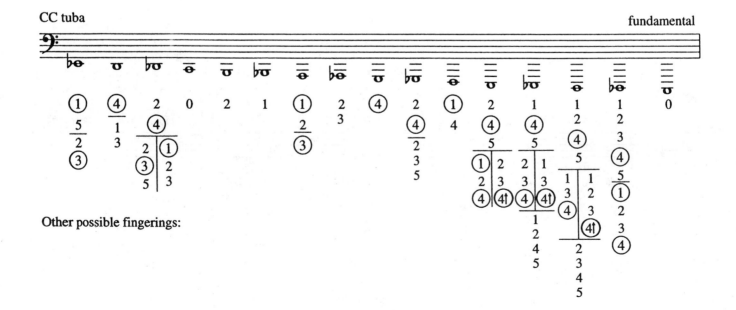

It is obvious that all tubas, except perhaps for inexpensive models intended for beginners, should be made with at least four valves. The four-valve system does have its limitations, however. The semitone above the fundamental is almost unusable due to sharpness, and it is only through the addition of a fifth valve that truly accurate intonation and a centered sound can be achieved.

In a five-valve system, the first four valves function as in the four-valve system. The fifth valve lowers the fundamental either five-quarters of a tone or two whole tones, depending on the length of the valve slide. The former is sometimes known as a *flat whole step* system and the latter as a *2/3* system (the 2/3 refers to the fifth valve's intervallic similarity to the normal 2–3 fingering, which also lowers the fundamental by two tones). Either system is effective, and the choice of one over the other is a matter of individual preference.

In the flat whole step mode, the fifth valve is used as follows (choose the fingering that yields the best intonation):

CC tuba

Other possible fingerings:

The fingering pattern for the 2/3 system is as follows:

CC tuba

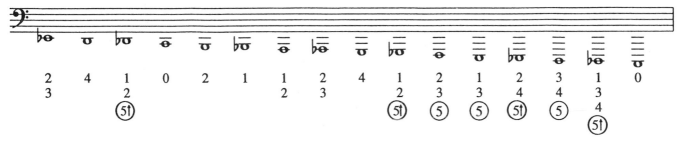

Well-known tubist Roger Bobo has recommended that in the latter system a trigger mechanism be fitted to the fifth valve slide to facilitate its adjustment.

Another difference in five-valve systems is how the fifth valve is operated. On many tubas, an actuating lever is placed adjacent to the thumb ring, with linkage connecting it to the fifth valve. Other models have a spatula attached directly to the fifth valve, which is operated with the left hand. The disadvantage of the latter arrangement is that the left hand is not free to adjust valve slides when the fifth valve is in use. Roger Bobo has advocated a dual linkage that would enable the player to operate the valve with either hand, as desired.

■ THE AUTOMATIC COMPENSATING SYSTEM

An entirely different approach to the problem of low-register intonation is the compensating system, devised in 1874 by English acoustician David Blaikley, which is incorporated in some baritones, euphoniums, and tubas.[3] In this system, corrective lengths of tubing are automatically added when the fourth (compensating) valve is used in combination with the other valves. While the Blaikley system does not solve all intonation problems, it works quite well. Previously, it was only available in top-action instruments of somewhat smaller bore than those used in American symphony orchestras. Tubas of this type are the principal instrument in British orchestras, bands, and brass ensembles (although regular large-bore rotary and piston-valve BB♭ and CC tubas are used for certain orchestral works). Recently, the Besson firm introduced the excellent model 983, which is front-action and of large bore for an EE♭. It would be very interesting to see if the Blaikley system works well on large-bore orchestral CC tubas, but as yet these have not been made available.

■ INTONATION

In addition to the intonation difficulties of the lower range, the tubist must be prepared to cope with some problem notes in the middle and upper registers. No absolute rules can be set, for individual instruments vary in this respect. This is a fertile period in the development of the tuba, and one of the prime goals is improved intonation.

Faulty intonation can be corrected by substituting an alternate fingering, moving a valve slide, or combining these measures. Whenever possible, it is preferable to adjust a note mechanically because of the negative effect on tone and stability caused by trying to force an off-center note into tune with the embouchure. Through careful practice,

[3] The Blaikley system is discussed more fully in Chapter 6.

tubists learn to incorporate the necessary slide movements or alternate fingering into their normal techniques.

The current trend among manufacturers of high-quality tubas is to shorten the outer tubes of the valve slides (as is customary with the horn) to allow more room for slide adjustment. The following chart applies to this type of instrument. On older tubas, more use of alternate fingerings may be necessary.

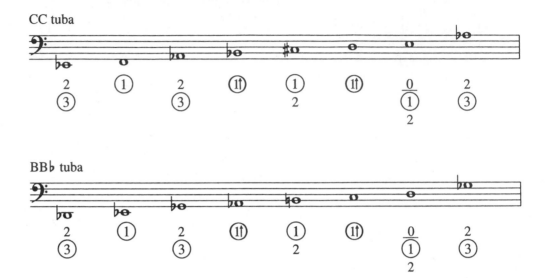

The fifth harmonic might be flat when played open:

If it is, it may be played 1–2 while pulling out the first valve slide. The 1–2 combination tends to be sharp an octave lower, and some adjustment of the slide will probably be necessary to correct it. An electronic tuner should be used to determine the best means of correction for other notes.

Regardless of how well the tubist can learn to play in tune when practicing, further adjustments will undoubtedly have to be made when performing in an ensemble. Within a brass section, the tubist must listen intently to the first trombone and first trumpet to provide a clear sense of pitch for the inner players to match. The ability of the tubist to balance and match the intonation of the first trumpet does a great deal to define the pitch center for the entire brass section.

■ BB♭ AND CC TUBAS

The preference of American orchestral tubists for the CC instrument is based on three factors. First, like the C trumpet, the CC tuba responds well in making "cold" entrances and is particularly responsive and flexible. Second, since orchestras frequently play in sharp keys, the awkward fingerings that would result if a BB♭ instrument were used is avoided. The third factor is that the timbre of the CC tuba projects with greater clarity. Some players find little difference in tone between the two instruments, but others, particularly German and Eastern European performers, have a definite preference for the tone of the BB♭.

The BB♭ tuba remains the primary band instrument, but CC tubas are sometimes found in bands and wind ensembles within schools of music, since tuba majors are

FIGURE 7.3
EE♭ tuba (Besson), played by
the late John Fletcher,
a legendary British tubist.

accustomed to playing the CC as their principal instrument. It is important, however, that, when parts are doubled by more than one player, the same key instrument is used, to avoid conflicts in intonation. At one time, bell-front (recording-bell) tubas were often seen in large bands, but these have been replaced by standard upright-bell models. The directionality of the forward radiating bell tended to lose the characteristic roundness of the tuba's timbre and to unbalance the brass section.

■ E♭ AND F TUBAS

E♭ and F tubas are predominantly used as auxiliary instruments to the normal CC when unusually high passages are encountered or when a lighter sound is desired (see Figures 7.3 and 7.4). The F is also widely found in performing solo literature because of its range and flexibility. The standardized use of large-bore E♭ (EE♭) tubas in Britain probably came about because the first British tubists were former euphonium players who sought an instrument that retained some of the euphonium's technical flexibility and response. A small-bore piston valve tuba in F was developed, and this provided an agreeable "bottom" to orchestral brass sections until the end of World War II.[4] Up to that time, smaller-bore trumpets, trombones, and French-type piston valve horns were mainly in use. As brass sections adopted larger instruments in the postwar years, British tubists changed to the brass band EE♭, which combines a fuller tone with much of the F's flexibility.

Rotary valve F tubas are often used on the European continent (particularly in German orchestras), along with contrabass models. The Vienna concert tuba,[5] like the Vienna horn, is a unique model related to instruments of an earlier epoch, in this case the first Wieprecht–Moritz instrument of the 1830s. Pitched in F, the Vienna tuba is viewed by Viennese players as a bass-contrabass, since its six rotary valves allow it to cover both ranges. The comparatively narrow bore and less flaring bell give this instrument a strong, clear sound in which higher partials are more present than in the timbres of other tubas.

[4] Ralph Vaughan Williams wrote his technically demanding *Bass Tuba Concerto* for the F tuba.
[5] The history and evolution of the Vienna concert tuba is discussed in Gerhard Zechmeister, "Die Entwicklung der Wiener Konzerttuba," *Brass Bulletin*, 75 (1991), pp. 44–47. (Translations in English and French are included.)

FIGURE 7.4
F tuba (Miraphone),
played by Scott
Mendoker, New
York freelance
artist and faculty
member at Rutgers
University.

This is felt to integrate better within the traditional Viennese brass sound than the darker and more massive tone of other tubas, which tends to drop out of the section's blended timbres.

An important application of the E♭ and F tubas is in the brass quintet, where their lighter timbres can contribute a more effective balance than a contrabass. In fact, the ideal brass ensemble instrument is the large-bore EE♭. This instrument has sufficient fullness and resonance of tone to support the brass ensemble while creating a superb balance and clarity in the overall sound. It seems to give the entire ensemble greater resonance and offer superior agility and clarity in fast-moving passages. Unfortunately, many brass quintets suffer from an imbalance created by the consuming tone of large BB♭ or CC tubas, and this is often accepted without question.[6] If a contrabass must be used, it should be one of the smaller sizes.

■ THE FRENCH SIX-VALVE C TUBA

Although practically obsolete today, the French C tuba is of interest because of the large body of solo literature and orchestral parts written for it by French composers. In reality, it is an extended-range tenor tuba pitched one tone higher than the euphonium and of somewhat greater bore. Through the addition of two sets of valves (one for each hand), a full four octaves is obtainable, from the lowest notes of the contrabass CC into the normal euphonium range. Parts for this unusual instrument have caused confusion, since neither the range nor the technical demands are well suited to bass and contrabass tubas. French solo literature is often neglected for this reason.

The concept of a tenor-sized bass for the brass section is not as peculiar as it may seem. French composers have always shown a predilection for mixtures of clearly defined timbres rather than blended sound. The French C tuba was well suited to this aesthetic while offering additional possibilities as a solo instrument. Such parts as are found

---

[6] A clear idea of the ideal balance that can be achieved with an EE♭ may be gained by listening to recordings of the great Philip Jones Brass Ensemble (currently available recordings are listed in Appendix B). The superb player on these recordings was the legendary John Fletcher, former tubist of the London Symphony Orchestra.

in Stravinsky's *Petrushka* and *The Rite of Spring* and the *Bydlo* solo in Ravel's transcription of Mussorgsky's *Pictures at an Exhibition*[7] were specifically written for this unique instrument and are an indication of its capabilities.

In French orchestras today, six-valve F or CC contrabass tubas are used for the majority of the repertoire, while the French C is reserved for solos originally written for it.

■ THE TUBA MUTE

Richard Strauss was the first to write for the muted tuba, in *Don Quixote* (1897). Since composers now call for a muted timbre with some frequency, a mute is considered a necessary part of the tubist's regular equipment. The problem is to find a mute that fits the bell taper accurately and plays in tune. Tuba mutes are normally in straight-mute form, but a few of the other types (such as cup mutes and practice mutes) have now become available.

■ NOTATION

Lacking any historical convention that the fundamental must be written as C (as with the horn and trumpet), the BB♭, E♭, and F tubas function as nontransposing instruments, with the player using the appropriate fingering to yield concert pitch. When more than one tuba is used, such as the CC or F, the player must learn a different set of fingerings for each instrument. There are exceptions to this practice. In British brass bands, all instruments except the bass trombone are considered transposing instruments and read treble clef. The bass tuba in E♭ is treated as a transposing instrument in much of the French solo literature, although parts for the six-valve C tuba are also usually included. (In French C tuba parts, there is some use of the nontransposed treble clef.) This is often the practice in French band scores and in some of Verdi's operas.

In order to have access to a greater variety of study material, it is important for tubists to develop the ability to read down an octave. This brings trombone and euphonium literature into a practicable range. It is also helpful to be able to read treble clef in order to perform etudes and solos written for trumpet and horn.

■ THE GOLDEN AGE OF THE TUBA

The last three and a half decades have seen more activity in the tuba world than in any period of its history. Today's generation of tubists is no longer content to remain in the background and has broken through barriers that were considered impassable 50 years ago. There are now several internationally recognized soloists, but the most striking aspect of the movement is the incredibly high standard of playing that is now taken for granted. Interesting new solo works are constantly appearing that exploit the possibilities of the tuba and the virtuosity of the player in previously unimagined ways. Undoubtedly, this evolution will continue into the future, with more recognition and opportunities for the solo tuba as each new generation of tubists carries the movement forward.

RECOMMENDED LITERATURE FOR TUBA[8]

Complete Methods

*Arban: *Arban–Bell Method* (C. Colin)

*Arban: *Famous Method for Slide and Valve Trombone and Baritone,* ed. Randall and Mantia (read octave down) (C. Fischer)

*Arban/Young: *Arban Complete Method for Tuba* (Encore Music)

Beeler: *Method,* 2 vols. (Warner Bros.)

*Bobo: *Mastering the Tuba,* 3 vols. (BIM)

[7] Today, the Stravinsky parts are usually played on an F or EE♭ tuba. *Bydlo* is either played on F, EE♭, or euphonium (tenor tuba). The solo is written in the tuba part.
[8] Essential material is noted with an asterisk. Repertoire lists appear in the texts by Bell, Bevan, Griffiths, and Morris.

Geib: *Method* (C. Fischer)

*Lelong: *Méthode* (Billaudot)

Elementary Methods

*Arban: *Method,* 1st and 2nd year, ed. Prescott (C. Fischer)

*Bell: *Foundation to Tuba Playing* (C. Fischer)

Endresen: *Method for E♭ Tuba* (M. M. Cole)

Hovey: *Rubank Elementary Method* (Rubank)

Kuhn-Cimera: *Method* (Belwin)

Studies

Medium to Medium-Difficult

Bell: *Blazhevich Interpretations* (C. Colin)

Bell: *William Bell Daily Routine for Tuba* (Encore)

*Bobo: *Mastering the Tuba,* (BIM)

Bordogni: *43 Bel Canto Studies,* transcribed Roberts (R. King)

*Bordogni/Rochut: *Melodious Etudes,* books 1 and 2, (for trombone) (C. Fischer)

Bordogni/W. Jacobs: *Legato Etudes* (Encore)

Bordogni/W. Jacobs: *Low Legato Etudes* (Encore)

*Bourgeois: *Per Tuba ad Astra* (Brass Wind Publications)

Carnaud: *25 Études* (Salabert)

*Carnaud: *25 exercises sur la gamme* (Salabert)

*Concone: *Legato Etudes,* ed. Shoemaker (C. Fischer)

Endresen: *Supplementary Studies* (Rubank)

Fink: *Studies in Legato* (C. Fischer)

Getchell: *Practical Studies,* 2 vols. (Belwin-Mills)

Girard: *15 études sur le phrase* (Billaudot)

Girard: *50 études faciles et progressives,* 2 vols. (Billaudot)

*Green: *Tuba Eurhythmics* (Warwick)

*Gregson: *20 Supplementary Tunes for Tuba* (Brass Wind Publications)

Gower and Voxman: *Rubank Advanced Method,* 2 vols. (Rubank)

*Hilgers: *Daily Exercises* (Reift)

W. Jacobs: *Warm-Up Studies* (Encore)

*Johnson: *The Tuneful Tuba* (easy–very easy) (Brass Wind Publications)

Knaub: *Progressive Techniques* (Belwin)

Lawrance: *Featuring Melody for Tuba* (Brass Wind Publications)

Little: *Embouchure Builder* (Pro Art)

*Pares: *Scales* (Rubank)

Ridgeon: *Eight Graded Lip Flexibilities for Tuba* (Brass Wind Publications)

Ronka: *Modern Daily Warm-Ups and Drills* (C. Fischer)

*Schlossberg: *Daily Drills and Technical Studies* (trombone) (M. Baron) (8va) (medium to difficult)

Sear: *Etudes* (Cor)

Skornicka and Boltz: *Rubank Intermediate Method* (Rubank)

Street: *Scales and Arpeggios* (Boosey & Hawkes)

Uber: *25 Early Studies* (Southern)

Williams: *Little Classics* (Colin)

Difficult

Bach: *Bach for Tuba,* transcribed Bixby and Bobo (Western International)

*Blazhevich: *70 Studies* (R. King)

*Bordogni/Rochut: *Melodies Etudes,* book 3 (for trombone) (C. Fischer)

Cimera: *73 Advanced Studies* (Belwin-Mills)

Gallay: *30 Studies* (R. King)

Gallay: *40 Preludes* (R. King)

Girard: *15 études de concours* (Billaudot)

*W. Jacobs: *Low-Register Development for Tuba* (Encore)

*Kopprasch: *60 Studies* (R. King) (medium to difficult)

Kuehn: *28 Advanced Studies* (Southern)

Kuehn: *60 Musical Studies,* 2 vols. (Southern)

Paudert: *18 Etudes* (Encore)

Robinson: *Advanced Conditioning Studies* (Whaling)

*Snedecor: *Low Etudes* (Pas Music)

Tyrrell: *40 Advanced Studies* (Boosey & Hawkes)

Uber: *Concert Etudes* (Southern)

Vasiliev: *24 Melodious Etudes* (R. King)

Unaccompanied Tuba

Difficult

Agrell: *Eccentric Dances* (BIM)

Anonymous: *Hijazker Longa* (Whaling)

Adler: *Canto VII* (Boosey & Hawkes)

*Arnold: *Fantasy* (Faber)

Bach: *Six Short Solo Suites* (R. King)

Croley: *Variazioni* (Philharmusica)

Dragonetti: *Concert Etude* (Philharmusica)

Dubrovay: *Caprice for Tuba* (Simrock)

Frackenpohl: *Studies on Christmas Carols* (Kendor)

Gallagher: *Sonata Brève* (BIM)

Globokar: *Echanges* (Peters)

Gregson: *Alarum pour tuba solo* (Intrada)

Haddad: *Short Suite* (Seesaw)

Hartley: *Music for Tuba* (Philharmusica)

Hartley: *Suite* (Presser)

Kagel: *Mirum* (Universal)

Khoudoyan: *Elégie* (BIM)

Kraft: *Encounters II* (BIM)

Másson: *Aeolus* (BIM)

Másson: *Boreas* (BIM)

Penderecki: *Capriccio* (Schott)

Penn: *3 Essays* (Seesaw)

*Persichetti: *Parable* (Presser)

*Persichetti: *Serenade No. 12* (Presser)

Poore: *Vox Superius* (Arts Lab)

Powell: *Midnight Realities* (BIM)

Presser: *8 Episodes* (Presser)

Reck: *5 Studies* (Peters)

Slavicky: *Echoes* (BIM)

Stevens: *Remembrance* (BIM)

Stevens: *Salve Venere, Salve Marte* (BIM)

Szentpali: *Caprices* (Nos. 1, 2, 3) (BIM)

Szentpali: *Variations for a Hungarian Children's Song* (BIM)

Tisné: *Monodie III* (Billaudot)

Tuthill: *Tiny Tunes for Tuba* (Presser)

Wilder: *Convalescence Suite* (Margun Music)

Tuba and Piano

Easy

Adams: *The Holy City* (Kjos)

Bach: *Air and Bourée*, arranged by Bell and Swanson (C. Fischer)

Bach: *Gavotte*, arranged by Smith (Belwin-Mills)

Bell: *Gavotte* (C. Fischer)

Bell: *Jig Elephantine* (C. Fischer)

Bell: *Low-Down Bass* (C. Fischer)

Bell: *Melodious Etude* (Belwin-Mills)

Bell: *Nautical John* (C. Fischer)

Bizet: *Toreador's Song*, arranged by Holmes (Rubank)

Daellenbach: *Beginning Tuba Solos* (with cassette accompaniment) (H. Leonard)

Daellenbach: *Easy Tuba Solos* (with cassette accompaniment) (H. Leonard)

Gregson and Ridgeon: *Nine Miniatures for E♭ Bass/Tuba* (Brass Wind Publications)

Grieg: *In the Hall of the Mountain King*, arranged by Holmes (Rubank)

Handel: *Honor and Arms from Samson* (Schirmer)

Keynotes Album for E♭ Bass/Tuba (Brass Wind Publications)

Kreisler: *Rondo* (Southern)

Lawrance: *Easy Winners for Tuba* (with CD accompaniment) (Brass Wind Publications)

Lawrance: *Six Modern Pieces for E♭ Bass/Tuba* (Brass Wind Publications)

Schumann: *The Jolly Farmer* (C. Fischer)

Up-Front Album for E♭ Bass/Tuba (2 vols.) (Brass Wind Publications)

*Wekselblatt (ed.): *First Solos for the Tuba Player* (Schirmer)

Medium to Medium-Difficult

Albeniz: *Cancion Catalan* (Reift)

Albeniz: *Love Song* (Reift)

Albeniz: *Malaguena* (Reift)

Albeniz: *Orientale* (Reift)

Beethoven: *Variations on a Theme by Handel*, **arranged by Bell** (C. Fischer)

*Benson: *Arioso* (Belwin)

*Benson: *Helix* (C. Fischer)

N. Clarke: *Sketches from Don Quixote for Tuba* (Brass Wind Publications)

Capuzzi: *Andante and Rondo* (Hinrichsen)

Daellenbach: *Intermediate Tuba Solos* (with cassette accompaniment) (H. Leonard)

Davis: *Variations on a Theme of Robert Schumann* (Southern)

*Fletcher: *BB♭ Bass Solos* (Chester)

*Fletcher: *E♭ Bass Solos* (Chester)

*Fletcher: *Tuba Solos* (Tuba in C) (Chester)

*Haddad: *Suite* (Shawnee)

*Jackman: *3 Tuba Rags* (Novello)

*Jacob: *6 Little Tuba Pieces* (Emerson Ed.)

*Jacob: *Tuba Suite* (Boosey & Hawkes)

Lawrance: *Winners Galore for Tuba* (Brass Wind Publications)

Mozart (Morris): *O Isis and Osiris* (BIM)

Ostling (ed.): *Tuba Solos*, 2 vols. (Belwin)

Ostrander (ed.): *Concert Album* (Editions Musicus)

* Perantoni: *Master Solos* (H. Leonard)

Phillips: *8 Bel Canto Songs* (Shawnee)

*Proctor: *Tuber Music* (Brass Wind Publications)

*Ramskill: *From Vivaldi to Fats Waller for E♭ Bass/Tuba* (Brass Wind Publications)

Reed: *Fantasia a due* (Belwin)

Senaille: *Introduction and Allegro Spiritoso* (Hinrichsen)

Top-Line Album for the E♭ Bass/Tuba (Brass Wind Publications)

Voxman (ed.): *Concert and Contest Collection* (Rubank)

*Wekselblatt (ed.): *Solos for the Tuba Player* (Schirmer)

Difficult

*Albinoni: *Concerto in D Minor* (Reift)

*Arutiunian: *Concerto* (BIM)

Baader-Nobs: *Bifurcation* (BIM)

Bach: *Choral Prelude BWV 659* (Reift)

Bach: *Sonata No. 2* (Reift)

Barat: *Introduction and Dance*, arranged by Smith (Southern)

Baska: *Tuba Sonata* (Presser)

Bellstedt: *Introduction and Tarantella* (Southern)

Beversdorf: *Sonata* (Southern)

*Bourgeois: *Concerto for Bass Tuba* (Brass Wind Publications)

*Bourgeois: *Fantasy Pieces for Tuba* (Brass Wind Publications)

*Broughton: *Sonata* (Masters)

Boda: *Sonatina* (R. King)

Bozza: *Concertino* (A. Leduc)

Chappot: *Concerto* (Reift)

Chebrou: *Tubafolia-Concerto* (BIM)

Childs: *Seaview* (M. M. Cole)

Croley: *3 Espressioni* (Philharmusica)

Filas: *Sonate* (BIM)

Frackenpohl: *Sonata* (Kendor)

Gower: *Sonata* (BIM)

*Gregson: *Concerto* (Novello)

Grunelius: *Drei Lyrische Szenen* (Walhall)

Grunelius: *Tuba-Triptychon* (Walhall)

Gulya: *Burlesque* (BIM)

Hartley: *Sonatina* (Fema Music)

*Hindemith: *Sonate* (Schott)

*Horovitz: *Tuba Concerto* (Studio)

Ionel: *Concerto No. 1* (BIM)

Ionel: *Fantezie nocturna* (BIM)

Ionel: *Galop* (BIM)

Ionel: *Konzertstück* (BIM)

Ionel: *Musical Joke (Gluma Muzicala)* (BIM)

Ionel: *Rondo International* (BIM)

Ionel: *Rumanian Dances Nos. 1–6* (BIM)

Ionel: *Visare (Dreaming)* (BIM)

*Jacob: *Bagatelles* (Emerson Ed.)

Jacobsen: *Tubabuffo* (Swensk)

Jevtic: *Balkan's Ayers Rock* (BIM)

Jevtic: *Concerto* (BIM)

Joubert: *Zénobie la Perdix* (Martin)

Kellaway: *Dr. Martin Luther King, in Memoriam* (BIM)

Kellaway: *Morning Song* (BIM)

Kellaway: *Songs of Ascent* (BIM)

Kellaway: *Westwood Song* (BIM)

Koetsier: *Concertino, op.77* (BIM)

Koetsier: *Sonatina* (Donemus)

Krol: *Falstaff Concerto* (BIM)

*Lebedev: *Concert Allegro* (Editions Musicus)

Madsen: *Konzert* (Musikk-Huset)

Madsen: *Sonata, op. 34* (Musikk-Huset)

Madsen: *Sonate, op. 25* (Musikk-Huset)

Másson: *Maes Howe* (Tuba Concerto with orchestra) (BIM)

Meier: *Eclipse finale?* (BIM)

Mortimer: *Tuba Concerto* (Reift)

Nelybel: *Concert Piece* (E. C. Kerby)

Newsome: *Basso Brazilio* (Obrasso)

Newton: *Millennium* (Studio)

Pauer: *Tubonetta* (BIM)

Plog: *Statements* (BIM)

Plog: *Three Miniatures* (BIM)

Plog: *Tuba Concerto* (BIM)

Proust: *Tuba Blues* (Combre)

Reynolds: *Sonata* (C. Fischer)

Rodgers: *Chaconne* (BIM)

Sowerby: *Chaconne* (C. Fischer)

Saglietti: *Concertissimo* (BIM)

Saglietti: *Concerto* (BIM)

*Salzedo: *Sonata* (Chester)

*Steptoe: *Concerto for Tuba* (Stainer & Bell)

*H. Stevens: *Sonatina* (Southern)

J. Stevens: *Journey* (BIM)

J. Stevens: *Liberation of Sisyphus* (BIM)

T. Stevens: *Variations in Olden Style* (BIM)

Strukow: *Concerto* (BIM)

Strukow: *Elégie* (BIM)

Szentpali: *Concerto* (BIM)

Szentpali: *Création* (BIM)

Thomson: *Jay Rozen: Portrait and Fugue for Bass Tuba and Piano* (Heilman)

Uber: *Sonata* (Editions Musicus)

Uber: *Sonatina* (Southern)

*Vaughan Williams: *Concerto* (Oxford)

*Vaughan Williams: *6 Studies in English Folksong* (Galaxy)

White: *Basingstoke* (Warwick)

*White: *Sonata* (Ludwig)

*Wilder: *Sonata* (Mentor)

*Wilder: *Suite No. 1* (Margun)

J. Williams: *Concerto* (H. Leonard)

Zamecnik: *Concertino* (BIM)

Books on the Tuba[9]

Bell, William. *Encyclopedia of Literature for the Tuba.* New York: Charles Colin, 1967.

*Bevan, Clifford. *The Tuba Family.* New York: Scribner's, 1978.

Bird, Gary. *Program Notes for the Solo Tuba.* Bloomington, Ind.: Indiana University Press, 1994.

Cummings, Barton. *The Contemporary Tuba.* New London, Conn.: Whaling Music, 1984.

*Frederiksen, Brian. *Arnold Jacobs: Song and Wind.* WindSong Press Limited, 1996.

Griffiths, John R. *The Low Brass Guide.* Hackensack, N.J.: Jerona Music, 1980.

Heyde, Herbert. *Trompeten, Posaunen, Tuben.* Leipzig: VEB Deutscher Verlag für Musik, 1980.

* Jones, Philip. *John Fletcher, Tuba Extraordinary: A Celebration.* London: John Fletcher Trust, 1997.

Little, Donald C. *Practical Hints on Playing the Tuba.* Melville, N.Y.: Belwin-Mills, 1984.

Mason, J. Kent. *The Tuba Handbook.* Toronto: Sonante, 1977.

Morris, R. Winston. *Tuba Music Guide.* Evanston, Ill.: The Instrumentalist Co., 1973.

*Morris, R. Winston, and Edward R. Goldstein. *The Tuba Source Book.* Bloomington, Ind.: Indiana University Press.

Nelson, Mark. *The Tuba as a Solo Instrument: Composer Biographies.* Annandale, Va.: Tuba-Euphonium Press, 1995.

*Phillips, Harvey, and William Winkle. *The Art of Tuba and Euphonium Playing.* Secaucus, N.J.: Summy-Birchard, 1992.

Preinsperger, Ewald. *Solo Tuba und Blasorchester: Verzeichnis von über 300 Solowerken für Eine oder mehrere Tuben und Blasorchester.* Vienna, Austria: Musik Verlag J. Kliment, 1993.

Randolph, David Mark. "New Techniques in the Avant-Garde Repertoire for Solo Tuba." D.M.A. thesis, University of Rochester, Rochester, N.Y., 1978. UM 78-11, 493.

Rose, W. H. *Studio Class Manual for Tuba and Euphonium.* Houston, Tex.: Iola, 1980.

Sorenson, Richard A. "Tuba Pedagogy: A Study of Selected Method Books, 1840–1911." Ph.D. dissertation, University of Colorado, 1972. UM 73-1832.

Stauffer, Donald W. *A Treatise on the Tuba.* Birmingham, Ala.: Stauffer Press, 1989.

*Stewart, Dee. *Arnold Jacobs: The Legacy of a Master.* Northfield, Ill.: The Instrumentalist Publishing Co., 1987.

Whitehead, Geoffrey I. *A College-Level Tuba Curriculum: Developed Through the Study of the Teaching Techniques of William Bell, Harvey Phillips, and Daniel Perantoni at Indiana University.* Lewiston, N.Y.: E. Mellen Press, 2003.

[9]Many interesting articles appear in the *ITEA Journal* (published by the International Tuba Euphonium Association) and other periodicals listed in Appendix C.

CHAPTER 8

OTHER BRASS INSTRUMENTS

■ FLUGELHORN

The flugelhorn derives its name from the curved horn used for signaling by the flügelmeister during hunts in 18th century Germany. Subsequently adopted as the *halbmond* (half-moon, denoting its shape) for military purposes, it was later modified to the bugle shape we know today (see Figure 8.1). In 1810, an English bandmaster, Joseph Halliday, fitted the instrument with keys, and in this form it was known as the Royal Kent bugle. In Germany, the instrument was known as *Klappenflügelhorn*. When valves replaced the key system, the flugelhorn found its modern form; models are now made with both piston and rotary valves.

Piston valve flugelhorns are constructed basically in a bugle shape but with a very widely wrapped bell section and the mouthpipe going directly into the first valve. Models with rotary valves are played on the side, in the manner of the rotary valve trumpet. Although the Bb flugelhorn covers the same range as the trumpet, its tone is almost totally opposite, due to its broad, conically shaped bell and deep, conical mouthpiece. The bell profile is very close to that of 19th century European bugles. The sweet, softly mellow timbre has many musical uses. It plays an important role in British brass bands, where it contributes to the mellow sonority of the overall sound and is featured in many solo passages. British brass ensembles, such as the Philip Jones Brass Ensemble, have also used the instrument in effective ways in the scoring, and this has enriched the tone colors available to this type of ensemble. Flugelhorns are now routinely written for in large brass ensemble compositions and arrangements. Occasionally, the flugelhorn is called for in orchestral music. The instrument creates a particularly haunting effect in the opening of Ralph Vaughan Williams's Ninth Symphony. Other composers who have made impressive use of the flugelhorn are Stravinsky, in *Threni*, and Respighi, in *The Pines of Rome*, where offstage flugelhorns are used to dramatic effect to evoke the sound of the ancient Roman *buccina* (the parts are often played on trumpets, however, negating this imaginative effect).

In American and British wind bands, flugelhorns are used only when required by the score, but they form a regular part of traditional European bands. It is in the brass band that the flugelhorn has come into its own and undergone the most development. The timbre of the flugelhorn, while capable of blending with any other brass band instrument, is unique and distinctive. The instrument provides an important resource for solo passages, and this is exploited in very creative ways by composers of brass band music. The mere presence of this rich timbre contributes to the overall quality of the brass band sound. It is therefore not surprising that most of the important developments in mouthpieces and instruments have come from this source.

An Eb flugelhorn is also made in Europe, known as the *petit bugle* in France, and *Pikkolo* in Germany. In the jazz field, the flugelhorn has come into prominence as a solo

FIGURE 8.1
Flugelhorn
(Besson).

voice and is considered a normal part of the trumpeter's equipment. Several internationally known jazz soloists play flugelhorn exclusively.[1]

A word should be said about flugelhorn mouthpieces. The instrument requires a much deeper and more conical mouthpiece than that used for the trumpet. The Denis Wick flugelhorn mouthpieces (2F or 4F for European instruments, 2Fl or 4Fl with large fitting for American and Japanese instruments) offer the richest tone quality currently available and are highly recommended.

■ ALTO (TENOR) HORN

The primary use today of the E♭ alto horn (tenor horn in Britain) is in the brass band, where the standard instrumentation calls for a section of three (see Figure 8.2). Alto horns were once popular in American concert bands as a substitute for the French horn, but as horn players became more plentiful the alto horn fell into disuse. Bell-front versions were once widely used in American marching bands—again substituting for the French horn—but these have largely been replaced by derivative instruments, such as the marching mellophone (now usually in F)[2] and the B♭ marching French horn.

The somewhat confusing designations for instruments of the alto horn family should be kept in mind:

Key	United States	Britain	Germany	France	Italy
E♭	Alto horn	Tenor horn	Althorn	Alto	Genis
B♭	Baritone	Baritone	Tenorhorn	Baryton	Flicorno tenore
B♭	Euphonium	Euphonium	Baryton	Basse	Eufonio

Based on Clifford Bevan, *The Tuba Family* (New York: Scribner's, 1978).

[1]For additional information on the flugelhorn, see Frederick Allan Beck, "The Flugelhorn: Its History and Literature" (D.M.A. thesis, University of Rochester, 1979), UM 79-21, 124.
[2]Substitutes for the French horn in marching bands are discussed later in this chapter.

FIGURE 8.2
E♭ alto (tenor) horn, played by British soloist Gordon Higginbottom.

During the era when alto horns were played in concert bands, it was found that constructing the instrument in a round, hornlike shape would result in a better imitation of horn sound. The new instrument was termed *mellophone* (in England, *tenor cor*) and was equipped with right-hand piston valves and a mouthpiece that was somewhat larger and more cup-shaped than that of the horn. Although easy to play, it lacked the true tone color of the horn, and gradually declined in use in American bands as a greater number of horn players appeared.

German alto horns are usually constructed in the traditional oval shape with rotary valves; these instruments have a somewhat fuller and sturdier tone. It was for this instrument that Hindemith composed his 1943 *Sonata für Althorn*, although it is now usually performed on the French horn.

■ BASS TRUMPET

Natural bass trumpets, usually in E♭ or B♭, were commonly found in German cavalry bands in the early 19th century. After the invention of valves, chromatic instruments of this type continued to be a feature of mounted bands throughout the century. The chief interest in the bass trumpet today is that Richard Wagner, seeking a broader spectrum of timbres, wrote for it in *Der Ring des Nibelungen*. Modern bass trumpets are built in C or B♭, with rotary or piston valves (see Figure 8.3). Some German makers also produce rotary valve models in E♭. Due to the size of its mouthpiece, the bass trumpet is always played by a trombonist rather than a trumpeter. The instrument produces a clearly

FIGURE 8.3
Bass trumpet
(Bach).

defined tone, quite distinct from that of the trombone. It was this quality that was exploited in Wagner's scoring.

◼ VALVE TROMBONE

The valve trombone (see Figure 8.4) flourished in the years following the introduction of valves. In France, in particular, the valve instrument was for a time favored over the slide instrument for its capacity for legato. In central Europe, valve trombones replaced slide trombones in the Vienna *Hofoper* in the mid-1830s and continued in use until 1883, when slide instruments were reinstated by order of the director.[3] Valve instruments were also used at the Paris Opera from 1866 to 1873.[4] A part for valve trombone that doubles the first trombone was included by Berlioz in *Marche Hongroise,* from *The Damnation of Faust* (1846). In 1852, the French inventor Adolphe Sax created a valve trombone with six independent valves (three valves for each hand) that had a brief vogue. Alto valve trombones in E♭ and F were also used at this time.

After an early flirtation with the valve instrument, German orchestras remained committed to the slide trombone, which had by then been enlarged in bore and bell dimensions. This was not true, however, in Vienna and Prague. In the latter musical centers, valve trombones were in use from the late 1820s. Their use in Prague may have continued into the early 20th century. Trombonist-author Ken Shifren has concluded that it is likely that composers such as Smetana and Dvořák intended their trombone parts for valve instruments.

Eventually, however, the valve trombone failed to hold its place against the slide trombone in orchestras. The tone of the valve instrument came to be viewed as rather hard and shallow in comparison with the rounder, deeper tone of the large-bore German slide trombone; and the instrument was thought to lack the smoothness and refinement of the small-bore French trombone. Also, the inherent intonation difficulties in the valve system and the lack of an effective means of correction (other than the lip) made the instrument unequal to the almost total pitch control afforded by the movable slide.

In bands, the valve trombone continued in popularity. Deficiencies aside, the instrument was sometimes preferred for the technical facility it offered. Italian bands, especially, were noted for dazzling technical displays by their all-rotary-valve brass sections. Valve trombones also found acceptance in circumstances where the use of a moving slide was difficult or impossible, such as mounted cavalry bands, where one hand must be free to hold the reins.

In the 20th century, the valve trombone has found an important niche in jazz, where its agility has made it a favorite solo instrument.

[3] Gerhard Zechmeister, "Die Stellung der (Contra) Bass-posaune im Wiener Klangstil," *Brass Bulletin,* 102 (1998), pp. 19–28.
[4] Important new research on the history and use of the valve trombone is presented in Ken Shifren's, "The Valve Trombone," *Brass Bulletin,* 111 (2000), pp. 126–144, 112 (2000), pp. 118–126.

FIGURE 8.4
Valve trombone
(Conn).

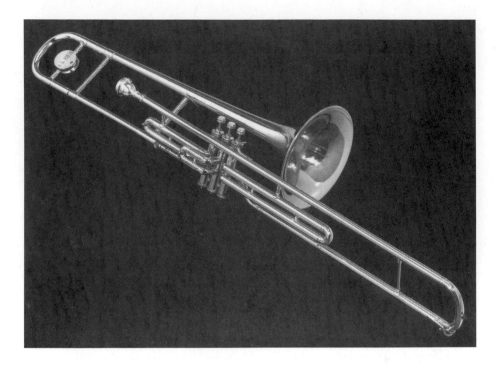

Valve trombones have been made with both piston and rotary valves. Rotary valve models sometimes have the bell angled upward to increase the directionality of the sound toward the audience.

■ CONTRABASS TROMBONE

Apparently an *Octav-Posaune* existed during the Renaissance, but how and to what extent the instrument was actually used remains obscure. Wagner called for a contrabass trombone in the score to *Der Ring des Nibelungen,* and an instrument pitched an octave below the B♭ tenor trombone was specially constructed by the instrument maker Moritz of Berlin in 1860 to play this work. The instrument utilized double tubing in its slide so that movements of the slide would be doubled in actual extension and thus be comparable to those of the tenor trombone. Contrabass parts also occur in operas by Verdi and Puccini. These were intended for a four-valve piston or rotary valve instrument known as the *cimbasso* (see Figures 8.5 and 8.6).

Today, both the contrabass slide trombone and the *cimbasso* are common in professional orchestral and opera circles. The slide instruments have evolved from an instrument designed by Hans Kunitz in 1959. This was a large-bore F trombone with two independent valves for C and D (see Figure 8.7). When the valves are used together, the instrument is pitched in low B♭. Development of this basic idea has led to new instruments using different tunings for the in-line valves, open-wrap designs, and thinner bells reinforced by a metal rim around the edge known as a *garland* or *Kranz.* One instrument made by the German firm of Thein uses D and low B♭ as the tuning of the independent valves; depressing both valves places the instrument in low A♭.

The *cimbasso* is a valve instrument pitched in F or E♭, with five rotary or piston valves. The instrument stands vertically on a spike, with the bell facing forward. The valves are positioned at the front, so they can be operated by the right hand, as on the tuba (the fifth valve is usually played by the left hand). Although rotary valve instruments by German makers[5] are most common, the Italian firm of Kalison has introduced

[5]German firms producing rotary valve *cimbassi* are Meinl Weston, R. Meinl, and Thein. The Italian firm Kalison makes a piston valve *cimbasso.*

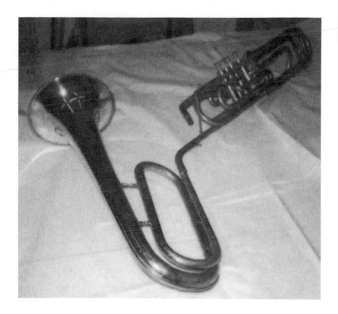

FIGURE 8.5
Piston valve cimbasso (Kalison).

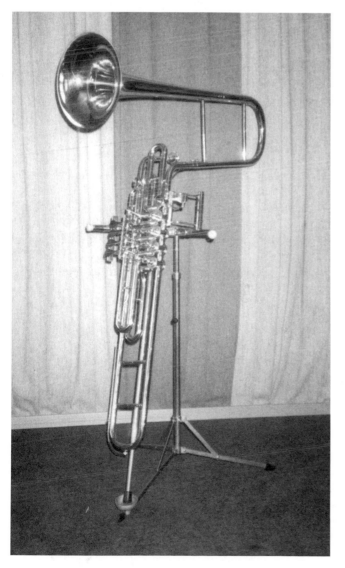

FIGURE 8.6
Rotary valve cimbasso (Meinl Weston).

FIGURE 8.7
Bass trombone in F (Kunitz
system).

a traditional model with four piston valves and a fifth rotary valve. A Viennese model
has been developed based on an earlier example that utilizes six valves, a set of three for
each hand. The reintroduction of the *cimbasso* has solved the difficulties of the technical
passages written for it in Italian opera. The slide contrabass trombone has also made
parts originally intended for this instrument readily playable, and bass trombonists
have made further use of it for low-register passages. The tricky glissando in Bartók's
Concerto for Orchestra has been rendered harmless through the use of this instrument.

■ HISTORICAL BRASS

The past four decades have witnessed a phenomenal revival of instruments that had previously been unused for two centuries or more. From the first uncertain attempts, performances of early music have progressed to the point that today's leading ensembles
routinely attain first-rate professional standards of precision, technique, and intonation
(see Figures 8.8, 8.9, and 8.10). The underlying principle in such performances is the
desire to hear music as it would have been heard by the composer and audiences of the
composer's time. The cornerstone of the early music revival is the use of authentic
instruments, whose timbres and techniques differ markedly from their modern coun-
terparts. Of equal importance is the employment of stylistic procedures that musicians
of the time would probably have followed. In this way, historical performances attempt
to convey a more faithful realization of the composer's intentions.

The success of this approach is demonstrated by the fact that new recordings
of Baroque music played on modern instruments are increasingly rare, and authentic
performances are now part of the recording and concertizing mainstream, with a

FIGURE 8.8
Natural trumpet (William Bull 1680), played by Crispian Steele-Perkins.

FIGURE 8.9
Natural trumpets, played by (left to right) David Staff and Michael Laird before a performance of Beethoven's Third Symphony at Queen Elizabeth Hall, London.

FIGURE 8.10
Sackbuts and cornets, played by His Majesties Sagbutts & Cornetts.

number of groups having attained international status. The movement has now reached well into the 19th century, and one wonders just how far the quest for authenticity will ultimately extend.

Reconstructions of natural trumpets and horns are a feature of orchestras specializing in Baroque and Classical performance. A number of outstanding soloists are active on the Baroque trumpet, including Michael Laird, Crispian Steele-Perkins, Friedemann Immer, David Staff, and Niklaus Eklund.[6] Trumpeters no longer need to ponder how Bach's trumpet parts may have sounded in his time; they can now listen to a number of representative recordings or attend live performances in which historical instruments are featured. The Baroque solo literature is also well represented. The Haydn concerto has been recorded using reconstructions of Weidinger's keyed trumpet. Excellent performances are also to be heard via recordings on Baroque or Classical hand horns,[7] and early valve trumpets are beginning to be revived for performances of solo and orchestral works from the 19th century.

In Renaissance music, the cornett[8] and sackbut are now widely used in various types of consort. Through the efforts of Don Smithers, Michael Laird, the late instrument maker Christopher Monk, Jeremy West, Bruce Dickey, and others, the cornett has regained its position as an agile, virtuoso solo voice in 16th and 17th century music. Consorts of cornetts and sackbuts bring a light, stylish character to pieces by the Gabrielis, Matthew Locke, John Adson, and others. Performers in modern brass ensembles can gain much stylistic insight by listening to such performances.

In recognizing the tremendous achievements of today's early music movement, some critical points must be noted as well. Problems of authenticity are more apparent in the brass than in other areas. Gone are such anachronistic expedients as the use of modern trombones with reformed bells in place of genuine sackbuts. Today, most ensembles use reasonable reproductions of authentic sackbuts. One common problem of authenticity, however, is the widespread use of modern mouthpieces on historical instruments. Although there are a few individuals who make use of reconstructions of early mouthpieces, the majority of players utilize regular mouthpieces intended for modern instruments. There are striking differences between the two in timbre and playing qualities. The mouthpieces often used today on natural horn usually have cups of greater air volume and inner rim diameter (sometimes with a wide rim) than historical examples. The latter were usually made from rolled metal sheet (although similar, lathe-turned examples were also made in the 19th century) in an entirely conical shape with a very narrow rim. Modern mouthpieces produce a much more robust and weighty sound and lose most of the subtle charm of the authentic instrument's timbre. Modern trumpet mouthpieces are made for the valve trumpet, which is far shorter in tube length and intended to compete in timbre and decibel level within the contemporary symphony orchestra playing Mahler, Wagner, and Stravinsky. Mouthpieces of this type brighten and restrict to some extent the timbre of the natural trumpet. Baroque mouthpieces were actually much larger than contemporary mouthpieces, with broad rims, bowl-like cups, and a sharp opening into the bore. This produced a deeper, broader, and more resonant timbre that complements other historical instruments and contributes vibrant color to a Baroque orchestra.

A further problem of authenticity involves the use of vent holes (once called *clarino holes*)[9], which are commonly incorporated into reconstructions of Baroque trumpets to correct the pitch of certain harmonics. By opening different vents, the 11th and 13th har-

---

[6] A listing of recommended historical brass recordings is included in Appendix B.

[7] Several first-rate recordings of the Mozart and Haydn horn concertos played on hand horn are available today along with other solo works originally written for this instrument.

[8] Although the cornett is made of leather-covered wood and has finger holes, its method of tone production is that of a brass instrument.

[9] Vent holes were invented c. 1962 by Otto Steinkopf, a maker of historical woodwinds, in conjunction with brass instrument maker Helmut Finke, who produced the first Baroque trumpets with this feature.

monics (written F and A) can be altered to conform to the diatonic scale. In the current four-vent hole Baroque trumpet, many other notes are played with open vents. The vents also aid the production of higher pitches. These additions were unknown during the 17th and 18th centuries, when players were taught to lip the harmonics into tune.[10] Aside from the authenticity issue, vent holes affect the timbre of the instrument, making the sound brighter and thinner than that of a true natural trumpet.

Vent holes are also used on reproductions of Baroque horns. The evidence suggests that Baroque horn parts were played with the instrument held high and no hand in the bell. As an alternative to vent holes, the technique of handstopping is sometimes employed. Although this technique may have existed to a limited extent in the later Baroque period, it did not become a standard practice until after c. 1750. The unevenness between stopped and open tones—while appropriate in the Classical period and later music—sounds anachronistic within the context of Baroque music. Along with handstopping, copies of early 19th century handhorns are sometimes used in Baroque performances rather than the smaller, less developed instruments of Bach's time.

Vent holes and the use of handstopping in Baroque music are the result of the perceived need to produce intonation that is acceptable to modern audiences. In the author's view, the natural intonation of the open harmonics contributes a certain rustic quality to the Baroque horn, which is lost when handstopping or vent holes are used. And if authenticity is indeed the goal, one might ask whether the natural trumpet should not be played with the same techniques as the great 17th and 18th century masters John Shore, Valentine Snow, and Gottfried Reiche. Compromises of this sort raise a deeper question: Are performers and audiences sincere in wishing to hear music performed as it actually was in its own time, or must it be made to conform to 20th century ears for commercial and other nonartistic reasons?

These issues aside, there are splendid historical performances taking place today and available on recordings. It is important for brass players to carefully study these performances to gain stylistic and conceptual insights into performing music of earlier periods.

■ BRASS IN THE MARCHING BAND

Aside from military and community bands, marching bands in the United States are in reality football and competition bands, specialized for performance in the open air. In Britain, bandsmen take the same instruments[11] on the march as they play in concerts, but the trend toward specialization in America has created a demand for instruments specifically designed for outdoor performance. In earlier years, this took the form of bell-front baritones, alto horns, and Sousaphones to increase the directionality of sound and provide a more equal balance of parts within the band's brass section. Today, largely due to the drum corps influence, an entire range of new instruments known as *marching brass* has been created.

Various alternatives to the French horn have been tried over the years, since the horn is fragile, expensive, and basically unsuited to the needs of high school and college marching bands. For a number for years, the E♭ alto horn[12] served as a substitute. This instrument offered (especially in upright form) a hornlike timbre and, with high-quality instruments, good intonation. Following the stylistic trend toward the drum corps, however, many directors changed over to instruments that produced a more powerful sound with greater directionality.

Trumpets built in low F or E♭ were tried, but these were found to be entirely unsat-

---

[10] A point raised by Don Smithers, Klaus Wogram, and John Bowsher in "Playing the Baroque Trumpet," *Scientific American* (April 1986), pp. 108–115.

[11] French horns, cornets, and upright euphoniums and tubas are used in British military bands.

[12] Some alto horns are pitched in F and supplied with an E♭ tuning slide. The alto horn is also known as the *altonium*.

isfactory in tone and intonation. Next came the circular, forward-facing mellophonium and the frumpet, both of which also suffered from intonation problems. Today, the most widely used instruments are the marching mellophone, in F, and the marching French horn, in B♭ (in the same key as the regular B♭ horn), also made in F. The marching French horn retains more of the regular French horn's round construction and bell flare in a forward-radiating pattern. Each of the newer instruments has its advocates, and only careful trial and error will establish their relative merits. Intonation is the critical factor, and this is where most of the problems occur.

Regular horn mouthpieces work on marching French horns, but a larger shank is required for the marching mellophone. In such cases, horn players can use a mouthpiece adapter or try to play on the mouthpiece supplied with the instrument. While the instrument will play better in tune and sound fuller with the mellophone mouthpiece, the broad rim and wide diameter often prove problematic for horn players in switching between this and their normal horn mouthpiece.

Also resulting from the drum corps influence are compact, bugle-shaped marching baritones, euphoniums, and (valve) trombones. A number of years ago, Sousaphones of fiberglass made their appearance, offering lower cost and lighter weight. Unfortunately, the fiberglass instruments do not compare well with brass Sousaphones in fullness and quality of timbre. Therefore, many college bands have returned to the conventional brass instruments, despite the cost. Euphoniums and small upright tubas with convertible leadpipes are also popular. These are played bell-forward, resting on the player's shoulder.

Even with the best-quality marching brass instruments, intonation is still a significant problem. Intonation difficulties probably stem from compromises in the instruments' basic tapers, plus the usual problems of three-valve systems.[13] Because every brand of instrument differs in its intonation (to say nothing of disparities between instruments of the same maker), each instrument must be tested individually. The use of a tuner is essential in evaluating instruments and making corrections.

It is customary for many of these instruments to be fitted with a ring on the first valve slide, and this is essential, but usually none is provided on the third valve slide. This allows the first valve tubing to be extended to lower the slightly sharp 1–2 combination, but it does little for the very sharp 1–3 and 1–2–3 combinations (the best solution for this would be the addition of a fourth valve). At least one new instrument has a trigger fitted to the main tuning slide to aid intonation adjustment. Alternate fingerings can also be used; the following intonation charts show these possibilities.

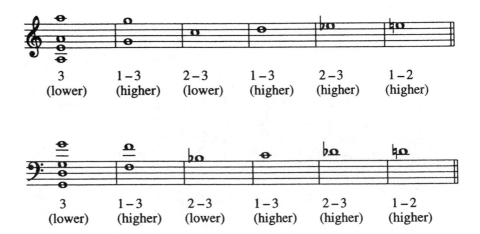

| 3 | 1–3 | 2–3 | 1–3 | 2–3 | 1–2 |
| (lower) | (higher) | (lower) | (higher) | (higher) | (higher) |

| 3 | 1–3 | 2–3 | 1–3 | 2–3 | 1–2 |
| (lower) | (higher) | (lower) | (higher) | (higher) | (higher) |

---

[13] This problem is discussed under "Intonation" in Chapters 2, 6, and 7.

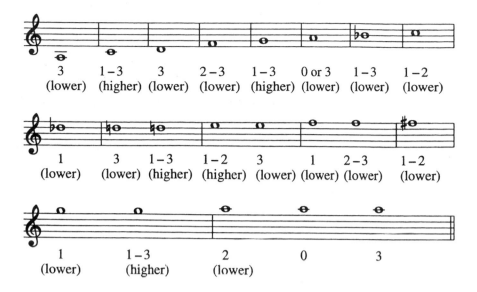

3	1 – 3	3	2 – 3	1 – 3	0 or 3	1 – 3	1 – 2
(lower)	(higher)	(lower)	(lower)	(higher)	(lower)	(lower)	(lower)

1	3	1 – 3	1 – 2	3	1	2 – 3	1 – 2
(lower)	(lower)	(higher)	(higher)	(lower)	(lower)	(lower)	(lower)

1	1 – 3	2	0	3
(lower)	(higher)	(lower)		

■ SUGGESTIONS FOR MARCHING BAND DIRECTORS

Brass players in marching bands should strive for an unforced, well-articulated, and sustained sound. A crisp and uniform attack gives sharpness and excitement to the sound and focuses it as it is heard in the distance. Good balance and sustaining work together to contribute resonance and fullness to the sound. Many bands actually lose sound by encouraging a heavy emphasis from note to note (rather than a sustaining approach of "blowing through the notes") and inattention to balance within and between sections. Smaller bands can often convey an impression of greater size by using their sound well.

In addition to stressing the sustained approach, it is important to emphasize that notes and chords be played as broadly as possible due to the absence of ambience in the outdoor environment. A good policy is to make certain that notes do not diminish before their release and to designate the beginning of the following beat as the release point. The latter will ensure notes of full duration. Notes and chords that are symmetrical or rectangular in shape sound best in the marching band style. It is the combination of balance, sustaining, and a broad style that brings resonance and fullness to brass in the open air.

One of the most common problems in marching bands today is poor intonation and tone quality. Intonation difficulties are most obvious in the alto range with the various substitutes for French horn. In addition to careful tuning, the use of octave and chord studies as a daily warm-up will do much to improve the sound. These should be played at low- to medium-volume levels while concentrating on an unforced, balanced, and in-tune sound. Careful listening and matching will lead to an improved concept of sound that will carry over into the performance. Poor tone is often caused by trying to play too loudly. It is much better if each section is encouraged to use a team approach and project a clear and balanced sound. Brilliance and definition are gained by using clearly pronounced consonants ("Tu"). This clarifies the beginnings of notes and chords and brings excitement to the sound.

THE HISTORICAL DEVELOPMENT OF BRASS INSTRUMENTS

THE HISTORICAL OUTLINES that follow note the principal points in the development of the major brass instruments. The outlines are aligned horizontally and chronologically to show concurrent developments of the trumpet, horn, trombone, baritone, euphonium, and tuba. This offers an overall view of the historical development of the brass family as a group.

Museum collections often give a rather incoherent picture of this development by displaying instruments (like the omnitonic horn) that are interesting visually but were little used in actual practice. Written accounts, too, sometimes leave the reader in doubt as to which instrument is likely to have been played in an orchestra in a particular era. The goal here has been to convey an accurate impression of the main instruments in use in each period. Important solo compositions have also been noted along the way. In the interest of space, the outlines have been kept as concise as possible. For those interested in pursuing the history of brass instruments, the following books are recommended (other sources are listed in the bibliography).

GENERAL REFERENCES

Baines, Anthony. *Brass Instruments: Their History and Development.* London: Faber & Faber, 1976.

Carse, Adam. *Musical Wind Instruments.* London: Macmillan, 1940. Reprint: Da Capo Press, 1965.

Herbert, Trevor, and John Wallace, eds. *The Cambridge Companion to Brass Instruments.* Cambridge, UK: Cambridge University Press, 1997.

Heyde, Herbert. *Hörner und Zinken.* Leipzig: VEB Deutscher Verlag für Musik, 1982.

Heyde, Herbert. *Trompeten, Posaunen, Tuben.* Leipzig: VEB Deutscher Verlag für Musik, 1980.

Mende, Emilie. *Pictorial Family Tree of Brass Instruments in Europe Since the Early Middle Ages.* Moudon, Switzerland: Editions BIM, 1978.

SPECIFIC INSTRUMENTS

Trumpet and Cornet

Altenburg, Detlef. *Untersuchungen zur Geschichte der Trompete in Zeitalter der Clarinblaskunst (1500–1800).* Regensburg, Germany: G. Bosse, 1973.

Altenburg, Johann Ernst. *Essay on an Introduction to the Heroic and Musical Trumpeters' and Kettledrummers' Art* (1795). Nashville, Tenn.: The Brass Press, 1974.

Barclay, R. L. *The Art of the Trumpet-Maker: The Materials, Tools, and Techniques of the Seventeenth and Eighteenth Centuries in Nuremberg.* Oxford, UK: Clarendon Press, 1992.

Bate, Philip. *The Trumpet and Trombone: An Outline of Their History, Development, and Construction,* 2nd ed. London: Ernest Benn, 1978; New York: Norton, 1978.

Bendinelli, Cesare. *The Entire Art of Trumpet Playing (1614).* Nashville, Tenn.: Brass Press, 1975.

Brownlow, Art. *The Last Trumpet: A History of the English Slide Trumpet.* Stuyvesant, N.Y.: Pendragon Press, 1996.

Cassone, Gabriel. *La Tromba*. Varese, Italy: Zecchini, 2002.

Clarke, Herbert L. *How I Became a Cornetist*. Kenosha, Wis.: Leblanc Educational Publications, n.d.

Dahlqvist, Reine. *The Keyed Trumpet and Its Greatest Virtuoso, Anton Weidinger*. Nashville, Tenn.: Brass Press, 1975.

Eichborn, Hermann. *The Old Art of Clarino Playing on Trumpets*. Trans. by Bryan A. Simms. Denver, Colo.: Tromba Publications, 1976.

Eldredge, Niles. *A Brief History of Piston-Valved Cornets*. New York: Historic Brass Society, 2002. [Reprinted from 2002 *Historic Brass Society Journal* 14:337–390.]

Enrico, Eugene. *The Orchestra at San Petronio in the Baroque Era*. Washington, D.C.: Smithsonian Institution Press, 1976.

Fantini, Girolamo. *Modo per imparare a sonare di Tromba tanto di Guerra quanto Musicalmente in Organo, con Tromba sordina, con Cimbalo e con orgn'altro strumento* (1638). New York: Performers' Facsimiles, 2002. Nashville, Tenn.: The Brass Press, 1972.

Farley, Robert, and John Hutchins. *Natural Trumpet Studies*. Oakham, Rutland, England: Brass Wind Publications.

Handel's Trumpeter: The Diary of John Grano (c. 1692–1748). Stuyvesant, N.Y.: Pendragon Press, 1998.

Harper, Thomas. *Instructions for the Trumpet (1837)*. Homer, N.Y.: Spring Tree Enterprises, 1988.

Laird, Michael. *BrassWorkBook for Natural Trumpet*. Gt. Dunmow, England: Brass Works.

Lindner, Andreas. *Die Kaiserlichen Hoftrompeter und HofPauker in 18. und 19. Jahrhundert*. Tutzing, Germany: H. Schneider, 1999.

Mathez, Jean-Pierre. *Joseph Jean-Baptiste Laurent Arban, 1825–1889: Portrait d'un musicien Française du XIXe Siècle*. Moudon, Switzerland: Editions BIM, 1977.

Naylor, Tom L. *The Trumpet and Trombone in Graphic Arts, 1500–1800*. Nashville, Tenn.: The Brass Press, 1979.

Seraphinoff, Richard, and Robert Barclay. *Making a Natural Trumpet: An Illustrated Workshop Guide*. Edinburgh University Collection of Historic Musical Instruments, 2003.

Smithers, Don L. *The Music and History of the Baroque Trumpet Before 1721*. London: J.M. Dent, 1973.

Steele-Perkins, Crispian. *The Trumpet*. London: Kahn & Averill, 2001.

Tarr, Edward. *The Art of Baroque Trumpet Playing: Exercises from the Schola Cantoris Basiliensis (Die Kunst des Barocktrompetenspiels: Übungen aus der Schola Cantorum)*. Mainz/New York: Schott, 1999.

Horn

Coar, Birchard. *A Critical Study of the Nineteenth-Century Horn Virtuosi in France*. DeKalb, Ill.: Coar, 1952.

Coar, Birchard. *The French Horn*. DeKalb, Ill.: Coar, 1947.

Fitzpatrick, Horace. *The Horn and Horn-Playing and the Austro-Bohemian Tradition from 1680–1830*. London: Oxford University Press, 1970.

Gregory, Robin. *The Horn: A Comprehensive Guide to the Modern Instrument and Its Music*. London: Faber & Faber, 1961.

Humphries, John. *The Early Horn: A Practical Guide*. Cambridge, UK: Cambridge University Press, 2000.

Janetzky, Kurt, and Bernhard Brüchle. *The Horn*. Portland, Ore.: Amadeus Press, 1988.

Morley-Pegge, Reginald. *The French Horn*. London: Ernest Benn, 1973.

Pizka, Hans. *Das Horn bei Mozart*. Kirchheim bei München: Hans Pizka Edition, 1980.

Tuckwell, Barry. *Horn*. New York: Schirmer Books, 1983.

Trombone

Fischer, Henry George. *The Renaissance Sackbut and Its Use Today*. New York: Metropolitan Museum of Art, 1984.

Gregory, Robin. *The Trombone: The Instrument and Its Music*. New York: Praeger, 1973.

Guion, David M. *The Trombone: Its History and Music 1697–1811*. New York: Gordon & Breach, 1988.

Lane, G. B.: *The Trombone in the Middle Ages and the Renaissance*. Bloomington, Ind.: Indiana University Press, 1982.

Smith, David. "Trombone Technique in the Early Seventeenth Century." D.M.A. thesis, Stanford University, 1981.

Tracy, Bruce Alan. "The Contrabass Trombone: Its Development and Use." D.M.A. Thesis, University of Illinois, 1990.

Wigness, C. Robert. *The Soloistic Use of the Trombone in Eighteenth-Century Vienna*. Nashville, Tenn.: The Brass Press, 1978.

Baritone, Euphonium, and Tuba

Bevan, Clifford. *The Tuba Family*. New York: Scribner's, 1978.

Trumpet and Cornet[1]	Horn	Trombone	Baritone, Euphonium, and Tuba
		Antiquity	
Straight trumpets made of wood, bronze, and silver. Greek salpinx, Roman tuba, lituus, and buccina.	Scandinavian *lur* (bronze), Hebrew *schofar*, Roman cornu, and various animal horns.		

(continued)

[1] The cornet is grouped with the trumpet in the interest of space. Actually, they have different origins. The cornet dates from ca. 1828, when Halary-Antoine added valves to the German post horn. Since the period of Arban (1869–1889), the pedagogy and history of the cornet and trumpet have been intertwined.

Trumpet and Cornet	Horn	Trombone	Baritone, Euphonium, and Tuba
		Middle Ages	
Trumpets reappeared during the Crusades, probably derived from the Saracens. *Ca. 1300. Buisine, trumba, trombono, trombetta, trummet.* Medieval trumpeters played only on the lowest harmonics.			
		Renaissance	
Ca. 1400–1413. The S-shaped trumpet was developed, followed by the folded trumpet and slide trumpet. The latter enabled the player to produce notes between the harmonics by sliding the instrument in and out on the mouthpipe.		*Ca. 1450.* The trombone developed from the slide trumpet. Both the exact date and the identity of the originator of the movable slide are unknown. The connected double tubes of the slide represented a significant advance over the awkward slide trumpet and reduced the distances between notes, greatly improving technique. The smaller slide movements also rendered tenor-range instruments practicable. These were known as the *saque-boute* or *trompone.*	
Ca. 1500. Corps of trumpeters were maintained by the large courts. Eventually, such large ensembles played in up to five parts (but with little harmonic variety). Players began to specialize in high and low ranges.	Two types of hunting horn were widely used: the curved horn and the helical horn. The latter was made of coiled metal and is the immediate predecessor of the *trompe de chasse.*	*Ca. 1540.* The earliest surviving instruments date from the mid-16th century. Three types were used in this period: an "ordinary" sackbut in B♭ (*gemeine-posaune*), an E♭ alto (*mittel-posaune*), and a bass (*grosse-posaune*), also known as *quart-* or *quint-posaune,* indicating its intervallic distance from the B♭ *gemeine-posaune.* Trombones in other keys were sometimes made, probably for transposition, and were also identified by interval from the "ordinary" in B♭.	
		17th Century	
Ca. 1600. Instrument makers centered in Nuremberg produced improved natural trumpets designed to function well	Hunting horns were occasionally used on the stage in operas, usually depicting hunting scenes.	*Ca. 1600.* The same pattern continued during the 17th century with the addition of a contrabass instrument	

Trumpet and Cornet	Horn	Trombone	Baritone, Euphonium, and Tuba
on the upper harmonics. The pitch was usually D or E♭, with terminal crooks added for lower keys. Lacking a tuning slide, natural trumpets were tuned by inserting small lengths of tubing to extend the mouthpiece. *Ca. 1600.* Increasing use was made of trumpets in church music, often in combination with strings. Praetorius's *In dulci jubilo* (1618) calls for six trumpets. *1620.* Florid parts in the high register were written by Samuel Scheidt in his setting of *In dulci jubilo* and Heinrich Schütz's *Buccinate in neomenia Tuba* (1629).		(*octav-posaune*), although it is unclear to what extent it was actually used. Sackbuts were regularly used in all types of ensemble, from large court bands to small mixed consorts, where it could blend with the softest instruments. A "vocal" style was cultivated that was free of any influence from the trumpet. The capacity to blend with voices caused the sackbut to be widely used in church music. It was also common in municipal bands, along with cornett and shawms, or in a consort of two cornetts and three sackbuts. Venetian composers such as Giovanni Gabrieli and Massaino wrote for the instrument regularly, occasionally calling for exceptionally large forces.	
	Ca. 1660. The hoop-shaped *cor de chasse* or *trompe de chasse* became a feature of hunting tradition in France.		
Ca. 1665–1700. Beginning with Maurizio Cazzati, composers associated with the basilica of San Petronio in Bologna produced an important body of works for solo trumpet and strings. The style reached its apex near the end of the century in the solo concertos of Giuseppe Torelli, Domenico Gabrielli, and Giacomo Perti. These works are widely performed today.	*Ca. 1680.* A larger-wound *trompe de chasse* made its appearance in France. This instrument had a circumference large enough to fit over the body for carrying on horseback.		
Ca. 1680–1695. The trumpet was widely used as a solo instrument in central Europe by composers such as Heinrich Biber and Johann Schmelzer. In England, Henry Purcell and others made extensive use of the trumpet in stage works. Purcell's *Sonata in D for Trumpet and Strings* (1694) is an important solo piece.	*1680–1682.* Franz Anton, Count von Sporck of Bohemia, became interested in the *cor de chasse* during a visit to France. He had two of his servants, Wenzel Sweda and Peter Röllig, trained to play the instrument and established a tradition of horn playing in central Europe.	*Ca. 1685.* A small trombone pitched an octave above the tenor made its appearance in central Europe and was used mostly for playing chorale melodies in trombone ensembles.	

18th Century

Trumpet and Cornet	Horn	Trombone	Baritone, Euphonium, and Tuba
	Ca. 1700–1710. Viennese instrument maker Michael Leichnambschneider was probably the first to produce terminal crooks to	Although there may have been diminished use of the trombone generally during the 18th century, the instrument continued	

(*continued*)

| | | Trumpet and Cornet | Horn | Trombone | Baritone, Euphonium, and Tuba |

Trumpet and Cornet

Horn

put the horn into different keys. The crooks consisted of various lengths of coiled tubing that were inserted between the mouthpiece and instrument. For lower keys, the crooks could be coupled together, although the instrument became farther away from the player. Once the crook was in place, the horn was played in accordance with the natural harmonic series, which sounded in the chosen key.

1705. Two horns were used in the orchestra for the opera *Octavia* by Reinhard Keiser.

Trombone

to flourish in an important soloistic role (at least) at the Viennese Imperial Court. Following the pattern established in the 17th century by Antonio Bertali (1605–1669), composers such as Johann Joseph Fux (1660–1741), Marc Antonio Ziani (1653–1715), Franz Tuma (1704–1774), and Georg Reutter (1708–1772) used the trombone in virtuosic fashion in vocal and instrumental works. The style reached its peak in the concertos of Georg Christoph Wagenseil (1715–1777) and Johann Georg Albrechtsberger (1736–1809). Concertos were also written by Salzburg composers Michael Haydn (1737–1806) and Leopold Mozart (1719–1787). This interesting chapter in the trombone's history is described in detail in C. Robert Wigness's *The Soloistic Use of the Trombone in Eighteenth-Century Vienna* (Nashville, Tenn.: Brass Press, 1978).

Baritone, Euphonium, and Tuba

Ca. 1716–1750. The Baroque trumpet reached its zenith in the works of Johann Sebastian Bach, who was well served by Leipzig trumpeter Gottfried Reiche. In his portrait, Reiche holds a coiled instrument known as a *jägertrompete,* probably by Nuremberg instrument maker J. W. Haas. Apparently, these were occasionally used in place of the more common long trumpet.

Ca. 1717. Handel's *Water Music,* which included parts for a pair of horns, was performed. During the Baroque era, horn parts focused on the upper portion of the harmonic series and were played without the hand in the bell.

Ca. 1750. Anton Joseph Hampel, a hornist of Dresden, developed the technique of filling in the spaces between the notes of the harmonic series by various degrees of handstopping, rendering the horn chromatic. The procedure is as follows:

Ca. 1755. Concerto by Georg Christoph Wagenseil (alto trombone).

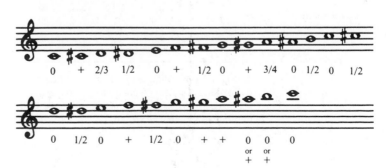

Trumpet and Cornet	Horn	Trombone	Baritone, Euphonium, and Tuba
Ca. 1760. The high clarino style of trumpet playing declined, not from lack of ability on the players' part, but as a function of broad changes in compositional style. Henceforth, trumpets played a supporting role in the orchestra, although two late concertos were written in the earlier clarino style (Leopold Mozart, 1762; Michael Haydn, 1764).	Although there was an unevenness of timbre between stopped and open tones, handstopping became the standard horn technique until well after the invention of valves. Placing the hand in the bell altered the tone, and a darker and softer timbre became accepted as traditional horn tone. To improve on the limitations of terminal crooks, Hampel invented a new structural format that incorporated a fixed mouthpipe and located the crook in the middle of the instrument. The new instrument, made by Johann Werner (Dresden), was known as the *inventionshorn.*	*Ca. 1762. Concerto* by Leopold Mozart (alto trombone). *1763. Larghetto* by Michael Haydn (alto trombone). *1764. Divertimento in D* by Michael Haydn (alto trombone). [Solo movements also published under the title *Concerto.*]	
	1762. Horn Concerto No. 1 by Franz Joseph Haydn.		
Ca. 1777. Handstopping, first used on the horn in 1750 and by this time normal practice, was applied to the trumpet by Michael Wöggerl. Notes of the harmonic series could be lowered a half or full tone by covering the bell with the hand, although a veiled tone resulted. Stop trumpets were curved or made quite short to increase the bell's accessibility; they followed the *inventionshorn* in locating the crook in the middle of the instrument, thereby eliminating terminal crooks.	*1750–1776.* J. G. Haltenhof (Hanau am Main) developed the tuning slide that was applied to the *inventionshorn.* *1780.* Parisian instrument makers Joseph and Lucien-Joseph Raoux brought out a structurally improved *inventionshorn,* calling their new model *cor solo.* Designed for solo playing, it had crooks only for the common solo keys: G, F, E, E♭, and D	*1769.* Concerto by Johann Georg Albrechtsberger (alto trombone). *Ca. 1780.* The trombone began to be used in opera to lend dramatic effect to certain scenes, as in Mozart's *Don Giovanni* and *The Magic Flute.*	
1795. Trumpeter's and Kettledrummer's Art by Ernst Altenburg was published. This is an important source concerning the natural trumpet and clarino style (see translation by Edward Tarr [Nashville, Tenn.: Brass Press, 1974]).	*1781–1791.* Concertos for horn—Wolfgang Amadeus Mozart: *Rondo in E♭,* K.371, 1781; *Concerto in E♭,* K.417, 1783 (No. 2); *Concerto in E♭,* K.447, 1786 (No. 3); *Concerto in E♭,* K.495, 1786 (No. 4); *Concerto in D,* K.412, 1791 (No. 1).		
1795. Viennese trumpeter Anton Weidinger gave solo appearances, performing on a keyed trumpet of his own design. Haydn's *Trumpet Concerto* (1796) was composed for him, as was the concerto by Hummel (1803).	*Ca. 1795.* Terminal crooks once again became popular with orchestral players, but with individual crooks for each key instead of the cumbersome practice of coupling crooks together for the lower keys. English players, however, continued to use the earlier system of terminal crooks and couplers; their instruments were fitted with tuning slides.		

(continued)

Trumpet and Cornet	Horn	Trombone	Baritone, Euphonium, and Tuba
		19th Century	
Ca. 1800. The natural trumpet flourished in England later than elsewhere (through most of the 19th century) due to John Hyde's invention of a spring-slide mechanism that allowed the instrument's fundamental pitch to be lowered a half or whole tone without affecting the timbre. An active tradition of performing Handel's clarino parts on the natural trumpet was thereby maintained.	1800. Horn Sonata, Op. 17, by Ludwig van Beethoven. Written for virtuoso Giovanni Punto (Jan Václav Stich). Ca. 1800. Before the invention of valves, there were attempts to construct a chromatic horn. These included the keyed horn and omnitonic horn. Neither gained wide acceptance, and the hand horn continued as the primary orchestral and solo instrument, with players specializing in either high or low ranges. 1806. Concertino for Horn by Carl Maria von Weber; revised 1815. The cadenza includes horn chords.	Ca. 1800–1850. During the early 19th century, composers increasingly called for three trombones in the orchestra. Parts were included in Beethoven's 5th and 9th symphonies. The normal trio of E♭ alto, B♭ tenor, and F bass began to give way because alto parts were often performed on the tenor. A large-bore trombone in B♭ was occasionally substituted for the bass in F. The alto trombone was retained (as it is today in central Europe) for parts requiring a high tessitura and light balances.	(The valved low brass have no direct predecessors. The instruments they replaced were the serpent [the bass of the conetto family and its more developed form, the bass horn] and the ophicleide, which was derived from the keyed bugle.)

■ THE DEVELOPMENT OF VALVES

In 1788, Charles Clagget was granted a patent for a "chromatic trumpet," which in fact consisted of two instruments, each with its own fundamental and a switching mechanism to direct the single mouthpiece to one side or the other. Although the invention was demonstrated, it failed to achieve any acceptance and should not, therefore, be considered a stage in the development of the valve.

The history of the valve begins with an article in the *Allgemeine musikalische Zeitung* of May 3, 1815, by G. B. Bierey, which reported on a new invention by horn player Heinrich Stölzel. Through the use of two "levers," a chromatic scale of almost three octaves could be obtained. The author described the timbre of the valve notes as "clear and strong," comparable to the natural tones. By 1818, Stölzel had joined the court orchestra in Berlin, when Friedrich Blühmel turned up, claiming that the invention was his. A joint 10-year patent was granted to Stölzel and Blühmel; we will probably never know which of them was responsible for the original idea.

The joint patent of 1818 was for both a tubular and a square-shaped (box) valve. In the tubular valve (Stölzel's), the air column was directed downward through the valve tube and out the bottom. Valves of this type were popular during the first half of the century and were known as Stölzel valves. The square valve (Blühmel's) had the advantage of more direct windways but was slower in action.[2]

---

[2] An important source of information on the early development of the valve is the account by Prussian bandmaster Wilhelm Wieprecht (1845), who knew both Stölzel and Blühmel. Relevant passages are translated in Anthony Baines, *Brass Instruments* (London, Faber & Faber, 1976), pp. 207–212. The most detailed study available is Herbert Heyde's series of articles, "Zur Frühgeschichte der Ventile und Ventilinstrumente in Deutschland (1814–1833)," *Brass Bulletin* 24 (1978), pp. 9–33; 25 (1979), pp. 41–50; 26 (1979), pp. 69–82; 27 (1979), pp. 51–59 (translations in English and French are included).

In 1828, Stölzel and Blühmel were unsuccessful in obtaining patents for rotary valves. Of similar design, the valves were apparently developed quite early, but, for some reason, Stölzel and Blühmel chose not to include them in the 1818 patent. Wieprecht stated that the rotary valve was immediately improved in Prague, a comment that lends credence to a story found in the papers of instrument maker Karl Nödel that credits hornist Joseph Kail with the invention of the rotary valve rather than Josef Riedl, who patented it in 1832.[3] According to Nödel, his father (also an instrument maker) and other old Viennese makers always maintained that Kail, a professor at the Prague Conservatory, invented the rotary valve in 1827, having gotten the idea from a beer tap. Kail apparently described his idea to Josef Riedl during a visit to Vienna, and Riedl proceeded to manufacture the valves, eventually securing a patent.[4]

Another valve in use today (but only on the Vienna horn) is the double-piston valve, which was patented in 1830 by Viennese instrument maker Leopold Uhlmann as an improved version of an earlier design by Christian Friedrich Sattler of Leipzig. With attached twin pistons, the air column flows from the bottom of one piston (like the Stölzel valve) and, after going through the requisite length of tubing, reenters the bottom of the second piston. This action is believed to contribute to the exceptionally smooth slurs and free tone of the Vienna horn.

In 1835, Wilhelm Wieprecht and instrument maker J. G. Moritz introduced improved piston valves known as *Berliner-Pumpen*, which featured unconstricted airways. Although they had a rather slow action, they were widely used in military bands in Germany and northern Europe (particularly on low brass instruments) and continued to be made into the beginning of the present century.

There were other experiments, such as the transverse spring slide by John Shaw and disc-type valves by Halary-Antoine, Shaw, and Köhler, but these had no significant impact on the development of the valve.

The final stage of development was reached in 1839, when François Périnet, a Parisian instrument maker, brought the piston valve into the form we know today. Thus the three modern valves—piston, rotary, and Vienna—were developed in the 1830s and have come down to the present era essentially unchanged. A new invention is the valve developed by Orla Ed Thayer. This valve has proved effective as a change valve for the F and other attachments on the trombone.

Trumpet and Cornet	Horn	Trombone	Baritone, Euphonium, and Tuba
		19th Century	
Ca. 1826. Spontini brought a German valve trumpet to Paris, where it gained acceptance and was copied. Berlioz was the first to use the new instrument in the overture *Les francs-juges* of the same year. During this period, valve trumpets were often used beside natural trumpets. As the	*Ca. 1825.* Although valve horns made their appearance, players preferred to use hand technique whenever possible on the new instruments. The valves served to avoid the most obvious inequalities of timbre inherent in the hand horn technique. French instrument makers often produced	As trombones were being increasingly used in orchestras, several trombonists attained fame as soloists. The first of these was Friedrich August Belcke (1795–1874).	

(*continued*)

---

[3] Nödel's statement is reproduced in Bernhard Brüchle and Kurt Janetzky, *Kulturgeschichte des Horns* (Tutzing, Germany: Hans Schneider, 1976), pp. 252–253.

[4] Another source, T. Rode, writing in the *Neue Berliner Musikzeitung* in 1860, says that Kail improved the rotary valve in 1829. Whether there is any connection between the Stölzel and Blühmel rotary valve and the Kail valve or (if the Nödel story is true) this is a case of independent conception remains unclear. Another early type of rotary valve was made by Nathan Adams of Boston as early as 1825.

Trumpet and Cornet	Horn	Trombone	Baritone, Euphonium, and Tuba
valve trumpet developed during the 19th century, instruments were produced with Stölzel, piston, rotary, and Vienna valves. The usual key was F or G, and crooks were added for lower keys.	horns with removable valves, and a third valve was considered unnecessary.		
Ca. 1828. Jean-Louis Antoine (Halary)[5] modified the (round) German post horn to become a valve instrument, calling it *cornet à pistons.* Two Stölzel valves were fitted, and it was wound (in B♭) so that the bell projected forward. The cornet gained rapid popularity as a solo instrument because of its chromatic agility, and it was often used (in a pair) along with trumpets in works by French composers.	*1835.* Halevy's *La juive* was the first score to call for valve horns. A pair of hand horns and a pair of valve horns was customary.	*Ca. 1828.* The new valve trombone was introduced, and, while it received some acceptance in bands, it was little used in orchestras in Germany. However, for a time significant use was made of this instrument in Paris, Vienna, and Prague. Following in the virtuoso tradition of Belcke were Karl Traugott Queisser (1800–1846) and Antoine Guillaume Dieppo (1808–1878). The latter taught at the Paris Conservatory and produced a *méthode complète* in 1840.	*Ca. 1828.* Tenor- and baritone-range instruments with valves appeared in German military bands during the late 1820s. These may be considered the first versions of the modern German *tenorhorn* and *baryton.*
		1837. Concertino by Ferdinand David (1810–1873).	*Ca. 1835.* The first tuba, a five-valve (*Berliner-pumpen*) instrument in F, was invented by Berlin bandmaster Wilhelm Wieprecht and instrument maker Johann Gottfried Moritz. *1838.* Moritz produced a tenor tuba in B♭.
		1839. C. F. Sattler of Leipzig introduced the first B♭–F trombone. The change to the F attachment was (as it is today) made by a rotary valve.	*1842–1845.* Parisian inventor Adolphe Sax produced his complete family of saxhorns, receiving a patent in 1845. These ranged from the E♭ soprano to the B♭ contrabass. Aside from the quality of their construction, the saxhorns' success can be attributed to their adoption by the French Army and by the famous Distin family quintet (who popularized them in England, where they were taken up by

[5] J.-L. Antoine took over the Halary business and adopted the name. His son, Jules-Leon Antoine, later joined him as a partner.

Trumpet and Cornet	Horn	Trombone	Baritone, Euphonium, and Tuba
			the developing brass band movement). Modern low brass instruments with piston valves evolved from the saxhorn.
			1843. The *Euphonion* was introduced by Sommer of Weimar. A similar instrument, identified as the *Sommerophone,* was exhibited in 1851 at the Crystal Palace in London.
			1845. Contrabass tubas in B♭ and C with rotary valves rather than *Berliner-pumpen* were manufactured by the Bohemian firm of Červený. The tuba was rapidly accepted in orchestras in Germany, but the ophicleide maintained its place in France and England until late in the century. Tubas found acceptance in bands everywhere.
Ca. 1850–1890. Possibly due to the influence of the B♭ cornet, with its advantage of more widely spaced harmonics, trumpeters gradually moved away from the long F and G trumpets toward instruments built in B♭ or C. Stölzel valves declined in popularity, and instruments were made with three piston or rotary valves.	*1849.* Robert Schumann was an important early advocate for the valve horn. His *Adagio and Allegro* for solo horn and piano and *Konzertstück* for four horns and orchestra demand the full capacity of the valve instrument. *1865. Trio for Violin, Horn, and Piano,* op. 40, by Johannes Brahms.	*Ca. 1850.* From the mid-19th century, German trombones became larger in bore and bell and took on their traditional wide-bow construction. French trombones of the Courtois type retained a smaller bore and bell taper. Large bass trombones in F or B♭/F became the rule in German sections. A smaller bass trombone in G was used in brass bands and orchestras in England for almost a century.	*Ca. 1840–1880.* Berlioz and Wagner were early champions of the tuba. The latter wrote for it in *The Flying Dutchman* (1843), and it was included in Berlioz's *Damnation of Faust,* composed three years later. The bass tuba in F was normally used, but the contrabass was occasionally specified, as in Wagner's *Ring.* In France, a small C tuba (pitched above the F bass) with six valves finally replaced the ophicleide.
1864. Jean-Baptiste Arban's *Grande méthode complète pour cornet à pistons et de saxhorn* was published in Paris. Arban's influence as performer and teacher had wide impact on both cornetists and trumpeters, which	*Ca. 1865.* During the second half of the 19th century, horns were typically built (in Germany) in F with three rotary valves and either terminal or slide crooks. Players preferred to use the high		

(continued)

Trumpet and Cornet	Horn	Trombone	Baritone, Euphonium, and Tuba
extends to the present. His method forms the basis of most modern teaching of the instruments.	B♭, A, G, E, and E♭ crooks when in those keys in order to retain the timbre of the open tones and avoid awkward fingerings. Henri Kling, in his *Horn-Schule* (1865), cited examples for the use of crooks and disparaged the practice of trying to play everything on the F crook, which was now theoretically possible through the use of valves. In France, horns with terminal G crook and ascending third valve (which put the horn in F) were preferred, and English players used French instruments with descending third valve and F crook. Uhlmann's ca. 1830 Vienna horn with double piston valves and terminal crook was (and still is) the standard instrument of the Imperial (now State) Opera and Vienna Philharmonic.		
1871. Julius Kosleck, Professor at the Berlin *Hoch-Schule,* gave a demonstration of clarino playing that aroused interest in reviving this art. Later, in 1884–1885, he caused a stir by performing the Bach parts on a two-valve straight trumpet in A. English players had similar instruments made by G. Silvani. Teste, of the Paris Opera, performed the *Magnificat* on a three-valve G trumpet (1885) made by Besson. Mahillion produced a successful D trumpet in 1892, and Alexander an F for the second "Brandenburg" Concerto in 1894. The great Belgian trumpeter Théo Charlier performed the second "Brandenburg" Concerto on April 17,		*1876.* A contrabass trombone in B♭ with double-tubed slide was constructed for Wagner's *Ring* (composed 1848–1874; performed Bayreuth, 1876).	*1874.* A compensating system (still in use) to correct intonation when valves are used in combination was invented by David Blaikley of Boosey and Co. This significantly improved low brass instruments used in England and is a contributing factor to the high quality of British brass bands.

Trumpet and Cornet	Horn	Trombone	Baritone, Euphonium, and Tuba
1889, in Anvers and on Nov. 17, 1901, in Liège. Charlier used a G trumpet made by Mahillon for these performances. The various high trumpets were often called Bach trumpets.			
	1882–1883. First Concerto for Horn, op. 11, by Richard Strauss.		*Ca. 1880.* Červený introduced a very large-bore tuba known as a *Kaiserbass.* This became the prototype for most modern rotary valve orchestral tubas in C and B♭.
Ca. 1890. The modern form of the orchestral trumpet became established. Piston valve trumpets were generally found in France, England, and the United States; rotary valve trumpets in Germany, Austria, and Italy. Instruments in C were favored by French and Viennese trumpeters, while the B♭ was common elsewhere. (The long F trumpet survived into the early 20th century in England.)	*1897.* Edmund Gumpert, in collaboration with the instrument firm of Eduard Kruspe, developed the first F–B♭ double horn, a compensating type that was soon followed by the full double. (The idea had been partially anticipated by Gautrot, who designed a compensating system to correct intonation in 1865.)	*Ca. 1890–1920.* During these years, small-bore Courtois-type trombones were popular in France and England and in bands in the United States. Players in American symphony orchestras preferred large-bore German instruments, and these influenced the development of the modern American symphonic trombone (which combines the best features of French and German instruments).	

20th Century

Trumpet and Cornet	Horn	Trombone	Baritone, Euphonium, and Tuba
Ca. 1905. The Belgian firm of Mahillon constructed a piccolo B♭ trumpet intended for Bach's second "Brandenburg" Concerto.	At the beginning of the century, single F, B♭, and double horns were in simultaneous use.		*1900–present.* German low brass instruments continued in the 20th century essentially unchanged from their 19th century counterparts. Band instruments such as the E♭ *althorn, tenorhorn,* and *baryton* (the latter two equivalent to the baritone and euphonium) were wrapped in an oval form with rotary valves and remain the same today. German tubas became accepted in many countries as the standard orchestral instrument. In England, an agile piston valve tuba in F (Ralph Vaughan Williams wrote his *Bass Tuba Concerto*
Ca. 1929. Larger-bore piston valve B♭ trumpets based on the Besson model replaced smaller-bore instruments in American orchestras. Through the influence of Georges Mager, principal trumpet of the Boston Symphony (1920–1950), the C trumpet became increasingly common. By the late 1940s, it had largely replaced the B♭ as the standard orchestral instrument.	*Ca. 1928.* Hornist Louis Vuillermoz developed a compensating double horn (piston valve) based on the ascending third valve principle. This became the standard orchestral horn in France and parts of Belgium until ca. 1974.

1942. Second Concerto for Horn by Richard Strauss.

Ca. 1945–1950. In England, French-type | *Ca. 1939.* The trombone gained widespread popularity through the influence of bandleaders such as Tommy Dorsey and Glenn Miller and its use in jazz. Tommy Dorsey, in particular, left his mark on all trombonists for his remarkable control and smooth legato.

Ca. 1950. American-type orchestral trombones became standardized throughout the world, in | |

(continued)

Trumpet and Cornet	Horn	Trombone	Baritone, Euphonium, and Tuba
Ca. 1959. Improved high trumpets were developed, bringing the Baroque literature into the sphere of regular orchestral players rather than specialists. *Ca. 1960.* French virtuoso Maurice André brought the trumpet into a new era as a popular solo instrument through worldwide appearances and recordings. *Ca. 1961.* Performances on natural trumpets were revived to lend an authentic timbre and style to Baroque music. The standard of performance has now risen to a very high level, and there are several internationally recognized soloists on natural trumpet. Replicas of Baroque instruments are readily available.	piston valve horns were gradually replaced by German single B♭s and doubles (a change regretted by many). *Ca. 1950–1957.* English horn player Dennis Brain achieved world renown as a soloist, establishing the horn as a major solo instrument. *Ca. 1958.* The first practical B♭–F alto double descant horn was developed by Richard Merewether. Double descants are also made in F–F alto, B♭–E♭ alto, and B♭–B♭ soprano. Single descants are most commonly built in F or G alto and B♭ soprano. *1965.* Richard Merewether introduced the triple horn in F–B♭–F alto.	some cases (as in England) displacing traditional small-bore instruments, in Germany and Austria, but German trombones continued their independent line of development. *Ca. 1952.* Several American bass trombonists were frustrated by the limitations of the B♭–F instrument in producing good notes immediately above the pedal range. They experimented with an additional length of tubing connected to the F attachment by a second valve that lowered the pitch to E. This was later altered to E♭ or D, and the dependent double-trigger bass trombone soon became standardized. *Ca. 1965.* Hans Kunitz invented the in-line independent double-valve large bass–contrabass trombone, tuned F/C–D–B♭. *Ca. 1970.* Dr. B. P. Leonard independently invented the in-line design. From Leonard's patented design, tuned B♭/G–E–D, other versions, tuned B♭/F–G–E♭ and B♭/F–G♭–D, were developed and produced commercially as bass trombones.	[1954] for this instrument) was favored up to World War II. Since then, the brass band–type E♭ is standard, with occasional use of a B♭ contrabass for certain works. The small French C tuba was used for some years but has now given way to more conventional instruments in Parisian orchestras, usually a German-type six-valve F or contrabass. The C instrument is still used for high solos, as in Mussorgsky–Ravel's *Pictures at an Exhibition* and Stravinsky's *Petrouchka.* German tubas were widely used in American orchestras (though not in bands) from the late 19th century onward. Some large-bore piston valve tubas were made by domestic firms early in the century and are greatly prized today.
Present. Trumpet sections composed of C trumpets are now standard in American orchestras, but the B♭ is used in certain repertoires. English and German players generally prefer the B♭, while C trumpets are widely used in France and Austria. Trumpets with piston valves are most common, but rotary valve instruments are the mainstay of orchestras in Germany	*Present.* The F–B♭ full double is the standard orchestral instrument today. Exceptions are the single F horn used in the Vienna Philharmonic (there is renewed interest elsewhere in this horn) and the occasional single B♭ or triple horn. Double or triple descant horns are usually used for high-register work.	*Present.* Large-bore tenors with and without F attachment and in-line double-rotor bass trombones are used in orchestras and bands today. While small-bore trombones are rare, medium and medium-large bores are widely used by students and in the jazz and recording fields. Alto trombones are used for certain repertoire (particularly in Germany). Modern versions of traditional	American tubists established the trend of using the C contrabass as the primary instrument, reserving the bass in F for high-register passages, and this pattern has been followed elsewhere (although the B♭ contrabass is preferred in some countries). At present, large-bore piston valve C tubas based on early 20th century models have come into wide orchestral use, and

Trumpet and Cornet	Horn	Trombone	Baritone, Euphonium, and Tuba
and Austria and have been adopted by American players for certain repertoire. B♭ cornets and trumpets are invariably used in bands. Baroque parts are now usually played on the piccolo B♭/A trumpet. Present-day trumpets are available in the following keys: B♭, C, D, E♭, E, F, G, (piccolo) A, B♭, C. Some are built in one key with slides for other keys, e.g., D/E♭, G/F/E, and piccolo B♭/A. German-type rotary valve trumpets follow the same format in keys.		German trombones are preferred in Central Europe. The valve trombone is now found only in jazz, where it is an important solo instrument. Parts for contrabass trombone are usually played on the bass trombone, due to the increased capability of the in-line double-valve instrument, but there is increased use of modern forms of the contrabass instrument.	improved rotary valve instruments now offer a viable choice in instrument type. Orchestral-type rotary valve tubas are widely used in bands in the United States. Marching bands use the Sousaphone. British-type euphoniums are preferred in American concert bands, while traditional narrow-bore baritones and alto (tenor) horns are now used only in brass bands. At present, brass bands, modeled on the British tradition, are gaining popularity in America and Scandinavia. There is also some use of "American-bore" baritones (larger), usually as substitutes for the euphonium.

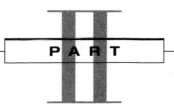

PART II

TECHNIQUE

TONE PRODUCTION

THE MOST VITAL attribute a brass player can have is an effective and reliable production of sound over the entire compass of the instrument. Not only is this the basis of one's ability to play the instrument, but it is also the cornerstone of a performer's confidence. Whether playing in the high or low ranges, loud or soft, notes must respond easily and dependably with a clear and resonant sound. Tone production consists of several elements that must be understood and brought together into a concept of how to play the instrument.

This is not a complex process in which each muscular function must be analyzed and controlled consciously. On the contrary, it is important that a practical concept of how to produce sound is developed and then transformed into a straightforward procedure that enables the player to achieve consistently good results. Brass students sometimes become obsessed with an analytical approach to playing. This often leads to what has been referred to by Adolph Herseth, former principal trumpet of the Chicago Symphony Orchestra, as "paralysis by analysis." The best approach is a natural, commonsense method that is based on sound principles and focused on musical results.

It should be recognized, however, that good brass players have different concepts and methods of playing; ultimately, a method of tone production must be judged on the basis of its results, and it has been amply demonstrated that brass players play successfully by using somewhat different approaches. Presented in this chapter is a method of playing as it is taught by the author. It is a proven method that works well for both beginners and advanced players who feel the need for a more consistent and reliable basis for their playing.

Musical sound on brass instruments is created by pitch vibration. Pitch vibration is in turn created by the motion of the air stream, which sets the embouchure into vibration at specific frequencies. To these fundamental elements is added articulation. Since air is the motive element in brass playing, how the air is moved by the respiratory system will be considered first.

■ THE AIR

Before presenting a practical approach to moving the air in and out of the lungs as this applies to brass playing, it would be helpful to discuss respiration in a general way, since misconceptions abound in musical circles. Air is moved in and out of the lungs by a process of expansion and reduction. This is accomplished by the respiratory muscles. Certain of these muscles work together to create various degrees of expansion to bring air into the lungs, and others bring about a reduction to expel air (under various levels of pressure) out of the lungs. The two procedures are called *inspiration* (taking in the air) and *expiration* (blowing out the air).

The lungs are contained within a flexible structure known as the *rib cage*. Within the lower ribs is a domed-shaped sheet of muscle called the *diaphragm*, which contracts upon inspiration (in normal breathing the muscular action of the diaphragm applies only to inspiration, not expiration). When the diaphragm contracts upon breathing in, the dome

FIGURE 10.1
Diagram based on
Frank H. Netter,
M.D., *Atlas of
Human Anatomy*
(Summit, N.J.:
CIBA-Geigy Corp.,
1989).

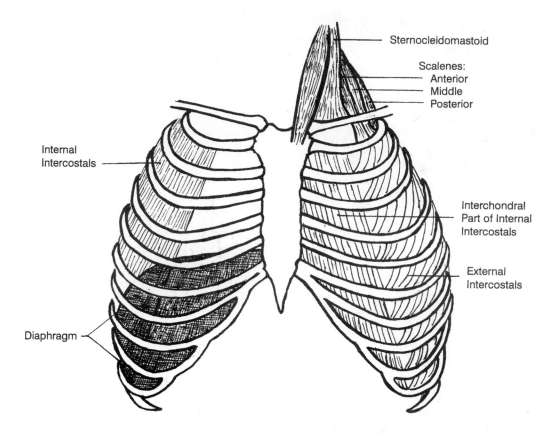

descends, vertically increasing the size of the thoracic cavity (the part of the trunk between the head and the abdomen). With the downward contraction of the diaphragm, the abdominal contents are forced downward; this also elevates the lower ribs, thus increasing the diameter of the rib cage at that level. The actual movement of the diaphragm is about one centimeter in normal *tidal* (quiet) breathing. In *active* breathing (known as forced inspiration and expiration), the movement can be up to 10 times greater.[1]

The other primary respiratory muscles that bring about expansion during inspiration are the external intercostal muscles and the interchondral part of the internal intercostals (see Figure 10.1). These muscles are attached between the ribs. The ribs slant downward and forward; when the intercostals contract upon inspiration, the ribs are pulled (rotated) upward and outward, increasing the diameter of the rib cage. In addition to the primary muscles of inspiration (diaphragm, external intercostals, and interchondral part of the internal intercostals), accessory muscles may also participate in the three-dimensional process of expansion. While these are little used in quiet breathing, they play an important role in the active breathing required in brass playing as well as in vigorous exercise. The sternocleidomastoids elevate (raise) the sternum at the same time as the scalenes (anterior, middle, and posterior) lift the first two (uppermost) ribs. This serves to further increase the size of the thoracic cavity and, consequently, the volume of air inhaled. The degree to which the accessory muscles participate in inspiration depends on how large a volume of air must be taken in. These muscles are more active in playing the tuba and low brass instruments than with the high brass.

Before inspiration, the pressure inside the lungs is equal to atmospheric pressure. As a result of the expansion created by the contraction of the muscles of inspiration, the intrathoracic pressure falls below atmospheric pressure and air flows into the lungs to equalize the pressure difference.

In quiet breathing, expiration is by passive recoil of the lungs and chest wall. The diaphragm and other muscles of inspiration release, allowing the lungs and chest wall

[1]John B. West, *Respiratory Physiology—The Essentials*, 4th ed.: Baltimore: Williams & Wilkins, 1990.

(through their natural elasticity) to return to their preinspiration position. Again, in the active respiration used when playing brass instruments or in exercise, contractions occur in the muscles of expiration. As in other areas of the body, respiratory muscles work together in groups. The abdominal muscles (rectus abdominis, obliquus externus, obliquus internus, and transversus abdominis) raise the intra-abdominal pressure by contracting on the lower ribs and compressing the abdominal contents; this pushes the released diaphragm upward toward its position prior to inspiration. It should be emphasized that this, like all of the muscular actions associated with respiration, are unconscious; by inspiring or expiring air, the respiratory musculature automatically becomes active in accordance with the demand placed on the respiratory system. Along with the contraction of the abdominal muscles, the internal intercostals (except for the interchondral part) contract, increasing the intrathoracic pressure by pulling the ribs down and in; this decreases the diameter of the rib cage and the volume of the thorax.

In light of the foregoing discussion of respiration, it would be well to dispel several common misconceptions about breathing as it pertains to brass playing. First among these is confusion over the role of the diaphragm in expiration. In normal breathing, the diaphragm functions as a muscle of inspiration, contracting on inspiration and releasing on expiration. In playing a brass instrument, the diaphragm can be either inactive or active on expiration, depending on the method of expiration chosen by the player. In the description of the four approaches to expiration that follows, in three of them the diaphragm releases as it does in normal breathing. In only one of the methods does the diaphragm continue its contraction, thus shifting the necessary reduction to the internal intercostal muscles in coordination with the transverse and oblique abdominal muscles. This method of expiration is discussed later in the chapter.

The second misconception about breathing as it relates to brass playing is that the shoulders should not be raised during inspiration. Although it is true that the shoulders should not consciously be raised and the breath taken from the chest, the normal elevation and expansion of the rib cage as the lungs are filled causes the shoulders to rise. This should not be resisted. If this natural motion is obstructed, there will be a significant decrease in the volume of air that can be inhaled. There will be a similar decrease in the volume of air if, as is often suggested, only the lower thorax is filled and the chest left out of the process of inspiration. In fact, it is essential to take air into the chest area, but secondary to filling the lower part of the lungs. If one thinks of filling the lungs from the bottom up, including the chest area, a more effective breath will be taken.

■ A PRACTICAL APPROACH

Having formed a general impression of how the respiratory system works, a procedure that is both effective and easy to use must be devised for taking in and blowing out the air. The two starting points of effective respiration are posture and relaxation. In order for the expansion that must occur on inspiration to take place without encumbrance, *the body must be upright and relaxed*. The body's respiratory system functions within a regime of gravity; therefore, it must be balanced in an erect position, not bent, in order to create the conditions that permit unimpeded expansion and reduction. When seated, it is essential to stay upright and *not rest on the back of the chair*. The latter position obstructs the rotational motion of the ribs in expanding and elevating during inspiration. Of equal importance is that *the body must remain relaxed*. Bodily tension inhibits the inflow and outflow of air and resists the respiratory system's natural movements. *Tension is the brass player's enemy.*

One of the principal problems facing brass teachers is the need to alter the student's natural tendency to start the breath from the chest. By filling only the chest, an inadequate volume of air will result. Even more destructive, however, is that exhalation tension will be created. This is an automatic reflex to a shallow chest breath. Tension is created in the upper thorax that quickly spreads to the muscles of the neck surrounding the trachea and throat, constricting the windway and obstructing the outflow of the air.

The windway must remain open, with the neck muscles and throat uninvolved in the process of blowing the air outward.

The way to avoid this and to establish a diaphragmatic breath is to have the student place his or her left hand on the stomach area and the right hand on the chest. The student should breathe in with a feeling of starting the breath from the stomach area, allowing the left hand to be moved outward as far as it will go, then filling the chest area, raising somewhat the right hand. In reality, the lungs are contained in the rib cage; it is the diaphragm's contraction that is being read by the left hand. As the diaphragm contracts, there is an outward movement around the waist. It is important in avoiding upper thorax tension that the left hand be moved outward all the way before topping up the air in the chest. A good mental image is that of filling a glass of water from bottom to top.

A related but somewhat different approach to taking in the air is to direct the intake to the middle of the back. The method of filling from bottom to top discussed in the preceding paragraph might be described as a vertical breath. Some players (and the author is among them) feel that a more effective breath can be taken by thinking of this process as a horizontal one, by using mental imagery. In this type of breath, the player imagines that the air is taken in horizontally through an opening in the middle of the back. Another way of accomplishing this is to think of bringing in the air horizontally through the mouth but directing it to the middle of the back. Either one of these procedures is equally effective. Some players favor the back breath but concentrate on expanding the lower back. This can be done by creating a feeling of pulling the lower back apart (to the left and right). Players who prefer the horizontal breath believe that air support on expiration is greatly improved by this method, and it is recommended.

An alternative way of thinking about inspiration is to visualize a quantity of air to be inhaled. Since air is essentially infinite, this cannot be done unless a way can be found to visualize a certain quantity of air as a finite form. Any common item of sufficient (or greater) size that represents the desired volume of air to be inhaled can serve for this purpose. A ball, balloon, or bag will work well enough. For example, if the student is asked to visualize a volume of air the size of a basketball and to inhale that quantity of air into the lungs, a full volume of air will be taken in. Of course, the volume of air contained in a basketball is much greater than the actual volume of air it is necessary to inhale, but the mental image will help the student take a full breath and experience what it feels like to have the lungs full of air.

There is an important relationship between the volume of air that has been inhaled and the effectiveness of the expiration. Expiration is most efficient when the lungs are full. This efficiency decreases sharply as the volume of air within the lungs becomes smaller (or was small in the first place). When a full volume of air has been inhaled, there is a natural outward propulsion of the air that is created by the recoil of the lungs and chest wall. This is the basis of the expiratory motion of the air; to this is added the (unconscious) contraction of the internal intercostal and abdominal muscles, which reduces under pressure the volume of the thoracic cavity, creating a more forceful outflow. The expiratory muscles can act more effectively when the lungs are full, since they are contracting on the volume of air contained in the lungs. If the volume of air is low, their ability to move air out of the lungs is compromised.

It is also important that the windway offer the least friction to the inflow of air. By thinking of inhaling with a feeling of "oh" in the mouth, the tongue will drop to the bottom of the mouth and the passage for the air will be open. "Oh" also encourages a feeling of relaxation on inspiration. Despite the fact that the expansion that occurs on inspiration is created by contracting muscles, the mind recognizes this action as a feeling of letting go and relaxing, as in a yawn. Relaxation is essential for good inspiration.

Before moving on to expiration, there is one more matter to consider: how fast the breath is taken. There are two schools of thought on this question. One approach regulates the intake of air to a beat of the music being performed. The upbeat serves for the intake of air, and it is felt that this synchronizes the preparatory steps to starting the note within time and facilitates a good attack. In all but the slowest tempos, breathing on the upbeat promotes a certain momentum to the breath, aiding a fuller inspiration. The second approach is to increase the duration of the breath without reference to a beat of the music. Depending on the tempo, the player breathes in for approximately two and a half beats. In fast tempos, an entire bar might be used for the breath. If the longer breath is made the norm and used at the beginning and wherever this is permitted in the music, a more relaxed and fuller breath will result, even in those places where only one beat is available for a breath. This is the main argument for the longer breath versus the one-beat breath. Tension is sometimes created by trying to take a full breath in only one beat. The long breath allows ample time to fill the lungs comfortably with a feeling of re-laxation. Since the long breath requires a more advanced sense of timing, it is probably best to start beginners with the one-beat breath and to introduce the longer breath at a later point in their development.

■ EXPIRATION

Expiration as it applies to brass playing should be conceived of as air in motion. It is the active motion of the air that creates stable pitch vibration in the mouthpiece and pro-duces a good quality of sound. This can be accomplished by thinking of moving the air as "wind."[2] Wind, as we observe it in nature, is air in motion. If the player visualizes cre-ating wind in motion when blowing the air outward, the respiratory system will re-spond to produce an effective air stream.

There are three components of the expiratory outflow of air: *volume* (the quantity of the air), *velocity* (this determines the pitch), and *pressure* (the force of the air). In order for the embouchure to be vibrated at various speeds to produce higher and lower pitches corresponding to the requisite cycles per second of the notes to be played, faster or slower air must be delivered to the embouchure. When ascending, the velocity of the air must be increased; in descending it must decrease. In addition to the correct velocity, each note requires the right balance of volume and pressure. These mixtures vary through the range and also between instruments. In general, low brass instruments re-quire comparatively more volume and less pressure than the high brass, which require more wind pressure as well as volume in the high register to support the rapid vibration of the embouchure. Low notes require air of slower velocity, greater volume, and only sufficient pressure to stabilize them. Dynamics, too, require subtle adjustments in the mixture of volume and pressure to maintain good pitch.

The player should think of creating both air volume and wind pressure when blow-ing the air outward, seeking an easily produced, in-tune, and good-quality sound. Tak-ing a note in the middle register as a base level of pressure and volume, both the pres-sure and volume should be raised in ascending to the upper register. In descending from the middle register to the lower register, the volume of air should be increased along with sufficient pressure to maintain an even dynamic level and a stable pitch and sound. Players sometimes have difficulty with the lower register, caused by decreasing (rather than increasing) the volume of air or not maintaining sufficient air pressure to stabilize the notes.

Four different approaches are used by brass players in blowing the air outward. The choice of which technique a brass player chooses has to do with the degree of resistance in the instrument, the range in which it plays, and which technique works best for the

---

[2] The concept of moving air as wind in brass playing is one of a number of important pedagogical principles developed by the great tubist Arnold Jacobs. Mr. Jacobs' work has had wide-ranging influence on modern brass playing. See M. Dee Stewart, *Arnold Jacobs: The Legacy of a Master* (Northfield, Ill.: The Instrumentalist Publishing Co., 1987); Kevin Kelly with Arnold Jacobs and David Cugell, M.D., "The Dynamics of Breathing," *The Instrumentalist* (December 1983), pp. 6–12; Bill Russo, "An Interview with Arnold Jacobs," *The Instrumentalist* (February 1973) (the latter two articles are reprinted in the Stewart book); Arnold Jacobs, "Arnold Jacobs Master Class," *The Instrumentalist* (June 1991); Arnold Jacobs, "Mind over Metal," *The Instrumentalist* (October 1992); Brian Frederiksen, "Arnold Jacobs—A Bibliography," *ITG Journal* (May 1993); Brian Frederiksen, *Arnold Jacobs: Song and Wind* (Gurnee, Ill.: WindSong Press, 1996).

player. The essential element that all four procedures have in common is that they are all processes of reduction to move air to support the pitch vibration of the embouchure.

The first mode of expiration follows the natural action of the respiratory system described earlier. As the player thinks of blowing outward, the respiratory system unconsciously brings about the necessary reduction to propel the air. Because it is dependent on the recoil of the lungs and chest wall to a large extent, a full breath is required. The resultant air flow might be described as high volume, low pressure.

The second means of expiration is similar to the first but adds a conscious contraction of the abdominal muscles—particularly the rectus abdominis, the vertical muscles at the front of the torso. As discussed earlier, there is an unconscious contraction of the abdominal muscles (during expiration) that aids the recoil of the released diaphragm. To this is added a conscious contraction of these muscles, with a feeling of pushing inward and upward. Sometimes the conscious contraction is reserved for high or loud passages, rather than maintained as a constant effort.[3] The effect of this is to raise the pressure somewhat, creating an outflow that is high volume, medium pressure.

The third procedure for expiration is often used when there is a feeling of resistance from the instrument. In the other three techniques of expiration, the diaphragm releases (as it does in common non-brass-playing respiration). In the third method, the inspiratory contraction of the diaphragm is consciously retained on expiration, thereby resisting the automatic contraction of the abdominal muscles. This action shifts the reduction to a strong contraction of the internal intercostal muscles and the transverse and oblique abdominal muscles. This results in a substantial increase in the air stream's outflow pressure. Although the physiological explanation of this process is complex, this mode of expiration is very simple to use. The player simply thinks of keeping the expanded area of the waist (stomach area) pushing outward while the air is blown outward. Players who use this means of expiration often speak of supporting from the diaphragm. Sometimes a "floor" is visualized in the waist area, with the air moving outward above it. It is unfortunate that in the literature this process has been confused with a rigid, isometric tension in which very little air is moved. In fact, it is a dynamic process of reduction through which air is moved with greater pressure than in the other three methods. It is therefore often preferred by trumpet and horn players, who require significant air pressure to support the vibration of the embouchure and to overcome the resistance of the instrument in the high range. As was seen in Chapter 1, brass instruments function with less acoustical efficiency in the high register. The air stream that results from this method of expiration may be said to be of high pressure and medium air volume.

The fourth approach to expiration is less common than the first three and is sometimes used by tuba and other low brass players. The idea is to compress the air before it is moved out of the lungs. To accomplish this, after the lungs are filled with air, the stomach area (through a contraction of rectus abdominis) is pulled inward, pushing the diaphragm upward and compressing the air into the chest immediately before blowing outward. This results in a large volume of air being moved under low-to-medium pressure that works well on the tuba.[4]

Another important concept common to all four approaches is that the air should be blown *directly and horizontally forward*. This can best be accomplished by directing the air to a point of arrival across the room.

■ THE EMBOUCHURE AND THE FIRST STEPS IN PLAYING

Sound and pitch are created in the mouthpiece by the vibration of the embouchure. To generate pitch vibration, the lips must be formed in such a way that they can be brought into oscillation by the motion of the air stream. The mouthpiece must be placed on the

[3]See Frøydis Ree Wekre, *Thoughts on Playing the Horn Well* (Oslo: Frøydis Ree Wekre, 1994).
[4]This method was one of the procedures taught by the late Arnold Jacobs. A similar technique is described in Antonio Iervolino, "Breathing Technique," *The Horn Call* (Vol. 12, no. 2, April 1982), pp. 19–25.

FIGURE 10.2
The TRU-VU transparent mouthpiece demonstrated by Peter Sullivan, trombonist with the Orchestre Symphonique de Montréal.

embouchure formation so that optimal vibration is encouraged and an air seal is formed. This isolates the oscillating parts of the lips from the facial musculature outside the mouthpiece; the latter support and regulate the formation inside the mouthpiece. An important step forward in our understanding of what takes place within the mouthpiece was taken by Ellis Wean.[5] Around 1985–86 Wean made a videotape of top professional brass players using high-quality transparent mouthpieces of his own manufacture (see Figure 10.2) playing scales, intervals, and arpeggios on the instrument while a strobe light isolated the actual vibratory motion of the lips. This motion was revealed to be an opening and closing of the embouchure for each complete oscillation. The number of oscillations corresponds to the frequency of the pitch played (for example, A = 440 oscillations per second).

To form an effective embouchure, bring the jaw forward so that the upper and lower teeth are more or less aligned. A small space should be made between the teeth for the air stream to pass through. Next, take a piece of paper and hold it about a foot and a half from the lips. Blow a stream of air at the paper while saying "tu" ("too"), causing the paper to fold back. Keep the "u" ("oo") going while continuing to blow, until the air runs out.[6] This will give the right feeling of blowing the air forward while forming an embouchure. The "u" formation that is created when pronouncing "tu" brings the lips into a slightly pursed configuration that creates a cushion for the mouthpiece to rest on. Not only does this protect the lips from mouthpiece pressure, but the "u" contracts the lips and facial muscles in such a way that the embouchure will vibrate in response to the motion of the air stream (see Figures 10.3 and 10.4).[7]

---

[5] Ellis Wean is presently tubist of the Vancouver Symphony Orchestra.
[6] Blowing outward toward a piece of paper is suggested in Dale Clevenger, Mark McDunn, and Harold Rusch, *The Dale Clevenger French Horn Methods* (Park Ridge, Ill.: Neil A. Kjos, 1974).
[7] The contraction of the embouchure and facial musculature can be observed by lightly pressing a finger against the upper lip and pronouncing the syllables "tee," "tah," "toh," and "tu." It will be observed that the musculature contracts only with "tu" (the "u" vowel). The same observation should be made at the lower lip and at the sides of the mouth.

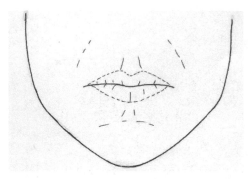

FIGURE 10.3   Natural lip formation.

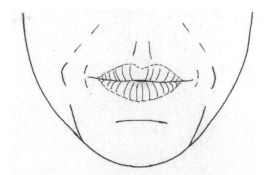

FIGURE 10.4   Embouchure formation.

It is important in forming the embouchure that the corners of the mouth not be allowed to pull outward as in a smile. If this happens, the pursed "u" formation becomes distorted and the embouchure cannot function effectively. To prevent this and to form a stable embouchure, it is necessary to contract the modioli. These are the junctures (*modiolus* means "hub") of the strands of facial muscles found just beyond each corner of the mouth (about one-third of an inch from each corner). These must contract[8] and *adhere to the sides of the teeth.* This becomes the primary lateral support for the embouchure, keeping it in position as the player moves from one range to another.

After understanding the role of the modioli, the width of the embouchure when pronouncing "tu" needs to be considered and optimized. As the modioli contract and adhere to the sides of the teeth, the horizontal width of the embouchure must be set to favor vibration throughout the range of the instrument. If the embouchure's width is too narrow (overly puckered), the embouchure will be unresponsive and difficult to set into vibration, especially in the high range. If the width is too wide, the overtautness of the embouchure will cause it to be brittle and inflexible, with insufficient cushion for the mouthpiece. To find the optimum embouchure width, close the lips normally, as shown in Figure 10.3. Then pronounce "tu" and firm the musculature around the "tu" formation without pulling the lips outward or bringing them in toward the center. The resultant width should more or less match the width of the mouth when the lips are closed naturally. This procedure will create the responsive and flexible semipuckered embouchure shown in Figure 10.4.

It is similarly important that the cheeks or chin not be allowed to inflate. This also causes problems, and the inflation prevents the facial musculature from contracting and supporting the embouchure formation inside the mouthpiece.

The next step is to place the mouthpiece in the best position for the embouchure to vibrate easily in a controlled way (see Figures 10.5 through 10.12). Mouthpiece placement is an important consideration, since embouchure difficulties often stem from an improper placement. The mouthpiece rim should be centered horizontally on the embouchure. This is the preferred position, but it should be recognized that many successful instrumentalists play slightly off-center due to variations in dental structure. The vertical placement is more critical, and this is usually described as proportions of upper and lower lip within the mouthpiece rim. These vary somewhat between instruments. An embouchure visualizer or transparent mouthpiece is helpful in checking vertical placement. For the trumpet, an equal proportion of upper and lower lip in the mouthpiece is generally preferred, although players often use a slightly higher place-

---

[8]The contraction of the modioli can be felt by pushing in with the fingers at the sides of the mouth, about a third of an inch beyond the mouth corners. It is essential that the modioli adhere to the sides of the teeth to bring stability to the embouchure.

FIGURE 10.5
Peter Bond, Metropolitan Opera Orchestra.

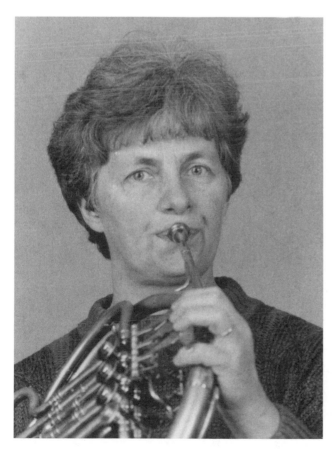

FIGURE 10.6
Norwegian horn soloist Frøydis Ree Wekre.

FIGURE 10.7
SSgt. Steven Kellner, Principal Euphonium, United States Marine Band.

FIGURE 10.8
Arnold Jacobs, Former Principal Tuba, Chicago Symphony Orchestra.

ment, about 60 percent upper and 40 percent lower lip. In earlier periods, a one-third upper/two-thirds lower placement was often recommended, but this is generally not encouraged today because of the possibility that the upper rim of the mouthpiece will slide down onto the upper lip and impede vibration. This is the primary concern for trumpet and horn players. If the inner edge of the mouthpiece rim slips down or is placed on the red of the upper lip, the opening and closing motion of the lip will be affected and the embouchure will not be reliable. For the horn, a two-thirds upper lip and one-third lower lip placement has always been used, and this continues to be favored today. This is necessary for the wide range covered by the horn and because of the depth of the horn mouthpiece. It should be noted that with the mouthpiece placed this high, the bottom inner edge of the rim comes slightly onto the red of the lower lip. This is normal and desirable in the horn embouchure. Most trombone, euphonium, and tuba players use a placement somewhat above half and half, but the latter is advocated by some trombonists. In addition to Figure 10.2, Figures 10.9 through 10.12 illustrate typical placements for each instrument.

The lower lip should serve as the "seat" of the mouthpiece on the embouchure and should bear the minimum pressure necessary to create an air seal. After having practiced a few times forming the embouchure and placing the mouthpiece, the player is ready to produce the first sounds. This should be done initially with the mouthpiece alone. In making sound on the mouthpiece, the same process is used as on the instrument. The mouthpiece, however, does not provide any pitch centers; pitch must be created by the player. Hold the mouthpiece at the bottom of the shank with two or three fingers and the thumb. Place the mouthpiece lightly on the embouchure. Inhale by opening the sides of the embouchure beyond the mouthpiece rim, and blow the air out by creating wind while pronouncing "tu." Keep the "u" going while blowing outward. A sound should result. If this does not occur the first time, keep trying. Sometimes placing a finger partially over the end of the shank or cupping the hands around the end of the shank will help to get the sound started by increasing the resistance.[9] Whatever pitch results, try to hold on to it. Control and stability will be gained by holding long notes, whatever pitch results. It is a mistake to insist that specific pitches be played in these initial attempts. Once notes can be played with some reliability, one can gradually focus on specific notes in the instrument's middle register.[10] It is important that the pressure of the mouthpiece against the embouchure be no greater than that required to form an air seal. Excessive mouthpiece pressure thwarts the normal functioning of the embouchure and causes it to tire quickly.

A word should be said about breathing when the mouthpiece is in place on the embouchure. The most common way of doing this is to release the playing pressure of the mouthpiece against the embouchure while leaving the mouthpiece rim lightly touching the lips. Open the lips at each side of the mouthpiece and draw in the air. It is important that the embouchure not be distorted when taking in the air. Do not stretch the lips backward to make an opening for the inflow of air. This distorts the embouchure position within the mouthpiece so that when playing is resumed, the lips are stretched out of position. A less common approach is to drop the jaw and bring the air in below the mouthpiece.

Having gained some confidence in playing long notes on the mouthpiece, the next step is to learn to change pitch. This can be done on the mouthpiece by sliding (slurring) back and forth from one note to another, beginning with the intervals of a major second or minor third and continuing to a few wider intervals and melodies. To change pitch on brass instruments, adjustments are made in the velocity of the air stream and in the oral

---

[9] Using a BERP (buzz extension resistance piece) or Buzz Aid is often helpful to beginners when making their first sounds. The added resistance makes it easier to get the sound started. Once the player gains control over playing pitches on the mouthpiece, it is preferable to use the mouthpiece alone without any added resistance.
[10] Recommended starting pitches are given in Chapter 12 along with suggestions for teaching young beginners.

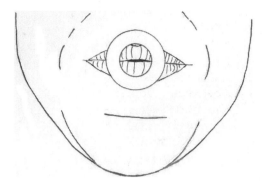

FIGURE 10.9

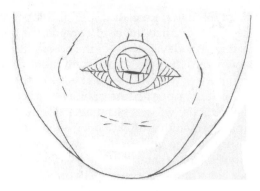

FIGURE 10.10

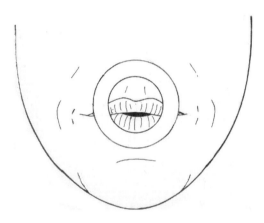

FIGURE 10.11

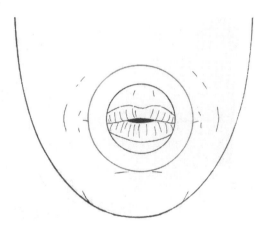

FIGURE 10.12

cavity by changing vowel formations.[11] The space in the mouth is made variable by raising and lowering the tongue. The basic "tu" position establishes a medium-sized oral cavity. From here, the mouth space can be made smaller by raising the tongue and made larger by lowering it. Every player already has the skill to do this through the mastery of speech. If the "u" of "tu"[12] is modified by mixing in progressively more of the "ee" vowel, the tongue will automatically rise toward the roof of the mouth, making a gradually smaller windway for the air to go through. To go lower from the "u" vowel, more "ah" or "oh" are added to cause the tongue to descend and create a larger passage for the air. The changes of vowel take place within the mouth. As has been seen earlier, the "u" vowel (as in "tu") causes the embouchure and facial muscles to contract in exactly the right way. Therefore, to maintain the embouchure's formation and contraction, vowel

[11] The variations of the oral cavity created by changing vowels have been confirmed by X-ray in the research of Bengt Belfrage, Mats Haverling, and Hans Bergstedt, *Practice Methods for Brass Players Based on Physiological Factors* (Stockholm: AB Nordiska Musikförlaget—Edition Wilhelm Hansen, 1982).

[12] The French "u" vowel as it was presented in a syllable by Arban is closer to "tew" or "tiyu" in English. In German it is usually written as "tü." Individual players should experiment to determine whether one of these or an English "too" will work better.

changes should be approached as mixed vowels, forming, for example, a combination of "u" and "ee" or "u" and "ah." In this way, the embouchure will retain its formation and support while the space inside the mouth changes for higher or lower pitches. The windway vowels are shown in the following table, arranged from high to low.

Mix some "u" into the vowels at right to maintain the contraction and formation of the embouchure	"ieess" or "iss" This brings the tongue close to the roof of the mouth for the highest notes.
	"eee"
	"ee"
	"e"
	"ue" "ü" For the middle register.
	"u"
	"ah"
	"awe"
	"oh" Creates the most open windway for the lowest notes.

In the highest register, the tongue moves very close to the roof of the mouth. When the "e" vowel will go no higher, the vowel should change to a different sound. By phonating the sound "ieess" ("eeess"), the tongue will flatten and rise closer to the roof of the mouth. This should be reserved only for the very highest notes.

In tonguing, the consonant "t" is combined with the appropriate mixed vowel, depending on the pitch of the note to be played, forming a syllable to start the sound. The changes of vowel are more than just raising and lowering the tongue. Different vowels also produce subtle changes of shape in the tongue, aiding the production of sound and timbre on different pitches. In general, the tongue should flatten, with its sides contacting the teeth to left and right, and a channel should be formed for the air to pass through. When the vowel, air velocity, pressure, and volume are well adjusted for a high note, the note seems to play with remarkable ease. There may be (as the author suspects) an acoustical phenomenon that has not yet been investigated that links the pitches formed in the mouth with pitch response in the instrument. It is hoped that acoustical research will be forthcoming in this area.

Once the concept of changing vowels is incorporated into a player's basic technique, it usually becomes an unconscious and automatic process concerned with centering the sound and pitch of the notes. The ability to change pitch can be learned on the mouthpiece, and this will carry over to the instrument. The basic procedures may be summarized as follows.

To go higher:

1. Increase the velocity, volume, and pressure of the air stream.
2. Change to a higher mixed vowel (see table).

To go lower:

1. Decrease the velocity of the air stream, but increase the volume of the air with enough pressure to stabilize the notes.
2. Change to a lower mixed vowel (see table).

Once the player can produce stable notes on the mouthpiece and change pitches, practice should be directed toward starting notes with a clear attack (by pronouncing "tu"). After some further practice with the mouthpiece, it is time to move to the instrument and to begin work with an elementary method.

■ ATTACK AND TONGUING

Sound commences when the embouchure vibrates in response to the motion of the air stream. The action of the tongue contributes a clear and controlled beginning to the sound. It also creates different effects in how the beginnings of notes sound through the use of varied styles of attack. In actuality, the tongue adds variable pulsations to the already moving air stream. This is done by pronouncing a syllable into the mouthpiece. The activating syllable is a combination of the consonant "t" and the vowel "u." "Tu" and "ta" are common syllables; these provide a clear, definite beginning to the sound. When a softer attack is desired, the syllables are pronounced less sharply, or the consonant is changed to a "d," as in "du." Although some players prefer to change to a softer consonant, others use only the "t" consonant but modify the syllables from very hard to soft by pronouncing them with greater or lesser force. The sound of a musical passage is first visualized (heard in the mind's ear), and the syllables are then pronounced with the appropriate degree of hardness. In tonguing various patterns within musical passages, a new syllable is pronounced for every tongued note.

The syllables "tu" and "du" can be recommended, since these syllables also create a reliable embouchure formation through the optimum muscular contractions associated with speech. However, some players find that broader syllables, such as "ta" and "toh," work better, especially on low brass instruments. These syllables will not automatically form and contract the embouchure as they are pronounced. Therefore, players who use "ta" or "toh" must create the habit of forming the embouchure and contracting the appropriate muscles as a normal part of their preparation to play. If the "t" consonant is replaced with "d" in conjunction with the "ah" vowel ("da"), there is a tendency for the mouth to open in articulation, causing excessive jaw movement. It is suggested that beginning players start with "tu." Once the embouchure is established, low brass players should try the syllable "ta" or "toh" while remembering to keep the embouchure contracted.

For practice purposes and in warming up, breath attacks are helpful in encouraging a free outflow of air and responsiveness of the embouchure. In a breath attack, the sound is started without the tongue, solely by the motion of the air. There are two types of breath attack; each contributes different positive qualities to a player's tone production. The most common breath attack substitutes the consonant "h" for the "t" in "tu." Starting notes with "hu" promotes an open and relaxed windway and a free outflow of the air stream. Because the "h" consonant is less decisive than "t," notes will usually begin slightly late. This should be accepted by the player as a practice tool in exchange for the benefit provided by the breath attack. Players often start their warm-up with a breath attack and then change the consonant to "t" after a short period. The other breath attack substitutes the consonant "p" to form the syllable "pu." This, too, is suitable only for warming up. The "p" consonant causes the center of the lips to close and catch the air stream, setting the embouchure into vibration and stimulating an easy response. It is particularly useful for beginning students, who sometimes have difficulty starting the sound and tend to force notes to speak. This is because the lip aperture is frequently too far open with beginners and the air goes through the lips without setting them into vibration. By starting the first lessons with the syllable "pu," students will learn to make sound more easily on the instrument and avoid force.

It is best if inspiration, expiration, and attack are approached as a continuous action. Inspiration should flow smoothly into expiration, with no stop at the changeover point. There should be no hesitation at the tongue before an attack is made. If either of these interruptions occur, there is the likelihood that tension will be built up in the throat and

FIGURE 10.13
Tongue placement.

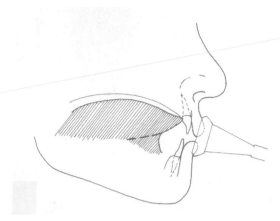

neck, impeding the free production of sound. To gain a continuous motion of inspiration into expiration, the student might visualize a wave coming onto a beach (inspiration) and then changing direction to return outward (expiration).

There is great variation among individual players in the placement of the tip of the tongue when starting notes. So great is the variation that it is impossible to lay down firm guidelines for this aspect of tone production. Figure 10.13 illustrates a common tongue placement, with the tip in the upper front corner of the mouth at the gum line of the upper teeth. In actuality, however, players often place the tip of the tongue on the back of the upper teeth or on the roof of the mouth. Some players do not think about tongue placement at all and only focus on pronouncing attack syllables, allowing the tongue to go to the most natural place. It is now generally agreed that players should not tongue between the teeth or lips.

To end a note, the basic procedure is to stop blowing. This is important; beginners often develop the habit of stopping the sound by replacing the tongue in its attack position with the note still sounding. This creates an unmusical and audible sound at the end of the note. The player should listen carefully to the end of the note and conclude it without any sound or variation in pitch. The so-called tongued release does have its place, however. Professional players often make use of it by adding a "t" at the end of the note ("tut") in very staccato passages. This produces a shortness and crispness that can be obtained in no other way.

A very helpful practice technique for attack and tonguing that is advocated by the distinguished trumpet teacher Vincent Cichowicz is the use of "wind patterns."[13] This is done without the instrument by saying "tu" on the rhythmic notation of the passage or piece without pitch. A full breath should be taken, and the player should blow through the notes in a sustained manner. No buzzing sound should be made, only the sound of the motion of the air in pronouncing "tu." By practicing wind patterns, the player will get the feel of articulating the notes freely, without tension. This will carry over to the instrument. Wind patterns can do a lot to improve a player's attack and tonguing as well as promote a more relaxed and natural approach to the instrument.

■ STYLES OF ATTACK AND SHAPING NOTES

The style or sound of the attack must be artistically modified in accordance with the repertoire being performed. It is inconceivable to use a single style of attack throughout the repertoire. Similarly, the *shape* of the note must be varied to fit the stylistic characteristics of different composers and musical periods. A note should be visualized as consisting of

[13] Air patterns and other important concepts are described in the following articles: Vincent Cichowicz, "Teaching the Concepts of Trumpet Playing," *The Instrumentalist* (January 1996), pp. 27–31; Wolfgang Guggenberger, "Vincent Cichowicz, Grand Master of Trumpet Teaching," *Brass Bulletin* 104 (1998), pp. 46–55.

three parts: a beginning (attack), middle, and end (release). As discussed earlier, different degrees of sharpness or smoothness can be imparted to the beginning of a note by pronouncing the attack syllable with greater or lesser force or by changing the consonant from a "t" to a "d" for a softer attack. The middle of the note can maintain a dynamic level that is equal to the attack or can swell or diminish after the attack, following a visualized contour that fits the musical context. The release can be abrupt, smooth, or tapered, depending on the desired effect.

To give a few examples: The style of attack and note shape used in Berlioz and Debussy are radically different from those used in Bruckner and Wagner. In French music (except where the composer indicates a different approach), a clear, bell-like attack should be sought, followed by an easing of the dynamic level of the middle of the note. In Bruckner and many other Germanic composers, a broader, less pronounced attack produced by using a softer consonant should continue into the rounder note shape common to singers. In the works of many other composers, a *symmetrically shaped note* is best. In this style of note, the volume remains even from the attack to the release; that is, the dynamic level of the attack, though clear, is not greater than that of the middle of the note or the release. This is the note shape that should be cultivated as a player's basic approach to attacking and shaping notes. Once this is mastered, the player should carefully study representative performances of specific works and emulate the specialized note shapes and styles of attack that fit the styles of various composers and periods.

■ MULTIPLE TONGUING

When normal single tonguing cannot cope with the pace demanded by a passage or sounds labored, a special technique is required. By utilizing the middle rear portion of the tongue for the second or third repetition, tonguing speed can be substantially increased. The syllables "tu-ku," "ta-ka," "tu-tu-ku," and "ta-ta-ka" are most often recommended for this purpose.[14] The main difficulty in double and triple tonguing is achieving a quality of sound and evenness that compare favorably with single tonguing. The problem comes from less air being moved by the syllables produced at the back of the tongue, causing weakness of the "k" syllable and inequality in the sound of double and triple tonguing.

This can be remedied in two ways. By substituting the syllables, "da-ga" and "da-da-ga" for "tu-ku" and "ta-ta-ka," more air will be moved forward, generating a stronger second or third syllable. The syllables should be pronounced fairly forward in the mouth. If double and triple tonguing are practiced *slowly and in direct comparison with single tonguing,* the syllables will gain in control, clarity, and strength, promoting equality between the syllables.

Each measure or pattern in an exercise should first be single tongued and then immediately repeated using double or triple syllables. The goal is to be unable to detect an important difference in the sound between the two procedures.

Another form of multiple tonguing is used by jazz players. "Doodle" or "lah-dah" tonguing is a smoother, legato form of double tonguing. This form of articulation has

---

[14]In certain passages, advanced players occasionally rearrange the order of triple tongue syllables to "tu-ku-tu," "ta-ka-ta," or "da-ga-da."

been used by many jazz trombonists and was popularized on the trumpet by Clark Terry.[15]

■ SLURRING

Slurring on brass instruments may be defined as smoothly moving between notes with no articulation. This can be done on the harmonic series, known as a *lip slur,* or with the valves. The primary consideration in making a slur is that the connection between notes be smooth and without any break in the sound. It is essential to keep the air in motion between notes, and it is helpful if the slur is approached as one sound going continuously into another.

Any interruption to the air flow or sound in the space between two slurred notes will ruin the quality of the slur. Valve slurs are particularly prone to this problem; care should be taken to move the air stream through the valve change. It is also important that the valve motion be quick because any interruption of the valve change will disrupt the motion of the air and be heard in the sound. Slurring should first be learned on the mouthpiece. By sliding from one note to another, any break in the motion of the air or the vibration will be revealed. It is best to slide slowly between notes at first, gradually bringing the change up to desired degree of quickness. Whenever problems with slurs occur, checking them on the mouthpiece in this way will correct the problem.

In order to retain an evenness of volume between slurred notes, it is necessary to increase the wind pressure when ascending, to compensate for the slightly greater resistance that is encountered on the higher pitch. The air flow must also rise for descending notes, to accommodate a more relaxed embouchure and lessened resistance. Sometimes it is useful (particularly in ascending) to crescendo on the lower note and let the momentum carry the sound to the higher note.

■ TROMBONE LEGATO

Because the medium for changing notes is a movable slide, the subject of legato on the trombone must be treated separately. Actually, the only true slurs available on the trombone are the lip slur (moving between two different notes of the same harmonic series), when the slide motion is opposite to the direction of the notes, and between adjacent positions in the same slide direction when there is a change of harmonic. Most of the time, however, the trombonist must depend on a refined legato tongue to create the effect of slurring. In practice, all four procedures are used in one integrated technique. The goal is a seamless legato in which the listener is unable to detect the means used to achieve it.

What has been said concerning slurring in general applies also to the trombone, particularly with lip slurs that take place in the same position. When the slide is moved, the problem of avoiding unwanted sound between notes becomes paramount. Quick slide motion is essential to avoid the slide's natural tendency to glissando.[16]

It is possible to achieve a clean slur between adjacent positions if the move involves a change from one series of harmonics to another. For example, a slur might be made

---

[15] Various jazz articulations and effects, including "doodle tonguing," are discussed in John McNeil, *The Art of Jazz Trumpet,* 2 vols. (Brooklyn, N.Y.: Gerard and Sarzin, 1993); Bill Watrous, *Trombonisms: An Extension of Standard Trombone Techniques and an Introduction to Some New Ones* (New York: Carl Fischer, 1983); and Jim Maxwell, *The First Trumpeter* (New York: Charles Colin, 1982).
[16] Slide movement is discussed in Chapter 5.

from A at the top of the bass staff (second position, fourth harmonic of the series on A) to D above (first position, sixth harmonic of the series on G) without using the tongue if the slide motion is quick. Another approach is through the direction of the motion of the slide in relation to the direction of the notes. A smooth slur might be achieved if the notes move downward as the slide is brought inward. The reverse—notes ascending, outward slide motion—is effective only in the upper register.

For all other slurring, legato tonguing must be employed through the use of a soft syllable, such as "du," "thu," or "loo." This is sometimes accompanied by placing the tongue on the roof of the mouth. To achieve a smooth legato, it is vital to keep the air stream moving. Students sometimes hesitate with the air between notes to avoid a glissando, when the real problem is that the slide motion is too slow.[17] Some teachers advocate almost always using the legato tongue in performance and reserving natural slurs for practice.

■ RANGE AND ENDURANCE

There is no magic secret for playing in the high register, and it does not involve a change in playing method. Rather, the high range should be viewed as the continuation of the upper middle register. It is important to remember that for each higher note that is added to the range, faster pitch vibrations are required. To create progressively faster vibrations, the velocity and pressure of the air must be increased, the vowel position must rise closer to the roof of the mouth, and the lips must become closer and be supported by the embouchure formation. The lower lip should bear any mouthpiece pressure.

What often occurs is that the increase in wind velocity, pressure, and volume is insufficient to vibrate the embouchure at the required pitch or that the vowel position is too low. This results in either no sound or a flat or forced note. In other cases, the embouchure becomes rigid and tight, resisting the air stream's effort to bring it into vibration. This is often accompanied by tension in the throat or excessive mouthpiece pressure. Sometimes, the embouchure formation is distorted by pulling back into a smile or some other contortion.

No progress in the upper register can be gained by trying to force the notes to sound. The best way to develop the upper register is to integrate high playing (in moderation) into the regular daily practice session. The embouchure develops (along with use of the air) in response to the demands of the material being played. Some of the regular daily exercise patterns should be continued upward to the top of the range. Slurring in the high range should be undertaken first. With each higher note, there needs to be a surge in air velocity, with its accompanying increase in air pressure and volume, allowing the embouchure to vibrate at the right pitch without force. The respiratory muscles must propel the air to create this surge. Of prime importance is that the tongue flatten so that its sides contact the teeth on either side and rise very close to the roof of the mouth, with only a slim channel for the air. This is accomplished by changing to a high "ee" or "ieess" ("eeess") vowel position. The air must go through this small channel with sufficient velocity for the embouchure to be supported in its vibration.[18] As stated earlier, there appears to be an acoustical relationship between the pitches formed in the mouth and the responsiveness of the instrument, particularly in the high register. When the vowel and air are well adjusted, the instrument responds with ease. The embouchure formation must support the lips coming closer together. The modioli (discussed earlier), in particular, must adhere to the sides of the teeth, preventing any tendency for the lips to be pulled outward into a smile. The bottom lip must serve as the seat of the embouchure, with the mouthpiece resting on it. This, along with the cushion created by the "tu" formation,

---

[17]Several books of studies for trombone legato may be recommended: Joannes Rochut, *Melodious Etudes,* vols. 1–3 (Carl Fischer); André LaFosse, *Méthode complète de trombone* à *coulisse* (Alphonse Leduc); Reginald H. Fink, *Studies in Legato for Trombone* (Carl Fischer); Blazhevich, *30 Legato Studies* (International).
[18]Some players feel that anchoring the tip of the tongue behind the lower teeth with the middle and rear of the tongue close to the roof of the mouth aids making entrances and playing in the highest register. The articulation is then made by the middle of the tongue against the roof of the mouth.

protects the upper lip from mouthpiece pressure. The latter should not be greater than that necessary to create an air seal.

It is best if daily playing in the high register is done at only a medium volume level. It is sometimes helpful to play the high-register material first on the mouthpiece and then on the instrument. If the notes are not forthcoming beyond a certain point, it is best to accept what has been accomplished for the current day and to continue the next day. Over time, this approach will produce improvement in the upper range.

The player's choice of etudes and solos played in daily practice should also be integrated into a progressive plan designed to strengthen and maintain the embouchure and respiratory muscles. This is the foundation of endurance. The embouchure builds strength as it plays challenging material. The same is true of the muscles used in expiration. The great cornetist Herbert L. Clarke coined the term *wind power* to describe his method of playing. This is a useful concept with regard to endurance. A player's wind power will be strengthened in proportion to the demands placed on it. In choosing the material to be played daily, thought should be given to the load placed on the embouchure and wind power. This should increase by carefully chosen increments. If too sharp a rate is attempted, the embouchure will not be able to cope with the demand and residual fatigue will set in.

Residual fatigue occurs when the embouchure is overstressed by heavy playing. The embouchure cannot fully recover overnight, and a residue of the previous day's fatigue is carried over into the next day. After several days of this, the embouchure will feel tired at the beginning of playing. When this occurs, the worst thing the player can do is to try to carry on with the normal routine. It is also unhelpful not to play at all. Both of these attempts to deal with the problem usually make matters worse. The best thing the player can do in these circumstances is to practice but to limit the material played to a light workout. This allows the embouchure to regain its equilibrium, and the next day should see some recovery.

The way to good endurance is through well-chosen material arranged in a progressive program for the daily practice session.

■ SUSTAINING AND CONTINUITY

The related concepts of sustaining and continuity are underlying principles of all good brass playing. It is important that notes retain an evenness of volume. Any "erosion" of a note detracts from the tone and reflects a poor mastery of style. This creates ensemble problems, as well, with balance and intonation since it is difficult to balance notes that are uneven in shape.[19] Another common error is to allow the note before a breath is taken to decrease in volume (unless the musical context calls for a diminuendo). This creates an abrupt, unfinished end to one phrase and upsets the continuity between phrases. What takes place is that the player unconsciously shifts the focus forward to the breath and leaves the note prior to it unshaped and unfinished. Care must be taken while practicing to develop the habit of sustaining up to the breathing point and making well-shaped notes at the ends of phrases. Both beginnings and ends of phrases must be carefully shaped.

The concept of sustaining must be applied to phrases as well as to individual notes. Brass players often speak of the need to "blow through the notes." The air stream must remain constant through the phrase, with the player resisting any tendency to allow the air pressure to drop when notes are tongued or changed during a slur.

19 The importance of sustaining in ensembles is discussed in Chapter 8 under "Suggestions for Marching Band Directors" and in Chapter 14.

Continuity is a function of sustaining and is concerned with the coherence of the line or phrase. In legato and slurred passages, each new note should flow from the one before it without a break. This can be accomplished by approaching the phrase as one long tone with regard to the delivery of air. In his complete method, the 19th century cornetist Saint-Jacome presented legato tonguing under the heading "Tonguing on the Sound."[20] This reflects a very clear concept of continuity: continuous sound uninterrupted by the tongue. Saint-Jacome's maxim might be diagrammed in the following way:

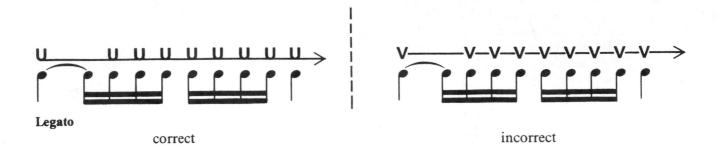

Legato

correct   incorrect

■ CONCEPT OF SOUND

A concept of sound is developed through careful listening. In the early stages, the teacher should lose no opportunity to play for and with the student. In this way, elements of the teacher's tone will be transferred to the student. While every great player has a unique and recognizable timbre and style of playing, many influences have contributed to this individual quality. The process through which a personal sound is developed is by studying a variety of models. This will not only enrich a player's concept of sound, but will bring out its own special qualities.

It is inaccurate to think of sound as a single entity. Actually, the timbre must be modified according to the repertoire being performed. What may be appropriate in one context may not be in another. By meticulous observation of how representative players and brass sections approach specific works (via recordings, concerts, and broadcasts), an overall concept of sound and interpretive style may be formed.

Mental imagery plays a vital role in this process. By visualizing in the mind a clear image of the sound, the player guides the physical aspects of tone production to reproduce that sound.[21]

■ VIBRATO

Vibrato should be viewed as a means of bringing added color to the sound. There are some contexts where it applies and others where it does not. For example, in the author's view, vibrato adds nothing to the inherent expressiveness of the horn timbre and robs it of its purity and natural beauty. At the same time, vibrato is a feature of the Czech and earlier French schools of horn playing, and this deserves respect. With other members of the brass family, vibrato can add character and sensitivity when used in specific areas of

---

[20] Louis Antoine Saint-Jacome (1830–1898), *Grand Method for Trumpet or Cornet* (New York: Carl Fischer, 1894), p. 110.

[21] See William H. Trusheim, "Mental Imagery and Musical Performance: An Inquiry into Imagery Use by Eminent Orchestral Brass Players" (Ed.D. dissertation, Rutgers University, 1987) and Dee Stewart, *Arnold Jacobs: The Legacy of a Master*. Another book that presents concepts of mental imagery is Paul Severson and Mark McDunn, *Brass Wind Artistry* (Athens, Ohio: Accura Music, 1983).

the repertoire, but the majority of the literature is best played with a pure, clear tone without vibrato. Exceptions to this approach are the euphonium and the cornet. Both instruments are traditionally played with vibrato, and they sound unnatural without it.

In orchestral playing, the expressive content of the music must be considered. In serious, ominous passages, vibrato is out of place. It is also out of place in the works of composers such as Wagner and Bruckner that were intended to be played without vibrato in the brass. It is important that a good sound be produced first without vibrato. From that basic approach, vibrato can be added in specific works where it is appropriate to lend expression and style without marring the essential quality of the player's sound. Vibrato must be controlled, and its speed should be varied within different musical contexts. In French music, for example, a light, quick vibrato gives a characteristic color to the sound. In Russian works, a deeply expressive vibrato that is more moderate in speed can add character to the music. The player should carefully study great performances of important works and consider whether vibrato is appropriate.

Five types of vibrato are currently in use: hand, diaphragm, slide, lip and jaw, and throat.

> *Hand vibrato*, which is only effective on the trumpet and cornet, is created by a gentle forward and backward movement from the right thumb resting on the bottom of the leadpipe. Because of its ease of control, it is the preferred means of vibrato on the cornet and trumpet. Since it is entirely visible, different speeds of vibrato are easily controlled. This method works well for players who alternately use or omit vibrato.

> *Diaphragm vibrato* consists of pulsations in the air stream (similar to that used on the flute). Although it can be effective, it tends to be difficult to control and consequently is only rarely used on brass instruments.

> *Slide vibrato* is commonly employed by trombonists in the jazz and studio fields and also occasionally used by symphonic players. Less subtle than vibrato produced by the lip and jaw (which is more typically employed on the trombone), it is produced by moving the slide slightly inward and outward according to the desired speed.

> *Lip-and-jaw vibrato* involves a subtle movement of the embouchure and jaw. It is the principal type of vibrato used on low brass instruments. Although it can also be applied to the trumpet, it tends to be heavy and less easily controlled than hand vibrato and can affect pitch. Orchestral trombonists, however, generally prefer lip-and-jaw vibrato for most of their work but have a perfected slide vibrato available when appropriate to the piece being performed.

> *Throat vibrato* is similar to diaphragm vibrato, in that an oscillation is introduced into the air stream. In this case, the oscillation occurs at the throat level rather than below.

■ SPECIAL EFFECTS

Composers sometimes call on brass players to produce specialized sounds. Two of the most common are the flutter tongue and the glissando. The *flutter tongue* is produced by thinking of rolling an "R" and allowing the tongue tip to vibrate as the air passes into the instrument. It is most effective in the middle range.

On valved brass instruments, when an obvious *glissando* effect is called for, lowering the valves halfway and sliding upward or downward will usually give the best results. Composers sometimes indicate when a valve glissando is to be used. Expressive glissandi of shorter duration can be rendered by elongating a slur or, if a less subtle effect is desired, by allowing the valves to come up with a deliberately slow action. Trombonists are frequently required to produce a slide glissando; this technique is discussed in Chapter 5.

New effects are occasionally found in the works of contemporary composers. These include singing or hissing through the instrument, playing with the water key open, and raising or lowering the pitch by the hand in the horn bell, among others.

■ HOW TO WARM UP AND PRACTICE EFFECTIVELY

The warm-up is an important element in brass playing. This is the time when all of the essential playing functions are brought into optimum condition before being applied to the demands of the literature. To plunge straight into a rehearsal or performance situation without adequate preparation is to invite difficulties. The warm-up should be extended, whenever time allows, to include exercises covering all phases of playing. These daily studies form the basis of a player's progress and maintain the level of skills already developed.

There are two approaches to warming up. Some brass players favor a flexible warm-up, choosing material at random. Others (and the author falls in this group) base their daily warm-up on a series of exercises that have been designed to bring the player's tone production up to peak form gradually. The flexible approach allows the player to vary the material according to the condition of the embouchure and the time available, but this can also be done in the second approach by having a large variety of daily exercises available. The common point between the two approaches is to avoid forcing the embouchure through set material when it is not up to it (due to heavy playing or a layoff). In such cases, it is better to work slowly and patiently, selecting the material in accordance with the condition of the embouchure. The goal is to try to gradually bring the embouchure into condition. It is important that the player plan the warm-up time carefully. If the player must travel to a rehearsal or concert, it is important to arrive early enough to have a calm, unhurried time period in which to warm up. When there is too little time for this, the player often must begin the rehearsal or concert with a feeling of not being completely warmed up—a frame of mind that is not conducive to confidence.

At the beginning of the warm-up, a few minutes should be devoted to playing on the mouthpiece alone. This helps center the pitch and gets the lips vibrating easily while stimulating a free production of sound. The mouthpiece might be played every so often as the warm-up and practice session proceed. Fluency and ease will be encouraged if the first portion of the warm-up consists of slurred material played only at a medium volume level. This should begin in the middle register and gradually work into the upper and lower ranges. After the instrument is responding easily and consistently, various tongued exercises may be added. By the end of the warm-up period, the entire compass should have been covered.

For those taking the flexible approach, warm-up material may be selected from various studies, melodies, intervals, scales, and arpeggios or can be improvised. Those who take the routine approach usually write or excerpt special material that (while offering a selection) is organized progressively.[22] The goal of the warm-up is to get the wind moving freely and the notes responding easily throughout the range, with a clear, centered tone. This should be achieved with an overall feeling of relaxation and ease in the production of sound.

Practice should be organized around a planned program of development. This should consist of daily work on basic skills, such as slurring, tonguing, multiple tonguing, scales, arpeggios, intervals, and flexibility, with any weak areas singled out for

[22] Warm-up and daily study material can be excerpted from Scott Whitener, *Warm-up and Daily Exercises for Horn* (in press, Balquidder Music); Max Schlossberg, *Daily Drills and Technical Studies* (M. Baron); Herbert L. Clarke, *Technical Studies* and *Clarke's Setting Up Drills* (Carl Fisher); Pierre Levet, *La technique journalière du corniste* (Lemoine); Michael Thompson, *Daily Warm-up Exercises* (Paxman); Frydis Ree Wekre, *Thoughts on Playing the Horn Well* (Wekre); Remington, *Warm-up Studies* (Accura); William Bell, *William Bell Daily Routine for Tuba* (Encore); Bobo, *Mastering the Tuba*, 3 vols. (BIM). With adjustments, many of the studies contained in these books can be used on all brass instruments, or individual studies can be developed for specific instruments based on them.

special attention. Those striving for orchestral careers should also incorporate transposition into their daily work. It is important to work patiently and positively with areas needing improvement. The second part of the practice session might be devoted to systematically working through important study literature for the instrument. The centerpiece of the practice session should be systematic and developmental work in the etude repertoire for the instrument. There is immense value in etudes, many of which were written by great players of the past. The variety of technical and musical challenges presented in etudes will expand one's ability to play the instrument in a way that no other literature can. The final portion of practice may include study of solo works, orchestral or band excerpts or parts, brass quintet or ensemble parts, and sight reading.

Flexibility is the key to successful practicing. The order of the practice session may be varied or portions omitted. Practice may be lengthened or shortened as necessary. At all times, the player should work calmly and patiently, stressing good tone production. Objectivity is needed to evaluate one's performance. Occasionally recording the practice session or segments of it can be helpful. The same should be done with concertos, solos, and orchestral excerpts. While areas needing improvement should be noted, it is also important in building confidence to acknowledge when something is played well. Building confidence is a vital aspect of practicing. Accuracy can only be developed through repetition, but it is of no use to practice beyond the tiring point. The best results will be achieved by working in a relaxed but thorough manner, always concentrating on establishing a solid foundation to one's playing while building confidence.

CHAPTER

PLAYING POSITION

IN THE EARLY STAGES of playing, the importance of the playing position is not always recognized by students. It should be understood, however, that *how the body is positioned when playing a brass instrument is the starting point of good tone production.*

Two vital factors must be considered. First, if there is to be free movement of the air during inhalation and exhalation, the body must be positioned in an upright posture so that the natural expansion and reduction of the thorax and abdomen can take place without restriction. It is essential not to lean on the back of the chair when playing seated, since this obstructs the rotational elevation and expansion of the rib cage. Any forward curvature of the posture will interfere with the breathing process and place a downward pressure on the lungs, reducing air capacity and creating tension. This, in turn, will impede the inflow of air on inspiration and constrict the outward motion of the air on expiration.

The second factor regarding playing position is the need for overall relaxation in both taking in and blowing out the air. An upright, but relaxed posture is the first requirement in learning to play a brass instrument. *The essential idea is to get the body into the right position and bring the instrument to the player.* Young players often do the reverse: place the instrument in a less than optimal position and adjust the body to the instrument. In the discussions that follow for each instrument, reference will be made to these common pitfalls in instrument placement.

Carefully study the photographs of leading professional players in this chapter. All the essentials of playing position are clearly revealed in these photographs. When playing, try to imitate the positions shown.

■ TRUMPET AND CORNET

Support the trumpet or cornet with the left hand, lightly gripping the valve casings (see Figures 11.1 through 11.5). How the fingers are positioned around the valve casings varies among professional players, but in general the third or little finger should be placed in the ring on the third valve slide. Place the thumb in the ring (or on the trigger, if one is present) of the first valve slide. If there is no ring or trigger, the thumb should wrap around the valve casings. Position the tips of the fingers of the right hand over, and lightly touch the valve caps. In order to press the valves straight down, the fingers must be curved. Turn the right thumb upward (with the thumbnail down) and rest it on the bottom of the leadpipe, between the first and second valves; this helps to balance and support the instrument and places the hand in the best position to operate the valves. The fingers move freely and quickly if the hand is placed in a position as if it were grasping a small object. Placing the pad of the thumb on the underside of the leadpipe encourages this position. Better valve action will also result if the little finger is kept free of the ring on the top of the leadpipe. Some players feel that they must keep the little finger in contact with the ring. In this case it is better to rest the finger on top of the ring rather than place it inside.

FIGURE 11.1
Playing position (trumpet): Raymond Mace, American Brass Quintet.

Quick valve motion is obviously an important aspect of technique. Players often, however, do not place enough emphasis on the valve stroke itself. There are only two positions of a valve: open and closed. As the piston slides between valve ports, a wall is presented to the air stream. To avoid this wall and make a clean slur or attack, it is vital that the piston move as quickly as possible between the two positions so that the windway is fully in position when the note starts. If the motion is even slightly sluggish, the effect (created by the partially occluded windway) can be heard in the sound. Therefore, the fingers must be rounded over the valve caps and the pistons struck smoothly straight downward. Sometimes it helps to keep the tips of the fingers very slightly above the valve caps to encourage a downward-striking motion. The piston will not return upward any faster than the valve spring pushes it. It is essential, therefore, to lift the fingers quickly so that they do not impede the piston's return motion. A helpful concept is to think of making the pistons bounce on their springs to ensure quick, clean valve action. Students sometimes unconsciously slow the valve motion when trying to play smoothly in slow tempos. This has the opposite effect, impairing the quality of the sound. Smoothness can

FIGURE 11.2
Playing position
(trumpet): British
trumpeter Philip
Jones.

only be attained by opening and closing the valves quickly. It is important to strive always for quick valve action, irrespective of the tempo or whether a passage is tongued or slurred.

The best position for the instrument is at a slight downward angle, as opposed to being held in a perfectly horizontal plane. The reason is that if the mouthpiece approaches the embouchure at too straight an angle to the face, mouthpiece pressure tends to be concentrated on the upper lip, an area where pressure should be minimized. In extreme cases, the mouth corners may turn upward to accept a mouthpiece angle that is too straight to the lips. This has a negative effect on embouchure, tone, and intonation. Players who adopt this position often have fairly brittle timbres and tend to play high on the pitch. It should be noted, however, that a small minority of players have an underbite. In these exceptional cases the instrument will take on a slightly elevated angle, usually with the head tilting somewhat downward.

For the majority of players, a slight downward angle allows the embouchure to oscillate freely and the bottom lip to serve as the base, or "seat," of the mouthpiece without undue mouthpiece pressure. One must be careful that the instrument is positioned only at a slight downward angle. If the downward angle increases, the lower lip will tend to recede and the upper lip is liable to overlap the lower lip, creating embouchure difficulties. Directors of marching bands and other groups sometimes insist that trumpets and trombones be held perfectly horizontal for visual effect. Rather than alter the embouchure to comply with this requirement, the angle can be raised with no harmful effect to the embouchure by simply tilting the head slightly backward until the instrument is level.

Use only the minimum effort necessary to hold the instrument, and the arms must remain as relaxed as possible. It is vital to sit in an upright position and not to lean against the back of the chair. When standing, try to avoid tension, and maintain an erect but relaxed posture. Practice time should be divided between sitting and standing to become equally comfortable in both positions.

Young players often point the instrument directly into the music stand and attempt to read over the bell. Aside from the negative effect on the sound, this habit tends to cause the trumpet to pull downward and the jaw to recede, affecting the embouchure.

FIGURE 11.3
Playing position
(trumpet): George
Coble, First
Trumpet, Syracuse
Symphony
Orchestra.

The solution is to place the stand slightly to the side so that it does not obstruct the radiation of sound from the bell. Most professional players keep the bell to the side of the music stand so that the sound can project freely into the performance space.

■ HORN

Of all the brass, the horn is the most susceptible to poor playing positions. Due to the horn's unique rear-radiating shape, the bell can easily be blocked by the body, resulting in a dull, unresonant timbre; or with the bell resting on the thigh, there can be a tendency to slump over the horn, diminishing the player's air capacity and hindering efficient respiration.

There are two methods of holding the horn: (1) keeping the body upright and holding the bell free and (2) resting the bell on the right thigh. The upright position has long been standard in Europe and Britain and there is a strong trend toward it in the United States, notably in the Chicago Symphony Orchestra and other major orchestras (Figures 11.6 through 11.8). This position has a definite advantage in that it allows the body to maintain an upright posture. This encourages the respiratory system to function

FIGURE 11.4
Hand position
(trumpet).

FIGURE 11.5
Playing position
(trumpet): Peter
Bond, Metropolitan
Orchestra.

FIGURE 11.6   Two views of playing position (horn): Dale Clevenger, Principal Horn, Chicago Symphony Orchestra.

FIGURE 11.7   Two views of playing position (horn): Norwegian soloist Frøydis Ree Wekre.

FIGURE 11.8
Playing position (horn): soloist Barry Tuckwell.

optimally. The timbre retains all of its partials, thus producing color and resonance in the sound, which projects well in the concert hall. By resting the bell on the right thigh, partials are absorbed; this damps some of the resonance of the sound, creating a more covered, darker quality.

In using either playing position, turn the chair slightly to the right. This enables the entire circumference of the bell to clear the body so that the sound can project rearward without obstruction. For those resting the bell, turning the chair allows the right leg to be brought back to a point where the bell rim can rest comfortably on top of the thigh.

The first three fingers of the left hand should be curved over the valve levers (the little finger may rest in the hook). The left thumb should rest on the B♭ valve lever on double horns or in the ring on single horns.

The position of the right hand is of critical importance in influencing response, tone, and intonation. The hand should be slightly cupped, with the thumb resting on top of the fingers (see Figures 11.9 and 11.10). The seemingly small matter of placing the thumb on top of the fingers enables the hand to form a new channel in the bell, which makes an important difference in how the horn plays and sounds. This makes sense acoustically, since the purpose of the hand is to narrow and extend the bell throat. With the thumb on top, the hand forms a more effective wall within the bell throat.

Sealing any space between the fingers (as in swimming), place the hand vertically into the bell. The back of the hand (where the knuckles are) must rest against the bell's far wall. The free space between the palm of the hand and the near wall can be closed down or opened to control intonation as well as to change the tone from a more covered quality to a brighter timbre. Opening the hand raises the pitch; closing it lowers the pitch. A helpful way to find the right degree of "cover" is first to close the bell so that the tone is somewhat muffled and then gradually open it until a resonant, clear sound results. Then, go past this point until the tone becomes harsh and sharp. Finally, go gradually back to the best position; this procedure will define for the player the desirable degree of "cover" to be used.

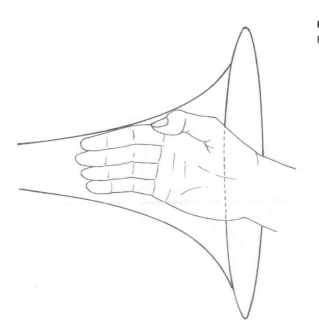

FIGURE 11.9
Right hand position (horn).

FIGURE 11.10
Right hand position (horn).

Several problems are frequently encountered among horn students. Aside from an incorrectly formed right hand position, the hand often unconsciously shifts away from the outer bell wall, creating a muffled tone. Students also sometimes try to put the hand too far into the bell. The hand should go into the bell as far as the knuckles. If it goes beyond this, the sound tends to dull and the instrument does not respond as easily.

A frequent problem encountered by teachers is when a student holds the horn so that the mouthpiece approaches the embouchure at too straight an angle. This is often caused by resting the bell too far out on the thigh. The horn is thereby tipped backward and the mouthpiece approaches the lips horizontally, disrupting the embouchure. On the horn, the mouthpiece and mouthpipe must assume a slightly downward angle (see Figures 11.6 and 11.7). By holding the horn so that the bell is basically perpendicular (vertical), the player will automatically achieve the proper angle of the mouthpipe in relation to the embouchure. Sometimes the horn is simply too large for a youngster to hold correctly. The only solution is gradually to perfect the position as the student grows, although it would be helpful if manufacturers made student instruments in more compactly wrapped patterns more widely available.

Another problem that often occurs with players who rest the bell on the thigh is that the mouthpiece is below the embouchure and the player must lean downward to reach it. If this occurs, a downward pressure is placed on the right lung, depressing it and limiting the volume of air the player can take in. It also sets up tension and resistance to the outflow of the air, in which the respiratory muscles must overcome the weight of the downward pressure on the lungs. This is the primary advantage of holding the bell free of the body. A relaxed, upright posture can be maintained and the instrument brought into this position. It is a case of adjusting the instrument to fit the posture of the player rather than compromising good posture to reach the instrument.

It should be noted that horn players are expected to stand when playing a solo, because the tone can be projected more clearly into the performance space and a better visual impression will be created. It is wise, therefore, frequently, if not always, to stand while practicing. In the standing position, care should be taken that the right hand position does not change.

■ TROMBONE

The most natural playing position for the trombonist is with the instrument held at a slight downward angle. Be careful not to lean the head to one side or the other. Keep the head erect, and bring the trombone to the embouchure rather than adapting the body to fit the instrument (see Figure 11.11).

Support the full weight of the trombone with the left hand and arm so that the right arm will be free of tension and able to move the slide quickly from position to position. Place the left index finger on the mouthpiece shank or receiver, and form the remaining fingers around the inner slide brace and the cork barrel. The left thumb should grasp the bottom of the bell brace or, on instruments fitted with F attachments, the rotary valve lever. The left index finger counteracts the pull to the left of the bell section (see Figure 11.12).

With the right hand, hold the outer slide brace at the bottom between the thumb and first two fingers. Usually, the third and fourth fingers curl under the lower portion of the slide. The slide is controlled through a combination of wrist and forearm motion. The right hand position sometimes varies slightly from this basic position.

Music stands often cause difficulties for trombonists. The best approach is to place the slide and bell to the left of the stand. The music can be read by looking to the right. The tone will project with more resonance when the bell is clear of the stand. Sometimes players try to place the slide beneath the stand. This is not an optimal position for projecting the sound, but, more critically, it causes an excessive downward angle at the mouthpiece, affecting the embouchure.

Slide Positions

The trombone slide has been compared to a violin string. Continuously variable in pitch, the exact placement of a position must be determined by careful listening. Some basic visual guidelines may be offered as a starting point, but these should not be taken as absolute, since instruments and individual players vary.

FIGURE 11.11 Two views of playing position (trombone): Jay Friedman, Principal Trombone, Chicago Symphony Orchestra.

Some of the positions are more clearly defined on the slide than others. The first, third, fourth, and sixth positions are fairly easy to locate. Less obvious are the second, fifth, and seventh positions, which require even greater reliance on the ear to place them precisely. (See Figures 11.13 to 11.19.)

There is some tendency to place the second position high (sharp), particularly when it occurs on a leading tone. The fifth position is rather awkward and depends heavily on the ear to find its exact center. Intonation problems are sometimes encountered in ensemble playing with this position. A good way to locate it is to match the fifth-position B♭ to the first-position B♭. Advanced players usually play the notes produced by the sixth and seventh positions in first and (altered) second position on the F attachment. It is, however, unwise for students to develop a dependency on the F attachment. Comparable ease and confidence should be sought on the longer positions as on the shorter ones.

FIGURE 11.12
Hand position
(trombone).

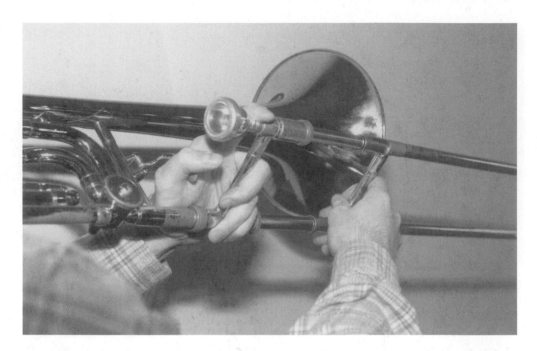

FIGURE 11.13 Trombone, first position: Slide fully in, lightly touching the corks or springs.

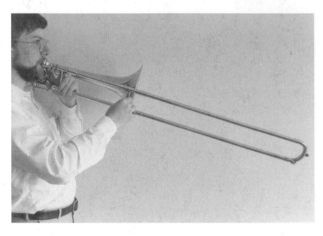

FIGURE 11.14 Trombone, third position: brace slightly above the bell rim.

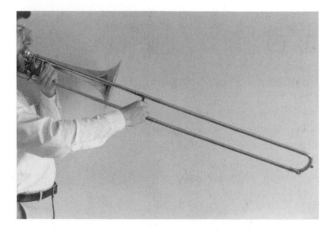

FIGURE 11.15 Trombone, fourth position: top of outer slide below the bell rim.

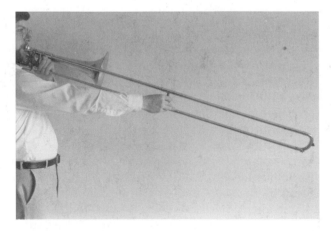

FIGURE 11.16 Trombone, sixth position: a comfortable arm's length.

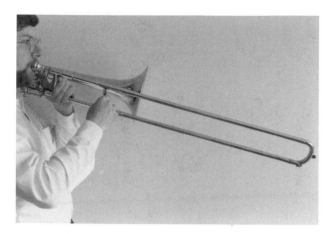

FIGURE 11.17 Trombone, second position: approximately one-third the distance between first and third positions.

FIGURE 11.18 Trombone, fifth position: approximately halfway between fourth and sixth positions.

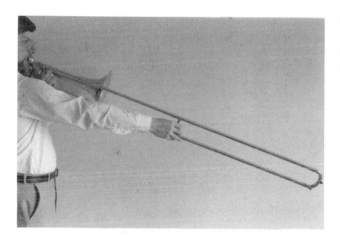

FIGURE 11.19 Trombone, seventh position: a stretched arm's length, exposing the slide stocking (boot).

■ BARITONE AND EUPHONIUM

Hold the baritone or euphonium diagonally across the body, with the lower bow pressed in to the waist to provide stability (Figures 11.20 and 11.21). It is important for the mouthpiece to be brought upward to the embouchure rather than allowing the instrument to rest on the lap or chair. If the instrument is too low, the player must bend forward to reach the mouthpiece, thereby restricting breathing. If necessary, a pillow, folded towel, or specially made stand[1] should be used to bring the instrument to the correct height. Mouthpiece pressure must also be monitored to make certain that the embouchure is not being used to help support the instrument.

On instruments with three top-action valves, round the fingers of the right hand and place them over the valve caps beneath the upper bow. The left arm must reach across the lower bow and grip some of the tubing on the right side. When a compensating fourth valve is located on the side, use the left index or middle finger to depress the valve. It is important that the left hand completely support the weight of the instrument so that the fingers of the right hand are free to press the valves.

On top-action designs having four in-line valves, the player has the option of placing all four fingers over the valves or operating the fourth valve with the left index

[1] The Stewart stand is designed for this purpose. A model is available for both euphonium and tuba.

FIGURE 11.20
Playing position (euphonium): SSgt. Steven Kellner, Principal Euphonium, United States Marine Band.

FIGURE 11.21
Playing position (euphonium): Brian Bowman, euphonium soloist, United States Air Force Band.

FIGURE 11.22   Two views of playing position (tuba): Arnold Jacobs, former Principal Tuba, Chicago Symphony Orchestra.

finger, because it is used in compensating models with the fourth valve at the side. The latter approach has an advantage because coordination is less effective between the middle and little fingers. By using the left index finger, the fourth valve action will usually be improved.

On euphoniums with side-action (front-action) valves, bring the right arm to the front of the instrument and grip the left side of the top bow with the left hand. If rings are provided on the tuning or valve slides to adjust intonation, the left hand may rest on one of these.

■ TUBA

The tuba should rest on the lap or the front the chair and be stabilized by the left arm and a gentle tension between the thighs (Figure 11.22). On tubas with top-action valves, place the fingers of the right hand over the valve caps. The left hand should grasp any tubing that can be comfortably reached on the right front of the instrument.

The right arm must reach around to the front of rotary and side-action (front-action) piston tubas, where the fingers rest on the valve levers or caps. Place the thumb in the ring; it is important that no tension (resulting from weight) is felt at the thumb, hand, or arm in order to promote good finger dexterity. The left hand should grasp the first valve slide, which will be moved in controlling intonation.

Some students have difficulty reaching the mouthpiece on larger tubas; in such cases, the player should use a cushion or some other means of bringing the embouchure and mouthpiece into alignment. There should be no tendency to lean back into the chair or to curve the torso. Some tubists consider that leaning the instrument slightly forward assists the free movement of the air and provides a greater feeling of control, but this is debatable.

■ KEYS TO A GOOD PLAYING POSITION

- Good posture is the starting point of good tone production.
- Place the body in a relaxed, upright posture.
- The basic idea is to get the body into an upright posture and bring the instrument to the player. Do not bend the body to fit the instrument.
- Do not lean on the back of the chair when playing seated; sit as if you were standing.
- Practice standing often or all the time (with the exception of the euphonium and tuba).
- Hold the instrument with minimum effort and remain as relaxed as possible.
- Hold the horn with the bell free of the body in an upright posture. Be sure the body does not bend downward.
- Make certain that the right hand position in the horn bell is correct (as described earlier in the chapter).
- Trumpets and trombones should not blow directly into the music stand. Do not aim the bell or slide beneath the stand. Keep the bell to the side of the stand (trombones must keep the slide and bell to the left side).
- Hold the trumpet, cornet, and trombone at a slight downward angle, rather than in a horizontal plane. Guard against excessive downward angles.
- The baritone, euphonium, and tuba must be held high enough so that the mouthpiece meets the embouchure without the player's having to bend downward.

GETTING STARTED

■ TEACHING YOUNG BEGINNERS

The general challenge of successfully teaching young beginners is a specialized area of study that goes beyond specific instrumental instruction. One of the most important aspects of teaching grade-school-age youngsters is that the teacher find ways of making the learning process *fun*. Brass instruments, in particular, can be discouraging in the early phases, so the teacher must be creative and enthusiastic in getting across good playing concepts in a manner that engages the student's imagination, interest, and sense of fun. For example, to convey the idea of moving sufficient air to support the vibration of the lips, a small balloon can be attached to the end of the mouthpiece shank. As the student produces sound on the mouthpiece, the balloon inflates, encouraging a positive outflow of the air. Another trick is to ask the student to blow through the instrument (without making sound) to expel water with the water key open. This will cause the student to increase the velocity, volume, and pressure of the air going through the instrument.[1] To introduce the idea of blowing steadily into the instrument, the teacher could place a small piece of tissue paper against a wall and ask the student to keep it in place only by blowing air against it.

The first 10 weeks of the student's experience with the instrument will largely determine success or failure. This is the period when the teacher's enthusiasm, creativity, and ability to see things in the way that a child sees them will make a major difference. It is also important during this period and at regular intervals thereafter to show the students where their ability to play an instrument will take them. Older students from the individual's high school or middle school should be brought in to play for the younger students. Also, visiting brass quintets or other ensembles can present educational programs. These can stimulate a great deal of interest and motivation. As soon as possible, trips to concerts or other performances should be organized. Sometimes, one significant performance will make a deep impression on a student and serve as a strong and continuing motivating image for the future.

Another consideration is that every teacher must be free to develop a personal teaching style and approach. While general goals can be established, each teacher must find an individual and imaginative way of communicating concepts and working with the students. The suggestions that follow in this chapter should be considered as material to be modified and developed creatively by each teacher. The general knowledge that can be applied to teaching youngsters could easily fill the pages of another book. Since that is beyond our scope, the discussion here will focus on specific issues relating to teaching brass instruments to beginners.

Before teaching begins, it is essential to make certain that students are provided with good-quality instruments and mouthpieces. Too often a youngster has to struggle with equipment that would present difficulties even to an advanced player. At any level, brass players are dependent on their equipment. Mouthpieces, especially, are of concern, and

---

[1] These techniques were developed by Peter DelVecchio.

those supplied with rental instruments are sometimes less than satisfactory. Horn mouthpieces, in particular, are often too small and not well designed. This makes learning to play the horn more difficult. The teacher should specify the mouthpieces that are to be provided with rental instruments, and the school should, if necessary, purchase appropriate mouthpieces to be loaned to students. It is also advisable to furnish parents with a list of recommended mouthpieces before they purchase an instrument (sometimes retailers will substitute a mouthpiece of the customer's choice for the one that normally comes with the instrument).

In selecting mouthpieces suitable for beginners, the main considerations are that the mouthpiece responds easily and that it produces a good tone. Mouthpieces of medium cup diameter and depth are best for this purpose. However, since youngsters vary in their lip configurations, teachers should have available a selection of mouthpieces that includes some larger sizes that can be loaned to students to try. A recommended list of suitable mouthpieces for young beginners is provided in Chapter 2, along with a discussion of the elements involved in selecting a mouthpiece.

The teacher should carefully check each instrument to determine if it is of reasonable quality and in acceptable condition. The following is a checklist that the teacher may follow in making this assessment.

1. *Mouthpiece.* Is the mouthpiece suitable for a beginning student?
   - The throat and backbore should be clean. Instructions for cleaning brass instruments are presented in Chapter 13.
   - There should be no dents at the bottom of the shank.
   - There should be no scrapes or gouges on the mouthpiece rim.
   - The plating should be in good condition.
   - The shank must fit the instrument's receiver.
   - Mouthpieces should be sterilized with alcohol before being given to the students.

2. *Valves.* The valves should be checked to see if they move freely.
   - If the instrument seems blocked up and does not play, check to see if each piston is in the correct valve casing (this is discussed in Chapter 13).
   - Valve casings should be free of dents.
   - If the instrument plays but the response and tone are uneven, valve alignment should be checked. This is especially important on rotary valve instruments. Valve alignment is discussed in Chapter 13.
   - Frayed or broken strings on rotary valves should be replaced.
   - On horns, the height of rotary valve keys should be adjusted to fit the students' hands. See Chapter 13.
   - The left hand grip on the horn should not be too wide (from the little-finger ring to the thumb ring or valve lever) for small hands. If necessary, the little-finger ring can be moved by a repair technician.
   - The valves should be oiled.

3. *Slides.*
   - Tuning and valve slides should move freely. All slides should be lubricated.
   - The trombone slide should move smoothly without binding and should be free of dents. The slide should be lubricated following the suggestions in Chapter 13.

4. *Dents.* There should be no dents in critical areas of the tubing, such as the leadpipe.

5. *Water keys.* The water-key spring and cork should be checked to be certain that an airtight seal is formed.

6. *Cases.* Instrument cases must provide adequate protection. Many dents are caused by the instrument's not fitting tightly inside the case. Also, there must be a secure place for the mouthpiece and other accessories so that nothing is loose inside the case that could dent the instrument.

Above all, the teacher should play each instrument to evaluate both condition and quality. The first consideration is whether the instrument's air seal is acceptable. Excessive wear of the valves and slides will cause leaking, which affects the instrument's response and tone. This can usually be detected as the instrument is played. A slow response, particularly in the upper register, combined with a dull and uneven tone are indications that the instrument may be leaking (although faulty valve alignment or a deficient water-key seal can also cause these symptoms). A leaking condition can be corrected, but it represents a major repair of considerable expense. If all of the previous criteria have been successfully met, the teacher should test intonation, response, tone quality, and evenness from register to register. Any instruments that do not meet the foregoing criteria should be returned to the rental firm or replaced if owned by the school. Once the teacher is confident that the instruments to be used by the class are satisfactory, teaching can begin.

■ ELEMENTARY BRASS CLASSES

Classes of the same instrument are generally more successful at the elementary level than classes of mixed instruments. The size of the class should be kept small because of the need for individual attention. In programs where private lessons can be offered as part of the regular curriculum, it is advisable to start students in pairs to take advantage of the positive motivation that results from the natural interaction between students.

Although some texts lay great stress on how students should be selected for instrumental classes, it is difficult to predict with accuracy whether a student will be successful on a particular brass instrument. Aside from reasonable pitch discrimination, the primary considerations are the type of lip structure and the teeth. Students who have larger, thicker lip structures are usually better suited to the low brass than to the horn or trumpet, but there are many exceptions. Perfectly even teeth are not essential, but protruding or missing teeth can cause problems. Far more important than physical factors are a student's interest and desire to learn combined with motivation to practice.

The First Lesson

No rigid plans should be set for the first few lessons. Better results will be gained if the teacher is free to approach each lesson creatively and flexibly, responding to the needs of the students and following a personal teaching style. The chief goal of the first lesson is to get each student to produce sound. This should begin with the mouthpiece alone. The first step might be to explain that sound is created on brass instruments by pitch vibration. Pitch vibration is made by blowing air through the lips formed in an embouchure in the mouthpiece. The best way to convey embouchure formation is to have each student hold a sheet of paper about one foot in front of the lips and blow at the paper, causing it to bend outward, while forming the lips as if saying "tu." Ask the student to keep the "tu" going until the air runs out. The "tu" naturally forms the lips into an effective embouchure (the "u" within "tu" brings the facial musculature into the semi-puckered formation necessary for vibration and creates a cushion for the mouthpiece to rest on). This little exercise also gets the student to blow a fast stream of air to an external point, thereby establishing the feeling of moving air as "wind" and creates a space between the teeth for the air to flow through. After experimenting with this exercise a few times, the teacher should show the students how to place the mouthpiece correctly for each instrument, following the guidelines presented in Chapter 10. As the students practice placing the mouthpiece, the teacher should remind them to keep a small space between the teeth for the air to pass through, as they did in the paper exercise.

Producing Sound

With the mouthpiece, the teacher should play a pitch and have the students try to imitate that sound. It is not important what pitch is produced at this point, only that some sound is made. *The objective is to have students experience that sound is produced by vibration and that vibration is caused by the motion of the air through the lips.*[2] The best syllable to use in this beginning stage is "pu." The "p" consonant, which temporarily replaces the "t," causes the lips to close and catch the air, setting the lips into vibration. "Pu" also encourages an easy response, helping students to avoid the tendency to try to force the lips to vibrate by blowing the air too forcefully. The next step is to try to lengthen the mouthpiece buzz, making a long, steady note. It is important to remind the students to blow the air freely outward, as they did when blowing the paper outward. Very gradually, perhaps over two lessons, the teacher should guide the mouthpiece buzzing toward the following middle-register pitches (holding them as long as possible):

Occasionally, a student will be found who has difficulty making any sound at all on the mouthpiece. This occurs when the lips are too far apart in the mouthpiece and the air goes through the lips without setting them into vibration. The teacher should demonstrate this problem and correct it by pronouncing "pu" clearly, explaining that the lips must catch the air. If this does not solve the problem, the teacher might demonstrate how to buzz the lips alone or into an embouchure visualizer and ask the student to imitate that sound. Once the student can make the lips buzz in some fashion, it should be possible to transfer the feeling of vibration to the mouthpiece. (In general, buzzing the lips without the mouthpiece is not recommended, since the lips function differently when the mouthpiece and instrument are involved. Also, there is a tendency for tension to develop in the throat when the lips are buzzed without the mouthpiece and when this approach is carried over to the instrument.) There are several ways of making the mouthpiece respond easier. Placing the tip of the index finger slightly over the end of the mouthpiece shank adds a little resistance that helps to stimulate vibration; alternatively, a BERP[3] or Buzz-Aid could be used. These devices increase resistance slightly, which aids the lips in vibrating. Also, the hand can be loosely cupped around the mouthpiece to provide a light resistance.

Sometimes students will only be able to produce pitches that are too high or too low. This is usually because the lips are being held too tight or too loose or because the vowel position is being set for a different range. If the pitch is too low, the teacher might demonstrate by blowing air outward while pronouncing "tu" with more "ee" in the "tu." The student should be asked to imitate the teacher and match the pitch of the air. This will raise the tongue in the mouth, and a higher pitch should result when going back to the mouthpiece. This usually takes several attempts. The reverse can be done if the pitch is too high, by bringing more "ah" into the "tu" syllable. By imitating the lower-pitched air, the student will bring the tongue position downward, aiding a lower pitch on the mouthpiece.[4] If the problem persists, it is best to go to the instrument. The pitch centers of the instrument will help the student to find the desired starting pitch.

Changing Pitch and Starting the Sound

Once there is some stability in the middle-register pitches played on the mouthpiece, the teacher should show the students how one can slide the mouthpiece's buzzing sound upward and downward by a note or two with a glissando effect. Again, the students

---

[2] Some very useful advice on teaching beginning brass players was presented in two lectures by the late Arnold Jacobs at the Second International Brass Congress at Indiana University in 1984. Texts of the lectures appear in M. Dee Stewart, *Arnold Jacobs: The Legacy of a Master* (Northfield, Ill.: The Instrumentalist Publishing Co., 1987), pp. 127–143. Some of the ideas presented here are based on concepts of Mr. Jacobs.
[3] Buzz extension resistance piece (BERP).
[4] Vowel positions in tone production are discussed in Chapter 10.

should try imitating the teacher's sound. Specific pitches are not important; rather, each student should experience the feeling of moving the pitch of the mouthpiece sound upward and downward.

This is an appropriate time to introduce the idea of starting the sound with the tongue, using a "tu" syllable. The "pu" syllable is helpful in the beginning to aid easy response and also as a warm-up syllable as the student advances. However, it cannot be used for regular articulation. The "p" consonant should be replaced by the "t" consonant at this point. In teaching students to start the sound with the tongue (by saying "tu") it is important to emphasize that it is *the air* that starts the sound; the role of the tongue is to help give a clear beginning to the sound. In actual practice, the tongue (in pronouncing "tu") creates a pulsation on the already-moving air stream that gives a clear beginning to a note. The tongue should not be used to stop the sound, since this makes an audible noise at the end of the note. The best way of ending a note is to stop blowing.

Transferring Sound Making to the Instrument

The students should now be ready to transfer sound making to the instrument. The teacher should first demonstrate how to assemble the instrument correctly (instrument assembly is discussed later in this chapter). Next, it is important to establish a good playing position, with each student following the recommendations presented in Chapter 11.

In making the first sounds on the instrument, it is again best not to insist that students begin on predetermined pitches. While the notes shown earlier are good starting tones and many students will have no difficulty carrying over the mouthpiece pitch to the instrument, if a student still seems inclined to produce a higher or lower pitch, it is better to work with this note. Once some pitch is produced, the student can gradually be guided to one of the recommended starting pitches. A good way of beginning the process is for the teacher to play a sound on the instrument and to ask the students to try to imitate it. As before, each note should be held as long as possible. This portion of the lesson should be directed to having the students play as many long tones as possible.

If a transparent mouthpiece is available, it would be helpful to reinforce the concept of pitch vibration by playing a note and allowing the students to observe the vibration taking place within the mouthpiece. This provides the student with a visual image of how sound is made on a brass instrument. An even greater impression will be made by asking the student to play on a transparent mouthpiece while looking into a mirror. This will help establish in the student's mind, from the beginning of the student's playing experience, the concept of moving air to create vibration.

Aural Imagery

One of the most important processes involved with learning to play a brass instrument is the formation of aural images. The research on mental imagery and brass performance has shown that sound memory and imitation are powerful tools that guide the development of the player.[5] One of the most effective things the teacher can do, therefore, is to demonstrate a poor sound on the instrument and to follow it with a good sound. This initiates a clear "sound image" in the mind of the student. This image will be recalled when the student attempts to produce sound. By imitating the teacher's sound, the student forms a mental sound image that functions like a "guidance system" in directing the physical aspects of sound production. It is beneficial to use the technique of demonstration and imitation frequently in beginning classes. When the teacher creates both a satisfactory and an unsatisfactory sound, a more clearly defined picture of what to strive for is conveyed to students.

---

[5]See William H. Trusheim, "Mental Imagery and Musical Performance: An Inquiry into Imagery Use by Eminent Orchestral Brass Players" (Ed.D. dissertation, Rutgers University, 1987).

Breathing

It is important right from the beginning for students to form the habit of working with sufficient air. With young beginners it is not necessary or desirable to explain the intricacies of how the respiratory system functions in playing brass instruments. What is needed is a means of getting the student to take in a sufficient amount of air and blow it out without tension or restriction. A little explanation is helpful—for example, that respiration consists of expansion and reduction, that the rib cage is flexible and expands with the intake of air, and that the waist area also expands as the diaphragm contracts downward to create more space for the lungs to fill with air. One of the most useful effective ways of getting the student to take in enough air is to suggest a mental image of a quantity of air to be inhaled. An inflated balloon, a plastic bag, or a ball can serve as a model to define a quantity of air. By visualizing an external quantity of air as a finite form, the student will be able to inhale more air in the most natural and effective way. It is of vital importance in this process for the body to be relaxed when the air is taken in.

Teachers often warn students not to raise the shoulders when breathing. While students do sometimes make large, shallow motions in breathing without bringing in much air, there will be some upward motion of the shoulders if a larger amount of air is taken in correctly (this is caused by the upward and outward rotation and expansion of the rib cage). If the emphasis is placed on taking in a mass of air that is determined by a visual image and the body is allowed to expand naturally, the resultant motion at the shoulders should be viewed as normal. It could also be mentioned that the lungs fill from the bottom upward: As the air fills the upper parts of the chest cavity, the shoulder areas will be elevated somewhat. To get the feeling of expanding low first, the student should be asked to place the left hand on his or her stomach. This could be called number one. The right hand can be placed on the chest and called number two. As the air is taken in, number one (the left hand) should be pushed outward as far as it will go; then the chest should be filled by allowing number two (the right hand) to rise. This will convey the feeling of filling from the bottom upward and avoid tension.

Natural means should also be used in blowing the air out. The body knows innately how to expel air from the lungs (this ability was called upon in the earlier blown-paper exercise). All that is necessary at this point is to encourage the student to blow a fast stream of air as "wind" without holding back the outflow or creating tension. The focus should be to blow an abundant quantity of fast air and to allow the body to accomplish this goal in its own natural way. It might be helpful to stress again that respiration on brass instruments consists of expansion to bring the air in and reduction to move the air out. At a later stage of advancement, the differing ways of blowing the air outward that are discussed in Chapter 10 can be explored.

The End of the First Lesson

Toward the end of the lesson, some attention should be given to connecting the sounds being produced with their notation. After giving clear practice instructions and the assignment for the next lesson, the teacher should briefly review the basic fundamentals that were presented in the lesson. A summary of these principles at the end of the lesson will help students to keep them in mind during practice. The lesson might conclude by demonstrating the proper method of lubricating the valves or trombone slide (see Chapter 13), removing accumulated condensation (discussed later in this chapter), disassembling the instrument, and placing it correctly in its case.

The Second Lesson

The second lesson should begin with a very brief review of the fundamentals covered in the first class. It is important to have the students play early in this lesson to take advantage of their natural eagerness to make sound. A main goal of the lesson is for the teacher to carefully observe the students to make certain that each individual is following the teacher's instructions and to watch for problems. Here are some potential problems.

- *Incorrect mouthpiece placement.* Watch especially for too low a placement that causes the upper rim to rest on the red part of the upper lip. (Horn students, in particular, often start with the mouthpiece placed too low on the upper lip; it is essential to use the conventional two-third upper, one-third lower placement.)

- *Stretched embouchure.*
  - Watch for any pulling of the lips outward in forming the embouchure. Forming the embouchure as if saying "tu" will help prevent this.
  - Students sometimes stretch (distort) the embouchure when taking a breath. Some practice drawing in air at the sides of the mouthpiece without stretching the lips back will help this problem.

- *Puffed-out (inflated) cheeks or other inflations.* When there is inflation, the muscles are not being contracted. If the student clearly pronounces "tu" when making sound, the muscles will be automatically contracted and this will generally avoid the inflation problem. If the problem persists, however, the teacher should place several rubber bands around the inflated area and have the student play. This enables the student to get the feel of playing with the cheeks or other inflated area held in. Once this feeling is created, students can usually achieve the necessary contractions by pronouncing "tu" clearly.

- *Poor playing position* (see Chapter 11). The angle of trumpet and trombone should be slightly downward from straight out. Also, students should not blow directly into the stand but to the side (with trombone, to the left of the stand).

- *Not taking a large enough breath.*

- *Excessive mouthpiece pressure.*

- *Blowing too hard.* Students sometimes try to force the lips to vibrate by blowing powerfully at the mouthpiece. By using the syllable "pu" as the starting sound, students can cultivate an easy response. This needs to be stressed. The air must move fast but not powerfully. The air should be moved horizontally forward and directed to a point across the room.

- *Too much embouchure tension.* The student should be reminded that the lip tissue inside the mouthpiece must be free to move in vibration. When the student pronounces "tu," the facial muscles support the pitch vibration inside the mouthpiece. Making the lips too tight causes the embouchure to become resistant to vibration.

- *Blowing outward from the throat.* The air should be moved outward from the waist.

The objectives of the second lesson are to add more notes, to change pitch, and to begin to learn simple tunes. Using the technique of demonstration and imitation, the teacher should have the students play various notes on the mouthpiece, holding each note as long as possible. More middle-range notes should be added to those attempted in the first lesson. Next, the teacher should demonstrate changing pitch with the mouthpiece and ask the students to try to imitate this sound. Once the students are able to change pitch to some degree, simple tunes in the middle register can be introduced (although this may not be possible until subsequent lessons). Buzzing melodies on the mouthpiece is of great value; it brings together all of the factors involved in tone production within a framework that is first conceived in the mind. In this way, playing tunes on the mouthpiece stimulates the basic aural-mental process that is involved in brass playing of visualizing a musical sound and then attempting to produce it. The practice of playing melodies on the mouthpiece should continue through the most advanced stages.

After spending a little time with the mouthpiece, the class should move to the instruments and begin working on some basic progressive material for the remainder of the lesson. For this purpose, one of the elementary methods listed in Chapters 3 through 7 or a band method could be used. Alternatively, the teacher could create some original exercises. At the conclusion of the lesson, the teacher should observe how each student disassembles the instrument and places it in its case, offering any necessary corrections.

Subsequent Lessons

Subsequent lessons should focus on establishing good tone production, exploring the instrument, developing the abilities to read and count, and quality of tone. Every lesson should contain some form of reinforcement of the basic concepts of tone production, perhaps using different words, and each student's progress should be carefully monitored by the teacher. Each individual should play alone at least once during the lesson to enable the teacher to observe what that student is doing. Sometimes, a student will play the notes of an exercise correctly, but with a poor approach to producing the sound. The teacher should be alert to this and place the emphasis on good tone production rather than on getting the notes. In tonguing, it is important to stress that the air must be kept moving between tongued notes rather than being interrupted by the tongue. It is helpful to convey the idea that the air must go through the tongue stroke and not be blocked by it. In repeated notes, the air must be blown steadily forward. Brass players refer to this concept as "blowing through the notes." A sustained, linear approach to exercises and tunes should be the rule. As the students begin to move upward in range, it is important to encourage them to use fast air on the higher notes, as opposed to slower air on the lower notes, and the idea of pitching the air in the mouth (through changes of vowel position) can be introduced. This is best done by asking students to imitate the pitch of the air stream as demonstrated by the teacher away from the instrument. To go higher in range, the air must first be blown faster (if the lips are to vibrate faster, the air must move faster). Following on the acceleration of the air, the pitch of the air stream must be generated by altering the vowel position. To go lower, the pitch of the air must descend by means of dropping the tongue. The stability of the lower notes can be increased by blowing horizontally forward to a distant point. This raises the volume and pressure of the air to stabilize the notes.

A good method is to play each tune or exercise first on the mouthpiece and then on the instrument, with the teacher demonstrating frequently. A good ear-training exercise (this could also be a short warm-up) is for the teacher to play random open tones in a musical manner and to ask the students to imitate what the teacher plays. It is important to introduce new material at each lesson. Students will realize a greater feeling of accomplishment by progressing through a number of exercises and tunes that achieve similar things than by remaining on the same material from class to class. Motivation is intimately linked to a sense of accomplishment. Familiar melodies and folk tunes are especially important, since students will unconsciously focus their thought patterns on the melodic sequence of the tune instead of on the mechanical aspects of producing sound. Melodic material should remain a part of a student's study routine throughout all levels. Melodies can be used to explore the instrument and to develop a feel for different keys. It is also worthwhile to encourage students to try to play notes of the harmonic series of each valve or slide position as well as bugle call-like melodies.

Method books should be worked through in a systematic way to ensure a steady line of development. Unfortunately, not all method books are organized in the most practical, progressive sequence, so it is often necessary to supplement the primary method with additional studies from other books or from material written by the teacher. Teachers should adapt both the study material and their approach to the needs of individual students.

Above all, teachers should strive to develop a concept of sound in each student by playing and demonstrating whenever possible. It is also rewarding to play recordings of brass artists and ensembles for the class and occasionally to bring in advanced students to perform. As early as possible, easy duets, trios, and quartets should be attempted, to lay the foundation of a sense of ensemble.

One of the main reasons students give up their study of a brass instrument is a feeling of lack of progress. This is often the result of poor practice habits. In the early stages, progress must be made rapidly. As youngsters advance in their ability to play, a sense of pride in this special skill develops and their motivation increases. Discouragement sets in if the process seems to be standing still. This is why effective principles of tone production need to be established from the beginning along with a purposeful practice routine. The importance of the latter cannot be overstressed. Gaining the support of parents is essential. All will go better if the teacher clearly explains to the parents what the student needs and what he or she is supposed to do. For example, a practice strategy should be developed.

- The student should, as far as possible, practice at the same time every day. In effect, this time should be reserved for practice.
- A music stand and a straight-backed chair need to be provided.
- Practice should take place in a well-lighted room that is free of distractions.
- A parent may need to help the student in the earlier phases.

Along with a practice strategy, there should be a systematic procedure for practicing the lesson:

- Spend the first 5 minutes buzzing on the mouthpiece. This could consist of tunes or exercises written by the teacher.
- With the assigned lesson material:
  - Say the note names in rhythm.
  - Say the note names in rhythm and do the fingerings at the same time.
  - Play the exercise or tune on the mouthpiece.
  - Play the exercise or tune on the instrument.

A well-organized course of study should be developed that, along with bringing in new material to stimulate interest, has been designed to ensure progress over a specified period of time. This should include regular evaluations to make certain that each student is progressing at a prescribed rate.

In spite of the best efforts, however, students will sometimes encounter problems with specific instruments. In such cases, the teacher might consider recommending a change to a different instrument. Many successful professional players began their study of music on a different instrument from the one with which they made their careers.

After a certain level has been reached, it is essential for students to have an opportunity to play in an elementary band or orchestra in addition to their weekly lesson(s). Membership in such a group offers a wealth of positive experiences and boosts motivation as well as providing an opportunity to learn new skills.

■ SURVIVING WHILE PLAYING A BRASS INSTRUMENT WITH BRACES

Students need a great deal of patience, support, and encouragement while trying to play with braces. There is a period of adjustment when the braces are first put on. Aside from the different feel to playing, the braces will tend to cut into the inside of the lips as a result of normal mouthpiece pressure. It is essential, therefore, that the embouchure formation create a cushion for the mouthpiece. This will be accomplished naturally if the lips are formed as if saying "tu." Various means have been devised to protect the inner lips from the braces. Brace Guard and brace wax are often used for this purpose. One of the most practical and effective shields can be made by cutting a rectangular piece of chamois skin to the right size and inserting it between the braces and the lips. Because it is very thin and made from animal membrane, it tends to interfere less with the embouchure while offering good protection. When the braces are taken off, there will be another (although shorter) period of adjustment that will require similar support and encouragement.

■ ASSEMBLING BRASS INSTRUMENTS

The following procedures should be followed in assembling brass instruments. The mouthpiece should be carefully inserted into the receiver and given a very slight turn to lock it in position. It must never be forced or tapped into the receiver. In assembling the trombone, *the slide should remain locked* to prevent it from accidentally falling out and becoming dented. While the left hand holds the bell section securely, the right hand should grasp the slide by both braces and insert the end into the bell lock receiver. The slide should be rotated so that an angle of 90 degrees (or slightly less) is formed and the locknut tightened. Particular care must be taken when removing trombones from their cases, since the slide rests in the case lid. The case should be laid flat and the lid opened evenly from end to end to avoid twisting the slide. With all brass instruments, it is important to remember to pull the main tuning slide out a half inch or so before beginning to play. From this position, the slide can be moved to conform to a tuning pitch.

■ REMOVING CONDENSATION

Condensation forms as warm breath is blown into the instrument. If this is not removed every so often, a gurgling sound will occur. The water can be removed almost silently by forming the lower lip around the mouthpiece rim and blowing with the water key open. One or more of the valve slides may require clearing as well, and these should be removed as necessary.

Removing water from the horn is slightly more involved. With the instrument resting on the left leg and held vertically so that the valves are downward and bell uppermost, the horn should be rotated to the right like a steering wheel, allowing any accumulated water to collect in the main tuning slide. The tuning slide should then be removed and the water poured out. Next, the horn should be returned to the inverted position so that water in the valve slides will run downward to the valves. The valves should be depressed to allow the water to enter the valves. With the third valve depressed, the horn should again be rotated to the right to direct the water into the third valve slide, which should be removed and emptied. Draining the valve slides will be easier if the water is poured in the opposite direction from the slide loop (see Figure 12.1).

The same procedure can be applied to the double horn, except that the F tuning slide must also be emptied. In clearing the valves, it is worth acquiring the knack of grasping both the F and B♭ third valve slides and emptying them together.

■ THE COLLEGE BRASS TECHNIQUES (METHODS) COURSE

The study of secondary instruments is obviously one of the most important aspects of a prospective instrument teacher's preparation. To be successful today, teachers need to have extensive knowledge of all the instruments and be able to convey effective principles of playing technique to their students. Considering the highly specialized and developed nature of brass playing today, greater demands are now placed on the college brass techniques or methods course than ever before.

There are two fundamental goals of the course:

- to provide detailed knowledge of the brass instruments and contemporary brass playing
- to prepare students to teach brass effectively by giving them a firm grasp of correct tone production and technique, both in concept and in practice

FIGURE 12.1
Removing water from the horn is slightly more involved.

The present text has been designed to meet both of these needs. In achieving the first objective, the content of the course can be enriched by incorporating information from the first nine chapters of this book. This will spur the students' interest in the subject and provide the depth of knowledge that today's brass teachers need to be effective. The chapters on tone production and playing position and the studies and ensembles found in Sections A, B, and C of this chapter work together to develop both a clear and practical concept of how to play brass instruments and the ability to play. Students should be encouraged to view the time and effort they spend in gaining knowledge and in learning to play as an investment for the future.

In the class material that follows, Section A consists of progressive studies to be played in unison, with some easy ensembles added at various points. The instructor should move at whatever pace seems appropriate to the class and remain on any material as long as it seems necessary. The choice of tempos is also totally at the discretion of the instructor; these will undoubtedly vary according to the ability level of each class. Typical classes are made up of both brass players learning the other brass instruments and nonbrass players. The brass-playing students will obviously develop at a somewhat faster rate, so the instructor must attempt to balance the pace between the two groups. My purpose has been to provide enough material so that both groups will feel challenged; the brass-playing students can go forward on their own and take advantage of the more advanced material. At the same time, a comfortable rate of progress for both brass players and nonbrass players has been built into the studies so that by playing together in class, all will develop at a reasonable pace.

Many of the studies should be played first with the mouthpiece alone and then on the instrument. In this way, students learn to center pitches accurately and their advancement will be faster. The great London Symphony trombonist Denis Wick aptly referred to mouthpiece playing as "lip solfège." In general, the horn should play the lower notation where possible, since playing in the middle and lower ranges is beneficial in the development of tone. When necessary, however, exercises can be played up an octave. Also, either the F or B♭ fingerings may be used. If a double horn is being used, the thumb valve must be depressed to use the B♭ fingerings. Beginning with exercise 89, common alternate positions are noted in the trombone part where appropriate. In learning fingerings and positions, it is helpful if students mentally practice the main fingering/position charts contained in Appendix D on a daily basis, with the goal of memorizing them. Although sixteenth notes frequently appear in the notation after exercise 129, the tempo should be very slow and can be subdivided as necessary.

Section B presents a series of ensembles that progress from easy to medium levels of difficulty. The instructor may wish to integrate these into Section A or work through this section as a unit, if time allows. There is great value in playing ensembles at any level. All ensembles appearing in this book have been scored for maximum flexibility of instrumentation so that they may be easily used in any brass class. The part number (1–4 or 1–5) of each line is shown as the circled number at the left. Trumpets are divided into two parts. The horn part usually doubles either the second trumpet or the trombone/euphonium line. Trombones and euphoniums may be used interchangeably. The bottom part is played by the tuba(s), but, in the event that no tuba is present in the class, this part has also been notated at the octave so that it can be played by a euphonium or trombone.

Section C is made up of 50 exercises for each instrument. These are intended to supplement the unison studies and ensembles used in class and to provide additional material for the student to practice at home. This material has been found to be particularly effective in moving the student's playing ability ahead in the shortest time period and establishing good tone production. Students should be encouraged to make a daily project of starting at the beginning or some other point and working down a page or two of these studies. In order to be able to include more exercises, an abbreviation has been used in the notation of some of the studies. In such cases, the study should be repeated by starting on the (stemless) note shown and playing in that key. (See, for example, number 28 for trumpet and cornet.) This procedure has the benefit of challenging the student to explore the instrument. This process develops control, technique, and confidence in a way that no other exercise can. The author was trained in this manner as a student and can attest to its effectiveness as a pedagogical procedure.

In addition to providing learning material for the college brass techniques course, the studies and ensembles presented in Sections A, B, and C can be used on the elementary, middle school, and secondary levels once the student begins a teaching career. The ensembles, in particular, are well suited to junior and senior high school brass ensembles. From the foundation that these pieces offer it will be possible to progress smoothly into the standard brass ensemble literature.

SECTION A

Unison Studies and Easy Ensembles for Class Use

Strive for a clear, freely produced sound on the mouthpiece.
Concentrate on in-tune pitches.

Repeat the first 11 exercises with instruments.

Buzz exercises 12–23 first on the mouthpiece; then play with instruments.

Slowly

Stabilize the sound and pitch by moving the air.

Remember to sustain the sound and blow through the notes.

(20) Hymn: *Abide with Me*
Legato

The Prince of Denmark's March Jeremiah Clarke (ca. 1674–1707)

(25) *Chester* William Billings (1746–1800)

Think of creating *wind* in moving the air outward.

(26)

*To perform No. 27 as a round, parts should be identified as 1, 2, 3, or 4.
To develop independence, parts should be changed.

(36) From the *Ninth Symphony* Ludwig van Beethoven (1770–1827)

From the *Third Symphony* Ludwig van Beethoven (1770–1827)

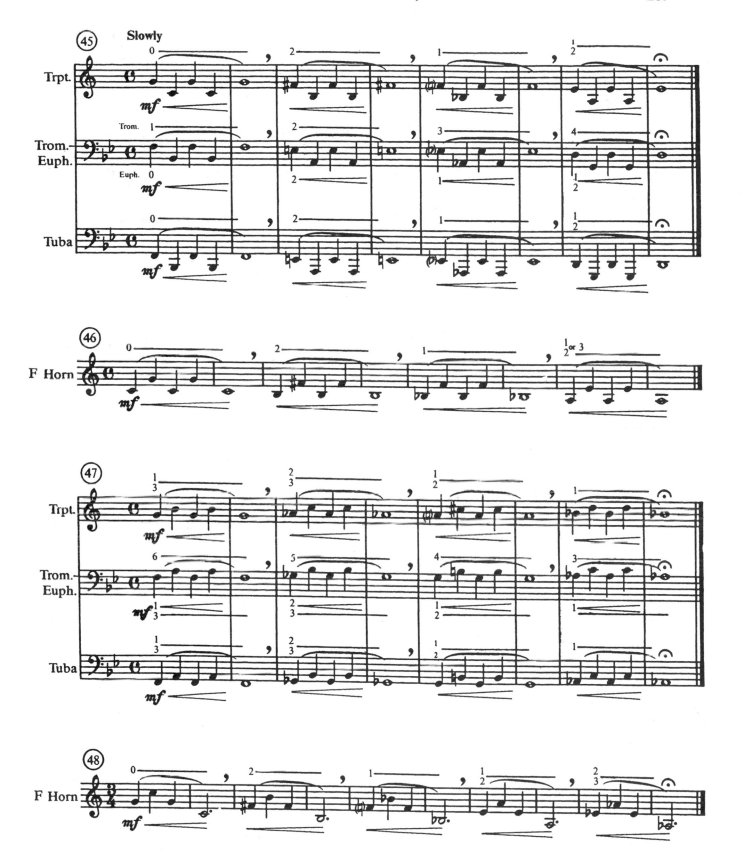

Trombone Legato. In addition to the lip slur, a slur can be made when changing from one set of partials to another:

Position:

The positions must be adjacent, however.

Partial number:

Trombone legato is discussed in Chapter 10.
(See also the harmonic fingering/position charts in Appendix D.)

A slur can also be made when the slide motion is opposite to the direction of the notes. For example:

Slide motion *inward,* direction of notes *downward:*

or

Slide motion *outward,* direction of notes *upward:*
(This is more effective in the upper register.)

In all other instances, the trombonist must use an exceptionally smooth legato tongue to create the illusion of a true slur:

Use whichever syllable produces the smoothest sound.

Trombone Legato Studies

59 *Advent Plainsong*

60 Slur Studies

Slowly

Remember to keep the air moving between notes when slurring.

61 Welsh Folk Song: *All Through the Night*
    Andante

English Folk Song: *Early in the Morning*

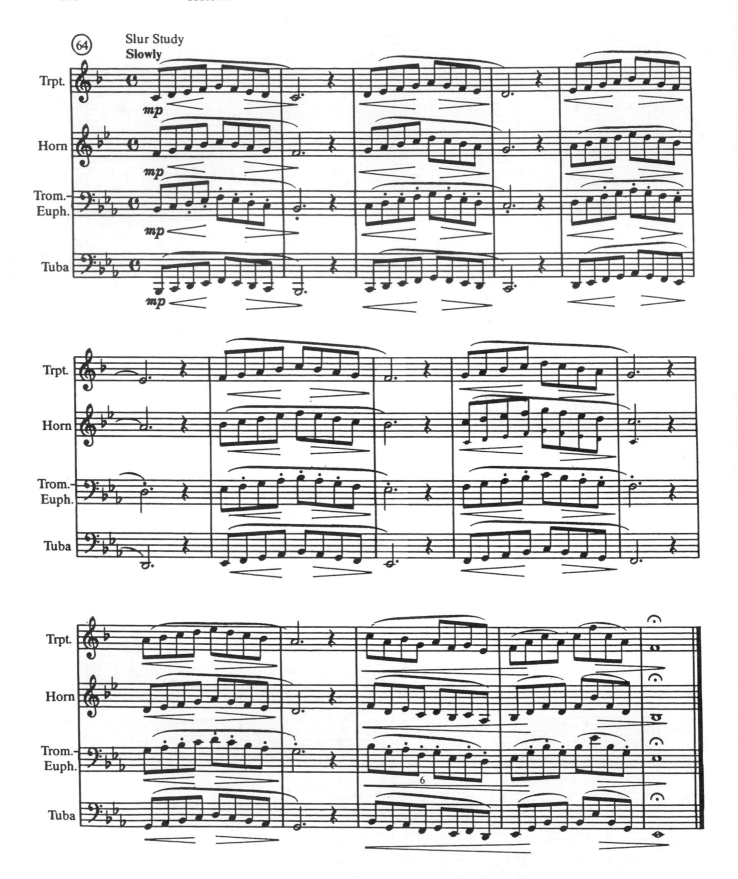

Largo from the *New World Symphony (No. 9)* Antonín Dvořák (1841–1904)

From number ⑥⑥ onward, all exercises should be taken in four as slowly as necessary.
As the ability of the class develops, these exercises should be repeated in a faster four or ₵

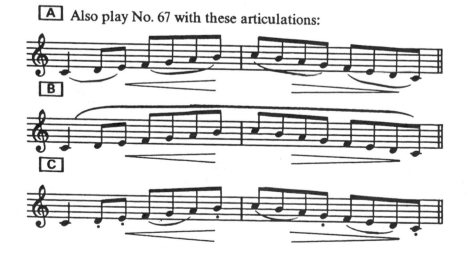

A Also play No. 67 with these articulations:

B

C

68 Pilgrim's Chorus from *Tannhäuser* Richard Wagner (1813–1883)

(71) Scottish Folk Song: *Ye Banks and Braes*
Sadly (slowly in 6)

Low Register

Strive to keep an even volume as the notes descend.
Slowly

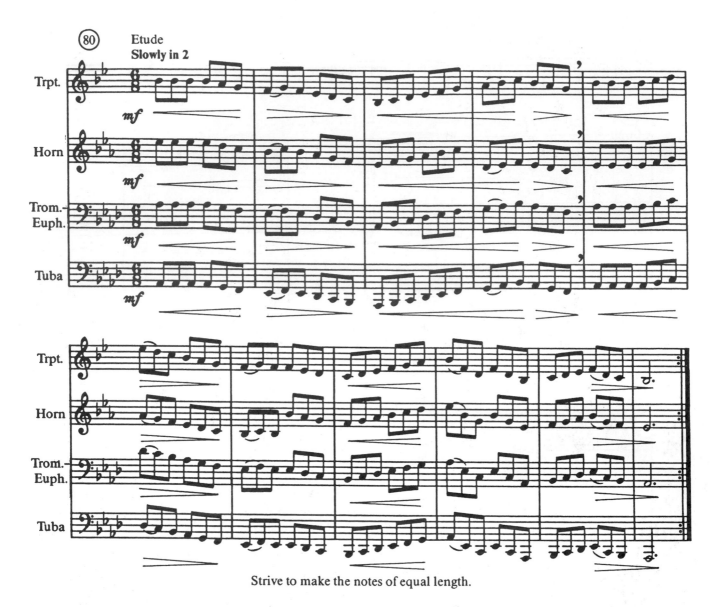

Strive to make the notes of equal length.

86 Arpeggio Study—Major

87 Arpeggio Study—Minor

88 Four-part chorale: *Christus, der ist mein Leben* J. S. Bach (1685–1750)

*In all ensembles the part number is shown by the circled numeral next to the instrument designation.

Alternate Positions for Trombone

mf Try to achieve an equality of sound between the normal and altered position.

Maintain the direction of slide motion where
possible by substituting alternate positions. (See Chapter 5.)

⑨⑦ Arpeggio Study—Minor
Slowly

Repeat: **A**   **B**

⑨⑧ Etude *In the style of a minuet*
In 3, but with a feeling of 1

99 Agnus Dei from *L'Arlesienne* (adapted) Georges Bizet (1838–1875)

Lip Slur Study
(104) **Slowly**

Now is the Month of Maying (adapted) Thomas Morley (1557–1602)

Moderate 2   Lightly, in a detached style

Major Scale

Since First I Saw Your Face (Abridged) Thomas Ford (d. 1648)

Studies in Staccato

Remember to keep the air moving in staccato playing.

Sea Chanty: *The Drunken Sailor*

The British Grenadiers
March tempo

Studies in Marcato

Sea Chanty: *Haul Away, Joe*

Slowly in 2

Welsh Folk Song: *Men of Harlech*

Studies in Legato Tonguing

English Folk Song: *The Wraggle–Taggle Gipseys*

Sea Chanty: *Rio Grande*

All studies from this point forward should be
played as slowly as necessary and may be subdivided.

(130) Major Scale
Slowly

Also play with these articulations.

A   B   C

(131) Relative Minor (melodic)
Slowly

Use articulations for No. 130.

(132) Arpeggio Study
Slowly

Also play with these articulations.

A   B   C

133   Interval Study

Also play with these articulations:

(134) Chromatic Scale
Not fast

A   B

(135) Lip Slur Study

Repeat in all valve combinations:
2, 1, 1–2, 2–3, 1–3, 1–2–3; positions: 2, 3, 4, 5, 6, 7

All studies may be subdivided as necessary.

Repeat in all valve combinations:
(omit 1–2–3)

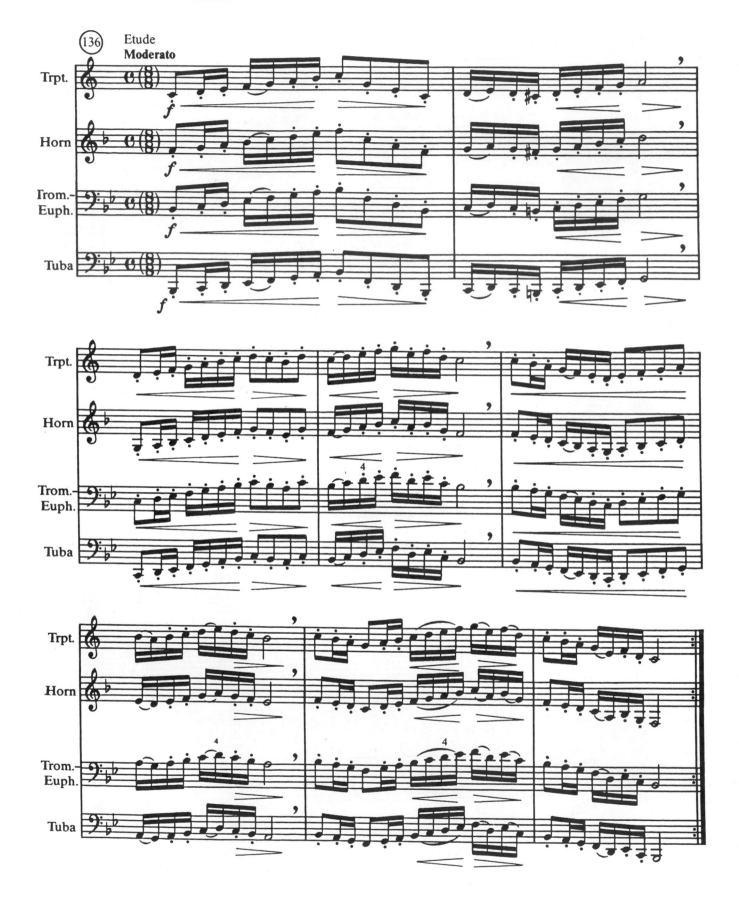

136 Etude
Moderato

Trpt.

Horn

Trom.-
Euph.

Tuba

(137) Double Tonguing (refer to Chapter 12)
Not fast

Exercises for double and triple tounging may also be practiced single-tongued.

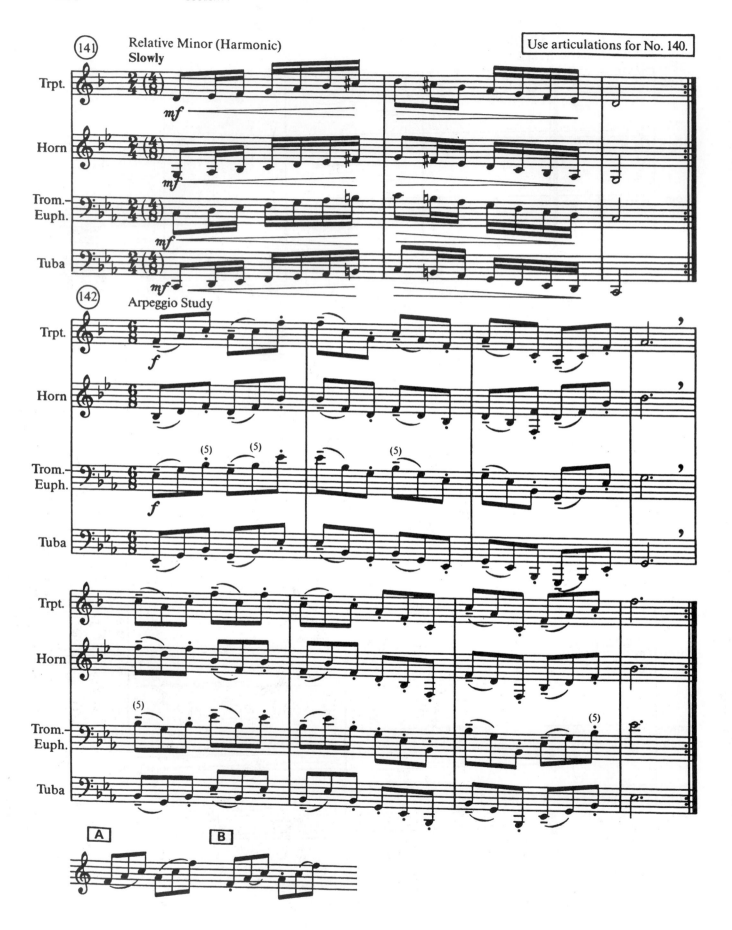

141 Relative Minor (Harmonic)
Slowly

Use articulations for No. 140.

142 Arpeggio Study

A   B

143 Interval Study

144 Lip Slur Study

Repeat in all valve combinations

Repeat in all valve combinations (omit 1-2-3).

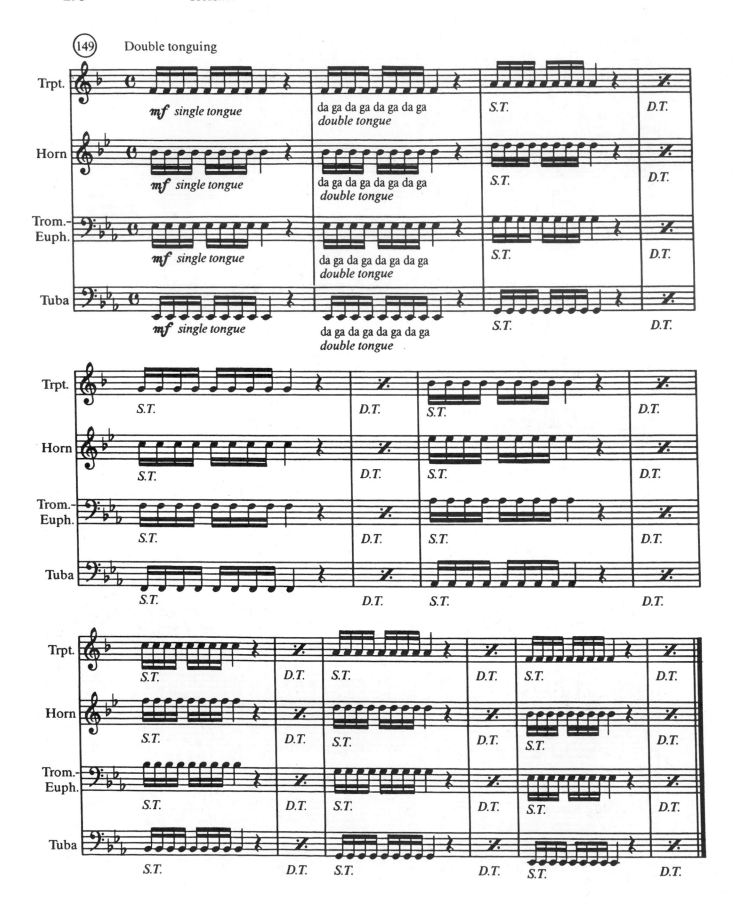

Exercises for double and triple tonguing may also be practiced single-tongued.

Scottish Folksong: *Loch Lomond*

Andante *legato*

Triple Tonguing

(160) *Rondeau* Jean Joseph Mouret (1682–1738)

Exercises for double and triple tonguing may also be practiced single-tongued.

Nos. 173 and 174: Use articulations for No. 161.

184 Relative Minor (Melodic)

Use articulations for No. 161.

185 Arpeggio (also slur)

186 Chromatic

Nos. 193 and 194: Use articulations for No. 161.

196 British Sailing Song: *Portsmouth*
Moderately

Nos. 197–200 may be omitted.

Additional Scales

197 Major

Progressive Ensembles

The Queen's Funeral March Henry Purcell (ca. 1659–1695)

* Parts are indicated by the circled number adjacent to the instrument designation.

Pavanne d'Angleterre Claude Gervaise (fl. 1540–1560)

La Mourisque Tylman Susato (ca. 1500–1561)

Bransle de villages Michael Praetorius (1571–1621)

Rather quick
Broad, but detached

L'arboscello ballo Furlano (1578) Giorgio Mainerio (fl. 16th cent.)

Moderato *broad, but not legato*

Danse du Roy Tylman Susato (ca. 1500–ca. 1561)

Courtly Masquing Ayre John Adson (ca. 1585–1640)

Tourdion (1547) Pierre Attaingnant (ca. 1494–ca. 1552)

Canzona (from the *Queen's Funeral Music*) Henry Purcell (ca. 1659–1695)

Courtly Masquing Ayre John Adson (ca. 1585–1640)

Gagliarda La Traditora Anonymous, ca 1520

Ballet Michael Praetorius (1571–1621)

Galliard Anthony Holborne (1584–1602)

In 1 or quick 3

Galliard (cont.)

Intrade Johann Pezel (1639–1694)

Intrade (cont.)

The tuba should play the upper octave if possible.

Bransle Simple Claude Gervaise (fl. 1540–1560)

Studies for Individual Practice
Trumpet and Cornet

Play all exercises on mouthpiece before playing on instrument.
Repeat often

28 Exercises should also be played in the keys of the notes indicated.

30 Exercises from 30 onward are more advanced.

slur and tongue

Horn

Play all exercises on the mouthpiece first.
All F Horn

29 Exercises should also be played in the keys of the notes indicated.

Exercises from 30 onward are more advanced.
30 Use double horn as desired.

Trombone and Euphonium

Play all exercises on the mouthpiece first.

Euphonium players should also play the exercises for trumpet and cornet.

mf Play often.

Stay on each exercise as long as necessary before moving on.

Exercises should also be played in the keys of the notes indicated.

Tuba

Play all exercises on the mouthpiece first.

Exercises from 30 onward are more advanced.

Exercises should also be played in the keys of the notes indicated.

INSTRUMENT CARE

■ WHY GOOD CARE IS IMPORTANT

Brass instruments are complex acoustical devices, and the process that takes place inside the tubing will function optimally only so long as the instrument remains in good condition. Most critical are the conical portions of the tubing, which must maintain an exact taper. As was shown in Chapter 1, it is the instrument's taper that determines the pitch placement of notes of the harmonic series. Equally important is its effect on response and tone quality. If any of the internal proportions of the tubing become altered at certain points because of grime or dents, the instrument's internal acoustical operation may be affected. It is also of primary importance that all moving parts work freely. Premature wear of valves and slides due to inadequate lubrication will ultimately lead to a deterioration of the air seal and a subsequent decline in the instrument's playing quality. Dents on the trombone slide create high spots that accelerate wear and destroy the smooth motion of the slide. Given adequate care, brass instruments will last for many years. A number of professional players have used a single instrument (with regular service and repair) for a substantial portion of their careers.

■ CLEANING

Grime collects most frequently in the instrument's mouthpiece and leadpipe; these should be cleaned regularly at two- or three-week intervals. A tapered mouthpiece brush should be used to clean the mouthpiece after running water through it. The mouthpiece's silver plating can be brightened with ordinary silver polish. It is best not to polish gold plating too frequently since the finish is prone to wear. For regular cleaning, the luster of gold plating can be restored by lightly rubbing it with liquid soap under warm water.[1]

The best way of cleaning the leadpipe and the instrument's other tubing is to run lukewarm water through it under strong pressure. To do this, the player needs to make up a special cleaning tube. First, obtain a length (about 2.5 feet) of plastic tubing that will fit inside the instrument's tubing. Plastic tubing of this type and an appropriate fitting that will attach it to a faucet are available at hardware/home improvement stores. A laundry tub, large sink, or bath tub should be used for cleaning. To prevent dents, towels or foam rubber can be placed where the instrument might come in contact with the tub or sink. After inserting the plastic tube slightly into the large end of the leadpipe or other tubing, adjust the taps so that high-pressure lukewarm water is forced through the tubing. Any collected grime will be washed out, with no danger to the soldered joints within the tubing. When done regularly, perhaps every three weeks or once a month, this method of cleaning will prevent a buildup of grime.

---

[1] Nickel silver mouthpieces present a problem in finding an effective cleaner. The author has been able to locate only one polish that works well. Happich *Simichrome* polish, a German product, is available in some hardware and home improvement stores. The Vermont Country Store, www.vermontcountrystore.com, regularly stocks this product.

Alternatively (especially when the instrument has not been cleaned for a long time), a flexible brush can be pushed carefully through the tubing. With this method, however, there is some risk of damaging the soldered joints between sections of tubing. It is important when applying a flexible brush that the tubing first be flushed with water and the brush end softened by soaking. Some flexible brushes come with a protective plastic coating, and this is to be preferred.

To do a thorough cleaning, the pistons and slides should be removed (rotary valve instruments may be cleaned with the valves in place) and lukewarm water forced through all subsections of tubing as well as the tuning and valve slides. *It is important that the temperature of the water not exceed lukewarm, or the instrument's lacquer finish might be damaged.* The interior of the valve casings of piston valve instruments can be wiped with a cleaning rod covered with a lint-free cloth (the rod must be completely covered to avoid damage to the valve casings). Special cleaners are available for this purpose. Otherwise, some valve oil added to the cloth will act as a solvent. All parts should be thoroughly rinsed and dried with a soft cloth.

Trombone slides require special handling to avoid damage. After separating the inner and outer slides, the outer slide may be cleaned by forcing water through it in the manner described earlier. The real danger is to the inner slide tubes. Smooth motion of the slide is dependent on the inner slide tubes' being aligned in parallel with each other; any jolt or pressure may distort this alignment, affecting the smoothness of the slide's motion. To be safe, the inner slide should be held by the side being cleaned. The water pressure method can be carefully used to clean the interior of the tubes. Alternatively, a long cloth attached to a string and weight (a fishing line and sinker work well) can be pulled from the stocking end toward the cork barrel. The inner slide tube's exteriors should be carefully wiped with a solvent or special cleaner. Old slide lubricant tends to collect in the cork or spring barrel, and this can be removed with a small brush.

■ LUBRICATION

The vulnerable point of every valved brass instrument is the air seal maintained by the valves. The problem is made more complex by the need for the valves to move freely and quickly. Inherent in these two parameters is a conflict. The degree of contact of the surfaces of the piston or rotor and its casing must be sufficient to be airtight yet loose enough for fast motion of the valve. A balance is created between these opposing requirements when the instrument is made. This is accomplished by lapping the valve piston or rotor into its casing with an abrasive compound until a specific clearance between the surfaces has been achieved. The degree of clearance is chosen as the best compromise between quick action and an effective air seal within the valve. The problem for the player is to try to prevent this clearance from increasing through wear, causing air leakage, as the valves are used under playing conditions. Once the valve seal leaks, the playing qualities of the instrument will decline. When one considers how many times the valves go up and down or rotate in a typical day of playing, the difficulty of preventing a deterioration of the instrument's air seal by wear over a period of time is obvious.

The only means of protecting the valves against wear is to use the best lubricants available. A valve lubricant works by creating a protective barrier between the piston or rotor surfaces and those of the casing. The viscosity of the lubricant must be determined with great accuracy by the manufacturer. If it is too high, the valve will not move quickly enough; if it is too low, the barrier will be insufficient to protect the valve or the barrier will break down. The best lubricants come in a selection of viscosities for each instrument. A number of formulations are on the market. Some are synthetic,[2] while others use petroleum as a base. Thin kerosene-based lubricants do not provide the necessary level

---

[2] The author has found Hetman synthetic lubricants to offer good protection and a fast, smooth action. The range of lubricants is available in various viscosities for each instrument.

of protection, although they offer fast action. The player should study the lubricant manufacturer's literature carefully and choose wisely. Above all, *premature valve wear can be prevented only by lubricating the valves every day.*

To lubricate valves, the following procedures may be used.

Piston Valves

Piston valves should first be cleaned with one of the special cleaners available or wiped with a soft cloth moistened with valve oil to remove any residue. Apply a light coat of valve lubricant to the piston's surfaces. Carefully insert the piston into the casing, following the alignment of the valve guides. The valve guides fit into the groove(s) on the side(s) of the casings (called the *keyway*). Do not rotate the piston in the casing, or the piston surface might be scratched. The pistons are stamped with the appropriate number to avoid inserting them into the wrong casing. *If the instrument does not play properly after assembly, it is probable that a piston has been inserted into the wrong casing.* This happens frequently with young students.

Rotary Valves

In lubricating rotary valves, it is important to apply lubricants that have been specifically formulated for this type of valve. Piston valve oil is too light and will not provide good results. In order to lubricate rotary valves, it is best if the lubricant containers have tubes to apply the lubricant; this makes reaching the places where the lubricant must be applied much easier. Two viscosities of lubricant must be used with rotary valves: a lighter viscosity for the rotor and casing surfaces, and a higher viscosity on the bearings and linkages. With the instrument laid flat, remove the valve caps and place a drop of the heavier lubricant on the end of each rotor shaft. The valves should be moved to encourage the lubricant to seep down between the shaft and the bearing plate to the bearing. After replacing the caps, turn the instrument over and apply some lubricant into the gaps between the stop-arm hubs and the lower bearing plates. Rotate the valves again to encourage the lubricant to go into the bearings. Next, each moving part of the valve-activating linkage should receive some lubricant. The valve levers turn on a rocker shaft; apply some lubricant to the shaft through the springs and at the ends of each lever (see Figure 13.1).

To maintain a quick action, it will occasionally be necessary to apply lubricant directly to the rotors and the casings. The lighter-viscosity lubricant should be used for this purpose. Lubricating the rotors must be done through the valve slides, so care must be taken to prevent slide grease (the valve lubricant acts as a solvent) from washing down into the valves, slowing their action. Hold the horn with the bell upward and the valve slides removed. Rotate the valves halfway and insert the tube on the lubricant bottle or a long eyedropper into the open tubes and release several drops of lubricant on the surface of the rotors. Replace the slides and turn the instrument to various positions while rapidly depressing the valves to spread the lubricant.

The Trombone Slide

One of the special silicone lubricants should be used on the trombone slide. The inner slide should be cleaned before applying new lubricant. After cleaning, place some small spots of lubricant along the slide and the stockings, and then spread it evenly over the slide surface. Next, the slide should be gently wiped so that only a light film remains. A fine mist of water can be periodically sprayed on the slide surface to maintain good action (plastic sprayers of the type available at garden stores may be used for this purpose).

Tuning and Valve Slides

Since the instrument's air seal is maintained by these slides as well as the valves, it is important to prevent wear by keeping them well lubricated. New products have appeared recently, and these are generally to be preferred over anhydrous lanolin, which has been

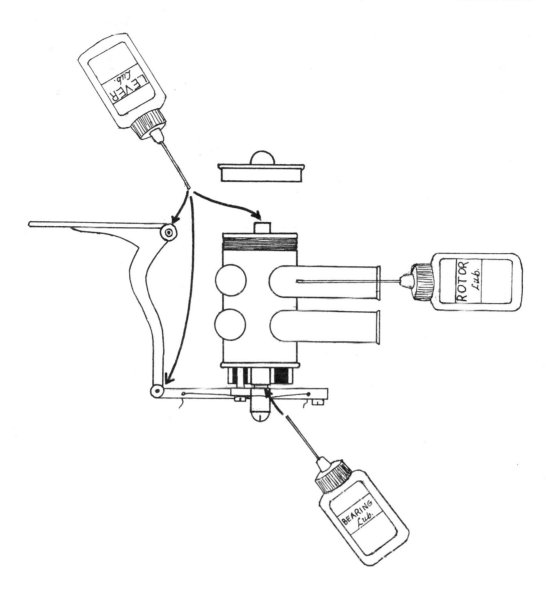

FIGURE 13.1
How to lubricate
rotary valves.

used for a number of years for this purpose. Petroleum jelly and gun grease have also been used in the past, but these have now been superseded by the new purpose-designed formulations. For slides that must be moved often in playing, such as trumpet first and third valve slides, one of the new light-viscosity synthetic lubricants should be applied. Regular slide grease is too heavy for this purpose.

On older instruments, slides tend to become worn and lose their air seal. These should be tightened by a repair technician. This requires special equipment that internally expands the inner slide tube to fit the outer tube. In severe cases, the slides can be replated, but, like valve replating, this should only be attempted by a very skilled craftsman. In a complete overhaul, it is advisable to have both valves and slides tightened or replated to reestablish the instrument's original air seal.

Before lubricating, the slide must be wiped with a clean cloth to remove any residue. Apply a light coating of the viscosity of slide lubricant that best matches the instrument's condition—higher viscosity for older instruments with more wear (this helps the air seal) and lighter lubricant for newer instruments. Make a ring with the lubricant completely around each inner slide tube about an inch from the end. The slide should be replaced and moved inward and outward several times; this will spread the lubricant evenly without forming a buildup at the end of the tube. Wipe off any excess lubricant. The valves should be depressed when inserting or withdrawing valve slides.

■ MISCELLANEOUS

Removing Stuck Mouthpieces and Slides

Jammed mouthpieces are a common occurrence in school bands, so it is advisable to have a mouthpiece puller available. This is an inexpensive tool that will remove the mouthpiece quickly and safely. The leadpipe or receiver can be damaged if any other method of removal is attempted. Frozen slides or severely stuck mouthpieces should generally be referred to a repair technician.

Piston and Rotary Valve Alignment

The valve ports of the piston must remain in correct alignment with those of the casing if there is to be minimal disturbance to the vibrating air column as it passes through the valves. On piston valve instruments, both vertical and radial alignment must be considered. The latter is maintained by the valve guides, which keep the piston from turning within the casing. Radial misalignment can occur only if the guides or keyways become worn.

The vertical alignment of piston valves is dependent on the thickness of the cork and felt bumpers. These become compressed with use and must be renewed periodically. Usually, a mark on the valve stem indicates the correct height of the bumpers. If no mark can be found, or in cases of radial misalignment, the instrument should be sent for repair.

Rotary valve alignment is maintained by the neoprene or cork bumpers located on the cork stop plate. To check this, the upper valve cap should be removed and the bearing plate inspected to see if one of the marks on the end of the rotor shaft lines up with the mark on the flange of the bearing plate with the valve at rest (closed). With the valve depressed (open), the other mark on the shaft should align with the mark on the bearing plate. If this is not the case, the bumper(s) must be replaced (or trimmed, if a high bumper is found). New neoprene or cork bumpers should be pressed into the cork stops and trimmed as necessary with a razor. Neoprene bumper material comes in different thicknesses, so it is important to make sure that the new bumpers match the original ones.

Removing Rotary Valves

Sometimes corrosion and accumulated grease from the slides slow the action of rotary valves to the point that lubrication does not help. The first step in such cases is to flush the valves with lukewarm water under high pressure (as described earlier under "Cleaning") and relubricate the valves with a light rotor lubricant on the rotor surfaces. In most instances, this will restore crisp action to the valve. In severe cases, the rotors must be removed, and both the inside of the casings and the rotors must be cleaned and lubricated. In general, because of the risk of damaging the valves in the removal process, this work should be left to a specialist. If this is not possible, the following procedure may be used: After taking off the strings or disconnecting the mechanical linkage, remove the upper valve cap and invert the instrument so that the stop-arm hub and screw are upward. Turn the stop-arm screw outward several times. While keeping the palm of the hand underneath the upper bearing plate (to catch the rotor when it falls), lightly and carefully tap the head of the screw with a hard leather or wooden hammer (alternatively, a block of wood can be placed on the screw and gently tapped with a metal hammer). Support the instrument with the arm to absorb any shock. As the rotor is forced downward, the upper bearing plate will drop into your hand; the stop-arm screw and hub can then be taken off and the rotor removed. Clean the interior of the casing and the rotor with one of the new cleaners for valves or a solvent and a soft cloth. After lubricating the rotor and casing, replace the rotor. The next step is critical: The mark on the upper bearing plate must be aligned with the mark on the casing. Carefully start the plate into the casing (be certain that it goes in straight), and gently tap the raised flange at the center until the

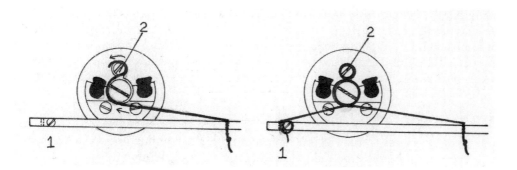

FIGURE 13.2
Restringing rotary
valves.

plate is fully seated. The rotor should be checked for free rotation. If the plate is tilted even slightly, the rotor will bind. (If binding occurs, the bearing plate must be removed and inserted again.) If all is well, replace the stop arm and then tighten the screw.

Restringing Rotary Valves

The restringing procedure can be seen in Figure 13.2. It is best to begin with the middle valve to make the adjustment of the valve keys easier. Special cord designed for the purpose should be used. If this is unavailable, 20- to 27-pound test fishing line may be substituted (linen or Dacron line is preferable to that made from nylon). One end of a six-inch length should be knotted and threaded in a figure-8 pattern. Once the string is correctly threaded, pull it taut and tighten setscrew number 1. To adjust the height of the valve keys, depress the key to the desired position and tighten setscrew number 2. *To change the height, it is only necessary to loosen setscrew number 2.* Adjust the height of the other valve keys to match the middle valve. Special stringing jigs are available that make adjusting the height of the valve levers easier.

Water Keys

Periodically, water keys should be checked to make certain that the spring has not weakened and that the cork makes an adequate air seal. Worn corks and springs should be replaced. A new cork of the exact size should be pressed into the water-key cup (add a drop of glue if the cork will not seat securely). It is a good idea for schools to maintain a supply of the correct springs and corks for each instrument. In an emergency, a worn cork can be turned upside down to form a temporary seal.

Using Piston Valves

On piston valve instruments, it is important that the valves be pushed straight down with the fingertips. If the middle part of the finger is used, pressure tends to be exerted on one side of the valve casing, causing it to go out of round and accelerating wear to that side of the piston.

Dents

Dents are a constant concern. Tubing dents can cause poor response, affect the instrument's intonation, and create other problems. Dents in a valve casing will affect valve action and seriously damage the piston or rotor. Aside from careless handling, many dents occur within the case. Loose mouthpieces and other items moving within the case are particularly destructive; make sure that the mouthpiece is kept in its place and that any other items are secure. It is essential that well-designed, hard cases be provided with every instrument. The fit of the instrument within the case should be inspected to make certain that the instrument cannot shift, causing dents as the case is transported. During rehearsal breaks, *instruments must never be left on chairs but must be returned to their cases.* Trombonists and trumpeters who use more than one trumpet should purchase one of the purpose-designed stands for instruments to rest on when not in use. The trombone slide, in particular, is extremely vulnerable to being knocked over and dented.

Advice on Repairs

A less-than-competent repair technician can do more harm than good to a brass instrument. Every effort should be made to locate a skilled professional technician. Professional players can usually recommend such a person. If none can be found locally, it might be advisable to send the instrument to a specialist. Also, some manufacturers will take their own instruments in for service. Repairs vary in complexity: valve replating, problems with trombone slides, and dent removal that entails taking the instrument apart should only be attempted by an expert. Horns, in particular, require special skills and equipment that are often beyond those of the average technician.

NOTES FOR CONDUCTORS

■ HOW THE BRASS SECTION IS ORGANIZED

The brass section is organized around a group of principal players who have the responsibility of directing all aspects of their respective sections' performance. Since full rehearsals offer little opportunity for concentrated work on intonation, balance, precision, and uniformity of style, a prime duty of the principal is to oversee sectional rehearsals as needed to develop these qualities. The principal is responsible to the conductor for the overall performance of the section, so it is important not only that the individual be the best player in the section but that he or she possess genuine qualities of leadership. The morale and effectiveness of the section are dependent on positive leadership. This is usually found in an individual who has the personal ability to set a high standard of performance and who also can direct positively and work in harmony with members of the section. The best principals often lead by example, try to be helpful to their section colleagues, and, above all, convey an air of humility. Additionally, it is important that principals of the brass section communicate well with each other to promote better ensemble playing between their respective sections.

A few orchestras have more than one principal, each holding equal status. In most others, the third or fourth trumpeter, fifth horn, or extra trombone usually also serves as an assistant first,[1] playing the less important works on the program and providing relief to the principal in taxing pieces. The terms *associate principal* and *co-principal* are sometime used to designate a position higher than assistant principal (but below the principal) whose duties are to lighten the load of the principal by sharing some of the first parts, at the principal's discretion.

Orchestral brass sections usually consist of three or four trumpets, five or six horns, three or four tenor trombones, one bass trombone, and one tuba. There are usually three cornet and two trumpet parts in bands, although the present trend among composers is to write for a single section of trumpets (or cornets), identified as first, second, third, etc., following the standard orchestral practice. In the traditional band format, the first cornet part includes most of the solo work, so this should go to the principal. The trumpets often perform independent of the cornets, but the first trumpet and first cornet parts are frequently doubled. For this reason, the player next in ability after the principal should be assigned the first trumpet part, with the remaining players filling out the lower parts. In scores that specify three or four trumpets in place of cornets, the first cornetist and first trumpeter should take the first two parts. Band conductors should review the scoring of each composition in order to assign parts to best advantage. The traditional use of both trumpets and cornets was intended to create a contrast of sound and playing style within the band. This is also a feature of some orchestral works by French composers (Berlioz, Franck, Debussy). Naturally, the intended contrast is lost when all of the parts are played on trumpets. Whenever possible, the conductor should endeavor to

---

[1] In Britain, assistants who play the less important parts of a work to provide relief for the principals are called *bumpers*.

have cornet parts played on cornets and should become familiar with the differences in timbre and playing style between the two instruments. If the conductor can bring out these differences, the work (whether for band or orchestra) will take on an entirely new character. (The cornet is discussed in Chapter 3.)

In horn sections, the two players of highest ability and best upper range should be assigned the first and third parts. Players who have good low registers should be given the second and fourth parts. This arrangement is suggested because horn parts are traditionally written for sections composed of two pairs of high and low players. Although today most players have sufficient range to cover all parts, there is some specialization in the professional field of high and low horns. The pairs are sometimes called upon to perform separately, and solos may occur in both the first and third parts. At other times, the third may be written to double the first. When all four play together, the usual voicing from upper to lower is 1–3–2–4. A similar pattern is followed in bands. In auditioning horn players it is important to choose material that reflects the players' specialization. Fourth horn players, for example, must develop a highly controlled and strong low register. As a result, they cannot be expected to perform in the upper register in the same manner as a first or third player.

The third trombone part is conceived specifically for the bass trombone, a much larger instrument than the two tenors, with extended low range. Bass trombone parts often diverge from the other two parts, and in these circumstances the instrument should be treated as a solo voice. Since the bass trombone and tuba often double or play in octaves, two schools of thought have arisen as to what the bass trombone timbre should be. One point of view is that the bass trombone must blend with the tuba. This has led to the use of ever-larger mouthpieces and instruments in the quest to darken the sound by reducing the presence of upper partials in the timbre. The more traditional view is that the blend and balance of the three-part trombone section is sacrificed if the bass trombone timbre moves too far in the direction of the tuba. In effect, the bass trombone sound seems to drop from the trombone section down into a two-part tuba and bass trombone section. The traditional concept of timbre when the bass trombone doubles the tuba is that the resultant sound should be a mixture, not a blend, of the two individual sounds. The bass trombone clarifies and puts a cutting edge on the less-defined tuba timbre. It is important to the overall effect of the brass section for conductors to consider this question and to articulate their wishes to their players.

■ ACHIEVING A GOOD BRASS SOUND

The best results will be achieved if the conductor approaches the brass section as a brass ensemble within the orchestra or band rather than as autonomous sections. This approach was strongly encouraged for all sections of the Berlin Philharmonic by Herbert von Karajan, who considered the orchestra a collection of individual ensembles. In working with the brass, balance is of primary importance since it strongly influences the quality of the sound that will be produced by the section. A sense of balance is also critical in developing good intonation. Intonation and balance go hand in hand. When good balance is the norm, irregularities of intonation can be heard more clearly by the players, making correction easier.

Each player must develop the habit of listening to the highest voice and matching its dynamic level precisely. When individual sections perform alone, players on the lower parts should adjust to the principal. The first trumpet establishes the volume level when the entire brass section plays together. When the low brass are called upon to play alone, all should match the principal trombone. A good brass section has an equality of sound from top to bottom.

Volume is another factor that affects intonation. There is a far greater margin of error at high volumes than at lower levels, and faults in intonation tend to be covered up by the mass of sound. When a passage sounds out of tune, a good corrective procedure is to repeat it slowly at a *mezzo forte* level. This affords the players both an opportunity to hear more clearly and sufficient time to make corrections. It is also a good practice to single out any chords needing correction. In extreme cases, the root might be played and then the fifth and third added. Octaves, too, often need to be singled out and checked. Better unisons will be achieved if section players approach such passages by reinforcing the principal rather than playing out boldly. The same approach can be used to good effect in passages written in octaves.

Another conceptual element that strongly influences the quality of sound is a sustained and linear style of playing, as opposed to a more vertical approach. This contributes continuity and direction to musical lines and encourages a refined and balanced sound. Attention must also be given to making certain that the length and shape of notes, attacks, and releases are uniform.

To ensure that the full resonance of the brass section is heard by the audience, trumpeters and trombonists should hold their instruments so that the bells are clear of the music stands. The music stand blocks the sound and absorbs partials when the sound is directed into it, destroying the clarity, balance, and tone quality of the brass section.

■ SEATING PROBLEMS

It is regrettable that in many ensembles little thought seems to be given to the best way of seating brass players so that they can adequately hear both themselves and each other. Playing in such groups is unpleasant and unrewarding. Among the worst and most frequent problems is to place the trumpets in front of the trombones. The first trumpeter can hear very little other than the sound radiating from the trombone bell in back of his or her head, and the first trombonist, who must balance and tune with the first trumpet, has difficulty in hearing this part. Even worse is to position the horns in front of trumpets or trombones.

The poorest location for horns is in the center of the ensemble, another common placement. The horn bell is low and to the side of the player, where its rear-directed sound is absorbed by the clothing and bodies of the players seated behind. In such a setup, horn players can barely hear their own sounds, and their ability to judge volume and intonation accurately is severely impaired. It also promotes severe fatigue, and the player finds the experience unrewarding. The most satisfactory position for the horns is at the rear or side of the ensemble, where their sound is unimpeded and can be reflected by one of the stage walls.

Because the horn bell goes to the player's right, it is customary for the principal to be seated on the left end of the section so that the players to the right can hear the principal's sound clearly.[2] This arrangement is not universal, however. Some prefer the greater sense of support from the lower parts that is gained by sitting to the section's right. In this arrangement, the principal also has an advantage in projection since the sound can be bounced off a reflective wall without any absorption from an adjacent player. This has been the traditional formation of the horn section in the Vienna Philharmonic Orchestra, and it was favored by the great English horn players Aubrey and Dennis Brain. A third approach is to place the third and fourth horns immediately behind the first and second. This plan works well enough and affords a viable alternative when a lateral layout is impractical.

The trombone section requires similar consideration. The principal trombonist normally sits on the right of the section so that the bell (rather than the slide) is closest to the second player to the left. In this way, the principal's sound can be heard across the section. The bass trombonist should be next to the tuba to facilitate playing parts that are doubled.

Suggested seating plans for various types of ensemble are shown in Figures 14.1 through 14.6. Following these plans will allow members of the brass section to hear each

[2] All suggestions for lateral placement refer to "stage" left or right, that is, from the players' perspective, looking outward from the stage toward the conductor and audience.

FIGURE 14.1
Seating chart:
orchestra.

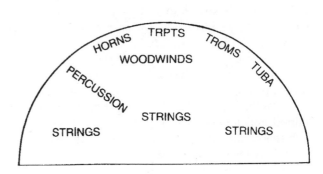

FIGURE 14.2
Seating chart:
band.

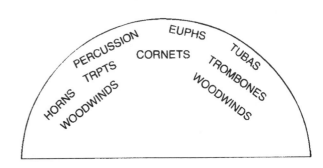

FIGURE 14.3
Seating chart:
brass quintet.

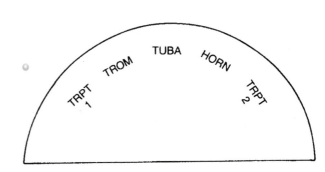

FIGURE 14.4
Seating chart:
brass quintet
(alternate).

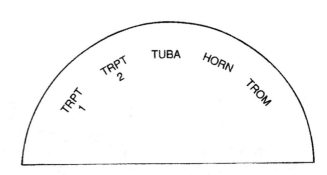

other with reasonable clarity and project a well-balanced and vibrant brass sound to the audience.

■ CONDUCTING BRASS PLAYERS

A basic problem for the conductor is securing the arrival of sound from various distances at the point when the beat is felt. Given experience, brass players usually develop the knack of focusing their sound to the conductor's beat while compensating for any lags caused by distance. It is a subtle process of anticipation. This process is aided if the

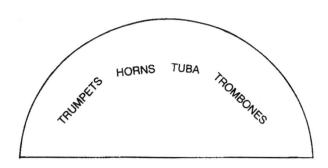

FIGURE 14.5
Seating chart:
brass ensemble.

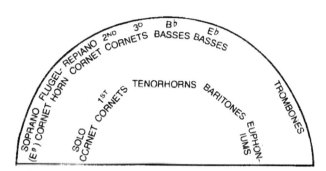

FIGURE 14.6
Seating chart:
brass band.

conductor refuses to accept late attacks and provides feedback to guide the players. To avoid ragged attacks, it is helpful if the conductor gains eye contact with the brass before the entrance and breathes on the preparation beat. Clearly defined beats are to be preferred when bringing in the brass.

Inexperienced conductors often create difficulties by demanding excessively soft dynamics. There is a minimum volume necessary for tone and security on brass instruments, and notes may fail to respond if this point is passed. High passages, in particular, require a certain effort and will be placed at risk if too low a dynamic is demanded by the conductor. Also, it should be recognized that even the very best brass players miss notes occasionally. It does no good to make a public issue out of a missed note.

Brass players respond positively to conductors who are knowledgeable about their instruments and ask for more than the notes. By attempting to bring out varied stylistic and tonal concepts of brass playing as they apply to the literature, the conductor will generate interest and commitment that will carry over into the performance. To take an obvious example, a more brilliant timbre and sharper attack should be used in Berlioz than in Brahms, which requires a dark, round tone and broad attack. Similarly, the full, sonorous sound one strives for in Bruckner is totally wrong in the works of Stravinsky.

The question of vibrato must also be carefully considered by the conductor. In general, a clear, pure sound without any vibrato gives greater resonance and color to many brass passages, especially in chordal textures. Certain compositions, however, such as works by Debussy, Ravel, and other French composers, require a light, quick vibrato to give them their vibrant color and style. There are other instances in the literature where the use of vibrato will enhance the expressive and stylistic effect of a composition. The speed of vibrato should be controlled and variable to create these contrasting sounds.

The choice of instruments can also contribute to the effectiveness of a performance. Rotary valve trumpets lend a broader, rounder sonority to works by Wagner, Bruckner, and other Germanic composers. The use of cornets in *Le Carnaval Romaine* and *Symphonie fantastique* is essential if the contrast (to the trumpets) intended by Berlioz is to be realized.

To gain an understanding of the various concepts and styles of brass playing, the conductor should make a study of representative recordings and seek out live performances, carefully analyzing the approach of each brass section to specific areas of the literature.

THE WORLD OF BRASS

FIGURE A.1
Chicago Symphony Orchestra: trumpets, trombones, horns (note the use of rotary valve trumpets and an alto trombone).

FIGURE A.2
London Symphony Orchestra: trumpets and trombones.

FIGURE A.3
Vienna Philhar-
monic: trumpets
and horns (note the
use of rotary valve
trumpets and single
F Vienna horns).

FIGURE A.4
Vienna Philhar-
monic: trombones
and tuba (the two
trombonists near-
est the tuba are us-
ing traditional Ger-
man trombones).

FIGURE A.5
Orchestre symphonique de Montréal: trumpets, trombones, tuba.

FIGURE A.6
Royal Philharmonic Orchestra, London: horns.

FIGURE A.7
Philip Jones Brass
Ensemble (quintet).

FIGURE A.8
Chicago Chamber
Brass.

FIGURE A.9
Stockholm Chamber Brass.

FIGURE A.10
Philip Jones Brass Ensemble (large ensemble).

FIGURE A.11   Black Dyke Mills Band.

FIGURE A.12   The United States Marine Band, "The President's Own": director, Colonel John R. Bourgeois.

FIGURE A.13 The Central band of Her Majesty's Royal Air Force: principal director of music, Wing Commander Eric Banks, M.B.E., F.L.C.M., L.R.A.M., L.G.S.M., R.A.F.

FIGURE A.14
Trumpeters from the Household Cavalry, Buckingham Palace, London.

FIGURE A.15 Trumpeters from the Household Cavalry, Buckingham Palace, London.

SELECTED BRASS RECORDINGS[1]

Solo Trumpet

Maurice André
EMI 69152, Trumpet concertos

EMI 73374 (2 CD), "Music for Trumpet"

Erato 92124, Italian Baroque concertos

Erato 92861, "Ultimate Trumpet Collection"

DG 413853, Telemann, Handel, Vivaldi

EMI 66961, Hummel, Telemann, L. Mozart

Ole Antonsen
EMI 85452, Concertos

Simax 1041, Recital pieces with piano

Eric Aubier
Adda 590027, Tomasi, Desenclos, Jolivet

Pierre Verany 730064, "Concerti Italiani"

Thierry Caens
Pierre Verany 788092, "Wind Music from a Golden Age"

Kevin Cobb
Summit 401, "One"

Timofei Dokshitser
Marcophon 904, Brandt, Gliere

Marcophon 914, "Scherzo Virtuoso"

Marcophon 915, "Arabesque"

Reinhold Friedrich
Capriccio 10436, Classical trumpet concertos

Capriccio 10598, Concertos for keyed trumpet

Capriccio 10439, Solos

Armando Ghitalla
Crystal 760, Trumpet concertos

Ludwig Güttler
Capriccio 10016, "Chamber Music for Trumpet"

Berlin Classics 1036, Haydn, Telemann, Leopold Mozart

Hakan Hardenberger
Philips 464028, Telemann Trumpet concertos

Philips 465460, Haydn concerto

Bis 287, "Virtuoso Trumpet"

Bis 1109, French solos

Adolph Herseth
DG 41504, Haydn concerto

David Hickman
Summit 118, Telemann, Hertel

Crystal 668, Halsey Stevens, Kent Kennan

Miroslav Kejmar (Czech Philharmonic)
Supraphon CO-72511, Vejvanovsky sonatas

Harry Kvabaek
Simax 1088, Trumpet & organ

Michael Laird
Argo 433 415 2, Purcell, Clarke, Charpentier (with Peter Hurford, organ)

Hannes, Wolfgang, and Bernhard Läubin
DG 431817, Telemann, Albinoni, Franceschini

Jens Lindemann
Marquis Classics 305, "Rising Sun"

Wynton Marsalis
Sony 42137, "Carnaval"

Sony 47193, Honegger, Halsey Stevens, Bozza

Columbia, 44726, Hummel, Jolivet, Levy

[1]Some specialists in brass recordings: www.tapmusic.com; www.paxman.co.uk (horn); www.spaeth-schmid.de; www.koebl.de; www.french-horn.com; www.bernelmusic.com (brass band)

Raymond Mase
Summit 148, "Trumpet in Our Time"

Summit 185, "Trumpet Vocalise"

Rafael Mendez
Summit 177, 178, Solos

Jean-François Michel
Marcophon 917, Trumpet and organ

Marcophon 919, Solos

Maurice Murphy (London Symphony)
Collins 30082, Haydn, Hummel, Arutunian

Sergei Nakariakov
Teldec 10788, Baroque trumpet concertos

Teldec 90846, Trumpet concertos

Teldec 85558, Russian concertos

Anthony Plog
Summit 108, "Colors of the Baroque"

Centaur 2068, Corelli, Hertel, Scarlatti

Crystal 663, Solos

Charles Schlueter
Kleos Classics 5122, Trumpet concertos

Kleos Classics 5126, Solos

Kleos Classics 5114, Solos and chamber music

Philip Smith
Summit 144, Orchestral Excerpts

Cala 516, "New York Legends"

Bernard Soustrot
Pierre Verany 788011, Hummel, Arutunian, Jolivet

Denon CD-7544, Michael Haydn, Albinoni

Angel CDC-47140, Baroque works

Crispian Steele-Perkins
Innovative 821, Haydn, Neruda, Torelli

MCA McAD-5844 and IMP Masters, Trumpet concertos

ASV Quicksilva QS 6081, Baroque trumpet concertos

Priory PRCD 189, "The King's Trumpeter"

Thomas Stevens
Crystal 665, "Sonatas"

Crystal 761, Solos

Alan Stringer
London Serenata 430633, Haydn concerto

Robert Sullivan
Summit 319, "Treasures for Trumpet"

Edward Tarr
Christophorus 74559, Fasch, Telemann, Handel

Guy Touvron
RCA 60858, Haydn, Hummel, Neruda

RCA 61200, Molter concertos

Forlane 16569, Various solos

John Wallace
Nimbus 5065, Hummel, Neruda

Nimbus 5010, Haydn

Nimbus 7012, Corelli, Torelli, Vivaldi, Purcell

James Watson
Doyen 036, Solos with brass band

*John Wilbraham, Edward Tarr, Maurice André,
Bernard Soustrot*
Seraphim 69731, "Favorite Trumpet Concertos"

Helmut Wobisch
Vanguard Classics OVC 2008, "The Virtuoso Trumpet"

Allen Vizzuti
DeHaske 991787, "Vizzuti meets Arban"

George Vosburgh
Four Winds 3018, 3024, Various solos and concertos

Cornet[2]

Maurice André
Erato ECD-99091, "La Belle époque" (Cornet solos)

Herbert L. Clarke
Crystal 450, Cornet solos (recorded 1904–1921)

Philip McCann
Chandos 4501, "The World's Most Beautiful Melodies"

Chandos 4502, "More of the World's Most Beautiful Melodies"

Chandos 4503, "The World's Most Beautiful Melodies," Vol. 3

Leonard Smith
Walking Frog 312, Cornet solos

Roger Webster
Polyphonic 086, Cornet solos with Brighouse and Rastrick
   Brass Band

SPS 21253, Cornet solos with brass band

Polyphonic 018, Cornet solos

Horn

Georges Barboteu
Sotone 102, "Parisian Horn Music"

---

[2]For additional cornet cornet recordings, see Historic Brass Recordings Recorded before 1950 below.

Hermann Baumann
Philips 464016, Gliere Concerto and other works

Teldec 94525, "Virtuoso Horn"

Philips 422346, Haydn concertos

Dennis Brain
Testament 1022, Beethoven Sonata, Schumann Adagio and Allegro

EMI 66950, Mozart concertos

EMI 67783, Strauss concertos, Hindemith concerto

BBC Legends 4048, Brahms Trio, Dukas, Marais

BBC Legends 4164, Hindemith, Vinter, chamber music

BBC Legends 4066, Schubert, Haydn concerto

Claire Briggs (City of Birmingham Symphony Orchestra)
Classics for Pleasure 4589, Mozart concertos

Timothy Brown
Hänssler 98.316, Mozart horn concertos

Philips 422833, Mozart horn quintet

Jeffery Bryant (Royal Philharmonic)
Intersound 2848/Tring TRP047, Mozart concertos

MCA Classics 10099, Britten Serenade

Vitali Buyanovsky
PRS 0045, PRS 0050, PRS 0046, solos and concertos

Gregory Cass (Orchestre de la Suisse Romande)
Gallo 741, Cherubini, Schumann, Rossini, Maxwell Davies

Alan Civil
Philips 464717, Mozart concertos

Dale Clevenger
Sony 44906, Mozart concertos

Teldec 8.42960 Haydn concertos

DG 415104, Mozart concerto No. 3

Philip Farkas
Coronet 1293, Bozza, Schumann, Gallay (cassette)

Summit 176, "Shared Reflections"

Peter Francomb
Pan Classics 510095, Stich, Rosetti, Foerster concertos

Norbert Hauptmann (Berlin Philharmonic)
DG 289 457 725, Classic performance of Strauss Concerto No. 2

Sony SK 53267, Later recording of Strauss Concerto No. 2

Michael Höltzel
M D&G 3240908, "Romantic Music for Horn"

Ifor James
EBS 6052, Haydn Concertos, Neruda concerto

EBS 6063, Strauss concertos

EBS 6040, Miscellaneous program

EBS 6062, Mozart concertos

AVM AVZ-3034, Beethoven Sonata, Cherubini, Danzi

EBS 6040, "Meditations"

EBS 6045, Rosetti concertos

EBS 6092, Telemann concerto

David Krehbiel
Summit 141, Orchestral Excerpts

Peter Landgren
Elan 82260, Schumann, Rheinberger

Frank Lloyd
Chandos 9150, Mozart concertos

Merlin MRFD 92092, "The Virtuoso Horn"

Marie-Luise Neunecker
Novalis 150030, Mozart concertos

Koch Schwann 3-1357, Gliere concerto and other pieces

Koch Schwann 364122, Schoeck concerto

HNNM03, Hindemith concerto

EMI 5 56183, Strauss concertos and Britten Serenade

Francis Orval
Marcophon 7042, Bach cello suites

Marcophon 936, Mozart concertos

David Pyatt
EMI Eminence EMX 2238, Strauss concertos

Erato 0630-17074, Mozart horn concertos and quintet

Erato 3984-21632, "David Pyatt Recital"

John Pigneguy
Hyperion CDA 66172, Malcolm Arnold, Fantasy for Horn

Bruno Schneider (Orchestre de la Suisse Romande)
Claves 50-9010, Strauss concerto No. 2

Marcophon 7010, Solos

Gerd Seifert (Berlin Philharmonic)
DG 429817, Mozart concertos

Sony 45800, Strauss concerto No. 1

Nimbus 5487, Mozart horn quintet

Stephen Stirling and Tim Caister
Naxos 8553204, Vivaldi concertos for two horns

Michael Thompson
Nimbus 5010, Haydn concertos

Nimbus 5018, Concertos by Vivaldi, Rosetti, Leopold Mozart

Naxos 553592, Mozart concertos

Naxos 553570, Danzi sonata

EMI 5 55452, Tippett sonata for 4 horns (with Jeffery Bryant, Richard Watkins, and Hugh Seenan)

Wolfgang Tomböck
Naxos 557471, "The Art of the Vienna Horn"

Barry Tuckwell
Etcetera 1121, Horn music of Czerny
Etcetera 1135, Dukas, Poulenc, Bozza
EMI 769569, Mozart concertos
Philips 30370, Strauss concertos
EMI 69395, Various concertos
ASV 716, Music of Koechlin

Radovan Vlatkovich
EMI 764851, Mozart concertos

Richard Watkins
IMP Classics 865, Mozart concertos
Conifer 75605-51228, Malcolm Arnold Concerto No. 1
Conifer CDCF 172, Malcolm Arnold Concerto No. 2
Chandos 9379, Gliere concerto
Marco Polo 8.223513, Ernest Tomlinson's Rhapsody and Rondo

Jonathan Williams
ASV CDCOE-805, Mozart concertos

Frøydis Ree Wekre
Crystal 377, Schumann, Tomasi, Cherubini
Simax 1100, Norwegian horn concertos

Gail Williams
Summit 139, Nelhybel, Reynolds, Musgrave, Wilder

Trombone

Joseph Alessi
Summit 130, "Slide Area"
Summit 309, "Beyond the End of the Century"
Summit 314, "Trombonastics"
Cala 508, "New York Legends"

Ronald Barron
Boston Brass 1002, "Hindemith on Trombone"
Boston Brass 1001, "Le Trombone Française"
Boston Brass 1004, "All American Trombone"
Boston Brass 1007, Alto trombone concertos

Michael Becquet
Koch Schwann 311127, Leopold Mozart concerto
Koch Schwann 313342, Miscellaneous program

Danny Bonvin
Marcophon 960, Wagenseil, Albrechtsberger

Ronald Borror
MHS 512214, 17th-century Italian sonatas

Ian Bousfield
Doyen 014, "Versatile Virtuoso"
Chandos 9960, Yoshimatsu trombone concerto

David Bruchez
Musique Suisses 89, David, Honegger, Martin

Pia Bucher
Marcophon 901, Wagenseil, Caldara, Pergolesi

Abbie Conant
Audite 97410, Guilmant, Marcello, Handel

Jay Friedman
Educational Brass Recordings 2000, "The Singing Trombone"

Vinko Globokar
Harmonia 905214, "Globokar by Globokar"

Thomas Horch
Audite 95437, 95440, 97479, 95435 Various solos

John Kitzman
Crystal 386, Creston, Hindemith, Pryor

Mark Lawrence
Summit 114, 121, "Golden Age of Brass"
D'Note 1012, "Trombonology"

Carl Lenthe
Summit 354, "Audition Window"

Christian Lindberg
Bis 568, Concertos by Rimsky-Korsakov, Tomasi, Rota
Bis 658, Concertos by Jacob, Howarth, Bourgeois
Bis 378, David, Grondahl, Guilmant
Bis 638, Martin, Bloch, Serocki
Bis 628, Creston, Zwilich, Walker, Schuller
Bis 788, Rouse, Chavez, Thomas
Bis 888, Holmboe, Larsson
Bis 1248, M. Haydn, Wagenseil, Albrechtsberger

Michael Powell
Music Minus One 3930, "Band Aids, Concert Favorites with Orchestra"
Music Minus One 3929, "Concert Favorites for Trombone"

Jacques Mauger
Doyen 027, Concertos by Bourgeois and Grafe and other works
Editions Passions 102, Solos with brass band
Editions Passions 991201, Solos with organ

Jean Raffard
Editions Passions 84005, Solos

Ralph Sauer
Summit 143, Orchestral Excerpts

Branimir Slokar
Claves 508407, Wagenseil, Martin, David, Tomasi
Claves 500906, Leopold Mozart, Albrechtsberger, Bellini
Marcophon 913, Rimsky-Korsakov and other works

Benny Sluchin
Adda 581087, "Contemporary Trombone"

Alain Trudel
Naxos 553716, "Art of the Trombone"

Euphonium

Roger Behrend
Walking Frog 269, "Elegance"

Brian Bowman
Klavier 11060, "American Variations"

Mark 37883, "Sacred Euphonium"

Crystal 393, Ross, Capuzzi, Boda, Adler (cassette)

Jean-Pierre Chevailler
Troy 201, "The Classical Euphonium"

Bob and Nick Childs
Doyen 001, "Childs Play"

Doyen 002, "Euphonium Music"

Doyen 022, "Welsh Wizards"

Doyen 061, "Premiere"

Michael Colburn
Summit 150, "Golden Age of Brass"

Neal Corwell
Nicolai 119, "Distant Images"

Steven Mead
Bocchino Music 102, "Bella Italia"

Polyphonic 217, "Bravura"

Polyphonic 131, "Concertino"

Polyphonic 095, "Essential"

Polyphonic 082, "Euphony"

Tuba

Oystein Baadsvik
Simax 1101, "Music for Tuba"

Bis 1285, "Tuba Carnival"

Roger Bobo
Crystal 125, "Bobissimo"

Crystal 690, "Tuba Libera"

Crystal 396, "Gravity is Light Today"

Floyd Cooley
Crystal 120, "Romantic Tuba"

Summit 156, "Schumann Fantasy"

Eugene Dowling
Pro Arte 595, Vaughan Williams, Arnold, Jacob, Handel

John Fletcher
RCA Gold Seal 60586, Vaughan Williams concerto

Chandos 4526, Gregson Concerto for Tuba and Brass Band

James Gourlay
Doyen 028, "Gourlay Plays Tuba"

Doyen 028, "East Meets West"

Patrick Harrild
Chandos 8740, Vaughan Williams concerto

Walter Hilgers
Marcophon 939, "Tubadour"

Marcophon 949, "Tubarogue"

Arnold Jacobs
Summit 267, "Portrait of an Artist"

Tommy Johnson
D'Note 3001, "Tubby the Tuba"

Michael Lind
Four Leaf 102, Arban, Gregson, Jacob

Bis 95, "No Title"

Caprice 21493, "Virtuoso Tuba"

Scott Mendoker
Summit 237, "Monument"

Mark Nelson
Crystal 691, Miscellaneous

Daniel Perantoni
Summit 163, Penderecki, McBeth, Arban

Harvey Phillips
GM 3017, Music by Peaslee

Sam Pilafian
Telarc 80281, "Travelin' Light"

Summit 190, "A Brassy Night at the Opera"

Summit 223, "Cool Brassy Night at the North Pole"

Gene Pokorny
Summit 129, "Tuba Tracks"

Melvyn Poore
Random Acoustics 005, "Groundwork"

Jim Self
Summit 132, "Changing Colors"

Performances on Historical Instruments

Timothy Brown
Virgin Classics 90845, Mozart Horn concertos (natural horn)

L'Oiseau Lyre 417610, Haydn Horn Concerto No. 1 (natural horn)

Calliope
Summit 112, Renaissance music (cornetts & sackbuts)

Elektra/Nonesuch 79039, "A Renaissance Revel" (cornetts & sackbuts)

Elektra/Nonesuch 79069, "An Italian Renaissance Revel" (cornetts & sackbuts)

Concerto Palatino

Harmonia mundi 901688, "Sonate e Canzoni" (music of Gabrieli played on cornetts & sackbuts)

Gabriele Cassone

Nuova Era 7128, "Trumpet in San Petronio" (natural trumpet)

Giulia 201008, Telemann concerto in D (natural trumpet)

Andrew Clark

Helios 55074, Hand horn

Deutsche Narturhorn Solisten

MD&G 6050762, Natural horn ensemble pieces

Bruce Dickey

Accent 9173, "Virtuoso Solo Music for Cornetto"

Niklas Eklund

Naxos 553531, 553593, 553735, 554375, 555099, "Art of the Baroque Trumpet"

Gottfried Reiche Consort

Ambitus 97865, "English Renaissance and Baroque Music" (cornetts & sackbuts; natural trumpets)

Lowell Greer

Harmonia Mundi 3957037, Beethoven sonata (natural horn)

Classical Express 3957012, Mozart concertos (natural horn)

Harmonia Mundi 907059, Mozart quintet (natural horn)

Haarlem Trumpet Consort

Teldec 8.42977, Works for natural trumpets

Gabrieli Consort and Players

Virgin Classics 7590062, "A Venetian Coronation, 1595" (cornetts & sackbuts)

Anthony Halstead

Nimbus 5190, Haydn horn concertos (natural horn)

Nimbus 5104, Mozart horn concertos (natural horn)

Nimbus 5180, Weber concertino (natural horn)

His Majesty's Sagbutts & Cornetts

Meridian 84233, Holborne, Adson, Locke

ASV 122, "Venice Preserved"

Meridian 84096, "Music from 17th Century Germany"

Hyperion 66894, "For His Majestys Sagbutts and Cornetts

Hyperion 66908, "The Canzonas and Sonatas from Sacrae Symphoniae 1597"

Friedemann Immer

L'Oiseau Lyre 417610, Haydn concerto (keyed trumpet)

Teldec 8.43673, Leopold Mozart concerto (natural trumpet)

MD&G L 3271, "Trompetenknozerte des Barock" (natural trumpet)

Deutsche Harmonia Mundi 77027, "Baroque Trumpet Music" (natural trumpets)

Michael Laird

DG (Archiv) 410500, Bach Brandenburg Concerto No. 2, with English Concert (natural trumpet)

L'Oiseau-Lyre 425-834 Trumpet music of Schmelzer and Biber with Crispian Steele-Perkins, David Staff and others.

New London Consort, Philip Pickett, Dir.

L'Oiseau-Lyre D103561, Tielman Susato: "Dansereye, 1551" (cornetts, sackbuts, natural trumpet)

L'Oiseau-Lyre 414633, Praetorius: "Dances from Terpsichore, 1612" (cornetts, sackbuts, natural trumpet)

Paul Plunkett

Move 3127, Baroque trumpet music (natural trumpet)

David Staff

Teldec 4509-91192, "Baroque Music of Bologna" (natural trumpet)

Crispian Steele-Perkins

EMI 476642, "Shore's Trumpet" (natural trumpet)

Hyperion A 66145, Biber Sonatas (natural trumpet)

Sony 6245, Stradella, Telemann, Albinoni, Handel (natural trumpet)

Crispian Steele-Perkins and Stephan Keavy

Hyperion 66255, "Italian Baroque Trumpet Music" (natural trumpets)

Edward Tarr

Christophorus 4003, 19th-century trumpet music (19th-century valve trumpet)

Michael Thompson

L'Oiseau Lyre 421429, Mozart quintet (natural horn)

Ensembles

American Horn Quartet

EBS 6008, Miscellaneous

EBS 6046, Various pieces

EBS 6038, Turner, Perkins, Bernstein, Hindemith

EBS 6050, Baroque program

American Brass Quintet

Summit 133, Ewazen, Sampson, Snow

Summit 275, "Classic American Brass"

Summit 181, "Fyre and Lightning"

Summit 133, "New American Brass"

Artic Brass Quintet

Simax 1074, Hindemith, Artunian, Plagge

Kudos 103, "Made in England"

Atlantic Brass Quintet

Summit 119, "A Musical Voyage"

Bayreuth Festival Horns (8 Bayreuther Festspiel-Hornisten)

Acanta 43800, Music of Wagner

Acanta 43469, Hunting music

Belgian Brass Soloists
Marcophon 923, Miscellaneous program

Berlin Philharmonic Horn Quartet
Koch-Schwann 311021, Schumann Konzertstück and other works

King KICC 39, "Live in Tokyo"

Berlin Trombone Quintet
Koch-Schwann 312062, 310089

Brass of Aquitaine & London
ASV 870, Copland, Lully, Adson, Gabrieli, Purcell

Brass Partout
Bis 1054, "Playgrounds for Angels"

British Tuba Quartet
Polyphonic 012, 020, 013, Miscellaneous

Canadian Brass
RCA 4733, "Greatest Hits"

Columbia 44931, Gabrieli, Monteverdi

RCA 14574, "High, Bright, Light & Clear"

Columbia 89731, "Art of the Fugue"

Chicago Chamber Brass
Pro Arte 805, "Fireworks for Brass"

Chicago Symphony Low Brass Section
Nonesuch 001, Orchestral excerpts (recorded 1971)

Crescendo
Crescendo 1: "Brass from the Past"

Crescendo 2: "Hymns of Faith"

Les Cuivres Française
Pierre Verany 793041, Poulenc Trio, Gabaye Récréation, Solos

Detmold Horn Quartet
MD&G 3098, Miscellaneous program

MD&G 3324, Bozza, Artôt, Wunderer

Eastman Brass Quintet
Allegretto 8154, "Renaissance Brass Music"

Eastern Brass Quintet
Klavier 11025, "Classical Brass"

Empire Brass Quintet
Telarc 80218, Organ and brass

Telarc 80257, "Royal Brass"

Telarc 80220, "Class Brass"

English Brass Ensemble
ASV 629, "Russian Brass"

ASV740, Bach, Elgar, Widor

L'Ensemble de Trombones de Paris
Crystal 223, Miscellaneous

L'Ensemble de Trompettes de Paris
CZO 404, Miscellaneous

CZO 197, Vivaldi's Four Seasons

Equale Brass
Nimbus 5004, Music by Arnold, Warlock, Poulenc, Bartok

European Brass Quintet
Pavane 7294, "Brass Meets Brass"

Fine Arts Brass Ensemble
Nimbus 5546, "Music for the English Courts"

Galliard Brass Ensemble
ASV 6035, "Carols for Brass"

German Brass
German Brass Productions 27302, Music of Samuel Scheidt

German Brass Productions 27301, "Spirit of Brass"

German Brass Productions 27305, "Bach 2000"

German Brass Productions 2183, "Bach Dimension"

German Brass Productions 1859, "Mit Bach ins 3. Jahrtausend"

Hallé Brass Quintet
Doyen 038, Music of Gregson

Harmonic Brass
HBQ07: "Jewels of Baroque"

Hänssler 98.123, "In dulci jubilo"

HR Brass (Brass Ensemble of the Frankfurt Radio Orchestra)
Capriccio 10361, Bach, Barber, Copland, Handel

Locke Brass Consort
Chandos 6573, "Fanfare"

Chandos 8419, Brass Music of Richard Strauss

CRD 3402, "Symphonic Marches for Concert Brass"

London Brass
Electrola 46442, "Modern Times"

Electrola 44136, Praetorius, Bartok, Shostakovich

Teldec 9031-77604, Music by Baroque composers

Teldec 2292-46443,"Christmas with London Brass"

Teldec 21920, Gabrieli and contemporaries

Teldec 76990, Music by Spanish composers

Teldec T2 46007, "Romantic Journey"

London Brass Virtuosi
Hyperion 66189, "Music for Brass and Percussion"

Hyperion 66879, "Royal Eurostar"

London Collegiate Brass
CRD 3444, Walton, Tippett, Britten, Ireland

CRD 3434, Elgar, Vaughan Williams, Holst

London Gabrieli Brass Ensemble
Hyperion 66517, "From the Steeples and the Mountains"

Hyperion 66470, 19th-century brass music

ASV- QS 6013, "Splendor of Baroque Brass"

Hyperion 67119, "Antique Brasses"

London Horn Sound
Cala 112, Miscellaneous

London Symphony Brass
Collins 13332, "Cathedral Brass"

Collins 12882, Copland, Bernstein, Cowell, Barber

Naxos 553609, 554129, Music of Gabrieli

London Trumpet Sound
Cala 113, 114, Miscellaneous

Meridian Arts Ensemble
Channel 2191, Lutoslawski, Arutunian, Jan Bach

Channel 9496, Miscellaneous

Channel 9796, New pieces with piano and drums

Millar Brass Ensemble
Koss Classics 1011, "A Chicago Tradition"

Delos 3171, "Brass Surround"

Crystal 433, Miscellaneous

Hornensemble der Hochschule Mozarteum
Koch-Schwann 3-1535, "Born for Horn"

Munich Trombone Quartet
Audite 97469, Miscellaneous

Netherlands Brass Quintet
Ottavo 48609, Miscellaneous

New Trombone Collective
Q disc 97034, Nine trombone ensemble

Philadelphia, Cleveland, Chicago Brass Ensembles
Sony 62353, "The Antiphonal Music of Gabrieli"

Phillip Jones Brass Ensemble
Decca 289467746 (2 CD), "Greatest Hits"

Decca B0000807 (2 CD), "Music of the Royal Court"

Decca 455666, Music of Handel

Decca 289470501 (2 CD), "The Twentieth Century Album"

Decca 473714, "British Music for Brass"

Decca 289473185 (2 CD), "The Lighter Side"

Marcophon 928, "Divertimento"

Marcophon 929, "Easy Winners"

Marcophon 927, "Fanfare"

Marcophon 926, "Festive Brass"

Claves 500600, "In Swizerland"

Marcophon 930, "La Battaglia"

Claves 508503, "Lollipops"

Chandos 6560, "Jubilate: Music for the Kings and Queens of England"

Chandos 8490, "PJBE Finale"

Marcophon 925, "Music for the Courts of Europe"

Prince of Wales Brass
ASV WHL2092, "Brass Around the World"

ASV WHL2083, "Christmas Fanfare"

Le Quatuor de Trombones Milliere
Editions Passions 30501, "Creations"

Quattromboni
Marcophon 921, Music for four trombones

Rheinland Philharmonic Orchestra Trombone Quartet
Bayer 100234, Music for four trombones

Royal Danish Brass
Rondo 8333, "Masterpieces for Brass"

Slokar Trombone Quartet
Claves 508402, German Baroque music

Marcophon 912, "Concert"

Marcophon 851, "Live"

Marcophon 944, "Jubilee"

Saint Louis Brass Quintet
Summit 120, "Baroque Brass"

Stockholm Chamber Brass
Bis 544, "Heavy Metal"

Bis 613, "Sounds of St. Petersburg" (Music of Viktor Ewald)

Bis 699, "Clockworks"

Stockholm Philharmonic Brass
Bis 223, Miscellaneous program

Süddeutsches Brass Ensemble
Marcophon 920, "Brass Symphony"

Südtiroler Brass Ensemble
Marcophon 952, 7041, Various large ensemble pieces

Summit Brass
Summit 127, "American Tribute"

Summit 138, "Delights"

Summit 115, Music of Hindemith

Summit 171, "Paving the Way"

Summit 101, Bach, Gabrieli

Summit 116, "Colors for Brass"

Summit 218, "Spirits of Fire"

Triton Trombone Quartet
Bis 644, German ensemble music

Vienna Trombone Quartet
Camerata 445, 573, Miscellaneous

Westphalian Trombone Quartet
MD&G 3295, Miscellaneous

Wiener Waldhorn Verein
Aricord 29408, "Makart Fanfares"

Young German Brass Quintet
Ram 59603, "Fresh Air"

Brass Band Recordings

Besses O' Th' Barn
Chandos 4529, "Hymns and Things"

Chandos 6571, "Around the World"

Chandos 4526, "Concertos for Brass" with Ifor James (horn) and
John Fletcher (tuba)

Black Dyke Mills
Chandos 8635, "Famous Marches"

Chandos 4516, "Celebrate 150 Years"

ASV 2039, "Walton-A Muse of Fire"

Chandos 6565, "World Famous Marches"

Chandos 4524, "The Great British Tradition"

Chandos 4524, "A Russian Festival"

Doyen 060, "Cathedral Brass"

Chandos 4517, "Kings of Brass"

Britannia Building Society
Doyen 004, "Rule Britannia"

Doyen 021, "Year of the Dragon"

Doyen 045, "Pines of Rome"

British Bandsman Concert
Chandos 4513, Miscellaneous

CWS Glasgow
Doyen 005, "Flower of Scotland"

Grimethorpe Colliery
Doyen 015, Miscellaneous

Doyen 013, "A Night at the Opera"

RCA 68757, "Brassed Off"

Chandos 4545, "Grimethorpe"

Chandos 4553, "Brass from the Masters, vol. 2"

Sellers Engineering
Chandos 4531, "Legend in Brass"

Chandos 4511, "The World of Brass"

Sovereign Soloists
Doyen 012, Miscellaneous

Williams Fairey Band
Chandos 4547, "Brass from the Masters, vol. 1"

Historic Brass Performances Recorded before 1950 (Reissued on Compact Disc)

Aubrey Brain
EMI 64198, Mozart Horn Concerto No.3; recorded 1940.

Sotone 104/EMI Classics CHS 764047, Bach Brandenburg
Concerto No. 1; recorded 1935.

EMI Classics CDH64495 and Testament SBT 1001, Brahms Horn
Trio; recorded 1933.

Herbert L. Clarke
Crystal 450, Cornet Solos, recorded 1904–1921

*Cornet Solos by Pioneer American Recording Artists
Made Prior to 1906*
ITG 004 (International Trumpet Guild), Liberati, Rogers, Levy,
Clarke, and others

George Eskdale
EMI Classics CHS 764047, First recording (1935) of Bach's
Brandenburg Concerto No. 2

Harry Glantz, Trumpet
RCA 09026-60929, Strauss's Ein Heldenleben with New York Philharmonic, conducted by Mengelberg (recorded 1928); also
included is Strauss's Don Quixote, conducted by Beecham,
recorded 1932.

Bruno Jaenicke, Horn
RCA 09026-60929, Strauss's Ein Heldenleben with New York Philharmonic, conducted by Mengelberg (recorded 1928); also
included is Strauss's Don Quixote, conducted by Beecham,
recorded 1932.

Jack MacKintosh
Choice Recordings 1, "The Cornet King" (recorded 1920s)

Georges Mager, Trumpet
RCA 09026-60929, First recording of Strauss's Also Sprach Zara-
thustra with Boston Symphony, conducted by Koussevitzky
(recorded 1935).

Pearl Gemm 9487, Prokofiev's Lt. Kijé with Boston Symphony,
conducted by Koussevitzky (recorded 1937) with Willem
Valkenier, Horn.

Pearl Gemm 9492, Roy Harris's Symphony No. 3 and other American works with Boston Symphony, conducted by Koussevitzky (recorded 1939) with Willem Valkenier, Horn.

Pearl Gemm 9408, Sibelius's Symphony No. 2 and No. 5 with Boston Symphony, conducted by Koussevitzky (recorded 1935
and 1936).

RCA 09026-61392, First recording of Mussorgsky-Ravel, Pictures
at an Exhibition with Boston Symphony, conducted by Koussevitzky (recorded 1930); also includes Ravel's Daphnis et
Chloé (recorded 1944\-1945).

Pearl PEA 9090, Debussy's La Mer with Boston Symphony, conducted by Koussevitzky (recorded 1938).

Harry Mortimer
Choice Recordings 2, "Fabulous Fodens" (recorded 1930s)

Arthur Pryor
Crystal 451, "Trombone Solos with the Sousa Band"

Karl Stiegler, Gottfried von Freiberg, Hans Berger
Pizka 04, "Great Hornists"

Vintage Gems
Choice Recordings 3, 78 r.p.m. recordings of great cornetists

SOURCES

Instrument Manufacturers[1]

Adaci: (Germany) www.exbrass.de (rotary valve trumpets & trombones)

Alexander: Bahnhofstrasse 9, Postfach 1166, DE-55116 Mainz, Germany. www.Gebr-alexander.de (horns and tubas)

Amati (Červený): (Czech Republic) www.amati.cz (tubas)

Amrein: Im Gleisdreieck 31, DE-23566 Lübeck, Germany. www.music-amrein.de (rotary and piston valve trumpets & trombones)

Ankerls Nachfolger A Küstner: Haberlgasse 11, A-1160 Vienna, Austria. Tel. 43 01 493 1714 (Vienna horns)

Atkinson: (US) www.akinsonhorns.com (horns)

B&M Symphonic (Walter Nirschl): (Germany) www.walternirschl.de (tubas)

B&S: (*see* Ja Musik Group)

B&S Challenger Trumpets: (Germany) (*see* Ja Musik Group). www.challenger-trumpets.com

B&S Tubas and Euphoniums: (Germany) (*see* Ja Musik Group). www.vogtlandische-musik.de

Bach: (US) (*see* Conn-Selmer) www.Bachbrass.com (trumpets & trombones)

Bauerfeind: (Germany) www.bauerfeind-ventile.de (valves)

Baumann: Kampenwandstrasse 71a, DE-83229 Aschau/Chiemgau., Germany. www.blechblasinstrumente.de (rotary valve trumpets)

Beck: (Germany) www.musikbeck.de (trumpets & flugelhorns)

Benge: (US) (*see* Conn-Selmer) www.bengebrass.com (trumpets & trombones)

Berg: 5875 Brown Rd. Dunster, B.C., Canada V0J 1J0. www.berghorns.com (horns)

Besson: (UK) (*see* The Music Group) www.besson.com

Blackburn: 1593 Highway 30 West, Decatur, TN 37322. www.blackburntrumpets.com (trumpets, leadpipes)

Blättler: Dorfbachstrasse 21, CH-6430, Switzerland. (alphorns)

Der Blechbläser: (Germany) www.der-blechblaeser.de (German trombones)

Blessing: (US) www.ekblessing.com

Boosey & Hawkes (Besson): (UK) (*see* The Music Group) www.besson.com (*see also* Boosey & Hawkes Music Shop)

Brass Atelier (Müller): CH-6289 Hämikon-Berg, Switzerland. Fax: 49 41 917 26 15

Calicchio Trumpets: 6409 Willoughby Ave., Hollywood, CA 90038. www.calicchio.com

Callet: (US) www.callet.com (trumpets)

Červený: (Czech Republic) (*see* Amati) (tubas)

Chicago Brass Works: (US) www.chicagobrassworks.com (trumpets)

Conn: (US) (*see* Conn-Selmer) www.cgconn.com

Conn-Selmer (Bach, Leblanc, Martin, King, Benge, Holton) (subsidiary of Steinway Musical Instruments): (US) www.conn-selmer.com

Cornford: (Germany) www.cornford.de (horns & trumpets)

Couesnon: 3 Ave. E. Couvrecelles-BP4, FR-02402 Chateau Thierry, France. Fax: 33 323 83 67 97 (trompes de chasse, horns)

Courtois: (France) (*see* Ja Musik Group) www.antoine-courtois.com

DEG Music Products. Box 968, Lake Geneva, WI 53147. www.degmusic.com

De Prins: Lammekensstraat 60, 2200 Borgerhout, Belgium.

Dubsek: (Austria) www.dubsek.at

Dürk: (Germany) www.duerkhorns.com (horns)

Eclipse Trumpets: (UK) www.eclipsetrumpets.com

Edwards: (US) www.edwards-instruments.com (trombones, trumpets)

Egger: (Switzerland) www.eggerinstruments.ch (trumpets)

Finke: (Germany) www.finkehorns.de (horns)

Freebell: (Germany) www.freebell.de (trumpets & flugelhorns)

Galileo Trumpets: (Germany) www.galileo-brass.de

Ganter: Manzinger Weg 7, DE-81214 Munich, Germany. www.musikhieber.de (rotary valve trumpets)

Getzen: P.O. Box 440, 530 S. County Rd. Highway H, Elkhorn, WI 53121. www.getzen.com

---

[1] Most manufacturers produce a range of instruments or mouthpieces. Where it has been considered helpful, a firm's specialty has been noted.

Glassl: Adam-Opel Strasse 12, DE-64569 Nauheim, Germany. Fax: 49 6152 6 97 16 (trombones)

Greenhoe: (US) www.greenhoe.com (trombones, trombone valves)

Gronitz: Haydnstrasse 10, DE-22761 Hamburg, Germany. www.gronitztuba.de (tubas)

Haag (Monschau): Kirchstrasse 15, CH-8280 Kreuzlingen, Switzerland. www.musikhaag.ch (trombones)

Haagston: Summerstrasse 3, A-3350 Austria. www.haagston.at (rotary valve trumpets, Vienna horns)

René Hagmann: (Switzerland) www.trombone.ch (trombone valves)

DeHaro: (US) www.deharohorn.com (horn leadpipes)

Wes Hatch: (US) www.weshatchhorns.com (horns)

Karl Hill (Kortesmaki): (US) Grand Rapids, MI

Hirsbrunner: Dorfgasse 6, CH-3454 Sumiswald, Switzerland. www.hirsbrunner.com (tubas)

Holton: (US) (*see* Conn-Selmer) www.leblancinc.com (horns)

Hans Hoyer: (Germany) (*see* Ja Musik Group) www.hans-hoyer.de (horns)

Inderbinen: (Switzerland) www.inderbinen.com

Ja Musik Group (B&S, Scherzer, Hoyer, VMI, Courtois, Wenzel Meinl): (Germany) www.ja-musik.com

Jiracek: (Czech Republic) www.volweb.cz (horns)

Jungwirth: AT-3564 Freischling 21, Austria. Fax: 43 2985 330324 (Vienna horns)

Jupiter: (US) www.jupitermusic.com

Kalison: Via Pellegrino Rossi 96, 20161 Milan, Italy. www.kalison.com (horns, tubas, cimbasso)

Kanstul: 1332 S. Claudina St., Anaheim, CA 92805. www.kanstul.net (trumpets)

King: (US) (*see* Conn-Selmer) www.kingwinds.com

Kordick: (Germany) www.kordick.com (trumpets)

Kröger: Saarstrasse 34, DE-54290 Trier, Germany. Fax: 49 651 492 62 (trumpets)

Kromat: Bahnhofstrasse 11, DE-27412 Wilstedt, Germany. www.hans-kromat.de (rotary valve trumpets & flugelhorns)

Kruspe: Am Schunkenhofe 5, DE-99848 Wutha-Farnroda, Germany. www.edkruspe.de (horns & German trombones)

Ricco Kühn: Chemnitzer Strasse 68, DE-09569 Oederan, Germany. www.riccokuehn.de (rotary valve trumpets & horns)

Kühnl & Hoyer: Neue Strasse 27, DE-91459 Markt Erlbach, Germany. www.kuehnl-hoyer.de (trombones)

Kunst: (Germany) www.kunst-brass.de (horns)

Kürner: Gemeindeplatz 1 A-4632 Pichl 44, Austria. Fax: 43 7247 86 76 17 (rotary valve trumpets)

Hub van Laar: (Netherlands) www.hubvanlarr.nl (trumpets)

Laskey: 270 Eisenhower Lane N, Suite 8, IL 60148. www.laskey.com (trumpets)

Lätzsch: Schmidtstrasse 24, DE-28203 Bremen, Germany. www.Laetzsch.com (German trombones, sackbuts)

Lawler: 131 Short Creek Rd., Decatur, TN 37322. www.lawlertrumpets.com (trumpets)

Lawson: P.O. Box 38, Boonsboro, MD 21713. www.lawsonhorns.com (horns & leadpipes)

LeBlanc: (US) (*see* Conn-Selmer) www.gleblancinc.com

Lechner: Gaisbergsiedlung 7, A-5500 Bischofshofen, Austria. www.musik-lechner.com (rotary valve trumpets)

Lewis Orchestral Horns: 1770 W. Berteau Ave., Chicago, IL. 60613. Email: swlewis@iwic.net

Josef Lidl: (Czech Republic) www.lidlmusic.cz (horns)

Mahillon: Rue du Transvaal 43, BE-1070 Brussels, Belgium. Fax: 32 2521 86 02

Martin: (US) (*see* Conn-Selmer) www.gleblancinc.com

McQueens: Sunset Business Center, Manchester Rd., GB-Kearsley, Bolton BL48RT England. Fax: 44 1204 7 94 600 (ceremonial trumpets & bugles)

Ewald Meinl: Postfach 1342, Jeschkenstrasse 26, DE-82524 Geretsried, Germany. www.ewaldmeinl.de (instrument bells)

Rudolf Meinl: Blumenstrasse 21, DE-91456, Diespeck/Aisch, Germany. http://212.227.240.153/rudolf-meinl/seite3.html (tubas)

Wenzel Meinl: (Germany) (*see* Ja Musik Group) www.meinl-weston.com (tubas, euphoniums, bass trumpets, cimbasso)

Meinlschmidt: (Germany) http://jm-gmbh.de (rotary valves)

Meinl-Weston: (Germany) (*see* Ja Musik Group) www.melton.de (tubas)

Meister Anton: Bonner Strasse 90, DE-50677 Köln, Germany. Fax: 49 8638 8 28 63

Melton: (Germany) (*see* Ja Musik Group) www.melton.de (tubas)

Berndt Meyer: Iglauer Str. 1, D-01279 Dresden, Germany. Trompetenmeyer@web.de; Fax: 25 99 678 (Heckel rotary valve trumpets)

Miraphone: Postfach 1129, DE-84464 Waldkraiburg, Germany. www.miraphone.de (tubas, euphoniums)

Horst Molter: Markstrasse 13, DE-67686 Mackenbach u. Kaiser, Germany. Tel: 49 6374 51 72 (rotary valve trumpets)

Monette: 6918 N.E. 79th Court, Portland, OR. www.monette.net (trumpets)

Josef Monke: Körnerstrasse 48-50, DE-50823 Köln-Ehrenfeld, Germany. www.josefmonke.de (rotary valve trumpets)

Karl Mönnich: Klingenthaler Strasse 55, DE-08265 Erlbach/Vogtland, Germany. Tel: 49 37 422 62 46 (German trombones)

Olds (Reynolds): (US) www.feolds.com

Orsi: (Italy) www.orsi-wind-instruments.it

Dieter Otto: Teisinger Berg 15, DE-84494 Neumarkt-St. Veit, Germany. www.otto-horn.de (horns)

Paxman: Unit B, Linton House, 164-180 Union St., GB-London SE1OLH England. www.paxman.co.uk (horns)

Martin Peter: Kirchsteig 5, DE-08258 Markneukirchen, Germany. Fax: 49 37 4 22 31 94 (rotary valve trumpets)

Pfretzschner: (Germany) Der Blechbläser, www.der-blechblaeser.de (German trombones)

Phaeton: (US) www.pjlamusic.com (trumpets)

Possegger: (Austria) http://members.aon.at/possegger (rotary & piston valve trumpets, trombones)

Michael Rath: Newsome Mill, Hart St., Huddersfield, West Yorkshire HD4 6LS England. www.rathtrombones.com (trombones)

Rauch: Prof. Kohts Vei 77, NO-1368, Stabekk, Norway. Email: norhorn@online.no (horns)

Reynolds: (*see* Olds)

Sandner Metallblasinstrumente: Ernst-Gläser-Strasse, DE-08265 Erlbach, Germany. Email: schallstueck@t-online.de (brass instrument bells)

Sarad: (US) www.saradmouthpiece.com (trumpets)

Schagerl: (Austria) www.schagerl.at (rotary valve trumpets)

Scherzer: (Germany) (*see* Ja Musik Group). www.scherzer -trumpets.com (rotary valve trumpets)

Schilke: 4520 James Pl., Melrose Park, IL 60160-1007. www .schilkemusic.com (trumpets)

Schmelzer Trombones: Diesel-Strasse 93, DE-41189 Mönchengladbach, Germany. Fax: 49 21 66 532 47 (trombones)

Engelbert Schmid: Kohlstattstrasse 8, DE-87757 Kirchheim-Tiefenried, Germany. www.corno.de (horns)

Martin Schmidt: (Germany) www.martin-schmidt-potsdam.de (rotary valve trumpets)

Schneider Alphornbau: Ebnetstrasse 9, CH-8308 Illnau, Switzerland. Tel: 41 52 347 22 10 (Alphorns)

Henri Selmer: (France) www.selmer.fr (trumpets, trombones)

Selmer: (US) (*see* Conn-Selmer) www.selmer.com

Shires: 4A Spaceway Lane, Hopedale, MA 01747. www.seshires .com (trombones)

Smith-Watkins: (UK) www.smithwatkins.com (trumpets & cornets)

Darin Sorley: (US) www.sorleyhorns.com (horns)

Spiri: (Switzerland) www.spiri.ch (trumpets)

Sterling: (UK) www.sterlingbrass.co.uk (euphoniums & cornets)

Stocker Alphornbau: (Switzerland) www.alphorn.com (alphorns)

Stomvi: Honiba, S.A., Antonio Mollé 10, ES 46920 Mislata, Valencia, Spain (trumpets)

Straub: Tettnanger Strasse 31, DE-88239 Wangen-Primisweiler, Germany. www.straubtrumpets.com (rotary valve trumpets)

Syhre: Cöthner Strasse 62a, DE-04155 Leipzig, Germany. Fax: 49 341 564 59 60

Taylor Trumpets: (UK) www.taylortrumpets.com (trumpets)

Thayer Valve International: (US) Box 475, 463 S.E. Moffitt Rd., Waldport, OR 97394. Fax: 541/563-5806 (trombone valves)

Thein: Rembertiring 40, DE-28203 Bremen, Germany. www.thein -brass.de (trumpets, trombones)

Throja Trombones: Der Blechbläser: (Germany) www.der -blechblaeser.de (German trombones)

VMI: (Germany) (*see* Ja Musik Group) www..ja-musik.com; www .vogtlaendische-musik.de (tubas and background brass)

Helmut Voigt: Siedlerweg 21, DE-08258 Markneukirchen, Germany. Fax: 49 37422 21 13 (German trombones & sackbuts)

Jürgen Voigt: Gewerbepark 22, DE-08258 Markneukirchen, Germany. Fax: 49 37422 4 52 14. www.vogtline.com (historical & modern trumpets, horns, trombones)

Wedgwood: (UK) www.deniswedgwood.com (trumpets)

Weril: (Brazil) www.weril.com.br

Wiener Hornmanufaktur: Postgasse 13, AT-1010 Vienna, Austria. Fax: 43 1 513 18 77 (Vienna & Kravka horns)

C.S. Willson: (Switzerland) www.swissprofi.ch/willson (euphoniums, tubas, horns, Rotax valves)

Worischek: (Germany) www.worischek.de (horns, also Pizka-model horns)

Yamaha: (US) www.yamaha.com

Yamaha: (International) www.global.yamaha.com

Historical Instruments

Alexander: Bahnhofstrasse 9, Postfach 1166, DE-55116 Mainz, Germany. www. Gebr-alexander.de (natural horns)

Couesnon: 3 Ave. E. Couvrecelles-BP4, FR-02402 Chateau Thierry, France. Fax: 33 323 83 67 97 (natural horns)

Dubsek: (Austria) www.dubsek.at (Baroque horns)

David Edwards: Fenns Lane, 5, Holly Ridge, GB West End, Surrey GU24 9Q England. Fax: 44 1483 489 630 (natural trumpets)

Egger: Turnerstrasse 32, CH-4058 Basel, Switzerland. www .eggerinstruments.ch (natural trumpets, horns, sackbuts, historical trumpet mouthpieces)

Endsley: (US) www.dmamusic.org (natural trumpets)

Finke: (Germany) www.finkehorns (natural trumpets & horns)

Glassl: Adam-Opel Strasse 12, DE-64569 Nauheim, Germany. Fax: 49 6152 6 97 16 (sackbuts)

Van der Heide: (Netherlands) www.geertjanvanderheide.NL (sackbuts)

Jiracek: (Czech Republic) www.volweb.cz (natural horns)

Jungwirth: AT-3564 Freischling 21, Austria. Fax: 43 2985 330324 (natural horns)

Kalison: Via Pellegrino Rossi 96, 20161 Milan, Italy. www.kalison .com (natural horns)

Stephen Keavy: 4 Friday Ct. GB-Thame, Oxon, OX9 3GA, England. Fax: 44 1844 261 814 (natural trumpets)

Josef Klier (JK): DE-91456 Diespeck, Germany. www.jk-klier.de (Baroque trumpet & sackbut mouthpieces)

Kunst: (Germany) www.kunst-brass.de (natural horns)

John McCann Cornetts: (US) www.mccann-cornetts.com (cornetts)

Ewald Meinl: Postfach 1342, Jeschkenstrasse 26, DE-82524 Geretsried, Germany. www.ewaldmeinl.de (natural trumpets, horns, sackbuts)

Monk Workshops: (UK) www.jeremywest.co.uk (cornetts, serpents)

Naumann: 39138 Bae court, Oconmowoc, WI 53066. Fax: 414/569-7689 (natural trumpets & mouthpieces)

Matthew Parker: 6, Greene Walk, GB-Berkhamsted, Herts HP4 2LW England. Fax: 44 442 872 761 (natural trumpets, corno da caccia)

Romera: Monsec 6, ES-08240 Manresa (Barcelona), Spain. www.romerabrass.com (Baroque trumpet & sackbut mouthpieces)

Engelbert Schmid: Kohlstattstrasse 8, DE-87757 Kirchheim-Tiefenried, Germany. www.corno.de (natural horns)

Werner Chr. Schmidt: Mosenstrasse 10, DE-08258 Markneukirchen, Germany. www.schmidt-brass.de (Baroque trumpet & sackbut mouthpieces)

Seraphinoff: 2256 Birdie Galyan Rd., Bloomington, IN 47408 (natural horns & mouthpieces)

Stewart: 140 E. Santa Clara #18, Arcadeia, CA 91006. Fax: 818/447-1904 (keyed brass, antique reproductions)

Syhre: Cöthner Strasse 62a, DE-04155 Leipzig, Germany. Fax: 49 341 564 59 60 (natural trumpets and horns)

Thein: Rembertiring 40, DE-28203 Bremen, Germany. www..thein-brass.de (natural trumpets, horns & sackbuts)

Bruno Tilz: Am Pfaffenbühl 4, DE-91413 Neustadt/Aisch, Germany. www.mundstuekbau-tilz.de (Baroque trumpet & sackbut mouthpieces)

Frank Tomes: 25 Church Path, Merton Park, GB-London SW19 3HS England. Email: earlybrass@hotmail.com Fax: 44 20 8587 9528 (natural trumpets, sackbuts)

Vanryne: Caversham, 50, Hemdean Rd. GB-Reading, Berks RG4 7SU, England. Fax: 44 118 947-3296 (Baroque and 19th-century trumpets)

Vintage Brass Reproductions: (US) http://mywebpages.comcast.net (Civil War period reproductions)

Helmut Voigt: Siedlerweg 21, DE-08258 Markneukirchen, Germany. Fax: 49 37422 21 13 (sackbuts)

Jürgen Voigt: Gewerbepark 22, DE-08258 Markneukirchen, Germany. Fax: 49 37422 4 52 14. www.vogtlinecom (historical & modern trumpets, horns, trombones)

Webb: Padbrook, Chaddington Lane, Bincknoll, GB-Wooton Bassett, Wilts. SN4 8QR England. http:// members.aol.com/wwwebbrass (natural trumpets, horns, historical trumpet & sackbut mouthpieces)

Mouthpieces

Alexander: Bahnhofstrasse 9, Postfach 1166, DE-55116 Mainz, Germany. www. Gebr-alexander.de (horn mouthpieces)

Bach: (US) (*see* Conn-Selmer) www. Bachbrass.com

Benterfa (mouthpieces made from wood): (France) members.aol.com/benterfa

Best Brass: (Japan) www5a.biglobe.ne.jp

Greg Black: 623 Eagle Rock Ave., West Orange, NJ 07052. www.gregblackmouthpieces.com

Blackburn: 1593 Highway 30 West, Decatur, TN 37322. www.blackburntrumpets.com (trumpet mouthpieces)

Böpple Musik, Siemensstrasse 17, DE-71254 Ditzingen, Germany. Fax: 49 7156 95 14 95

Breslmair: Halterzeile 25,A-2453 Sommerein, Austria. www.breslmair.at

Callet: (US) www.callet.com (trumpet mouthpieces)

Curry: (US) www.currympc.com (trumpet mouthpieces)

Dillon: 325 Fulton St., Woodbridge, NJ 07095. www.dillonmusic.com

Elliott: (US) www.dougelliotmouthpieces.com (component mouthpieces for low brass)

Endsley: (US) www.dmamusic.org (trumpet mouthpieces)

Fokus: (US) www.fokusmouthpieces.com (trumpet mouthpieces)

Giardinelli: 7845 Maltlage Dr., Liverpool, NY 13090. www.giardinelli.com

GR Technologies: (US) www.grmouthpieces.com (trumpet mouthpieces)

Griego: (US) http://griegomouthpieces.com (trombone mouthpieces)

Haefner Trumpet Mouthpieces: (US) www.trumpetpro.com

Houser: 10 Clyston Circle, R.D. #2, Norristown, Pa. 19403. www.housermouthpiece.com

Jerwyn Adjustable Cup Trumpet Mouthpiece: (UK) www.bill-lewington.com

Jet-Tone: (US) www.jet-tone.com

Kelly: (US) www.kellymouthpieces.com (transparent mouthpieces)

Josef Klier (JK): DE-91456 Diespeck, Germany. www.jk-klier.de

Laskey: 270 Eisenhower Lane N, Suite 8, IL 60148. www.laskey.com

Lawson: P.O. Box 38, Boonsboro, MD 21713. www.lawsonhorns.com (horn mouthpieces)

Lewington-McCann Cornet Mouthpiece: (UK) www.bill-lewington.com

Marcinkiewicz: (US) www.marcinkiewicz.com

Milahuis Trumpet Mouthpieces: (Netherlands) http://pw2.netcom.com

Monette: (US) www.monette.net (trumpet and trombone mouthpieces)

Rudy Muck: (US) (*see* Parduba) www.parduba.com (trumpet mouthpieces)

Najoom: (US) www.najoom.com (trumpet & cornet mouthpieces)

Northernbrass: (US) www.northernbrass.com (trumpet mouthpieces)

L'Olifant: (France) www.lolifantparis.com (horn mouthpieces)

Parduba: (US) www.parduba.com (trumpet mouthpieces)

Parke: (US) www.parke.net

Paxman: Unit B, Linton House, 164-180 Union St., GB-London SE1OLH England. www.paxman.co.uk (horn mouthpieces)

Paxman-Halstead-Chidell Horn Mouthpieces: (UK) www.horncups.com (horn mouthpieces)

Perantucci: (Germany) Robert Tucci Musikinstrumente. www.hornboerse.de

Purviance: (*see* Reeves).

Michael Rath: Newsome Mill, Hart St., Huddersfield, West Yorkshire HD4 6LS England. www.rathtrombones.com (trombone mouthpieces)

Reeves: 25574 Rye Canyon Rd., Suite D, Valencia, CA 91355. www.bobreeves.com (trumpet mouthpieces)

Romera: Monsec 6, ES-08240 Manresa (Barcelona), Spain. www.romerabrass.com

Sarad: (US) www.saradmouthpiece.com (adjustable cup and other trumpet mouthpieces)

Schilke: 4520 James Pl., Melrose Park, IL 60160-1007. www.schilkemusic.com .

Engelbert Schmid: Kohlstattstrasse 8, DE-87757 Kirchheim-Tiefenried, Germany. www.corno.de (horn mouthpieces) (*see also* Bruno Tilz)

Werner Chr. Schmidt: Mosenstrasse 10, DE-08258 Markneukirchen, Germany. www.schmidt-brass.de

René Spada: Scheunenstrasse 18, CH-3400 Burgdorf, Switzerland. Fax: 41 41 622 0179

Sparx Cornet Mouthpiece: (Canada) www.sparxmusic.com

Stein: Fuhrenkamp 29, DE-21244 Buchholz, Germany. Fax: 49 4181 3 45 20 (horn mouthpieces)

Stork: (US) www.storkcustom.com

Bruno Tilz: Am Pfaffenbühl 4, DE-91413 Neustadt/Aisch, Germany. www.mundstuekbau-tilz.de

Toshi: (Japan) www.eurus.dti.ne.jp/~toshi-tp (trumpet mouthpieces)

Tottle: (US) www.tottlebrass.com (trumpet mouthpieces)

Trumpet Lounge: (Japan) www.trumpetlounge.jp

Warburton: P.O. Box 1209, Geneva, Fla. 32732. www.warburton-usa.com.

Webb: Padbrook, Chaddington Lane, Bincknoll, GB-Wooton Bassett, Wilts. SN4 8QR England. http://members.aol.com/wwwebbrass (historical trumpet mouthpieces)

Wick: (UK) (see The Music Group) www.musicgroup.com; also www.deniswick.com

Wiener Hornmanufaktur: Postgasse 13, AT-1010 Vienna, Austria. Fax: 43 1 513 18 77 (Vienna horn mouthpieces)

Windhager: (Austria) www.whf.mouthpieces.at

Yamaha: (US) www.yamaha.com

Yamaha: (International) www.global.yamaha.com

Zottola: (US) Http://users.rcn.com/rakright

Brass Music

There are over 500 publishers who offer music for brass, many of them specializing in this area. There are also a number of firms that specialize in stocking brass music from all publishers:

Spaeth/Schmid Blechbläsernoten: (Germany) www.spaeth-schmid.de

Ulrich Köbl Blechbläsersortiment: (Germany) www.koebl.de

Robert King Music Sales: (US) www.rkingmusic.com

Boosey & Hawkes Music Shop: (UK) www.boosey.com

June Emerson Wind Music: (UK) www.juneemerson.co.uk

Hickey's Music Center: (US) www.hickeys.com

Sheet Music Service of Portland: (US) www.sheetmusicservice.com

TAP Music Sales: (US) www.tapmusic.com (brass recordings)

Editions BIM: (Switzerland) www.editions-bim.com

Simply Brass: (US) www.simplybrass.com (recordings & music)

Other Firms That Stock Brass Music

Luck's Music Library: (US) www.lucksmusic.net

Southern Ohio Music: (US) www.somusic.com

Sheetmusicplus: (US) www.sheetmusicplus.com

McNaughtan Musikverlag: (Germany) www.mcnaughtan.com

The Music Mart: (US) www.musicmart.com

Brand Edition Musikverlag: (Germany) www.edition-brand.de

Zimmermann Musikverlag: (Germany) www.zimmermann-frankfurt.de

Robert Ostermeyer Musikedition: (Germany) www.corno.de (horn music)

Schott Musikverlag: (Germany) www.schott-music.com

Wallhall Edition: (Germany) www.edition-wallhall.de

Max Hieber: (Germany) www.musikhieber.de

Publications

The Brass Herald: (UK) www.thebrassherald.com

The British Bandsman: (UK) www.britishbandsman.com

Historic Brass Society Journal: (US) Historic Brass Society. www.historicbrass.org

Historic Brass Society Newsletter: (US) Historic Brass Society. www.historicbrass.org

The Horn Call: (US) International Horn Society. www.hornsociety.org

The Horn Player: (UK) British Horn Society. www.british-horn.org

The Instrumentalist: (US) www.instrumentalistmagazine.com

ITA Journal: (US) International Trombone Association. www.ita-web.org

ITEA Journal: (US) International Tuba Euphonium Association. www.iteaonline.org

ITG Journal: (US) International Trumpet Guild. www.trumpetguild.org

Piszton: Hungarian Trumpet Organization. Email: tromba@axelers.hu

La Revue du Corniste: (France) Association Française du Cor. http://afcor.free.fr

The Trombonist Magazine: (UK) British Trombone Society. www.trombone-society.org.uk

Uilenspieghel: Dutch Horn Society. www.hoornistengenootschap.nl

Other Brass Organizations

Associazone Italiana Trombonisti (Association of Italian Trombonists): (Italy). Fax: 39 0125 658 003

Belgian Horn Society: (Belgium) www.hoorn.be

Danish Horn Club: (Denmark) www.hornklub.dk

Finnish Horn Club: (Finland) www.musicfinland.com/hornclub

Finnish Trombone and Tuba Association: (Finland) www.musicfinland.com

Internationale Posaunen-Vereinigung e.V. (German Trombone Association): (Germany). www.internationale-posaunenvereinigung.de

North American Brass Band Association: (US) www.nabba.org

Northwest Horn Society: (US) http://horn.campus.uidaho.edu

Norwegian Horn Club (Norsk Hornklubb): (Norway) Box 179 Sentrum N-0102 Oslo, Norway

Trompes de France Pays-Bas: (Netherlands) http:home.planet.nl

Swedish Horn Society: (Sweden) www.shs.home.se

Wiener Waldhornverein: (Austria) Postfach 134, AT-1080 Vienna, Austria. Fax: 43 2239 37 05

Miscellaneous

Bate Collection of Musical Instruments: (UK) www.ashmol.ox.ac.uk

Tony Bingham Old Music Instruments: 11 Pond St., GB-London NW3 2PN England. Fax: 44 20 7433 3662 (antique instruments)

The Brass Player's Museum, Springfield, Mass.: (US) http://neillins.com

Tom Crown Mutes: 3907 Howard Ave., Western Springs IL 60558. Fax: 708/246-6314

Edinburgh University Collection of Historic Musical Instruments: (UK) www.music.ed.ac.uk

Engemann-Dämpfer: Turmstrasse 3, DE-35104 Lichtenfels, Germany. Email: engemann-daempfer@t-online.de (mutes)

Hetman Lubricants: (US) www.hetman.com

Humes & Berg: (US) www.humes-berg.com (mutes)

Instrumentenmuseum Schloss-Kremsegg: (Austria) www.schloss-kremsegg.at

Jo-Ral Mutes: (US) www.jo-ral.com

Malone's Brass Technology: 7625 Havenhurst Ave. #47, Van Nuys, CA 91406. Email: bmbrtek@ad.com

National Music Museum: (US) www.usd.edu/smm

Trompetenmuseum Bad Säckingen: (Germany) www.trompeter-von-saeckingen.de

TrumCor Mutes: (US) www.trumcor.com

FINGERING/ POSITION CHARTS

Trumpet/Cornet

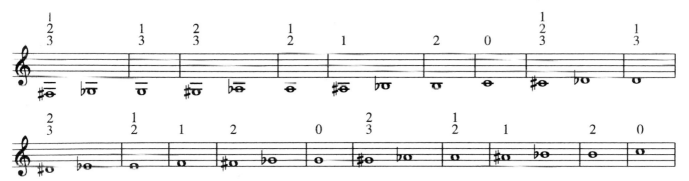

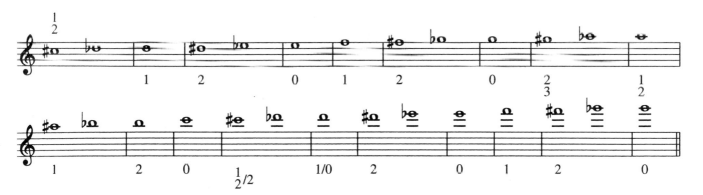

Single F Horn

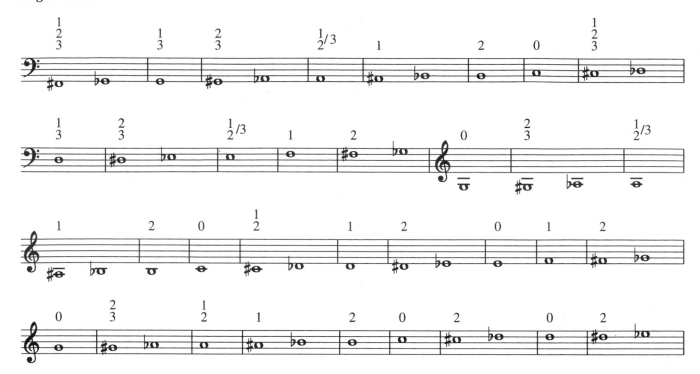

Single B♭ Horn

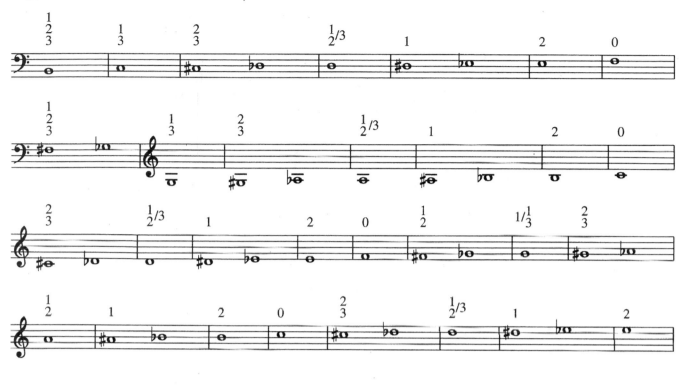

F/B♭ Double Horn
(pedal tones on B♭ side)

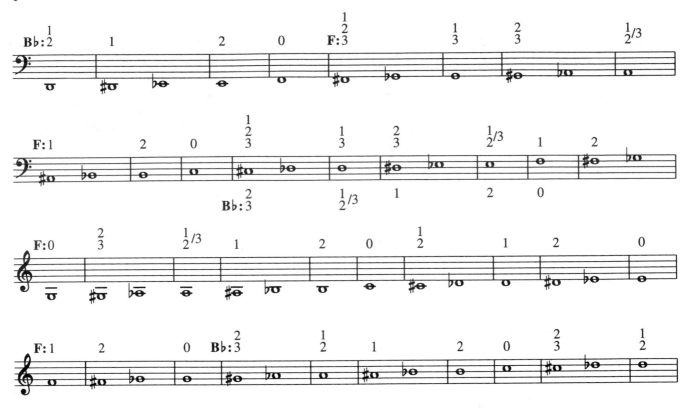

Trombone with F Attachment
(B♭ pedal tones)

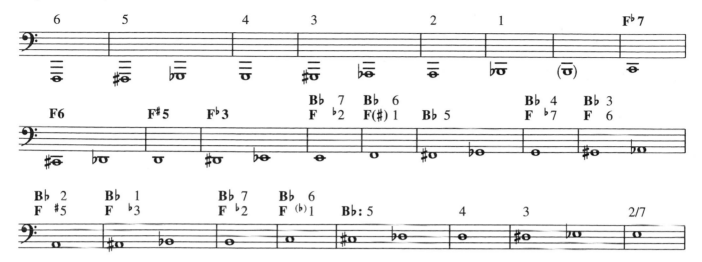

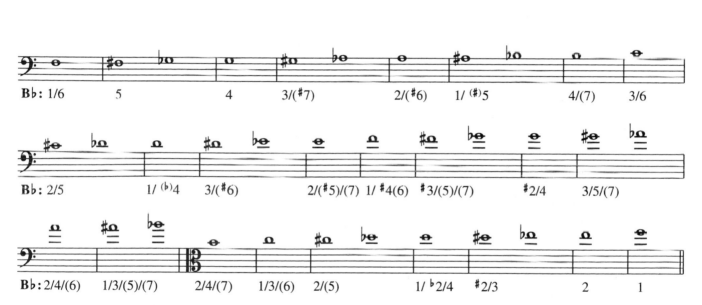

Euphonium [1]

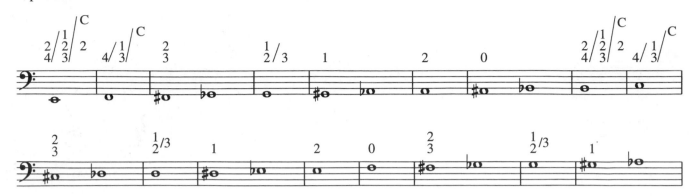

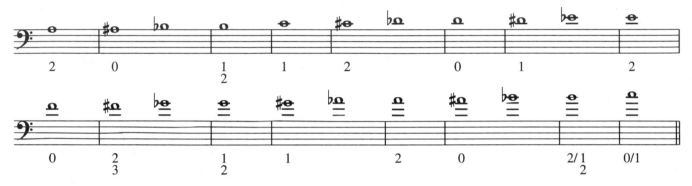

[1] Where they differ, fingerings are shown in the following order: four valve uncompensated euphonium; three valve; four valve compensating euphonium.
The letter C indicates that the fourth compensating valve should be depressed.

To facilitate intonation, valve slides of the fingerings circled should be pulled outward.
  ex. ①
    2 = pull 1st valve slide outward.
    4
When a valve slide is to be pushed inward, an arrow is added to the circle.
  ex. 1
    3 = push 4th valve slide inward.
    ④↑

Four-Valve B♭ Tuba

(All fingering charts for tuba were prepared by Scott Mendoker.)

Five-Valve CC Tuba
(5th valve lowers fundamental 5-quarters of a tone: "flat whole step system")

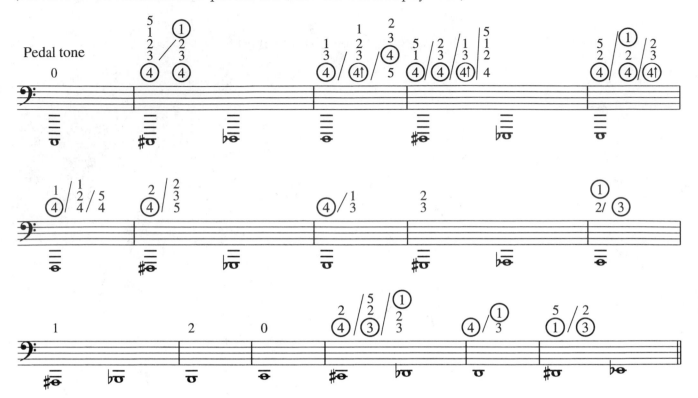

Five-Valve CC Tuba
(5th valve lowers fundamental two whole steps: 2/3 system)

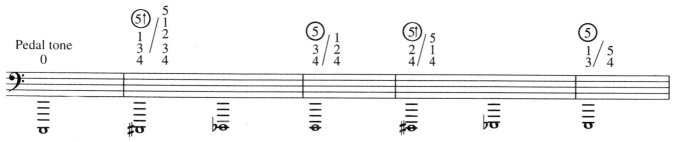

For intonation adjustment, the 1st valve slide should be pulled outward approximately one inch.

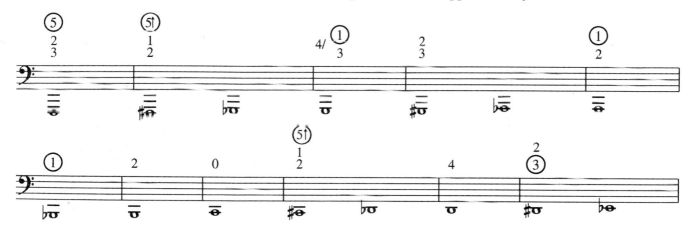

Both Systems

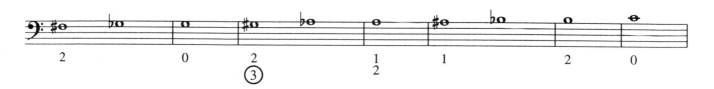

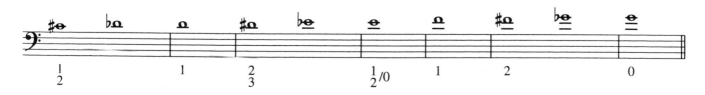

Four-Valve EE♭ Tuba

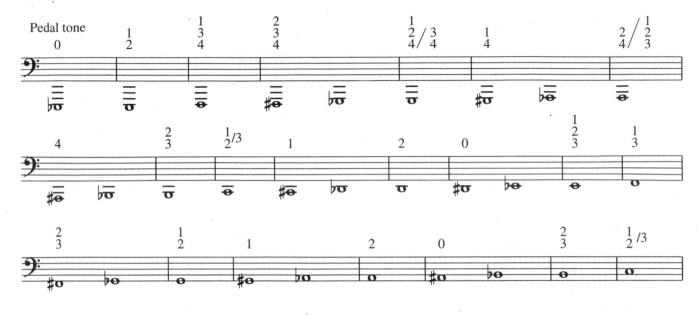

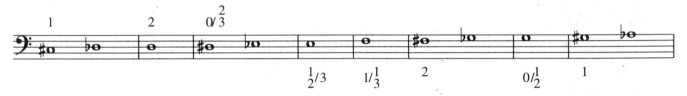

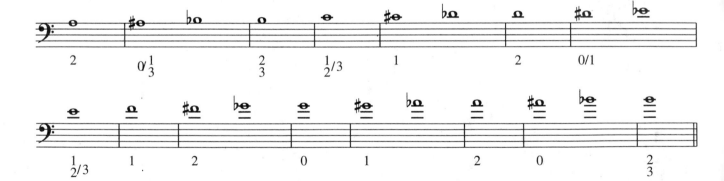

Five-Valve F Tuba/"2/3 System"

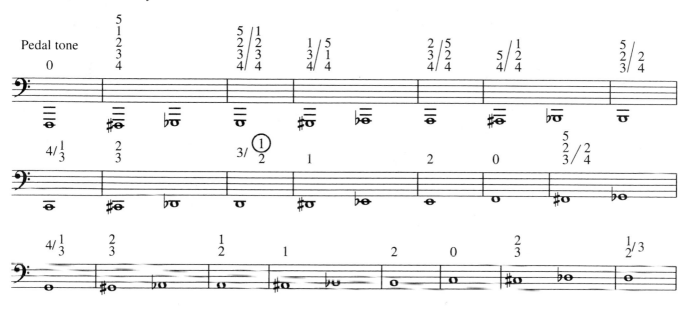

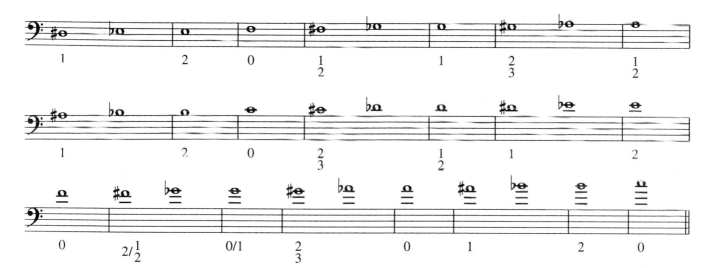

For intonation adjustment, the fifth valve slide should be pulled outward approximately 3 inches.

Five-Valve F Tuba
(5th valve lowers fundamental 5-quarters of a tone)

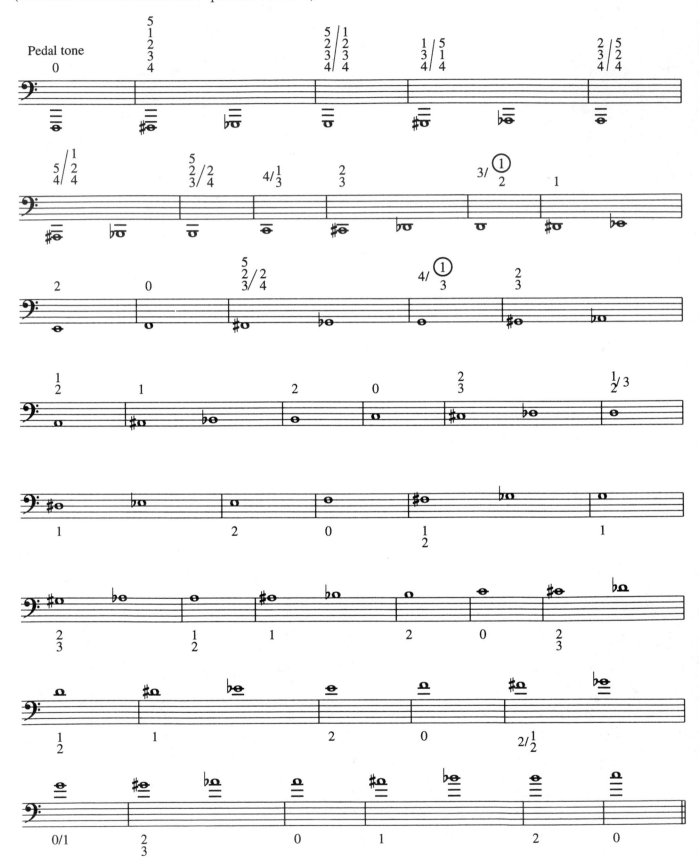

Harmonic Fingering Chart
Common fingerings are shown as whole notes.
Trumpet

Harmonic Fingering Chart
Common fingerings are shown as whole notes.

Horn in F

Harmonic Fingering Chart
Common fingerings are shown as whole notes.
Horn in B♭

Harmonic Fingering Chart

Common fingerings/positions are shown as whole notes.

Trombone or 3-Valve Baritone

Harmonic Fingering Chart

Common fingerings are shown as whole notes.

BB♭ Tuba 3-Valve

PARTS OF THE INSTRUMENTS

Trumpet

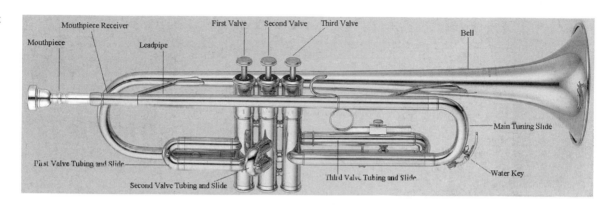

Mouthpiece
Mouthpiece Receiver
Leadpipe
First Valve
Second Valve
Third Valve
Bell
Main Tuning Slide
First Valve Tubing and Slide
Second Valve Tubing and Slide
Third Valve Tubing and Slide
Water Key

F/B♭ Double Horn

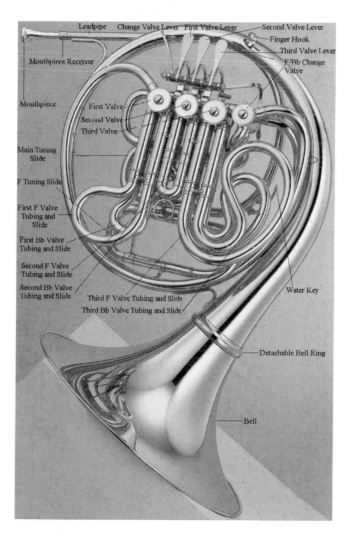

Leadpipe
Change Valve Lever
First Valve Lever
Second Valve Lever
Finger Hook
Third Valve Lever
F/Bb Change Valve
Mouthpiece Receiver
First Valve
Second Valve
Third Valve
Mouthpiece
Main Tuning Slide
F Tuning Slide
First F Valve Tubing and Slide
First Bb Valve Tubing and Slide
Second F Valve Tubing and Slide
Second Bb Valve Tubing and Slide
Third F Valve Tubing and Slide
Third Bb Valve Tubing and Slide
Water Key
Detachable Bell Ring
Bell

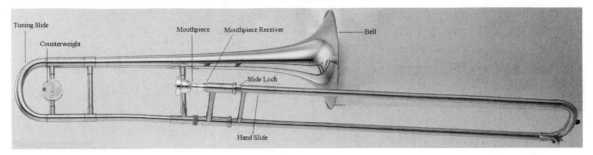

Trombone

Compensating
Euphonium

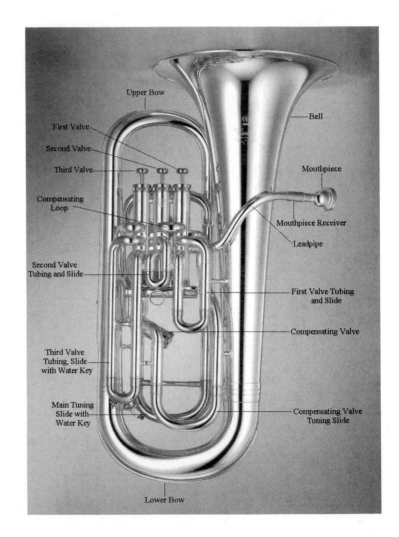

BB♭ Tuba

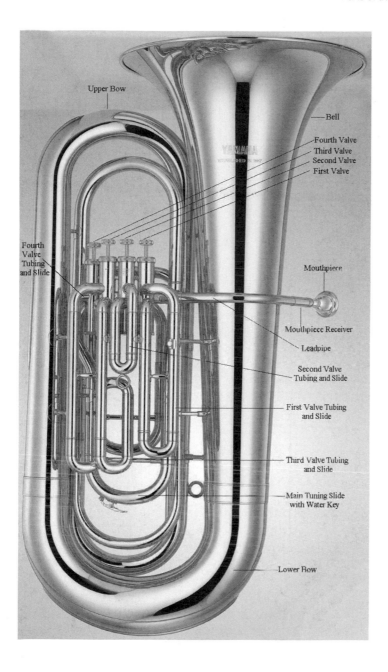

Upper Bow

Bell

Fourth Valve
Third Valve
Second Valve
First Valve

Fourth
Valve
Tubing
and Slide

Mouthpiece

Mouthpiece Receiver

Leadpipe

Second Valve
Tubing and Slide

First Valve Tubing
and Slide

Third Valve Tubing
and Slide

Main Tuning Slide
with Water Key

Lower Bow

BIBLIOGRAPHY

Books

Altenburg, Detlef. *Untersuchungen zur Geschichte der Trompete in Zeitalter der Clarinblaskunst (1500–1800)*. Regensburg, Germany: G. Bosse, 1973.

Altenburg, Johann Ernst. *Essay on an Introduction to the Heroic and Musical Trumpeters' and Kettledrummers' Art (1795)*. Nashville, Tenn.: The Brass Press, 1974.

Anderson, Paul G. *Brass Solo and Study Material Music Guide*. Evanston, Ill.: The Instrumentalist Co., 1976.

Arling, Harry J. *Trombone Chamber Music: An Annotated Bibliography*, 2nd ed. Nashville, Tenn.: The Brass Press, 1983.

Bach, Vincent. *The Art of Trumpet Playing*. Elkhart, Ind.: Vincent Bach Corporation, 1969.

Bach, Vincent. *Embouchure and Mouthpiece Manual*. Elkhart, Ind.: Vincent Bach Corporation, 1956.

Backus, John. *The Acoustical Foundations of Music*, 2nd ed. New York: Norton, 1977.

Bahr, Edward. R. *Trombone/Euphonium Discography*. Stevens Point, Wis.: Index Horse, 1988.

Baines, Anthony. *Brass Instruments: Their History and Development*. London: Faber & Faber, 1976.

Baker, David. *Contemporary Techniques for the Trombone*. 2 vols. New York: Charles Colin, 1974.

Barbour, J. Murray. *Trumpets, Horns, and Music*. East Lansing, Mich.: Michigan State University Press, 1964.

Barclay, R. L. *The Art of the Trumpet-Maker: The Materials, Tools, and Techniques of the Seventeenth and Eighteenth Centuries in Nuremberg*. Oxford, England: Clarendon Press, 1992.

Bate, Philip. *The Trumpet and Trombone: An Outline of Their History, Development, and Construction*, 2nd ed. London: Ernest Benn, Ltd., 1978; New York: Norton, 1978.

Bell, William. *Encyclopedia of Literature for the Tuba*. New York: Charles Colin, 1967.

Bellamah, Joseph L. *Brass Facts*. San Antonio, Tex.: Southern Music Co., 1961.

Benade, Arthur H. *Fundamentals of Musical Acoustics*. New York: Oxford University Press, 1976.

Bendinelli, Cesare. *The Entire Art of Trumpet Playing, 1614*. Nashville: The Brass Press, 1975.

Bevan, Clifford. *The Tuba Family*. New York: Scribner's, 1978.

Booth, Matthew. *Sound the Trumpet: The John Wilbraham Method*. London: Stainer & Bell, 2000.

Bourgue, Daniel. *Conversations About the Horn*. Paris: International Music Diffusion, 1996.

Bowman, Brian L. *Practical Hints on Playing the Baritone (Euphonium)*. Melville, N.Y.: Belwin-Mills, 1983.

Brass Anthology: A Collection of Articles Published in the Instrumentalist Magazine from 1946 to 1999. Northfield, Ill.: The Instrumentalist Co., 1999.

Brown, Merrill E. *Teaching the Successful High School Brass Section*. West Nyack, N.Y.: Parker Publishing Co., 1981.

Brownlow, Art. *The Last Trumpet: A History of the English Slide Trumpet*. Stuyvesant, N.Y.: Pendragon Press, 1996.

Brüchle, Bernhard. *Horn Bibliographie*. 3 vols. Wilhelmshaven, Germany: Heinrichshofen's Verlag, 1970.

Brüchle, Bernhard, and Janetzky, Kurt. *Kulturgeschichte des Horns*. Tutzing, Germany: Hans Schneider, 1976.

Bush, Irving. *Artistic Trumpet Technique and Study*. Hollywood, Cal.: Highland Music Co., 1962.

Bushouse, David. *Practical Hints on Playing the Horn*. Melville, N.Y.: Belwin-Mills, 1983.

Campos, Frank Gabriel. *Trumpet Technique*. New York: Oxford University Press, 2005.

Carse, Adam. *Musical Wind Instruments*. London: Macmillan, 1940. Reprint: New York: Da Capo Press, 1965.

Cassone, Gabriel. *La Tromba*. Varese, Italy: Zecchini, 2002.

Clarke, Herbert L. *How I Became a Cornetist*. Kenosha, Wis.: Leblanc Educational Publications, n.d.

Coar, Birchard. *A Critical Study of the Nineteenth-Century Horn Virtuosi in France*. DeKalb, Ill.: Coar, 1952.

Coar, Birchard. *The French Horn*. DeKalb, Ill.: Coar, 1947.

Cousins, Farquharson. *On Playing the Horn*. London: Samski Press (Distributed by Paxman Musical Instruments), 1983.

Cummings, Barton. *The Contemporary Tuba*. New London, Conn.: Whaling Music Publishers, 1984.

Dale, Delbert A. *Trumpet Technique*. London: Oxford University Press, 1967.

Dahlqvist, Reine. *The Keyed Trumpet and Its Greatest Virtuoso, Anton Weidinger*. Nashville, Tenn.: The Brass Press, 1975.

D'Ath, Norman W. *Cornet Playing*. London: Boosey & Hawkes, 1960.

Davidson, Louis. *Trumpet Techniques*. Rochester, N.Y.: Wind Music, Inc., 1970.

Davies, Rick. *Chappottin, Chocolate, and the Afro-Cuban Trumpet Style*. Lanham, Md.: Scarecrow Press, 2003.

Dempster, Stuart. *The Modern Trombone: A Definition of Its Idioms*. Athens, Ohio: Accura Music, 1994.

Devol, John. *Brass Music for the Church.* Plainview, N.Y.: Harold Branch, 1974.

Dokshizer, Timofei. *The Memoires of Timofei Dokshizer: An Autobiography.* Westfield, Mass.: International Trumpet Guild, 1997.

Domnich, H. *Méthode de premier et second cor.* Geneva, Switzerland: Minkoff Reprints, 1974.

Draper, F. C. *Notes on the Besson System of Automatic Compensation of Valved Brass Wind Instruments.* Edgware, England: Besson and Co., 1953).

Dundas, Richard J. *Twentieth Century Brass Musical Instruments in the United States,* rev. ed. Rutland, Vt.: R. Dundas, 1998.

Duvernoy, Frédéric. *Méthode pour le cor.* Geneva, Switzerland: Minkoff Reprints, 1972.

Eichborn, Hermann. *The Old Art of Clarino Playing on Trumpets.* Trans. by Bryan A. Simms. Denver, Colo.: Tromba Publications, 1976.

Eldredge, Niles. *A Brief History of Piston-Valved Cornets.* New York: Historic Brass Society, 2002. [Reprinted from 2002 *Historic Brass Society Journal* 14: 337–390.]

Eliason, Robert E. *Early American Brass Makers.* Nashville, Tenn.: The Brass Press, 1981.

Endsley, Gerald. *Comparative Mouthpiece Guide for Trumpet.* Denver, Colo.: Tromba Publications, 1980.

Enrico, Eugene. *The Orchestra at San Petronio in the Baroque Era.* Washington, D.C.: Smithsonian Institution Press, 1976.

Everett, Thomas G. *Annotated Guide to Bass Trombone Literature,* 3rd ed. Nashville, Tenn.: The Brass Press, 1985.

Fadle, Heinz. *Looking for the Natural Way: Thoughts on the Trombone and Brass Playing.* Detmold, Germany: Edition Piccolo, 1996.

Fako, Nancy Jordan. *Philip Farkas and His Horn: A Happy, Worthwhile Life.* Elmhurst, Ill.: Crescent Park Music Publications, 1998.

Fantini, Girolamo. *Modo per imparare a sonare di Tromba tanto di Guerra quanto Musicalmente in Organo, con Tromba sordina, con Cimbalo e con orgn'altro strumento (1638).* New York: Performers' Facsimiles, 2002; Nashville, Tenn.: The Brass Press, 1972.

Farkas, Philip. *The Art of Brass Playing.* Rochester, N.Y.: Wind Music, 1962.

Farkas, Philip. *The Art of Horn Playing.* Evanston, Ill.: Summy-Birchard, 1956.

Farkas, Philip. *The Art of Musicianship.* Bloomington, Ind.: Musical Publications, 1976.

Farkas, Philip. *A Photographic Study of 40 Virtuoso Horn Players' Embouchures.* Rochester, N.Y.: Wind Music, 1970.

Farley, Robert, and Hutchins, John. *Natural Trumpet Studies.* Oakham, Rutland, England: Brass Wind Publications.

Fink, Reginald H. *The Trombonist's Handbook.* Athens, Ohio: Accura Music, 1977.

Fischer, Henry George. *The Renaissance Sackbut and Its Use Today.* New York: Metropolitan Museum of Art, 1984.

Fitzpatrick, Horace. *The Horn and Horn-Playing and the Austro-Bohemian Tradition 1680–1830.* London: Oxford University Press, 1970.

Foster, Robert E. *Practical Hints on Playing the Trumpet/Cornet.* Melville, N.Y.: Belwin-Mills, 1983.

Fox, Fred. *Essentials of Brass Playing.* Pittsburgh, Pa.: Volkwein Bros., 1974.

Frederiksen, Brian. *Arnold Jacobs: Song and Wind.* WindSong Press Limited, 1996.

Gardner, Randy C. *Mastering the Horn's Low Register.* Richmond, Va.: International Opus, 2002.

Gourse, Leslie. *Blowing the Changes: The Art of the Jazz Horn Players.* New York: Franklin Watts, 1997.

Gregory, Robin. *The Horn.* London: Faber & Faber, 1969.

Gregory, Robin. *The Trombone.* New York: Faber & Faber, 1973.

Griffiths, John R. *The Low Brass Guide.* Hackensack, N.J.: Jerona Music Corp., 1980.

Guion, David M. *The Trombone: Its History and Music 1697–1811.* New York: Gordon & Breach, 1988.

Hajdinjak, Reinhard. *Solo-Trompete und Blasorchester: Verzeichnis von über 500 Solowerken für Trompete(n) und Blasorchester.* Vienna, Austria: J. Kliment, 1991.

Handel's Trumpeter: The Diary of John Grano (ca. 1692–1748). Stuyvesant, N.Y.: Pendragon Press, 1998.

Hanson, Fay. *Brass Playing.* New York: Carl Fischer, 1975

Harper, Thomas. *Instructions for the Trumpet (1837).* Homer, New York: Spring Tree Enterprises, 1988.

Harvey, Roger. *BrassWorkBook for Alto Trombone.* Gt. Dunmow, England: BrassWorks.

Harvey, Roger. *BrassWorkBook for Trombone Section.* Gt. Dunmow, England: BrassWorks.

Herbert, Trevor. *The British Brass Band: A Musical and Social History.* Oxford, England: Oxford University Press, 2000.

Herbert, Trevor, and John Wallace, eds. *The Cambridge Companion to Brass Instruments.* Cambridge, England: Cambridge University Press, 1997.

Heyde, Herbert. *Hörner und Zinken.* Leipzig, Germany: VEB Deutscher Verlag für Musik, 1982.

Heyde, Herbert. *Trompeten, Posaunen, Tuben.* Leipzig, Germany: VEB Deutscher Verlag für Musik, 1980.

Hill, Douglas. *Collected Thoughts on Teaching and Learning, Creativity, and Horn Performance.* Miami, Fla.: Warner Bros. Publications, 2001.

Hill, Douglas. *Extended Techniques for the Horn.* Hialeah, Fla.: Columbia Pictures Publications, 1983.

Hiller, Albert. *Trompetenmusiken aus drei Jahrhunderten (ca. 1600 nach 1900): Kompositionen für 1 bis 24 (Natur-) Trompeten mit und ohne Pauken.* Cologne, Germany: W. G. Haas, 1991.

Hernon, Michael. *French Horn Discography.* New York: Greenwood Press, 1986.

Humphries, John. *The Early Horn: A Practical Guide.* Cambridge, England: Cambridge University Press, 2000.

Janetzky, Kurt. *Das Horn: Eine Kleine Chronik seines Werdens und Wirkens.* Stuttgart, Germany: Hallweg Verlag, 1977.

Janetzky, Kurt, and Bernhard Brüchle. *The Horn.* Portland, Or.: Amadeus Press, 1988.

Johnson, Keith. *The Art of Trumpet Playing*. Ames, Iowa: Iowa State University Press, 1981.

Johnson, Keith: *Brass Performance and Pedagogy*. Upper Saddle River, N.J.: Prentice-Hall, 2002.

Jones, Philip. *John Fletcher, Tuba Extraordinary: A Celebration*. London: John Fletcher Trust, 1997.

Kagarice, Vern L. *Annotated Guide to Trombone Solos with Band and Orchestra*. Lebanon, Ind.: Studio P/R, 1974.

Kagarice, Vern L., et al. *Solos for the Student Trombonist: An Annotated Bibliography*. Nashville, Tenn.: The Brass Press, 1979.

Kaslow, David M. *Living Dangerously with the Horn: Thoughts on Life and Art*. Bloomington, Ind.: Birdalone Books, 1996.

Kay, Jackie. *Trumpet*. New York: Pantheon Books, 1998.

Kehle, Robert. *Alto Trombone Literature: An Annotated Guide*. Warwick, England: Warwick Music, 2000.

Kleinhammer, Edward. *The Art of Trombone Playing*. Evanston, Ill.: Summy-Birchard Company, 1996.

Kleinhammer, Edward. *Mastering the Trombone*. Hannover, Germany: Edition Piccolo, 1997.

Knaub, Donald. *Trombone Teaching Techniques*, 2nd ed. Athens, Ohio: Accura Music, 1977.

Laird, Michael. *BrassWorkBook for Natural Trumpet*. Gt. Dunmow, England: BrassWorks.

Lane, G. B. *The Trombone: An Annotated Bibliography*. Lanham, Md.: Scarecrow Press, 1999.

Lane, G. B. *The Trombone in the Middle Ages and the Renaissance*. Bloomington, Ind.: Indiana University Press, 1982.

Lawrence, Ian. *Brass in Your School*. London: Oxford University Press, 1975.

Lawson Brass Instruments. *French Horn Mouthpieces: Material and Design*. Boonsboro, Md.: Lawson, 1990.

Lawson, Walter A. *Development of New Mouthpipes for the French Horn*. Boonsboro, Md.: Lawson, n.d.

Lindner, Andreas. *Die Kaiserlichen Hoftrompeter und HofPauker in 18. und 19. Jahrhundert*. Tutzing, Germany: H. Schneider, 1999.

Little, Donald C. *Practical Hints on Playing the Tuba*. Melville, N.Y.: Belwin Mills, 1984.

Louder, Earle L. *Euphonium Music Guide*. Evanston, Ill.: The Instrumentalist Co., 1978.

Lowrey, Alvin. *Lowrey's International Trumpet Discography*. Columbia, S.C.: Camden House, 1990.

Lupica, Benedict. *The Magnificent Bone: A Comprehensive Study of the Slide Trombone*. New York: Vantage Press, 1974.

Macdonald, Donna. *The Odyssey of the Philip Jones Brass Ensemble*. Moudon, Switzerland: Éditions BIM, 1986.

Mason, J. Kent. *The Tuba Handbook*. Toronto: Sonante Publications, 1977.

Mathie, Gordon. *The Trumpet Teacher's Guide*. Cincinatti, Ohio: Queen City Brass Publications, 1984.

Maxted, George. *Talking About the Trombone*. London: J. Baker, 1970.

McBeth, Amy. *A Discography of 78 rpm–Era Recordings of the Horn: Solo and Chamber Music Literature with Commentary*. Westport, Conn.: Greenwood Press, 1997.

Meckna, Michael. *Twentieth-Century Brass Soloists*. Westport, Conn.: Greenwood Press, 1994.

Meek, Harold. *Horn and Conductor: Reminiscences of a Practitioner with a Few Words of Advice*. Rochester, N.Y.: University of Rochester Press, 1997.

Mende, Emilie. *Pictorial Family Tree of Brass Instruments in Europe Since the Early Middle Ages*. Moudon, Switzerland: Editions BIM, 1978.

Méndez, Rafael: *Prelude to Brass Playing*. Boston: Carl Fischer, 1961.

Merewether, Richard. *The Horn, the Horn . . . .* London: Paxman Musical Instruments, 1979.

Miles, David Royal. *An Annotated Bibliography of Selected Contemporary Euphonium Solo Literature by American Composers*. Tuba Press, 1992.

Morley-Pegge, Reginald. *The French Horn*. London: Ernest Benn, 1973.

Morris, R. Winston. *Tuba Music Guide*. Evanston, Ill.: The Instrumentalist Co., 1973.

Musique pour Trompette, 1st and 2nd eds. Paris: Alphonse Leduc, n.d.

Naylor, Tom L. *The Trumpet and Trombone in Graphic Arts, 1500–1800*. Nashville, Tenn.: The Brass Press, 1979.

Nelson, Mark. *The Tuba as a Solo Instrument: Composer Biographies*. Annandale, Va.: Tuba-Euphonium Press, 1995

Perspectives in Brass Scholarship: Proceedings of the International Historic Brass Symposium, Amherst, 1995. Stuyvesant, N.Y.: Pendragon Press, 1997.

Pettitt, Stephen. *Dennis Brain*. London: Robert Hale, 1976.

Phillips, Harvey, and W. Winkle. *The Art of Tuba and Euphonium Playing*. Secaucus, N.J.: Summy-Birchard (Warner Bros. Publications), 1992.

Pizka, Hans. *Das Horn bei Mozart*. Kirchheim bei München, Germany: Hans Pizka Edition, 1980.

Pizka, Hans. *Hornisten-Lexikon/Dictionary for Hornists 1986*. Kirchheim bei München, Germany: Hans Pizka Edition, 1986.

Poper, Roy. *Roy Poper's Guide to the Brasswind Methods of James Stamp*. Montrose, Cal.: Balquidder Music, 2001.

Porter, Maurice M. *The Embouchure*. London: Boosey & Hawkes, 1967.

Preinsperger, Ewald. *Solo-Tenorhorn und Blasorchester: Verzeichnis von über 500 Solowerken für ein oder mehrere Tenorhörner/Euphonien und Blasorchester*. Vienna, Austria: J. Kliment, 1995.

Preinsperger, Ewald. *Solo Tuba und Blasorchester: Verzeichnis von über 300 Solowerken für ein oder mehrere Tuben und Blasorchester*. Vienna, Austria: Musikverlag J. Kliment, 1993.

Prichard, Paul, ed. *The Business: The Essential Guide to Starting and Surviving As a Professional Hornplayer*. Surrey, England: Open Press Books, 1992.

Rasmussen, Mary. *A Teacher's Guide to the Literature for Brass Instruments*. Durham, N.H.: Brass Quarterly, 1968.

Reynolds, Verne. *The Horn Handbook*. Portland, Or.: Amadeus Press, 1997.

Rose, W. H. *Studio Class Manual for Tuba and Euphonium*. Houston, Tex.: Iola Publications, 1980.

Ryan, Marc. *Trumpet Records: An Illustrated History, with Discography*. Milford, N.H.: Big Nickel Publications, 1992.

Schöck, Ralf F. *Solo-Posaune und Blasorchester Verzeichnis von über 750 Solowerken für Eine oder Mehrere Posaunen und Blasorchester*. Vienna, Austria: Musikverlag J. Kliment, 1999.

Schuller, Gunther. *Horn Technique,* 2nd ed. London: Oxford University Press, 1992.

Schwarzl, Siefgried. *The Development of Horn Ensemble Music from the Romantic Era to the Present Time in Vienna and in Other Cultural Circles*. Vienna, Austria: Wiener Waldhornverein, 1987.

Secrist-Schmedes, Barbera. *Wind Chamber Music, for Two to Sixteen Winds: An Annotated Guide*. Lanham, Md.: Scarecrow Press, 2002.

Seraphinoff, Richard, and Robert Barclay. *Making a Natural Trumpet: An Illustrated Workshop Guide*. Edinburgh, England: Edinburgh University Collection of Historic Musical Instruments, 2003.

Severson, Paul, and Mark McDunn. *Brass Wind Artistry*. Athens, Ohio: Accura Music, 1983.

Sherman, Roger. *The Trumpeter's Handbook*. Athens, Ohio: Accura Music, 1979.

Skei, Allen B. *Woodwind, Brass, and Percussion Instruments of the Orchestra: A Bibliographic Guide*. New York: Garland Publishing, 1985.

Smithers, Don. *The Music and History of the Baroque Trumpet Before 1721*. London: J. M. Dent, 1973.

Snell, Howard. *The Trumpet: Its Practice and Performance: A Guide for Students*. Hollington, England: Rakeway Music, 1997.

Solos for the Student Trombonist. Nashville, Tenn.: The Brass Press, 1979.

Stauffer, Donald W. *A Treatise on the Tuba*. Birmingham, Ala.: Stauffer Press, 1989.

Steele-Perkins, Crispian. *The Trumpet*. London: Kahn & Averill, 2001.

Stewart, Dee. *Arnold Jacobs: The Legacy of a Master*. Northfield, Ill.: The Instrumentalist Co., 1987.

Stewart, Dee. *Philip Farkas: The Legacy of a Master*. Northfield, Ill.: The Instrumentalist Co., 1990.

Swain, John. *The Brass Instruments: A Reference Manual*. Portland, Maine: Manduca Music Publications, 1997.

Tarr, Edward. *East Meets West: The Russian Trumpet Tradition from the Time of Peter the Great to the October Revolution, with a Lexicon of Trumpeters Active in Russia from the Seventeenth to the Twentieth Centuries*. Hillsdale, N.Y.: Pendragon Press, 2000.

Tarr, Edward. *The Trumpet*. Portland, Or.: Amadeus Press, 1988.

Taylor, Arthur R. *Brass Bands*. London: Granada Publishing, Ltd., 1979.

Thévet, Lucien. *Méthode complète de cor*. Paris: Alphonse Leduc, 1960.

Tuckwell, Barry. *Horn*. New York: Schirmer Books, 1983.

Tuckwell, Barry. *Playing the Horn*. London: Oxford University Press, 1978.

Watson, J. Perry. *The Care and Feeding of a Community British Brass Band*. Farmingdale, N.Y.: Boosey & Hawkes, n.d.

Watson, J. Perry. *Starting a British Brass Band*. Grand Rapids, Mich.: Yamaha International Corporation, 1984.

Weast, Robert. *Famous Trumpet Players (from 1584 to the present)*. Johnston, Iowa: The Brass World.

Weast, Robert. *Keys to Natural Performance for Brass Players*. Des Moines, Iowa: The Brass World, 1979.

Webster, Gerald. *Piccolo Trumpet Method*. Nashville, Tenn.: The Brass Press, 1980.

Wekre, Frøydis Ree. *Thoughts on Playing the Horn Well*. Oslo, Norway: Frøydis Ree Wekre, 1994.

Weyse, Volker. *Solo-Horn und Blasorchester: Verzeichnis von über 200 Solowerken für ein oder mehrere Hörner (inklusiv Jagdhorn, Signalhorn, Alphorn, Lure) und Blasorchester*. Vienna, Austria: Kliment, 2000.

Whitehead, Geoffrey I. *A College-Level Tuba Curriculum: Developed Through the Study of the Teaching Techniques of William Bell, Harvey Phillips, and Daniel Perantoni at Indiana University*. Lewiston, N.Y.: E. Mellen Press, 2003.

Wick, Denis. *Trombone Technique,* 2nd ed. London: Oxford University Press, 1975.

Wigness, C. Robert. *The Soloistic Use of the Trombone in Eighteenth Century Vienna*. Nashville, Tenn.: The Brass Press, 1978.

Wilkins, Wayne. *The Index of French Horn Music*. Magnolia, Ark.: Music Register, 1978.

Winter, Denis. *Euphonium Music Guide*. New London, Conn.: Whaling Music Publishers, 1983.

Vaughan Williams, Ralph. *The Making of Music* Ithaca, N.Y.: Cornell University Press, 1955.

Yancich, Milan. *An Orchestra Musician's Odyssey: A View from the Rear*. Rochester, N.Y.: Wind Music, 1995.

Yancich, Milan. *A Practical Guide to French Horn Playing*. Rochester, N.Y.: Wind Music, 1971.

Yanow, Scott. *The Trumpet Kings: The Players who Shaped the Sound of Jazz Trumpet*. San Francisco: Backbeat Books, 2001.

Articles

Agrell, Jeffrey. "An Indexed Bibliography of Periodical Articles on the Horn," *The Horn Call,* 6(2) (May 1976), pp. 51–54; 7(1) (November 1976), pp. 45–51; 7(2) (May 1977), pp. 49–55.

Anderson, Stephen C. "The Alto Trombone, Then and Now," *The Instrumentalist* (November 1985), pp. 54–62.

Benade, Arthur H. "The Physics of Brasses," *Scientific American* (July 1973), pp. 24–35.

Cazalet, André. "The Horn, the Brasses and France," *Brass Bulletin,* 81 (1993), pp. 48–55.

Cichowicz, Vincent. "Teaching the Concepts of Trumpet Playing," *The Instrumentalist* (January 1996), pp. 27–31.

Čižek, Bohuslav. "Josef Kail (1795–1871)" (Part Two), *Brass Bulletin,* 74 (1991), pp. 24–29.

Droste, Paul. "Begged, Borrowed, and Stolen Solo Euphonium Literature." *The Instrumentalist*, (May 1981), pp. 30–32.

Everett, Thomas G. "Solo Literature for the Bass Trombone," in *Brass Anthology*. Evanston, Ill.: The Instrumentalist Co., 1976, pp. 587–590.

Guggenberger, Wolfgang. "Vincent Cichowicz, Grand Master of Trumpet Teaching." *Brass Bulletin*, 104 (1998), pp. 46–55.

Heyde, Herbert. "Zur Frühgeschichte der Ventile und Ventilinstrumente in Deutschland (1814–1833)," *Brass Bulletin*, 24 (1978), pp. 9–33; 25 (1979), pp. 41–50; 26 (1979), pp. 69–82; 27 (1979), pp. 51–59. (Translations in English and French are included.)

Louder, Earle L. "Original Solo Literature and Study Books for Euphonium." *The Instrumentalist* (May 1981), pp. 29–30.

Roberts, B. Lee. "Some Comments on the Physics of the Horn and Right Hand Technique," *The Horn Call*, 40(2) (May 1976), pp. 41–45.

Saeki, Shigeki. "A Historical Perspective of the Alto Trombone," *Brass Bulletin*, 115 (2001), pp. 96–101.

Shifren, Ken. "The Valve Trombone." *Brass Bulletin*, 111 (2000), pp. 126–144; 112 (2000), pp. 118–126.

Smithers, Don, Klaus Wogram, and John Bowsher. "Playing the Baroque Trumpet," *Scientific American* (April 1986), pp. 108–115.

Thévet, Lucien. "On the French School of Horn Playing," *Brass Bulletin*, 84 (1993), pp. 54–61.Turrentine, Edgar M. "The Physiological Aspect of Brasswind Performance Technique: A Bibliographic Essay," *NACWPI Journal*, 26(2) (November 1977), pp. 3–5.

Werden, David R. "Euphonium Mouthpieces—A Teacher's Guide," *The Instrumentalist* (May 1981), pp. 23–26.

Yeo, Douglas. "The Bass Trombone: Innovations on a Misunderstood Instrument," *The Instrumentalist* (November 1985), pp. 22–28.

Zechmeister, Gerhard. "Die Entwicklung der Wiener Konzerttuba," *Brass Bulletin*, 75 (1991), pp. 44–47. (Translations in English and French are included.)

Zechmeister, Gerhard. "Die Stellung der (Contra) Bass-posaune im Wiener Klangstil," *Brass Bulletin*, 102 (1998), pp. 19–28. (Translations in English and French are included.)

Dissertations and Theses

Anstutz, Allan Keith. "A Videofluorographic Study of the Teeth Aperture, Instrument Pivot, and Tongue Arch and Their Influence on Trumpet Performance." D.M.E. thesis, University of Oklahoma, 1970.

Bahr, Edward Richard. "A Discography of Classical Trombone/Euphonium Solo and Ensemble on Long-Playing Records Distributed in the United States." D.M.A. thesis, University of Oklahoma, 1980. UM 80-16, 922.

Beck, Frederick Allan. "The Flugelhorn: Its History and Literature." D.M.A. thesis, University of Rochester, 1979. UM 79-21,124.

Carnovale, August N. "A Comprehensive Performance Project in Trumpet Literature with an Essay on Published Music Composed Since ca. 1900 for Solo Trumpet Accompanied by Orchestra." D.M.A. thesis, University of Iowa, 1973. UM 74-16, 703.

Chesebro, Gayle M. "An Annotated List of Original Works for Horn Alone and for Horn with One Other Non-Keyboard Instrument." D.M.A. thesis, Indiana University, 1976.

Davidson, Todd. "The Introduction of the High Trumpet into the Late-Nineteenth and Early-Twentieth-Century Orchestra." D.M.A. thesis, Indiana University, 2002.

Hyatt, Jack H. "The Soprano and Piccolo Trumpets: Their History, Literature, and a Tutor." D.M.A. thesis, Boston University, 1974. UM 74-20, 473.

Keays, James Harvey. "An Investigation into the Origins of the Wagner Tuba." D.M.A. thesis, University of Illinois, 1977. UM 78-4044.

Meidt, Joseph Alexis. *A Cinefluorographic Investigation of Oral Adjustments for Various Aspects of Brass Instrument Performance.* Thesis: University of Iowa, 1967.

Randolph, David Mark. "New Techniques in the Avant-Garde Repertoire for Solo Tuba." D.M.A. thesis, University of Rochester, 1978. UM 78-11,493.

Schumacher, Stanley E. "An Analytical Study of Published Unaccompanied Solo Literature for Brass Instruments." Ph.D. dissertation, Ohio State University, 1976. UM 77-2497.

Senff, Thomas E. "An Annotated Bibliography of the Unaccompanied Solo Repertoire for Trombone." D.M.A. thesis, University of Illinois, 1976. UM 76-16,919.

Smith, Nicholas Edward. "The Horn Mute: An Acoustical and Historical Study." D.M.A. thesis, University of Rochester, 1980. UM 80 19,070.

Smith, David. "Trombone Technique in the Early Seventeenth Century." D.M.A. thesis, Stanford University, 1981.

Sorenson, Richard A. "Tuba Pedagogy: A Study of Selected Method Books, 1840–1911." Ph.D. dissertation, University of Colorado, 1972. UM 73-1832.

Tracy, Bruce Alan. "The Contrabass Trombone: Its Development and Use." D.M.A. Thesis, University of Illinois, 1990.

Trusheim, William H.. "Mental Imagery and Musical Performance: An Inquiry into Imagery Use by Eminent Orchestral Brass Players." Ed.D. dissertation, Rutgers University, 1987.

Whaley, David R. "The Microtonal Capability of the Horn." D.M.A. thesis, University of Illinois, 1975. UM 76-7010.